T0306071

Workers, Unions and Payment in Kind

Despite the dramatic expansion of consumer culture from the beginning of the eighteenth century onwards and the developments in retailing, advertising and credit relationships in the nineteenth and twentieth centuries, there were a significant number of working families in Britain who were not fully free to consume as they chose.

These employees were paid in truck, or in goods rather than currency. This book will explore and analyse the changing ways that truck and workplace deductions were experienced by different groups in British society, arguing that it was far more common than has previously been acknowledged. This analysis brings to light issues of class and gender; the discourse of free trade, popular politics and protest; the development of the trade union movement; and the use of the legal system as an instrument for bringing about social and legal change.

Christopher Frank is Associate Professor in the Department of History at the University of Manitoba, Canada.

Perspectives in Economic and Social History

Series Editors: Andrew August and Jari Eloranta

For more information about this series, please visit www.routledge.com/series/PESH

Workers, Unions and Payment in Kind

The Fight for Real Wages in Britain, 1820–1914

Christopher Frank

Routledge
Taylor & Francis Group

LONDON AND NEW YORK

First published 2020
by Routledge
2 Park Square, Milton Park, Abingdon, Oxon OX14 4RN

and by Routledge
605 Third Avenue, New York, NY 10017

First issued in paperback 2021

Routledge is an imprint of the Taylor & Francis Group, an informa business

British Library Cataloguing-in-Publication Data
A catalogue record for this book is available from the British Library

Library of Congress Cataloging-in-Publication Data
A catalog record for this book has been requested

ISBN 13: 978-1-03-208640-8 (pbk)
ISBN 13: 978-1-138-12106-5 (hbk)

Typeset in Bembo
by Apex CoVantage, LLC

For Sarah, Naomi, Martin and Julian

Contents

Abbreviations

Archive abbreviations

TNA   The National Archives, Kew

Reference guides

ODNB   *Oxford Dictionary of National Biography Online*

Newspapers and periodicals

NBDM   *North British Daily Mail*

Law journals

CP	*The Law Reports, Common Pleas Division*
JP	*Justice of the Peace Reports*
KB	*The Law Reports, King's Bench Division*
LJ	*Law Journal Reports*
LJQB	*Law Journal Reports, Queen's Bench*
LRQB	*Law Reports, Queen's Bench*

Trade unions and employers' organizations

NAUSAWC	National Amalgamated Union of Shop Assistants, Warehouse-men and Clerks
SSCC	South Scotland Chamber of Commerce
TUC	Trades Union Congress
WIC	Women's Industrial Council
WTUL	Women's Trade Union League

Truck and related statutes

4 Edward I, c. 1 (1465)
3 Henry VIII, c. 6 (1512)
8 Elizabeth I, c. 7 (1566)
14 Elizabeth I, c. 12 (1572)
1 Anne, c. 18 (1703)
9 Anne, c. 30 (1711)
10 Anne, c. 16 (1712)
1 George I, c. 15 (1715)
12 George I, c. 34 (1726)
13 George I, c. 23 (1727)
13 George II, c. 8 (1740)
22 George II, c. 27 (1749)
29 George II, c. 33 (1756)
30 George II, c. 12 (1757)
31 George II, c. 76 (1758)
10 George III, c. 53 (1770)
17 George III, c. 56 (1777)
19 George III, c. 49 (1779)
43 George III, c. 134 (1803)
47 George III, c. 68 (1807)
57 George III, c. 115 (1817)
58 George III, c. 51 (1818)
1 George IV, c. 93 (1820)
1 & 2 William IV, c. 36 (1831)
1 & 2 William IV, c. 37 (1831)
37 & 38 Victoria, c. 48 (1874)
46 & 47 Victoria, c. 31 (1883)
50 & 51 Victoria, c. 46 (1887)
50 & 51 Victoria, c. 58 (1887)
51 & 52 Victoria, c. 43 (1887)
57 & 58 Victoria, c. 52 (1894)
59 & 60 Victoria, c. 44 (1896)
2 Edward VII, c. 21 (1902)

x *Truck and related statutes*

Acknowledgements

At the end of this long project I am deeply indebted to many friends for their invaluable assistance and suggestions. My dear friends and respected colleagues Jamie Bronstein, Greg Smith, James Muir and Lynn MacKay have read and edited drafts, listened to presentations and discussed this project with me many times. Their thoughtful advice and useful insights have helped me often during the nine years of research and writing this book. I am a part of a vibrant and close-knit Department of History at the University of Manitoba that has an active colloquium committee, which has served as a sounding board for different parts of this monograph. I am grateful to Tina Chen, Roisin Cossar, Len Kuffert, David Churchill, Erik Thomson, Jorge Nállim, Mark Gabbert, Adele Perry, Julie Guard, James Hanley, Jennifer Dueck, Julie Gibbings, Jarvis Brownlie, Ben Baader, Joy Chadya, Barry Ferguson, Henry Heller, Esyllt Jones, Todd Scarth, Francis Carrol, Michael Kinnear and Mary Kinnear for being such supportive and kind colleagues. The research for this book was generously funded by the Social Science and Humanities Research Council of Canada, as well as the Rh Foundation, the Faculty of Arts, the Department of History, and the Institute for the Humanities at the University of Manitoba.

I have also benefited from the expertise and knowledge of the community of scholars who make up the Western Conference of British Studies, where this book has grown and developed for many years. Andy Muldoon, Marjorie-Levine Clark, Padraic Kennedy, Justin Olmstead, Jessica Sheetz-Nguyen, Thomas Prasch, Jodie Kreider, Derek Blakeley, Richard Follett, Robin Ganev, Timothy Jenks, Stephen Heathorn, Robin Ganev, Allison Abra, James Rosenheim, Robin Hermann, Jeanine Hurl-Eamon, Mark Klobas, and Michael Rutz have provided wonderful encouragement and constructive criticism. I am continually thankful to Douglas Hay, Nicholas Rogers and Paul Craven for their friendship and mentorship.

Some material in Chapter 1 was used previously in "Truck or Trade: Anti-Truck Societies and the Campaign Against the Payment of Wages in Goods in Mid-Nineteenth Century Britain." *Historical Studies in Industrial Relations* 27/28 (Spring/Autumn 2009): 1–40. My thanks to the publisher of this article for granting me permission to use these materials. I would also like to thank

Lisa Lavelle at Taylor & Francis for all of her assistance in the publication of this book.

This book was written during a very happy period of my life because of the love and support of a large family. I am appreciative of the encouragement of Marty and Janet Frank, Wayne and Naomi Elvins, and Julie, Bill, Stephen and Christopher Feighery. I owe so much in the completion of this project to my wonderful wife, Sarah Elvins. I am very blessed to be married to an accomplished historian who has given so much help and guidance to me while writing this book. It is much easier to hear and accept "Chris, you do not need a fourth example in this paragraph" from someone you love. Life while working on this book has been made joyful by the presence of my three children: Naomi, Martin and Julian.

Introduction

During the nineteenth century changes in retailing, advertising and credit relationships dramatically altered the way British people acquired, experienced and thought about material goods. Yet a significant number of working families, sometimes employed in leading sectors of the British economy, were not fully free to consume as they chose. Many of these employees were paid in "truck," or in goods or services rather than currency. Truck often took the form of employees being compelled, under the threat of dismissal, to receive and spend their wages at a company-owned store. This usually meant that they received less value for their wages and that their employers exercised greater control over their lives.

Employers also controlled employees' lives by reducing workers' wages through deductions for disciplinary fines or faulty workmanship (as determined by the employer). They took deductions from their workers' wages for providing workplace heat, light, fuel, equipment, materials, break rooms and "standing room." Owners sometimes forced labourers to pay subscriptions to sickness or benefit clubs run by the employer rather than to independent or trade-union-organized clubs of their choice. During the nineteenth and twentieth centuries many male and female manual labourers worked for wages that were appallingly low, yet often they did not even receive the full value of what little they earned. These practices have received little attention from historians despite the abundance of examples in the historical record. *This book explores the changing ways that truck and workplace deductions were experienced by different groups in British society, the discourses used to articulate their objections to these practices and the variety of industrial, legal and political strategies that they pursued to end them.* Some examples demonstrate the variety of ways in which employers deprived workers of their due pay.

On 13 November 1830 William Birch, a potter in Shelton, Staffordshire, swore under oath that he had spent the previous year working under contract for wages of 12s per week. Instead of receiving his wages in money he had been forced by his employer to accept 75% of his pay in flour, cheese, bacon, beef and shoes. The employer valued these items at as much as 40% greater than their actual market price, cutting deeply into the worth of Birch's pay. Birch and his family not only received less than the real value of his wages, but when they needed to pay rent they either had to persuade their landlord to accept some of these items in lieu of money or had to sell the items at a heavy discount to obtain cash.[1]

During the 1840s in South Staffordshire, at the large ironworks of Messrs. Lloyd and Co., paydays were once a fortnight. However, if employees wanted an advance on wages earned but not yet paid the cash office would provide them with a cheque drawn on the Birmingham Banking Company, which was over ten miles away from the workplace. Workers understood that these cheques were never to be cashed at the distant bank but were to be presented at the company-owned store. Here the worker could receive 4s of every £1 of the cheque's value in money; the remainder had to be taken in goods sold at inflated prices.[2]

In 1844 a Welsh wire manufacturer named Henry Hughes informed his employees that he expected them to purchase their provisions at his shop. Hughes told one of his employees, William Balton, to patronize his shop or be fired, even though the flour sold there was 8d a bushel more and the butter 3d a pound more than in other retail stores a mere 400 meters away. Balton's wife, Eliza, went to the shop every Monday and took flour, tobacco and other items which were recorded and then deducted from his wages. Eliza noted this was a hardship, stating "I should have gone to other shops if I had the money. I could have had them [the goods] cheaper." Another of Hughes' employees earned £8 of wages during the summer of 1844 but only received 16s of it in cash that he was free to spend where he pleased.[3]

In July of 1869 the *North British Daily Mail* reported that the Schotts Iron Company in Lanarkshire calculated the wages of its workers at the end of each month but insisted upon having an additional two weeks "lying time" before paying them, which meant they always held at least two weeks' wages in hand. Consequently, the reckoning period lasted between five and six weeks for the first pay. The employer gained cash flow advantages with long pay periods, but these created great difficulties for workers. Employees could take advances on wages that were earned but not yet paid, understanding that a high proportion of these advances had to be spent in a company-owned store, where the goods were sold at slightly higher prices than the shops in the nearby village. Failure to spend the advance at the company store, referred to as "sloping the store," would result in the refusal of future advances. The *North British Daily Mail* also reported that many mines and ironworks in western Scotland with long pay periods charged workers for advances on wages earned but not paid at a rate of 1s per £1, a fee called "poundage." The *North British Daily Mail* condemned this practice, observing "the miner, in fact, pays interest for getting a loan of his own money."[4]

In April of 1887 managers in the Rhymney Coal and Iron Company in Wales summoned the wives of employees to explain why they were spending insufficient amounts of their husbands' wages at the company store. These company officials reportedly hinted to the women that their husbands' employment could be in jeopardy if they did not deal in greater quantities at the store.[5]

Workers at the Rhymney Coal and Iron Company were informed regularly that if they wanted to remain in their employment they were not fully free to dispose of their hard-earned wages as they wished.

In 1899, in Dungloe, Ireland, local shopkeepers worked as agents paid on commission by large textile firms headquartered in Londonderry or Glasgow. These shopkeepers recruited local women to hand knit socks or hosiery or make shirts in their homes. The shopkeepers kept their costs low by paying the outworkers only in inferior goods from their stores and never money.[6] Similar arrangements existed in Cornwall and Somerset, where women knit Guernsey sweaters or made gloves in their homes and were paid in drapery goods or groceries.[7]

Employers who did not wish to keep a store had other methods of clawing back wages owed to employees, often through fines and charges. In 1909, Henry England, a Belfast hemstitcher and finisher, took deductions from the wages of his employees for the cost of thread and needles used in their work. England charged his workers for thread at a rate of 4 ¾d per cop, when it cost him only 3 ½d per cop.[8] England made money from selling his employees materials that went directly into the product that he later sold for an additional profit. In 1912, a Leicester boot manufacturer deducted 4d per week from pay packets for "standing room" in the workshop.[9] A Scottish clothing factory in 1902 deducted 6d a week from workers' wages to pay for the power that ran the machines. Another workplace deducted 1d per week from the wages of its largely female workforce for the use of a cloakroom in winter.[10] Trade union leader Mary MacArthur investigated a factory where 400 female employees had 2d deducted each week for "cook money." The women brought their own tea, milk, sugar and mugs to work, but they contributed to the wages of a cook who boiled the water for their tea. MacArthur remarked to the women that "[t]he cook must be a millionaire" if 400 women were paying 2d a week for her services. The women informed MacArthur that the cook only earned 8s a week and "does heaps of other work besides." MacArthur calculated that the firm profited nearly £150 a year from this deduction.[11] In 1906, the Haywood Brothers, pickle manufacturers, deducted ½d a week from all employees for cleaning water closets, 3d per week for tea and 1d a week for the four fires that they kept going to maintain the temperature in the factory mandated by the Factory Acts.[12] During the nineteenth and twentieth centuries, it was very common for employers to directly shift many of the ordinary expenses of doing business, maintaining the workplace, and complying with government regulations onto the backs of their employees.

Not only did employers claw back wages from workers to cover business expenses, they also used workers' pay as an insurance policy against accidently spoiled work, sometimes deducting the retail value of damaged products from the workers' wages or forcing them to purchase ruined items. In 1904, a London needle worker misheard a verbal instruction from a foreperson and stitched to the edge of the collar instead of leaving a border. Normally, her wages were 1s 9d for six dozen collars, but in this case her employer deducted the outrageous sum of £1 0s 6d from her pay for improperly sewing them.[13] Employers or forepeople determined whether a product was damaged, and the employee rarely had recourse for challenging the damage or deduction.

Employers used wage deductions to discipline and control employees. In 1907, Women's Trade Union League (WTUL) President Gertrude Tuckwell testified to a Parliamentary Departmental Committee about an employer deducting a fine of 5d from the wages of a woman for being 5 minutes late to work. The size of this fine suggests that the value of her time to her employer was 5s *per hour* (5d for 5 minutes × 12). Her employer actually paid her 5s *per week*.[14] At a clothing factory in Leeds, employees, mostly women, faced 3d deductions from their wages as a fine for "standing about in the doorway," 3d for leaving the factory without a bonnet or 2d for "saucy or abusive language."[15] Shop assistants employed in some London retail stores could also be fined 1d for poor dusting, 1s for laughing, 1s for talking, 1s for carelessness in serving, 3d for failing to promptly serve a customer, 6d for cleaning one's nails on the shop floor and 2s 6d for forgetting to address a member of the firm with the "customary terms of respect."[16] The employer was the prosecutor and judge who determined both guilt and the severity of the penalty. For shop assistants, this code of conduct did not end when their shift at work was concluded. Well into the twentieth century, many shop assistants "lived in," or received part of their remuneration in room and board provided by the employer, and they were also subject to disciplinary fines that regulated their behaviour in these domiciles.

The pages that follow contain numerous examples of similar cases in which workers had substantial portions of the wages they earned unfairly taken back by employers through a variety of dubious practices. The method and timing of calculating and paying wages could convey large advantages and provide employers with control over their workforce. Truck and deductions from workers' wages allowed employers to lessen the value of compensation of workers without explicitly lowering wages promised in the employment contract.

Because employers and employees rarely met as equals in the formation of contracts of employment, especially where trade union power was weak or non-existent, unscrupulous employers gamed the payment of wages. Employers who sought an edge against their competitors resorted to long pay periods, pressured employees to patronize employer-owned stores, used fines to discipline the workforce and deducted business expenses from the wages of their workers. This meant that labourers, especially the least organized, most precariously employed and lowest paid, were forced to make do with less than the value of the wages promised and earned. It is telling that truck and workplace fines were least likely to exist in regions and trades where workers had long-standing traditions of trade union organization. In places where workers had some power, they used it to prevent truck and theft of their wages.[17] Indeed, the rise and fall of the truck system and workplace fines and deductions tracks quite closely with the power of organized labour in Britain.

In addition to illustrating the ways in which employers used their financial power to cheat and control employees, this book examines the ways in which workers and others fought back against this abuse in all its forms. Some of this opposition was discursive; workers complained in public about paying high prices for inferior products available from their employers at company stores. Truck wages denied them the freedom to use their own resourcefulness and ingenuity to stretch their wages as far as they could.

Even in cases where a company store could provide products for employees at competitive prices, workers still opposed them because these shops deprived them of their liberty and autonomy. Receiving the full rewards of one's labour and being able to enjoy them as one pleased was an important criterion by which working people measured freedom and independence. Working class men and women frequently invoked the rhetoric of slavery and serfdom when articulating their grievances against truck and other dishonest practices. They insisted that long pays, company stores and disciplinary fines gave employers an unacceptably high degree of control over their lives. In October of 1829 an "Observer" wrote a letter to the *Birmingham Journal* linking the right to spend one's wages as one pleased with freedom and citizenship, describing a worker in receipt of truck wages:

> His condition is just so far above that of a slave, as that he is not subject to being bought and sold as chattels in the market, and this is nearly all the pre-eminence he has to boast. His life is one round of drudgery and toil without the reasonable gratification of even handling his hard-earned pittance. . . . Instead of the pleasure (the greatest, perhaps, that the life of a labouring man affords) of going as he was wont, and laying out his earnings at the market or the shop, where he was received with kindness and respect, and felt something of the just independence of a man and freeborn Briton, . . . he must now go crouching to the Tommy shop for his daily morsel, where he is neither allowed to choose or cheapen, and is treated more like a beggar asking alms than as a customer.[18]

Employers exercised authority over labourers in the workplace, and the latter resented the fact that this power extended to when it was time to enjoy the rewards of their labour.[19] The language of independence was often highly gendered, as opponents of truck also appropriated and modified the widely used political language of the family wage, insisting that the payment of wages in kind interfered with proper domestic roles and undermined the dignity and respectability of working class wives. The emphasis on freedom, autonomy and family harmony is often present in arguments against truck.

Shopkeepers also opposed the truck system, arguing that truck prevented workers from patronizing nearby retail shops, which damaged local economies and took money out of circulation. Truck prevented the rise of a respectable and rate-paying middle class, undermining civic life. Money-paying employers also objected to truck, complaining that it gave their competitors an unfair advantage and, if unchecked by the law, could force them to follow suit. Members of the clergy, as well as government inspectors of the mines and factories, who witnessed first-hand the impact that the truck system had on working class families, also frequently articulated the need for state intervention to stop these practices.

Toward the end of the nineteenth century, efforts to eliminate truck expanded to protest many of the deductions that employers took from the wages of their workers. Employees objected to paying for materials that went directly into the products that their bosses sold. Workers suspected that employers deducted more from their wages than the cost of the items or services being provided. Even more galling was when an employer deducted pay for disciplinary fines or damaged work. These deductions especially targeted low paid and non-unionized female or juvenile workers. Early female trade unions led the struggle for stronger legislation to prohibit such exactions, and the female factory inspectorate spent much of its time investigating workplace fines and deductions at the turn of the century, producing information that fuelled the anti-sweating campaigns of the era. A wide variety of workers in Britain during the nineteenth and twentieth centuries repeatedly articulated a desire to have their wages paid weekly, in cash, and with as few set-offs as possible.

Opposition to truck and workplace fines and deductions manifested in industrial action, public protests, pamphleteering, petitioning, lobbying, government and private investigations, Acts of Parliament and local and high court litigation. Examining the changing strategies and arguments used by opponents of truck, fines and deductions shows how different groups in British society understood transformations in retailing, credit, contract and consumption and how these were shaped by class and gender. It also adds to our knowledge of popular politics and protest as well as the development and political influence of both male and female branches of the trade union movement. Studying this struggle can illuminate the development of the regulatory state and the importance of the knowledge created by government inspectors, as well as how interest groups used the statute law and the legal system to force social change.

Securing effective legislative remedies was very difficult in a Parliament where the interests of labour were not well represented. Those who opposed the passage of laws to curtail truck and related practices frequently presented two – sometimes contradictory – arguments. Advocates of classical political economy argued that employers and workers should enjoy the freedom to make their own bargains and live with the consequences of those choices. If an employee agreed to sell his or her labour for uncertain quantities of bacon and cheese, it was not for the state to interfere. Agreements about the rules of the workplace and their enforcement, as well as deductions employers were allowed to take from wages, should be made by the interested parties free from outside intervention. If an employer sought to shift many of the risks and costs of doing business to employees, then those employees could always seek better remunerated employment elsewhere. In the 1820s and 1830s, the most forceful advocate of this position was Joseph Hume, who insisted in the House of Commons that "[t]he master and the workman ought to be at liberty to come to whatever agreement they thought proper respecting the wages one is to give

and the other to receive, and respecting the manner and time of paying them."
For over 150 years Hume's argument would remain the most common objection to state intervention against the truck system.[20] The remedy for workers against truck and large fines and deductions was not to be found in the law or state regulation but in their own power to refuse work from employers who engaged in these practices.

The second persistent argument against state regulation of truck and deductions from wages was rooted in paternalism. Truck-paying employers claimed that truck allowed them to exercise sumptuary control over employees, who when left to their own devices spent money in unwise ways. Policy makers and employers frequently discussed the effect that different methods and timing of wage payment had on the alcohol consumption of (especially male) workers.[21] Advocates on both sides of the debate stressed the importance of getting provisions into the hands of working class wives before their husbands drank the wages away. MP Robert Gordon argued against truck legislation in 1830 because

> there was a custom in those places [Dorset and Somerset] of employing the wives and daughters of the peasantry in making gloves, and giving them a certain portion of their earnings in clothes. Far from considering that a loss, he looked on it as an advantage to both parties. If the entire amount of wages were paid in money, it would fall into the hands of the husband, who was not always disposed to spend it in a manner most advantageous to his family.[22]

These sentiments were repeated for the remainder of the nineteenth century.

Other employers who kept company stores argued that their shops were a great convenience to the workforce which otherwise might have to travel great distances to provision themselves. Many common defences for truck, such as remote locations of workplaces or problems with the supply of hard currency, do not hold up to close scrutiny, especially as the nineteenth century progressed. The prominence of retail shopkeepers in the opposition to truck and their complaints about the unfair competition from "Tommy Shops" (shops owned by the employer or a shopkeeper in partnership with that employer) suggest that employers were not simply providing a service for workers where no other shopping options were available.

Truck-paying employers also claimed that company stores protected employees from the dangers of credit offered by retail shopkeepers, whom they charged with luring workers into debt and dependence. They questioned workers' ability to manage credit relationships with the same skill as members of the middle class.[23] Employers also stated that the savings in labour costs that came from the profits of company stores enabled them to continue employing workers in bad economic times.[24] In the twentieth century, employers used paternalism to defend deductions from wages. Fines allowed employers to teach employees proper conduct and discipline them without resorting to the harsher sanction of dismissing them.[25] Deductions taken from the pay of employees for subscriptions to compulsory employer-run benefit clubs protected workers from misfortune.[26] Truck and taking deductions from workers' wages were examples of the paternal care and commitment that masters provided to "their" labourers. Opponents of tougher laws against truck and deductions from wages seemed to embrace the contradictory position that workers should be trusted to make their own contracts of employment but not to spend their own money.

Those opposing the freedom of contract argument noted the obvious imbalances in the bargaining position of employers and employees that went beyond the greater economic power of the former. The law also shaped labour markets in ways that greatly favoured employers for much of the nineteenth century. The 1825 Combination Act, and the judiciary's interpretation of its terms, placed limitations upon the ability of workers to organize and negotiate advantageous terms of employment.[27] Master and servant statutes allowed employers to prosecute certain descriptions of employees before magistrates for breaking their employment contracts by leaving work before the term of the agreement was completed. Magistrates could sentence workers to up to two months' imprisonment with hard labour. Master and servant laws constricted when and how workers were allowed to bargain.[28] In cases where truck masters prosecuted workers under the master and servant law for leaving their employment before the term of service was completed, magistrates almost never accepted the defence that the employer had broken the contract first through the payment of truck wages.[29] The economic and legal obstacles that workers faced when bargaining meant that they often had to live with terms of employment that were to their disadvantage and could not easily leave if they felt mistreated by their employers.

Adam Smith himself identified laws prohibiting the payment of wages in truck as a legitimate state regulation on economic transactions. Smith saw that in real life, as opposed to abstract economic theory, truck was a means by which employers took advantage of their workers. In Chapter 10 of *An Inquiry into the Nature and Causes of the Wealth of Nations*, Smith writes:

> Whenever the legislature attempts to regulate the differences between masters and workmen, its counsellors are the masters. When the regulation, therefore, is in favour of the workmen, it is always just and equitable; but it is sometimes otherwise when in favour of the masters. Thus the law which obliges the masters in several different trades to pay their workmen in money, and not in goods, is quite just and equitable. It imposes no real hardship on the masters; it only obliges them to pay that value in money, which they pretended to pay, but did not always really pay, in goods.[30]

In June of 1830, J.C. Herries read Smith's words to the House of Commons to answer Joseph Hume's strident free trade arguments against laws the prohibiting truck.[31]

Free contract arguments put forward by those in favour of legalizing truck tend to ignore that the payment of truck wages was often a means of *evading* the terms of a contract. Employment agreements that explicitly exchanged labour for goods were rare. In most instances, an employee contracted to work for monetary wages, and the employer used his or her power over the worker to compel the employee to accept goods in lieu of the money promised.

Employers themselves frequently admitted that company stores impeded collective action by workers, leaving employees more tightly tied to the workplace.[32] Truck and related practices created workforces that were more disciplined and less unionized. They made workers less independent, mobile and free. Of course, beyond economic considerations and the law, for many workers the pull of family support networks, emotional rootedness in a community and uncertainty of finding better conditions elsewhere could cause them to endure great unfairness rather than quit and seek employment elsewhere. Furthermore, workers often faced difficulty obtaining new employment without a "character" certificate from their previous employer. Contemporaries often raised these points.[33] This book will shed light on the elasticity of "free trade" discourses and the disjuncture between the theory of freedom to contract and how it was experienced in workplaces and courts of law.

The chapters that follow will explore the struggles that led to the creation of laws to prohibit truck and regulate workplace deductions, as well as the efforts by many individuals to bring those statutes into effect. Legislation prohibiting truck has a history dating back all the way to the reign of Edward IV; a large number of statutes passed before the nineteenth century outlawed the practice in specific trades or regions, often temporarily. Economist George Hilton found that pressure to pass these statutes usually came from workers and employers objecting to rogue masters using truck to evade standard trade rates of pay. He observes that "the truck prohibitions enacted before 1817 were almost entirely adjuncts to the general process of trying to maintain standard rates in the face of various forces for instability."[34]

For most of the nineteenth century, the primary law prohibiting truck was the 1831 Truck Act, which passed Parliament thanks to the repeated efforts of Edward J. Littleton, a Whig MP from Staffordshire. Littleton's work in Parliament was assisted by public support from workers – and guilds, in Staffordshire, Gloucestershire and South Wales – who sought to maintain their level of real wages in the face of an expansion of the truck system between 1824 and 1830. Shopkeepers and money-paying employers from these areas also expressed alarm at the increase of truck and encouraged Littleton.[35] The 1831 Truck Act, which replaced earlier piecemeal legislation, made it illegal to pay servants or artificers in a range of occupations in anything but the "current coin of the realm." The Act allowed a worker who had been paid in truck to bring an action before two magistrates, neither of whom could be engaged in the same trade as the litigants. Magistrates could award the worker the full monetary value of any wages paid in truck and fine the employer £5 to £10 for the first offence, between £10 and £20 for the second and up to £100 for a third violation; magistrates had the discretion to award half of the fine, up to £20, to the informer.[36] Yet the Truck Act was widely considered to be a failure because of the limitations of its composition and the narrow judicial interpretation of its scope. It applied only to specifically listed trades, including mining, iron and steel manufacture, pottery, textiles, lace making and cutlery trades. The failure of the Act to include domestic servants, agricultural workers, casual labourers, railway workers or employees in Ireland was a very important omission. Deductions by the employer for medical care, fuel, equipment and rent remained legal provided they were part of a signed agreement.[37]

After repeated attempts by truck opponents to win new legislation to address the shortcomings of the 1831 Act, in 1887 a new Truck Act was passed. This new Truck Act expanded the protections of the 1831 Act to nearly all manual workers in Britain (including Ireland) and entrusted their enforcement to the inspectors of mines and factories. It was not immediately clear what impact the new law had upon workplace fines and deductions.[38] This confusion was addressed with the 1896 Truck Act, which regulated deductions from wages. It enacted that disciplinary fines on shop assistants and manual workers were only legal if they were authorized in a signed contract or a notice posted prominently in the workplace. The document had to list the specific acts or omissions for which a person could be fined and the amounts that would be taken for each offence. Employers could only fine workers for acts or omissions that harmed the business, and fines had to be "fair and reasonable having regard to all circumstances of the case." Employees had to receive written particulars of every fine levied, which employers had to record in a ledger that the inspectors of mines and factories could access. Employers could only make deductions for bad or negligent work if they were part of a signed contract with the worker or posted in a notice, and the amount deducted could not exceed the actual loss experienced by the employer. The amount taken also had to be "fair and reasonable having regard to all circumstances of the case," and an employer had to provide written particulars to the worker for every deduction. Deductions for tools, materials, light, heat or standing room were subject to the same conditions: there had to be a written contract or notice, the deductions could not exceed the actual cost to the employer, the amounts of the deductions had to be "fair and reasonable having regard to all circumstances of the case" and the employer had to provide the worker with written particulars for every deduction. Enforcement of this act was given to the Inspectors of the Mines and Factories, who had the power to prosecute violators before magistrates for a maximum penalty of 40 shillings per offence. There was also a civil procedure that allowed a worker to go before a magistrate and recover amounts illegally deducted from his or her wages.[39]

Neither these laws nor their impact has received scholarly attention. The only monograph-length treatment of the truck system in Britain is economist George Hilton's *The Truck System Including A History of the British Truck Acts 1465–1960* published in 1960. Hilton focuses primarily upon the effects of the 1831 Truck Act, devoting only four pages to the legislation passed in 1887 and 1896. Moreover, Hilton's work was influenced by the context in which he researched and wrote. Beginning in the 1950s, many employers and conservatives in Britain lobbied for the repeal of all laws against truck, arguing that they were anachronistic and imposed burdensome regulations on employers. Hilton's book and articles buttressed this endeavour by arguing that the laws against truck had always been ineffective and had a negligible impact upon its eventual decline, which he attributes to economic factors, the rise of organized labour and the demise of the trades in which truck was most likely to exist.[40] This interpretation of the truck law has persisted into modern times with little qualification.

Economist Elaine Tan has researched the operation of the truck system in several mines and ironworks and argues that it was not exploitative but rather mutually beneficial for workers and employers. She finds that the price differential between company stores and retail shops was not as great as has been argued by labour historians, as employers could not ruthlessly gouge their workers because of labour mobility. The mark-up in the company stores she examines is similar to, or less than, the costs of credit offered by small shopkeepers. This argument will be addressed further in Chapter 1, but it has many flaws. Her comparison focuses on the larger company stores, and contemporaries noted the mark-up was generally less in the greater workplaces than the smaller "Tommy shops." Additionally, it ignores that employers deliberately used long reckoning periods to push employees into a position where they were compelled to borrow their own money. Long pay periods meant that workers either took advances that they had to use for more expensive goods at the company store or obtained credit from shopkeepers. Weekly wages could have allowed workers to get the best deal of all. Further, she misunderstands the nature of the labour market in the nineteenth century, as well as the abundant evidence of employer coercion upon workers to use the company store. Most importantly, it ignores the voices of working people themselves. In nearly every investigation of the truck system in the nineteenth century, when employees felt free to speak without the threat of reprisals, they almost always condemned the truck system.[41] There is very little evidence that workers thought truck was mutually beneficial.

British historians of labour and popular politics have not investigated truck wages, fines and workplace deductions in sufficient depth. An institutional framework and a focus upon the problem of low wages has caused many prominent labour historians to pass over what was an important grievance for many vulnerable workers in the nineteenth and twentieth centuries. Labour historians sometimes address truck when the issue intersects with the trade union or workers under consideration, oftentimes describing its role in provoking industrial action or popular protest. They rarely offer more than a brief or local examination of the operation of the 1831 Truck Act, and the implications of the 1887 and 1896 Acts remain largely unexplored.[42]

This book will confirm that by many measures the laws against truck were in fact ineffective. The number of prosecutions brought under them fluctuated from year to year but were never large. Individual workers had a lot to lose by confronting an employer who had paid them in truck. The magistrates who enforced the laws were variable in their attitudes toward truck, and even when they found an employer guilty they were rarely willing to impose tough penalties. Whenever Truck Acts cases were appealed to the higher courts, judges who were ideologically hostile to regulatory legislation interpreted the Acts as narrowly as possible, circumscribing their scope and prohibitions, often in ways clearly at odds with legislative intent.

Despite these limitations, I argue that the laws had a greater effect on reducing truck and workplace fines and deductions than historians have realized. Workers, trade unions and allies coalesced around efforts to win legislation from parliament and to bring it into effect. The law legitimized and drew attention to their cause. These campaigns produced speeches, public meetings, protests, strikes, petitioning drives, pamphlets, newspaper editorials and exposés, parliamentary investigations and debate, reports by government inspectors, court cases and legislative proposals, all of which publicized the plight of workers who were cheated out of their wages by truck and unfair deductions. The passage of truck legislation, as well as public campaigns to strengthen it, caused many employers to voluntarily abandon truck, workplace fines and many objectionable deductions. By the end of the nineteenth century, paying workers in truck and cheating them out of their hard-earned wages were seen not only as technically illegal but also as dishonourable ways of doing business. Changes in the law have the power over time to change beliefs, customs and practices. During the nineteenth and twentieth centuries in the struggle over real wages, labour did not always win the results they wanted in the political and legal arenas, but in the long term they ultimately did win the argument. Without the legitimacy of the law, that would have been more difficult to achieve. This book will evaluate and examine that struggle.

Chapter 1 explores the repeated attempts by industrial workers, retail shopkeepers, money-paying employers and clergy in Staffordshire and Wales to use local magistrates' courts to end truck. The 1831 Truck Act made it illegal to pay servants or artificers in particular trades in anything but the current coin of the realm. Between 1842 and 1853, retail shopkeepers, industrial workers, money-paying employers and local clergy banded together in anti-truck societies to fund prosecutions under the Act. This strategy ultimately failed to permanently reduce the truck system in Staffordshire or Wales because of the limitations of the Act and the interpretation by magistrates and judges of its scope. Studying the obstacles to this local litigation strategy can shed light on the administration of summary justice by magistrates, as well as prevailing understandings of consumption, credit and contracts. The failure caused opponents of truck to shift their focus toward lobbying Parliament for more comprehensive legislation with tougher penalties. This chapter will examine the language that opponents of truck used to articulate their grievances. It will also analyse the seemingly contradictory use of free-market and paternalist rhetoric deployed by those who hoped to prevent the passage of additional anti-truck legislation.

In the 1860s and 1870s so-called New Model Unions became more publicly prominent, eventually forming the Trades Union Congress (TUC) and later the Parliamentary Committee of the TUC. Alexander MacDonald of the Miners' Association, a long-time opponent of the truck system, made significant efforts in the 1860s and 1870s to end truck and bring about the weekly payment of wages without deductions, as shown in Chapter 2. MacDonald won over editors of both the *North British Daily Mail* (*NBDM*) and the *Times* to the anti-truck cause. The *NBDM* found a shocking persistence of truck payments in Scotland and published its investigative findings during the months of June and July in 1869. Building upon the publicity from this report, MacDonald led large public meetings and lobbied government inspectors of the mines and factories as well as sympathetic MPs to pressure Parliament in action.

Their efforts eventually resulted in the 1871 Truck Commission, one of the most thorough Parliamentary investigations of the nineteenth century, in which commissioners asked 45,125 questions to 569 witnesses. This testimony (and the *NBDM* exposé) reveals the experiences of men and women who were paid in truck and how they felt about it. The Commission issued a report which supported most of organized labour's arguments against the truck system and largely endorsed its demand for the weekly payment of wages in the current coin of the realm (but not its desire to eliminate all deductions from wages). It also forcefully rejected the paternalist arguments that the keepers of company stores had used to defend their system. However, trade unions discovered that winning the argument was not the same as having the political strength to enact change. This chapter will examine how workers experienced truck, the debate over government regulation of wages and the power of organized labour.

The TUC persisted in its demands for legislation mandating the weekly payment of wages in the current coin of the realm without any deductions. By the late 1870s the issues of workplace fines and deductions from wages were becoming more pressing. Employees had no power to make sure that the deducted funds went toward their stated purpose. They disapproved of excessive deductions for sharpening tools, heat, light, power or equipment necessary to do their jobs and increasingly complained about arbitrary workplace fines. When abused by employers, these practices could be as profitable and useful for labour discipline as the truck system.

By the mid-1880s the Parliamentary Committee of the TUC found some new allies in Parliament, including Charles Bradlaugh and Donald Crawford, and they were assisted by revelations of the persistence of truck and poundage in Wales and Scotland. Chapter 3 will examine their efforts to obtain a tougher Truck Act from Parliament. Hilton and many other labour historians treat the 1887 Truck Act as an unnecessary afterthought, but in fact it was a piece of legislation that was fiercely debated and repeatedly amended by a wide range of diverse interests. The resulting compromise that was able to pass Parliament left labour unsatisfied, but it was an improvement over the 1831 Act. The legislation of 1887 expanded the scope of the Truck Act to include nearly all manual labourers (including those in Ireland), outlawed poundage, strengthened the language against compulsion and delegated its enforcement to inspectors of the mines and factories. It also placed some limitations upon deductions, and, in fact, Bradlaugh interpreted his Act to have placed restrictions upon workplace fines as well. The high courts did not share this interpretation.

Although the Factory Inspectorate and the Home Office received little encouragement from the high courts, they continued to invoke the 1887 Truck Act with employers who took excessive fines and deductions, threatening to prosecute them for not paying all wages owed to workers in the current coin of the realm. In the vanguard of these efforts was the female factory inspectorate, created in 1893 to focus upon the conditions of low-paid women workers in factories and sweated industries. These women, assisted in their efforts by Liberal MP Sir Charles Dilke and Gertrude Tuckwell of the WTUL, publicized numerous cases of outrageous injustices inflicted upon female employees by unscrupulous employers. Chapter 4 describes how these efforts culminated in the 1896 Truck Act. However, far from being grateful for this new law, workers and organized labour were outraged. Rather than perceiving the new law as regulating and prohibiting many different types of deductions from wages, they understood the law as "legalizing fines" and obnoxious set-offs, giving statutory sanction to practices that labour had believed were illegal.

Chapter 5 uses the efforts of the Factory Inspectorate to enforce the 1896 Truck Act as a window into understanding the experiences of low-paid workers in sweated industries as well as the ambitions of middle-class female inspectors who hoped to create more opportunities for women in the civil service. It will also provide insight into the push and pull between workers, unions, employers, parliament, the regulatory state and different levels of the British legal system. It demonstrates the ways in which the law could be used to reduce fines and deductions even in the absence of successful prosecutions.

Chapter 6 explains the efforts led by female trade unions and female factory inspectors to pressure the new Liberal government in 1906 to pass legislation that would outlaw most types of fines and deductions from wages. Female factory inspectors were able to use over a decade's worth of accumulated expert knowledge to build a compelling case that fines and deductions from wages for damaged work should be outlawed. A Departmental Committee on the Truck Acts investigated these issues between 1906 and 1908, but the Committee split in its recommendations between a group that wanted tighter regulation of these exactions and another that wanted to eliminate them altogether. While Parliament did not pass legislation based upon the conflicting recommendations of the Departmental Committee on the Truck Acts, in 1909 it did pass a new law that provided some assistance to a small number of poor workers who had been highly susceptible to having their wages reduced by fines and deductions. In 1909, Parliament passed the Trade Boards Act, which applied to workers in ready-made and bespoke tailoring, domestic chain making, card-box making and machine-made lace making and finishing. The legislation allowed for the creation of Trade Boards in the named industries where wages were deemed unacceptably low. These boards consisted of representatives of labour, representatives of employers and independent members appointed by the government and were empowered to establish minimum time rates of wages or minimum piece rates. The law contained a number of loopholes and limitations, but it did lead to significant improvements in pay for workers in these jobs.[43] Of particular relevance was Section six of the Trade Boards Act, which stated that the minimum wage rate decided by a Trade Board must be paid to the person employed "clear of all deductions." Labour and its allies were not satisfied with this legislation and continued to agitate for the abolition of fines and deductions. Reacting to protests, demonstrations and petitioning drives – led primarily by female trade unions – the Liberal government was in the early stages of drafting reform legislation when the Great War broke out, stalling progress on this front.

When evaluating the exploitation of working people, labour historians have often focused upon the struggle over control of the production process and the small rewards provided to employees for their labour. The fact that many workers could not even secure the low wages promised to them and faced great disadvantages in consumption is terrain that has been less explored by historians.[44] Not only were the wages of the poor tragically small, but they could not make a shilling go nearly as far as their middle-class counterparts could. This book is about the people who tried to change that.

Notes

1 *Cases of Distress and Oppression in the Staffordshire Potteries; By Labourers Wages Being Paid in Truck* (Market Place, Burslem: Brougham Printer, 1830), Case 6, p. 5. Goldsmith-Kress Library of Economic Literature, Reel #26355.

2 *Report of the Commissioner Appointed under the Provisions of the Act 5& 6 Victoria, c.99 to Enquire into the Operation of that Act and into the State of the Population in the Mining Districts, 1850* (London: W. Clowes and Sons, for HM Stationary Office, 1850), p. 21. Staffordshire Country Record Office, D260/M/F/5/18. For two other examples of employers using cheques in this way, see: *Walsall Free Press,* 21 November 1857, p. 3 and *The Glamorgan, Monmouth and Brecon Gazette Cardiff Advertiser, and Merthyr Guardian,* 9 September 1843, p. 1.

3 *The Monmouthshire Merlin and South Wales Advertiser,* 5 October 1844, 23 November 1844, p. 3.

4 *North British Daily Mail,* 3 July 1869, p. 5.

5 *Cardiff Times,* 30 April 1887.

6 *Factories and Workshops: Annual Report of the Chief Inspector of Factories and Workshops for the Year 1899* (London: HM Stationary Office, 1900), pp. 275–276. Parliamentary Papers [cd. 223].

7 *Factories and Workshops: Annual Report of the Chief Inspector of Factories and Workshops for the Year 1900* (London: HM Stationary Office, 1901), p. 404. Parliamentary Papers [cd. 668].

8 *Belfast Newsletter,* 11 September 1909. Gertrude Tuckwell Papers, London Metropolitan University Archives. For another example of a similar case, see *Factories and Workshops: Annual Report of the Chief Inspector of Factories for the Year 1899, Part II: Reports* (London: HM Stationary Office, 1900), p. 142. Parliamentary Papers [cd. 223].

9 *Leicester Post,* 16 December 1912. Gertrude Tuckwell Papers, London Metropolitan University Archives.

10 *Annual Report of the Chief Inspector of Factories . . . for the Year 1901, Part II: Reports* (1902), p. 149.

11 Mary MacArthur, "Trade Unions," in Tuckwell, Smith, MacArthur, Tennant, Adler, Anderson and Black, *Woman in Industry from Seven Points of View* (London: Duckworth and Co., 1908), p. 69.

12 The National Archives (TNA), LAB 14/47; *Annual Report of the Chief Inspector of Factories . . . for the Year 1901, Part II: Reports* (1902), p. 190.

13 *Factories and Workshops: Annual Report of the Chief Inspector of Factories for the Year 1904, Reports* (London: HM Stationary Office, 1905), p. 282. Parliamentary Papers [cd. 2569]. For similar examples of workers being charged for errors in production, see: *Factories and Workshops: Annual Report of the Chief Inspector of Factories for the Year 1902: Part I: Reports* (London: HM Stationary Office, 1903), pp. 189–191, Parliamentary Papers [cd 1610]; Rose Squire, *Thirty Years in the Public Service: An Industrial Retrospect* (London: Nisbet and Co, 1927), p. 106.

14 *Departmental Committee on the Truck Acts, Report of The Truck Committee, Vol. I: Report and Appendices* (London: HM Stationary Office, 1908), p. 20. Parliamentary Papers, [cd 4442].

15 *Departmental Committee on the Truck Acts, Report of The Truck Committee . . .* (1908), pp. 19–21.

16 *The Daily Chronicle,* 31 March 1898 in TNA, HO 45 9986 X68918.

17 *Report of the Commissioners Appointed to Inquire into the Truck System, Volume I: Report, Schedules, Supplement. Vol. II: Minutes of Evidence* (1871) *Parliamentary Papers,* XXXVI [c326–c327], xx. M. Curthoys, *Governments, Labour and the Law in Mid-Victorian Britain: Trade Union Legislation of the 1870s* (Oxford: Clarendon Press, 2003), p. 238.

18 *The Tommy, or Truck System, Exposed in Three Letters to the Editors of the Birmingham Journal* (Dudley: The Office of Hinton's Executors, 1829), p. 7. Goldsmith-Kress Library of Economic Literature, Reel #25792.

19 *A Report of the Proceedings of the Anti-Truck Meeting for the Staffordshire Potteries Held on the Pottery Race Ground on Monday 18 October 1830. William Ridgway, Esq. Chief Bailiff of Hanley and Shelton, in the Chair* (Hanley: Printed at the Mercury Office by T. Allbut, 1830), p. 4. Goldsmith-Kress Library of Economic Literature, Reel #26439; *Monmouthshire Merlin,* 9 December 1843, p. 3. Also see: *Wolverhampton Chronicle,* 13 March 1850, p. 4; "District News: The Truck System: Public Meeting at Bilston," Staffordshire Record Office, D260/M/F/5/18. For more on R.E. Heathcote (1780–1850), see: David Dyble, *The Turbulent Squire of Apedale: Richard Edensor Heathcote (1780–1850)* (Audley and District Family History Publications, 2010).

20 *Hansard Parliamentary Debates Online, House of Commons,* 23 June 1830, c.596; J.L. Hammond and Barbara Hammond, *The Town Labourer, 1760, 1832: The New Civilization* (London: Longmans, 1932 (orig 1917), p. 206.

21 *A Dispassionate and Succinct View of the Truck System as It Affects the Labourer, the Capitalist, the Landlord, and the State; with an Attempt to Answer the Query, "Is It a Subject for Legislative Interference?" Being a Reply to the Objectors to the System* (Birmingham: Printed by Thomas Knott, Jr., 1830), pp. 4–6, Goldsmith-Kress Library of Economic Literature, Reel #26456.

22 *Hansard Parliamentary Debates Online, House of Commons,* 5 July 1830, c.956.

23 *Hansard Parliamentary Debates Online, House of Commons,* 30 June 1830, c.601.

24 *Hansard Parliamentary Debates Online, House of Commons,* 23 June 1830, c.601.

25 *Departmental Committee on the Truck Acts: Minutes of Evidence, Vol. II* (1908), p. 22, questions 273–274; p. 23, questions 295–297; p. 29, questions 424–428; p. 30, Questions 439–447, 506; pp. 34–35, questions 530–533, 548–550; p. 32, Questions 487–489; p. 41, Questions 694, 708; p. 43, question 743; p. 66, questions 1368–1369; p. 73, Question 1501–1502; p. 74, Questions 1524–1526, 1539–1546, 1565; p. 71, questions 1467; p. 72, Questions 1489–1492; p. 175, Questions 4567–4571; p. 176, Questions 4593–4597, 4609–4613; p. 178, Questions 4655–4661, 4671–4672; p. 179, Question 4700; p. 367, Questions 9752–9755; p. 369, Question 9792; p. 370, Questions 9806–9808, 9811–9812, 9814. *Departmental Committee on the Truck Acts: Minutes of Evidence, Vol. III* (1908), p. 33,

Questions 10961–10962; p. 38, 11111–11117; pp. 51–52, Question 11522–11523; p. 55, Questions 11599–11603; p. 67, Question 11915; p. 233, Question 16025; p. 277, Question 17276; p. 290, Questions 17639–17641; p. 291, Question 17657.

26 *Report of the Truck Commission* (1871), pp. xiv, xlv–xlvii.

27 John Orth, *Combination and Conspiracy: A Legal History of Trade Unionism, 1721–1906* (Oxford: Clarendon Press, 1991).

28 Christopher Frank, *Master and Servant Law: Chartists, Trade Unions, Radical Lawyers and the Magistracy in England, 1840–1865* (Farnham: Ashgate Press, 2010); Marc Steinberg, *England's Great Transformation: Law, Labor, and the Industrial Revolution* (Chicago: University of Chicago Press, 2016); *Masters, Servants and Magistrates in Britain and Empire, 1562–1955*, Eds: Douglas Hay and Paul Craven (Chapel Hill: University of North Carolina Press, 2004); Robert Steinfeld, *Coercion, Contract and Free Labor in the Nineteenth Century* (Cambridge: Cambridge University Press, 2001).

29 Willibald Steinmetz, "Was There a De-Juridification of Employment Relations in Britain?" in Willibald Steinmetz (ed.), *Private Law and Social Inequality in the Industrial Age: Comparing the Legal Cultures of Britain, France, Germany and the United States* (London: Oxford University Press, 2000); Christopher Frank, "'Let But One of Them Come Before Me and I'll Commit Him': Trade Unions, Magistrates and the Law in Mid-Nineteenth Century Staffordshire," *Journal of British Studies* 44:1 (2005): 64–91.

30 Adam Smith, *An Inquiry into the Nature and Causes of the Wealth of Nations,* Book II, Chapter 10, Part II; Hammond and Hammond, *The Town Labourer, 1760–1832,* p. 214.

31 *Hansard Parliamentary Debates Online, House of Commons,* 5 July 1830, c.961.

32 *Some Remarks on the Injurious Effect of the Truck System with an Appendix Consisting of Affidavits* (Dudley: Stanley, Printer, 1830), p. 13.

33 *Select Committee on Payment of Wages Bill, and Payment of Wages (Hosiery) Bill: Report, Proceedings, Minutes of Evidence, Index* (London: HM Stationary Office, 1854), p. 7. *Parliamentary Papers* [cd. 382], Q. 363–364, 4210; *Select Committee on the Payment of Wages* (1842), Q. 337–341; *Commission of Inquiry into the Mines Act* (1852), p. 439; *Labour and the Poor in England and Wales, Vol. III,* 151; *Wolverhampton Chronicle,* 4, May 1842, p. 3; David Bailey, *The Truck System: A Book For Masters and Workmen* (London: Fred Pitman, 1859), pp. 6–7; *Hansard Parliamentary Debates Online, House of Commons,* 5 July 1830, c. 969; Friedrich Engels, *The Condition of the Working Class in England* (Stanford: Stanford University Press, 1958 (orig 1845)), pp. 204–207, 211.

34 George Hilton, *The Truck System Including a History of the British Truck Acts 1465–1960* (Cambridge: Heffer & Sons, 1960), p. 63.

35 Hilton, *The Truck System,* pp. 97–113, 115; George Hilton, "The Truck Act of 1831," *The Economic History Review* 10:3 (1958):470–479; D. Arlington, "A Squire's Examples: The Persistent Persuasion of Edward J. Littleton," *Western Speech* 38 (1974):162–169. Also see Elaine Tan, "Ideology, Interest Groups, and Institutional Change: The Case of the British Prohibition of Wages in Kind," *Journal of Institutional Economics* 1:2 (2005):175–191. Tan argues that a strong and under-explored motivation for the passage of the 1831 Truck Act was the desire by the state to eliminate private currency and defend its seigniorage rents. A problem with this interpretation is the fact that discussion of currency occupied a very tiny part of the debate inside and outside of Parliament in 1826–1831 and almost no part of the debate in the subsequent decades. Furthermore, if the state was an interested party the suppression of truck, why was it so resistant in the 1840s, 1850s and 1870s to passing reforms that would have made the 1831 Act more effective? See Elaine Tan, "Scrip as Private Money, Monetary Monopoly, and the Rent-Seeking State in Britain," *The Economic History Review* 64:1 (2011):237–255.

36 1 & 2 Will 4, c.37, s.4–5, 9, 23–24, 27; Hilton, *The Truck System,* p. 111.

37 1 & 2 William IV, c.36 (1831) repealed the piecemeal anti-truck provisions from Acts passed in 1465, 1566, 1572, 1703, 1711, 1712, 1715, 1726, 1740, 1749, 1756, 1757, 1777, 1779, 1817 and 1818. Once these Acts were repealed, 1 & 2 William IV, c.37 (1831)

applied new anti-truck penalties to a number of specifically listed trades. Hilton notes that by 1820, 24 Anti-Truck Acts were in effect. Of these, 19 were still in effect in 1830. In 1831 one was repealed by Parliament, and the remaining eighteen were repealed by 1 & 2 William IV, c.36 (1831), to be replaced by 1 & 2 William IV, c.37 (1831). See Hilton, *The Truck System*, pp. 7–8, 65–66. 1 & 2 Will 4, c.37, s.1, 3, 19, 20, 21; *The Times*, 5 June 1840.

38   50 & 51 Victoria, c.46.

39   59 & 60 Victoria, c.44.

40   Hilton, *The Truck System*; George Hilton, "The Truck System in the Nineteenth Century," *The Journal of Political Economy* 65:3 (January 1957):237–256; Hilton, "The Truck Act of 1831," pp. 470–479. Also see: Otto Kahn-Freund, "The Tangle of the Truck Acts," 4 *Industrial Law Review* 2 (1949–1950):1–9.

41   Elaine Tan, "Regulating Wages in Kind: Theory and Evidence from Britain," *Journal of Law, Economics, and Organization* 22:2 (2006):442–458.

42   George Barnsby, *The Working Class Movement in the Black Country from 1760 to 1867* (Wolverhampton: Integrated Publishing Services, 1977), p. 220; Alan B. Campbell, *The Lanarkshire Miners: A Social History of their Trade Union, 1775–1974* (Edinburgh: John Donald Publishers, Ltd., 1979); J.E. Williams, *The Derbyshire Miners: A Study in Industrial and Social History* (London: Unwin Brothers Limited, 1962), pp. 29–31, 61–63, 74, 90, 93, 97–98, 455; David Williams, *John Frost: A Study in Chartism* (London: Augustus M. Kelley, 1969), pp. 112–113; Edward Thompson, *The Making of the English Working Class* (London: Penguin, 1963), pp. 222, 270, 566, 591, 602; Sidney Webb and Beatrice Webb, *A History of Trade Unionism* (New York: Augustus M Kelly, 1965 (orig 1894)), pp. 50, 89, 371; J.L. Hammond and Barbara Hammond, *The Skilled Labourer, 1760–1832* (London: Longmans, Green and Co, 1919), pp. 20, 21, 26, 33, 157, 161, 163, 184, 228, 229, 235, 236, 258, 266; Hammond and Hammond, *The Town Labourer*, pp. 40–42, 65–71, 206, 214, 255; G.C. Allen, *The Industrial Development of Birmingham and the Black Country, 1860–1927* (London: George Allen and Unwin, Ltd., 1929), pp. 128, 144, 155–157, 171–172, 339; Gordon M. Wilson, *Alexander McDonald: Leader of the Miners* (Aberdeen: Aberdeen University Press, 1982), pp. 20, 36, 47, 64, 79, 80, 81, 99, 105, 106, 115, 129, 138, 161; John Rule, *The Experience of Labour in Eighteenth Century English Industry* (New York: St. Martin's Press, 1981), pp. 138–139; John Rule, *The Labouring Classes in Early Industrial England, 1750–1850* (London: Longman, 1986), Chapters 2 and 4; J.H. Morris and L.J. Williams, *The South Wales Coal Industry, 1841–1875* (Cardiff: University of Wales Press, 1958), pp. 224–225, 265–269; James Handley, *The Navvy in Scotland* (Cork: Cork University Press, 1970), Chapter 6; H.A. Clegg, Alan Fox, and A.F. Thompson, *A History of British Trades Unions Since 1889, Vol. I, 1889–1910* (Oxford: Clarendon Press, 1964), pp. 186, 227, 386, 397, 403; Engels, *Condition of the Working Class in England*, pp. 204–207, 211, 215, 285, 289; E.H. Hunt, *British Labour History, 1815–1914* (Atlantic Highlands, NJ: Humanities Press, 1981), pp. 61, 65, 68, 110, 195, 265; Also see the treatment of the 1831 Act by historians studying changing regimes of local law enforcement: Roger Swift, "The English Urban Magistracy and the Administration of Justice During the Early Nineteenth Century: Wolverhampton, 1815–1860," *Midland History* 17 (1992):75–92; David Philips, "The Black Country Magistracy, 1835–1860: A Changing Elite and the Exercise of Its Power," *Midland History* 3:2 (1976):161–190; D.C. Woods, "The Borough Magistracy and the Authority Structure in the Black Country, 1858–1875," *West Midlands Studies* 12 (1979).

43   Shiela C. Blackburn, "Curse or Cure? Why Was the Enactment of the Trade Boards Act so Controversial?" *British Journal of Industrial Relations* 47:2 (June 2009):214–239; Shelia Blackburn, "Must Low Pay Always Be with Us? The Origins of Britain's Minimum Wage Legislation," *Historical Studies in Industrial Relations* 23/24 (Spring/Autumn 2007):61–101; Simon Deakin and Francis Green, "One Hundred Years of British Minimum Wage Legislation," *British Journal of Industrial Relations* 47:2 (June 2009):205–213;

Sheila Blackburn, "'Between the Devil of Cheap Labour Competition and the Sea of Family Poverty?' Sweated Labour in Time and Place, 1840–1914," *Labour History Review* 71:2 (August 2006):91–101; Jessica S. Bean and George R. Boyer, "The Trade Boards Act of 1909 and the Alleviation of Household Poverty," *British Journal of Industrial Relations,* 47:2 (June 2009):240–264.

44 A Noteworthy exception: Peter Gurney, *Wanting and Having: Popular Politics and Liberal Consumerism in England, 1830–1870* (Manchester: Manchester University Press, 2015); Peter Gurney, *Co-Operative Culture and the Politics of Consumption in England, 1870–1930* (Manchester: Manchester University Press, 1996).

1 Anti-truck prosecution societies and the campaign against truck, 1831–1860

Introduction

This chapter will explore the arguments and strategies deployed during an especially active period of popular mobilization against truck in the 1840s and 1850s. The rhetoric and tactics of opponents reveal a great deal about the centrality of credit and consumption to people's sense of their own identities, independence and claims to political citizenship. Those mobilized against truck in the mid-nineteenth century included money-paying employers, shopkeepers and trade unionists who joined together in anti-truck associations throughout Staffordshire and Wales. By encouraging and funding anti-truck litigation under the 1831 Truck Act, they sought to use the legal system as a force for social and economic change.[1]

The failure of this litigation strategy to produce long-term results caused these organizations to shift their focus from institutions of local justice toward lobbying Parliament for more comprehensive legislation containing tougher penalties. For much of the nineteenth century, the debate over the appropriate role of the government in preventing truck took place in many different forums. The arguments over the enactment of additional anti-truck legislation highlight the significant gap that existed between the seemingly neutral language of "freedom to contract" and how employment agreements were actually experienced by workers. These debates also demonstrate the centrality of class and gender to how people made sense of the benefits and perils of consumption and credit during the mid-nineteenth century.

Reformers' efforts to win additional anti-truck statutes in the 1850s failed largely due to two arguments by opponents of further legislation. First, many Members of Parliament (MPs) expressed discomfort about interfering with freedom to contract and the employment relationship, arguing that if truck were a grievance for workers in a particular workplace, then they could always find other employment. Additionally, advocates of company stores defended truck in paternalistic terms by raising doubts about the ability of working-class men and women to manage their consumption and credit responsibly in the absence of the sumptuary control provided by the company store. When put together, opponents of further anti-truck legislation from the mid-1850s, all the way through the mid-1880s, adopted the apparently contradictory position of having confidence in the ability of workers to navigate labour markets but not consumer markets.

Truck and company stores in mid–nineteenth-century Britain

Truck encompassed a range of practices by which employers either directly paid their workers in goods or exercised compulsion over how they spent wages. In the eighteenth and early nineteenth centuries, truck often took the form of tickets redeemable at a company store, or "Tommy shop," owned by the employer or a shopkeeper in partnership with that employer.[2] Opponents objected to it because it compelled workers to purchase goods for higher prices than could be found in retail stores, thereby cheating them of the full value of their wages. At different points in the nineteenth century, investigators made comparisons, of variable reliability, between products sold at truck shops and local retail stores, estimating that the former were from 10% to 150% more expensive.[3]

To address critics who suggested that the form and quantity of wages was a matter for the contracting parties to decide for themselves, anti-truck advocates responded that laws against truck did not "interfere" with contracts but rather ensured their enforcement. Employment agreements never explicitly mentioned truck, and anti-truck advocates pointed out that the terms of a contract with a truck master could never be fixed or definite in terms. Workers in many trades could be imprisoned under master-and-servant laws for breaking their employment contracts, but truck allowed employers to reduce the value of their obligations under the agreement without penalty by raising prices at the company store.[4] Indeed, many observed that in periods of economic downturn, more employers adopted truck, and those already practicing it increased the proportion of wages that workers were expected to spend at the "Tommy shop."[5]

After the passage of the 1831 Truck Act some employers sought to preserve the advantages of truck by adopting methods of wage payment and advances that technically complied with the law but still pressured workers to spend their wages at the company store. These evasions usually involved long pay periods, often as long as one month to six weeks. Workers and their family members, however, were permitted to make weekly draws against wages earned but not yet paid. These advances were paid in cash (usually in an office connected to the company store) to avoid the penalties of the 1831 Act, but cash payments were permitted only with the (deniable) understanding that some or all of the wages advanced would be spent at the owner's shop. Failure to do so could result in the refusal of any future draws or even termination at the earliest opportunity.[6] The wife of a coal miner from Bilston, Staffordshire, told a reporter, "I get half money and half goods . . . if I do not spend 5s out of every 10s [in the shop] my husband will never have another day's work in the pit." Other women gave similar testimony.[7] This gave employers an advantage through lower labour costs and provided them with a powerful means to discipline and maintain an affordable workforce.

Elaine Tan has argued that in the nineteenth century the truck system was not exploitative, but rather mutually beneficial. She interprets the higher cost of goods in the company stores (which she argues was often exaggerated by opponents of truck) as the cost of receiving credit from the employer in the form of advances on wages at the store. In many cases this mark-up was less than the interest charged by local retailers when allowing workers to purchase goods on credit.[8] This argument is problematic because employers had considerable power to influence the workers' need for credit or advances through the establishment of long pay periods. Further, advances at the company store were almost always drawn against wages that were earned but not yet paid. Thus it seems wrong to conceptualize the wage advance as representing employer credit or a loan to the worker. One might equally consider that the worker was forced to loan the employer his or her labour for which the employer had not yet paid.

How widespread were company stores or the payment of wages in kind? According to a Parliamentary Select Committee, by 1854 the payment of truck wages in company stores was concentrated in the coal and iron industries of South Wales, south Staffordshire and western Scotland, but it was by no means confined to these areas or trades. In the mid-nineteenth century, truck was also practiced in parts of Nottinghamshire, Warwickshire, Derbyshire, Leicestershire and Yorkshire and was experienced by railway and canal workers, agricultural workers, framework knitters, nailers, potters and cutlery trade workers. In 1852, an inspector of the mines reported that the 18 largest mining and iron firms in Staffordshire and 12 of the 17 largest collieries and iron firms in Monmouthshire and Glamorganshire kept truck shops, a significant increase from just eight years earlier. In Bilston alone, there were more than 11 company stores dispensing truck wages to workers.[9] As late as 1871, the government estimated that over 500,000 people in Britain, including possibly 40% of Scottish miners, lived off truck.[10]

Arguments against truck, 1830–1860

Individuals from different social backgrounds used many arguments against truck. The most widely circulated anti-truck discourses were remarkably consistent, describing truck as a fraud against workers that violated their rights as consumers. The role that truck played in shaping local labour markets and regimes of workplace discipline, or in impeding union organizing, were not as frequently articulated until later in the century. Indeed, in the 1840s and 1850s, when these issues were raised, it was by employers as arguments in favour of truck. Anti-truck advocates stressed that the ability to spend wages as one chose was a fundamental right, part of what made a person a free and independent citizen. They also argued that being deprived of this right lowered both the living standards and habits of self-reliance of working-class families. Appropriating and modifying the political language of respectability, opponents of truck in the 1840s and 1850s also insisted that the payment of wages in kind interfered with proper domestic roles and degraded the working-class family.

Opponents of truck complained that the practice deprived workers of the right to use their own ingenuity to stretch their wages and manage their credit to the greatest advantage. Here, the language often portrayed truck as an attack upon the domestic sphere, by focusing upon women and the deterioration of the household. Opponents of truck and defenders of the company store both seemed to agree that, in most instances, ideally women managed the family budget and consumption. Commissioner of the Mines, Seymour Tremenheere, reported to Parliament that truck was "unjust and injurious" to miners' families in Staffordshire because

> a careful wife, obliged to deal at the truck shop, cannot make her husband's wages go as far as if she were at full liberty to exercise her judgment and experience as to where and when she should make her purchases.[11]

A South Wales newspaper editorial argued that truck demeaned miners' wives:

> For the woman ... she felt a humbleness that she had never felt before. It had been a pride for her to expend their weekly wages in providing for their children, but now she felt she was dependent on another – she could no longer exercise her experience, or bestow her patronage upon her neighbours – she must seek "the shop" for everything – take what is given to her – and dare not grumble lest retaliation should find out her husband.[12]

The *Monmouthshire Merlin* objected to truck because it "is degrading to the character of the wife and the dignity of women," and *The Times* added that it "interferes with ... proper liberties and domestic arrangements of the operative."[13]

Managing the family budget was seen as an important skill set often exercised by women, and one that could determine the credit-worthiness and material condition of the working-class family. Opponents of truck emphasized this point to stress that truck masters were reaching into the private sphere, a realm of life that should be beyond the purview of an employer, and humbling the working-class wife by interfering with her administration of household resources. Through this interference, truck masters undermined the dignity, pride and position of the working-class wives by taking away part of their authority. Adopting the language of domesticity was a common tactic among male working-class radicals as a means of claiming respectability and the full political rights of citizenship. This language drew attention to the ways in which truck worked against middle-class moral values.[14]

Government inspectors of mines, railways and factories also argued that truck reduced working-class families to a dependent state. They claimed that reliance upon the company store reduced incentive to adopt frugal habits, practice good household management and accumulate savings. In 1852, Tremenheere complained to Parliament that truck prevented workers from making contributions to benefit clubs or friendly societies. Some mine owners who paid truck wages countered that they sponsored funds to which employees made contributions from their wages, which provided payments to injured or sick members. The *Second Report on Children's Employment* (1843) noted that truck involved a double theft from a frugal worker because it allowed employers to earn interest on money that should have been paid out in wages, interest that could have gone to an industrious employee who deposited pay in a savings bank. The report's author argued that truck "encourages improvidence by preventing the chance of a habit of saving, for nobody can save food." This lack of savings

> prevents the family from obtaining a sufficient supply of clothes, and more comfortable furniture, – in proportion to the possession of which it is always found that the working man becomes more steady, careful, industrious and respectable. It therefore amounts to a prevention of good conduct.[15]

According to this argument, acquiring goods tethered a male worker to the world of respectability, grounding him and making him more reliable, compliant and hard working.

Although it had been illegal since 1842, another form of truck that observers argued was detrimental to the working-class family was the payment of wages at a public house (often owned by an employer or subcontractor). On the payday, the employer would have a large single note for the payment of all workers' wages, which could only be broken and divided by the landlord after the male workers had drunk a specified amount. It was argued that this practice encouraged drunkenness and undermined domestic life. Many argued that company stores encouraged drunkenness among men because "the husband is tempted to spend in drink the small sums of money that come into his hands . . . it is suggested that there is the shop for the wife to go to for all that is wanted at home" and the money portion of the wages were his to spend.[16] However, defenders of company stores argued that truck gave women more direct control over their families' wages by preventing their husbands from wasting their pay on drink.[17]

Consumption was only one part of a wife's domestic duties, which explains why opponents of truck emphasized the long waiting lines at truck shops, which took women from their families and the home. Because many such shops in Wales and Staffordshire allowed draws only once a week and held limited stock, on "draw days" there were frequently long lines of women outside from 5 a.m. until late in the evening.[18] This made careful consumption even more difficult because individuals were often pressured to rush in making their selections. Opponents of truck frequently emphasized this point, recounting (possibly apocryphal) stories of injuries to unattended children while their mothers waited in line.[19]

This was another rhetorical effort to portray truck masters as disrupters of the proper family order. These statements also reveal anxiety about women's role in consumption, which transgressed public private realms. More than one truck master responded that women waited outside their shops not due to long queues, but "generally for the sake of gossip."[20] Opponents also argued that, in truck districts, working-class homes were poorly kept and their children shabbily dressed and barely educated: thus truck had interfered with women's ability to conform to middle-class notions of their duties as wives and mothers.[21]

The language of the rights and independence of workers, as well as comparisons of truck to serfdom and slavery, was also pervasive in anti-truck discourses.[22] Truck was "an unjust encroachment on the rights and liberties of the working man-destroying to a great extent, his free agency, reducing him to the condition of a mere vassal."[23] The *Wolverhampton Chronicle* editorialized that "under the truck system, the labouring man is almost as much a slave as ever were the West Indian slaves" because under truck "he eats and drinks and wears what his master chooses."[24] A solicitor argued in court that a truck master was "a practical slave holder over 500 men who should be absolutely deprived of the power of spending their own money." This made them "literally like oxen and asses, dependent upon their masters' for food that they eat."[25] David Bailey, author of the 1859 pamphlet *The Truck System: A Book for Masters and Workmen*, argued a worker paid in truck could "never say 'I am a free man,' for he is not free to appropriate his own earnings as he pleases."[26] It was often suggested that choice in consumption was among the worker's last vestiges of independence in the industrial world. Employers had control over the workplace, and it was oppressive to permit this authority to extend further. The *Monmouthshire Merlin* called truck "repugnant to the manly pride and independent feelings of the workman," and stressed:

> The modern labourer is already too much of a machine ... confined within the forge, the mill, the mine, or the factory. It would be cruel to further deprive him of that independence that consists of that faculty of 'doing what he likes with his own' in his few moments of leisure ... without feeling the chain of dependence is forever around his neck.[27]

The Times argued that "the operatives would like control ... to stop at the mill; they expect to be controlled there, ... but at their home they would be their own masters." Truck forced "operatives to live perpetually within an invisible fence of mill law rule."[28]

Opponents of truck also complained about the quality and the narrow range of products offered by the truck shop as well as the inconvenience of not having cash for other needs.[29] Landlords in truck-paying districts complained of being forced to receive rent in truck.[30] To obtain money, workers often resold goods "purchased" at the truck shop at a heavy discount.[31] Tremenheere reported in 1852 that a Bilston pawnbroker showed him 51 pecks of flour bought at a discount from miners' wives. He also had purchased candles and sugar, which they had been forced to sell at a loss.[32] James Baird, a Scottish MP and owner of mines and ironworks in Lanarkshire, countered these examples by arguing before the 1854 Select Committee on the Payment of Wages that wives only resold goods from company stores in order to deceive their husbands by using the money to buy frivolous "articles of dress" or "gaudy caps" behind their backs, demonstrating the gendered anxieties about women's power in consumption.[33]

Anti-truck advocates rarely described its effect on union organizing or labour markets. Indeed, it was the truck-paying employers themselves who most often raised this point. The lack of ready cash impeded the ability of miners or ironworkers to pay dues to trade unions, and this was by design. Before the 1854 Select Committee, employers admitted that the payment of wages in truck undermined industrial action.[34] Baird testified that

> the delegates who have come to excite the men to strike have found the store a very powerful engine against the union; the moment they stop working, the store stopped advancing. It is not so with credit-giving shops; in fact, the credit-giving shops assist to support the men during a long strike.

He continued "the shop is a very powerful engine, because when it is shut against the men they cannot get credit at other places" because shopkeepers were reluctant to give credit to families that worked for truck masters.[35] Coal and iron owner Edward Cresswell introduced a truck shop into his works in 1849 following a 17-week strike in which the union was "supported entirely by the hucksters and shopkeepers in Tipton and the neighbourhood, encouraging them to hold out against their masters, . . . it was nearly our ruin."[36] This undercuts a common argument made by defenders of company stores that additional anti-truck legislation was unnecessary because if truck was really a grievance, workers would go on strike.[37]

Truck was also an impediment to labour mobility, as workers rarely were able to acquire the savings necessary to cover relocation costs or downtime between jobs. The debts to the company stores were usually not in themselves an insurmountable obstacle, because employers rarely advanced more than could be covered by the next pay period. Under section 6 of the 1831 Truck Act, an employer had no cause of action against a worker for goods delivered in place of wages.[38] In 1843, the directors of the Blaenavon Iron Company were informed that due to layoffs, the truck shop would have to absorb losses of £340 11s 11d in bad debts advanced to the workmen before their discharge.[39] Retail shopkeepers took a leading role in opposing truck, helping to organize anti-truck associations and producing pamphlets explaining its evils. Shopkeepers complained of the loss of patronage and argued that truck shops took money out of circulation, enriching coal and iron masters at the expense of the community.[40] The opening of a truck shop could "withdraw at once several thousand pounds per week from the business of independent shopkeepers." Shopkeepers in Aberdare, South Wales, argued that a new truck shop in 1850 caused the loss of nearly £3,000 per month in business from retail shop owners.[41] One shopkeeper wrote to a newspaper that "those who adopt the truck system become grocers, mercers, shoe dealers, dealers in hats . . . in short, monopolize every trade extant."[42] It was asserted that the Staffordshire miner receiving truck "wears tommy hats, and his wife and daughters tommy bonnets; they all have tommy shoes and tommy stockings . . . and tommy shirts, shifts, jackets, gowns and petticoats."[43] An 1843 government report suggested that since 1817, when truck became widespread in Bilston, "hundreds were bankrupted" as

> the markets became deserted, and the shops untenanted, and it is calculated on good authority that previously to the prevalence of the truck system, upwards of £5,000 of wages were expended in Bilston every Saturday night" and now "not more than £200 was so expended.

By the 1850s, four large truck-paying employers in Bilston saw between £2,000 and £3,000 of wages per week pass through their shops, money that did not circulate in the town.[44]

Shopkeepers argued that the existence of truck prevented the growth not only of a local retailing sector but also of a middle-class. One Welsh editorialist suggested that this "drops civilization . . . it prevents from rising the middle-man, the respectable tradesman, from whose sober, persevering, industrious habits, the working man would take an example." These sentiments were repeated by Tremenheere in his 1852 report and testimony before the 1854 Select Committee.[45] In the 1850 Commission of Inquiry into the Operation of the Mines Act, it was noted that the abandonment of truck by coal and iron companies in Merthyr, South Wales, had led to a "rapid increase in the respectable middle class."[46]

Truck was also represented as an unfair advantage given to disreputable producers over money-paying masters.[47] Truck masters who clawed back a portion of their workers' wages through inflated truck shop profits reduced their labour costs and undersold competitors, giving a 7–15% advantage.[48] Opponents feared that this would result in more employers adopting the practice. John Parsons wrote to the *Wolverhampton Chronicle* to defend his recently opened truck shop, explaining "it would never have been opened at all, had I not been driven to it in self-defense." These sentiments were often repeated.[49]

Attempts to enforce the 1831 Truck Act

Although truck was illegal in many trades, the laws outlawing it were difficult to enforce. In fact, the 1831 Truck Act had been such a failure in preventing truck that in September 1849 an attorney defending a gun-lock manufacturer accused of paying truck wages expressed wonder at the charges, as "the Truck Act might now be said to be a dead letter."[50] It was dangerous for a worker to prosecute an employer and almost certainly would lead to dismissal, or worse, being blacklisted in the region.[51] William Duignan, the Walsall solicitor who conducted most of the prosecutions for the South Staffordshire Anti-Truck Association between 1849 and 1852, testified that many of his clients in truck cases were left without work, as other masters refused to hire them.[52] Anti-truck associations in Staffordshire sought to help informants with payments and referrals to money-paying masters.[53] A worker had to decide quickly whether or not to take these risks, as the 1831 Act stated that an information had to be laid within 3 months of the offence.[54]

Even if a worker was prepared to risk losing employment to bring a prosecution, it was difficult to put a case in motion. In many regions, a miner was often unable to find two magistrates who were not engaged in the coal or iron trade and could hear the case.[55] Furthermore, magistrates were highly variable in their attitudes toward truck and interpretations of the 1831 Act. Some showed a great reluctance to convict or punish offenders with substantial fines. A correspondent for the *Morning Chronicle* visiting Staffordshire in 1849 noted, "Not a few magistrates themselves are notorious truck store keepers."[56] A speaker at a meeting in Bilston suggested that at local Petty Sessions truckmaster magistrates "commit poor women and children to prison for taking 3 or 4 lbs of coal from a spoil bank while they themselves were robbing their workmen of 5 to 20 per cent" of their wages.[57] Often magistrates "discouraged informations, . . . moralizing 'My man, you know you have had your masters' goods; and surely you ought to pay for them,'" treating truck prosecutions as a fraud against employers.[58] In cases where truck masters were found guilty, some magistrates were reluctant to award part of the penalty to the prosecutor for fear of "encouraging a system of espionage," or "creating a class of common informers."[59]

The fact that magistrates often refused to use their discretion and give part of the fine to the informer exacerbated the problem of legal costs, which in truck cases could be prohibitive despite the affordable justice promised by magistrates' summary proceedings. Magistrates who were qualified to hear a truck case were not always nearby and litigants often had to travel with their witnesses to have a case heard. The 1831 Truck Act was complex legislation, and employers usually hired solicitors to defend them, forcing workers to seek their own legal help. On average, a truck prosecution conducted by a solicitor might cost anywhere from £5 to £25.[60] This was well beyond the range of working-class families. Although magistrates could award costs in a successful case, these costs never met the full expenses. It was uncommon for an individual employee to bring a prosecution under the Truck Act in the absence of support from either an anti-truck association or a trade union.

Trade unions occasionally funded prosecutions, including some conducted by William Roberts, the Chartist solicitor. "The Miners' Attorney-General," as he was called by the unionized workers he regularly represented in labour-related matters during his remarkable career, conducted high-profile prosecutions of truck masters on behalf of organized labour in Staffordshire, Yorkshire and Wales.[61] These cases exposed many of the difficulties in obtaining prosecutions under the Act.

In May and June 1844, Roberts and William Broomhead were hired by the miners of Yorkshire to conduct truck prosecutions against mine owners, hoping to force owners to abandon their company stores. Roberts' recent legal victories on behalf of miners had been heavily publicized in the *Northern Star*, so his clients had expectations of success. Upon arriving in town, Roberts was escorted to the courthouse by a precession of over 200 miners, their families and a band playing "See the Conquering Hero Comes." The rest of the day did not live up to Roberts's triumphal entry. The mine owners' solicitors raised technical objections to the form and content of the documents containing the charges, called informations. The defence convinced the magistrates to dismiss one case because the information failed to state explicitly that the wages allegedly paid in goods had actually been earned, thus failing to establish an offence. In eight other cases, informations did not state the county where the offence occurred, thus failing to establish the magistrates' jurisdiction. Other cases were dismissed because the documents failed to list the precise times when the miners were allegedly paid in truck. After over a month of legal work, writing and re-writing a large number of informations, Roberts had managed to win a total of only £15 and some legal costs.[62]

Roberts was not the only attorney who found it difficult to write an information when prosecuting a truck case. Welsh solicitors John Owen and Charles James testified before the 1854 Select Committee about the difficulty of using the 1831 Act. Owen, who often brought truck prosecutions on behalf of Welsh miners, noted that cases were frequently "dismissed when the magistrates upheld some technical objection." James testified to the importance of "extreme particularity" in writing informations because employers often engaged solicitors who scrutinized forms before magistrates who were in some cases reluctant to rule against the employers.[63]

Since 1831, a number of short-lived anti-truck associations had periodically emerged in different parts of Staffordshire and Wales, with significant activity in 1842, 1844 and 1847. From 1849, these societies began a more sustained and coordinated effort to make the Act effective. In response to the spread of truck in south Staffordshire, between December 1849 and July 1850 anti-truck associations were created in Bilston, Walsall, Tipton, Dudley, Darlaston, Wednesbury and Halesowen. Delegates from the first five of these bodies held monthly meetings as the South Staffordshire Anti-Truck Association, which also corresponded with other anti-truck associations.[64] Members, who included retailers, money-paying masters, local clergymen and workers, paid weekly subscriptions. Shopkeepers contributed anywhere from 3d to 1s per week. Working-class men represented over one-third of the membership of the South Staffordshire Association as a whole, but did not all pay weekly subscriptions. More commonly, workers periodically raised funds at public houses.[65] One should not, though, discount the agency of the working-class within these organizations. Anti-truck advocate Joseph Linney and Duignan disputed the accusation that anti-truck agitation was largely the product of shopkeepers stirring up indifferent workers; they pointed out that although retailers and money-paying masters contributed most of the funds, this was because workers did not have the same level of discretionary income (indeed, workers paid in truck had hardly any). Nonetheless, at least two of the anti-truck societies, including Darlaston's, were initiated and almost entirely composed of working-class men. The complaints and evidence against truck masters were obtained through the efforts of workers, who brought the cases to the organization's solicitor for consideration.[66]

Between 1849 and 1851, the South Staffordshire Anti-Truck Association spent between £600 and £800 to fund 500–600 prosecutions and secured at least 250 convictions.[67] Most of these prosecutions were conducted by Duignan.[68] The Association funded these cases not only to inflict the law's penalties upon violators of the 1831 Act but also to publicly shame truck masters. A common procedure for Duignan was to bring many informations against a defendant, secure a few convictions and then agree to withdraw the remainder in return for a pledge to abandon truck. In one case he convinced a truck master not only to abandon his shop but also to become a subscriber to the Association.[69]

Despite the large number of prosecutions, by 1851 members doubted whether they had significantly reduced truck in Staffordshire. The inspector of the Mines estimated that these prosecutions had reduced the amount of truck paid by 5%, but Duignan argued that the figure was lower, and the Association secretary conceded that only two truck shops had been permanently closed. Indeed, lack of results caused the dissolution of most of the anti-truck associations in Staffordshire by late 1854.[70]

There were several reasons why the prosecutions in Staffordshire and Wales were unable to reduce truck significantly. Fines for a first offence were small and offending employers could avoid future convictions by making slight modifications to comply with the letter of the 1831 Act without losing the advantages of truck. These included moving the payhouse to a separate building near the shop and paying the workers in cash with the plausibly deniable understanding that this money still had to be spent at the company store. In most of these systems there was not a bona fide payment in cash, as the social compulsion to use the truck shop was clear to all, but hard to prove. Truck masters continually insisted that they kept shops for the benefit of their workers who were free to shop elsewhere.[71]

An 1851 prosecution funded by the Tredegar Anti-Truck Association in South Wales demonstrates the great difficulty of proving compulsion to use the company store. Solicitor Charles James brought an action against the Rhymney Iron and Coal Company for wages paid in truck to James Olding. Rhymney was a joint stock company that employed over 4,000 workers. The works had a store adjoining the pay office, and with the permission of the coal agent workers or family members were permitted to draw advances on their wages, which were settled monthly. The prosecutors alleged that while these advances were in money, the workers understood that they were expected to spend part of these advances in the company store. Before the court, James proved that a coal agent, David Humphries, kept a list of men whose families were not spending enough at the shop and he informed those on his list that unless they dealt in greater quantities at the store they "must stand the consequences." The judge admitted Humphries's statements as evidence of compulsion, and a verdict was delivered for the plaintiff for £17 2s 5d.[72] The Company appealed this case to the Court of Queen's Bench, which ruled that Humphries, despite being the link of communication between the employer and workers, did not speak for the employer in this instance. Justice Coleridge ruled that

> Humphries may have been the ordinary channel of communication between the men and their employers, but a master who usually communicates with his inferior servants by an upper servant is not on that account bound by every and any communication which that servant may make to those under him.[73]

The court ruled that the evidence of Humphries's statements should not be admitted, and therefore there was no evidence of compulsion.

The scope of the 1831 Act made it difficult to win prosecutions. In many mining areas, including parts of South Wales and south Staffordshire, mine owners contracted with subcontractors called "butties" to mine coal at a fixed rate per ton. The butty would then hire the miners, pay them and provide the small supplies. In some cases, several butties would join together and operate a public house or a Tommy shop and pay their workers partly in truck and pass the savings to the mine owner.[74] In many other instances, an employer would pay the butty partly in truck, which he would pass onto his workers, or he would be given financial incentives for having employees make purchases at the employer's store.[75] The miners paid in truck were employees of the butty, and therefore had no action against the mine owner, even though he was the primary beneficiary. Because the butty was often not much wealthier than the miners who worked under him and because he did not always have an interest in the company store, the prosecution of such men gradually came to be understood as having little impact upon the extent of truck.[76] Furthermore, it was difficult for butties to prosecute mine owners for paying them in truck to pass onto their own workers, because the scope of the 1831 Act was limited to artificers. A considerable amount of high court litigation determined that subcontractors were not "artificers" under the 1831 Act, and therefore were outside its protection.[77]

Efforts to secure new legislation, 1851–1855

The legal proceedings and public meetings held by anti-truck societies and trade unions in Staffordshire and Wales drew attention to the shortcomings of the 1831 Act. By mid-century, there was a substantial campaign to pressure Parliament for new legislation that would severely punish truck. In March 1851 a large petition against truck was signed throughout south Staffordshire, which complained of long pay periods that were driving families to take advances that needed to be spent in the company store. The petition also highlighted the paying of employees in cheques for sums under £1 that were redeemable at the company store but not expected to be cashed at an actual bank. According to the 1831 Truck Act, all cheques used for payment of wages had to be drawn on a bank within 15 miles of the workplace. This was often evaded by drawing the cheque for a small amount on a bank that was barely on the inside edge of this 15-mile limit, but allowing workers to use the cheque at the much closer company store. Petitioners also sought to extend the scope of the Truck Act to include truck payments to subcontractors, especially butties in the coal and iron industry, and workers in previously unprotected trades such as railway and canal workers.[78]

The petition was presented to Edward R. Littleton, the Whig MP for Walsall, and the son of the sponsor of the 1831 Act. Littleton's father supported the petition in general terms, conceding that his Act "failed in much of its object." He agreed that the fines were too small and pointed out that in 1831 all of the Act's supporters had believed that its scope included subcontractors and butties, failing to anticipate the narrow judicial interpretation of the statute. He expressed doubt as to the feasibility of eliminating cheques under £1 or long pay periods and thought that it would be difficult to protect employees who refused to take truck from reprisals.[79]

Littleton brought the petition to the attention of Sir George Grey, the Whig Home Secretary, who in autumn 1851 dispatched Mines' Inspector Tremenheere to investigate the nature and extent of truck. Tremenheere travelled widely in the regions affected by truck and his report of June 1852 described the hardships that it caused to working-class families, retailers and money-paying employers. It also laid bare the methods by which employers in these regions disguised truck in order to evade the 1831 Act. The report recommended changes to the law to eliminate some of the most common methods of evasion. He also recommended extending the period within which actions had to be brought to 6 months and allowing prosecutors to waive the requirement that neither of the adjudicating magistrates could be in the same trade as the litigants. He also suggested raising the penalties and increasing the stigma of the offence by making a second conviction a misdemeanour. Tremenheere forwarded, but did not endorse, additional recommendations by Duignan, including expanding the scope of the Truck Act to include subcontractors or butties, as well as railway and canal workers. Duignan also suggested mandating weekly paydays and outlawing the paying of wages in any shop on the employers' premises or in the form of cheques for small amounts.[80]

In July 1853, Lord Palmerston, by now Home Secretary, introduced a bill that went much further than Tremenheere's recommendations. Palmerston's bill raised the maximum penalty for a first offence from £10 to £20, and provided that an employer convicted of a second offence would be guilty of a misdemeanour and could incur a fine of up to £100. To encourage prosecutions the bill increased the time limit for bringing charges, mandated that half of the fine would go to the informer and permitted prosecutors to waive the conflict-of-interest restrictions on magistrates. The bill also would have made the Truck Act far more difficult to evade by fining employers who kept shops on their premises between £10 and £20 per day. It also would have made it a violation to stop money out of a worker's wages on payday to pay for goods purchased with advances if the employer had any interest in the profits on those products. It also proposed that cheques used by employers to pay their workmen must be greater than £5 and redeemable at a nearby bank. Lord Grey, who as Home Secretary had favoured truck reform, felt that the bill went too far in restricting the freedom of employers by preventing them from owning shops.[81] The bill did not receive a second reading before the parliamentary session expired, but it was put forward again in February of 1854 by Walsall Whig MP Charles Forster.[82] On 16 March 1854 the bill received a second reading and was referred to a Select Committee on the Payment of Wages. One week later, a bill promoted by Conservative MP Sir Henry Halford to abolish the exploitative practice of deducting frame rents from the wages of hosiery workers also received a second reading and was committed to the same Select Committee.[83]

The 1854 Select Committee, consisting of 16 members, included Halford, Forster and Conservative Scottish coal and ironmaster James Baird, along with Whig MPs Sir Joshua Walmsley of Leicestershire, Henry Bruce of Merthyr Tydfil and Lord Stanley.[84] The Committee met 17 times between 1 May and 21 July 1854, asking over 6,500 questions of 28 different witnesses, including employers, retail shopkeepers, workers, lawyers, journalists, magistrates, government inspectors and MPs. Due to the lateness of the session and divisions within the committee, its report was brief with few recommendations. The committee opposed the provisions of the Palmerston/Forster bill that would have outlawed employers keeping shops on their premises, put restrictions on the payment of workers' wages in cheques and encouraged prosecutions by guaranteeing half of the fine to the informer and lengthening the time limit for bringing prosecutions. The committee postponed making recommendations on any other parts of the bill.[85] In May 1855, the Truck Bill was reintroduced into Parliament, but shorn of clauses that the Select Committee opposed. By now the arguments of opponents of additional legislation had momentum and the bill did not receive a second reading.[86] The arguments against Parliament passing further legislation reveal much about prevailing understandings of the role of government and political economy, as well as concerns about consumer culture and credit relationships.

The arguments against further legislation

The campaigns for further anti-truck legislation in the mid-1850s were unsuccessful because of the strength of contradictory arguments rooted in both liberal political economy and traditional paternalism. Many coal and ironmasters with staunchly liberal free-market views when it came to forming contracts of employment saw no inconsistency with advocating company stores on the basis of paternalism and "protecting" working families from the dangers of the same free market. The inconsistency on this issue had existed for some time: years earlier the Radical MP William Ferrand had mocked many members of the Anti-Corn Law League for being notorious truck masters, resulting in a Select Committee Investigation on the Payment of Wages in 1842.[87]

Some defenders of truck not only argued against further legislation but even advocated repealing the 1831 Act in order to legalize the practice. They suggested that, by having restrictions on truck, Parliament ensured that only the most immoral employers used the truck system, which need not be oppressive.[88] Others stressed that if a truck master was able to use the system to undersell money-paying employers it could only benefit consumers.[89] They also questioned whether anti-truck legislation was an appropriate use of state authority. Many employers feared that regulating the mode of paying wages might lead to setting the level of wages.[90] A new law was unacceptable Parliamentary interference with the freedom of individuals to contract, preventing workers and masters from entering into "voluntary" agreements.[91] Many outside Parliament felt that to interfere was to deprive parties of basic freedoms. A solicitor defending an employer told the magistrate that the Truck Act was one of "the most loose, ill-constructed and unconstitutional acts ever passed" because it interfered with the freedom of individuals to make their own agreements.[92]

Lord Stanley and others argued that new legislation would be as inoperable as the 1831 Act because the only means of eliminating truck was through market forces, meaning workers refusing to accept employment from truck masters. Members of the Select Committee continually asked why, if workers objected to truck, did they not simply leave their employment and work for money-paying masters?[93] John Bright, a Manchester MP, complained in Parliament that a new Truck Act would distract workers "from the true remedy in their own hands."[94] S.H. Blackwell, who owned ironworks in Staffordshire and South Wales, noted that "you can scarcely call truck a wrong, when the workman has the power of leaving his master's employment, and he does not choose to exercise that power."[95] Others thought that if workers were opposed to truck, they could end the system through industrial action.[96] These arguments were based upon the flawed assumption that employers and workers met as juridical equals in the formation of employment contracts or that the later were always legally free to leave their work.[97]

Blackwell's assertion also ignored the difficulties in finding new work. It was not easy to uproot a working-class family and move to a new location, separating from networks of emotional and economic support, especially with little savings. Tremenheere, who had interviewed a number of mining families, observed

> a variety of circumstances constantly intervene to indispose a man to leave his work: for example, circumstances of relationship, acquaintance with a particular neighbourhood, and the difficulty of removing. Therefore a man

may voluntarily submit to what he considers . . . to be a hardship for a considerable time before he will remove.

Such points were often reiterated.[98]

Truck-paying masters also insisted that their shops existed for the benefit
of working families. Company stores allowed employers to regulate the sale of
alcohol to their workmen, which reduced lost workdays and protected family
budgets. An opponent of the 1831 Act noted,

> [E]veryone knows that the labouring classes with money in their pocket
> will quaff too many draughts in honour of their God Bacchus, to the terri-
> ble injury of themselves, their wives, and their families. . . . But the labourer
> paid in truck . . . cannot debauch himself unless he pawns the goods.[99]

One truck master insisted that "where men have more money to spend in the
public houses, it keeps them away from their work," and "if a man has money
in his pocket it is a thousand to one if he will go to work."[100]

Employers were quite open in admitting their use of truck as a means of
labour discipline, but they justified it on the grounds that it enabled the wives
to exercise better control over the family budget. The acting partner of the
Blaina Mine Works in Wales insisted that

> in the case of truck, women are able to receive the great part of the pro-
> duce of their husbands' wages, while in cases where the men get their
> money, and receive it themselves, they are too apt to spend it in drink.[101]

These sentiments were frequently repeated.[102] Already in 1843 the *Second Report
on Children's Employment* had noted that

> when the husband is of dissolute . . . habits and the wife a bad manager
> (either or both of which is a common case) tommy prevents the family
> from being destitute" and "many married women often express their satis-
> faction in the existence of a tommy shop, as far as they can understand its
> operation.[103]

Many truck masters asserted that where truck was practiced, "there was very
much less drunkenness, because women got the goods from the shop, and the
men could not get the money to spend."[104] Truck masters claimed that they
were the true protectors of the domestic harmony by preventing wives and
children from being at the mercy of their brutish, drunken and intemperate
husbands. Secure in their own paternalist position, employers condescendingly
dismissed workers' claims to Victorian manhood by challenging their abilities
to provide for their families.[105]

What anti-truck advocates perceived as tyrannical control over the liberty of
employees, truck masters defended as the exercise of paternal care. Employers

running company shops looked after "their" workers as common retailers never would, because while the shopkeeper

> does not care in the least degree for the condition of the person whom he supplies provided he pays his bill, the master has the same interest in the health and regularity of his workmen as he has in the health and regularity of his horses and oxen.[106]

Paternalist employers also argued that the advantage gained from truck allowed them to continue to employ "their men" in bad times.[107] Other employers suggested that they provided shops for workers because otherwise they would be unable to secure credit from local retailers, as in the case of a sub-contractor building a local barracks in Wales. His employees were largely itinerant single men, who would be unlikely to have credit extended to them.[108]

For some mine owners, this paternal interest required that they set up a shop because of the isolated locations of many mines. Some truck masters argued that without a company store, their workers would be forced to travel great distances to provision themselves.[109] While this might have held true in the eighteenth century, it is a more doubtful argument in the mid-nineteenth century and sceptics provided an abundance of examples from remote locations in Wales, Durham and Northumberland, where retail shops grew up rapidly near collieries and ironworks.[110] Indeed, setting up a shop or entering business as a huckster did not take large amounts of capital.[111]

Defenders of truck argued that the inclination to spend frivolously exposed workers who were paid in money to the dangers of credit extended by shop-keepers.[112] They demeaned the capacity of the working class, in particular working-class women, to negotiate the risks of credit.[113] Yet managing credit relations with local shopkeepers and retailers was an everyday part of life for working-class men and women who received wages in money. Depending upon the location, shopkeepers frequently extended credit.[114] For smaller independent shopkeepers this was a delicate balancing act, for they needed to extend credit to workers to secure business and compete with larger retailers, but this could also expose them to great risks. The extension of credit was done on highly personal terms, usually after a judgement about the respectability of the family, specifically, the housewife, in question. In fact, the ability to be taken on credit at the local shop was often a sign of working-class status.[115]

Working-class wives could also secure credit from shopkeepers, pawnbrokers, moneylenders and a variety of other sources in order to make ends meet. Credit was essential but it carried real dangers.[116] After 1846, small debtors could be brought before County Courts by their creditors and repeatedly imprisoned for periods of up to 6 weeks at a time. A high proportion of the business in the County Courts in the mid-nineteenth century consisted of shopkeepers' attempts to collect bad debts from working-class families.[117] In response to the accusation that workers were compelled to take truck against the threat of dismissal, one Select Committee member asked whether workers were more afraid of losing their employment or of being summoned by a shopkeeper to the County Court.[118] The manager of an iron works that paid workers in truck claimed to have started the company store because his men "were supplied by a class of inferior shopkeepers, chiefly on credit, and they were in bondage to those shopkeepers, who might charge whatever they pleased." He argued that the real compulsion and control came not from truck masters, but from shopkeepers, because "our men were very largely in debt, and were therefore in bondage to the shopkeepers and in terror of being taken to ... court if they did not continue their patronage."[119] Shopkeepers were accused of "endeavouring to get the workmen into their hands to such an extent as to keep them above the limit where imprisonment for debt is legal, that they might at least have that hold on them."[120] Truck-paying employers complained that shopkeepers advanced workers credit and, once the worker was in debt, the shopkeeper would "sell an inferior article and demand a higher price" against the threat of court action.[121] One attorney argued that it was "much better to receive goods from a master, a capitalist who could supply them cheaply than ... petty, miserable and paltry shopkeepers who were stimulating the present movement for their own ends."[122] Truck masters argued that *miners actually owed their souls to the local retailers* and not to the company stores.[123]

The success of these anti-truck arguments reveal what a highly flexible discourse "free trade" was for employers. The freest type of trade would have been to have paid workers in the current coin of the realm in the shortest reckoning period that was possible. Employers argued that any legislation mandating this would be an unacceptable interference with the market. The language of paternalism should have had no place in an economy dominated by ideas of the free market, yet employers deployed it to great effect to protect their exploitative methods of paying wages. Notions of free markets and freedom to contract were intended only to apply to productive relations and not to the workers' ability to spend his or her wages.

Opponents of truck legislation argued that the anti-truck associations were merely fronts for shopkeepers who wanted to eliminate competition from employers and ensnare workers into debt. They accused "sharper" attorneys of making money from costs by fomenting discontent among workers. Tipton ironmaster Edward Cresswell explained that employees who prosecuted him for paying wages in truck had been "seduced by the Anti-Truck Association to inform against us; they were not only seduced . . . but they were actually bribed to do so": after the men left his employment they "were supported for a considerable time by the Anti-Truck Association," neglecting to mention that this was due to the fact that they had been blacklisted.[124] Another defender of truck argued that

> if the workmen were left alone, they would be exceedingly satisfied with a well-conducted shop. . . . I believe that canvassing the workmen, and telling them they are much aggrieved, leads to agitation . . . which is calculated to create dissatisfaction.[125]

Ironmaster Blackwell argued "apparently the complaints come from the work-men, but in reality they come from the shopkeepers."[126]

The solicitors who conducted truck prosecutions were also subjected to abuse. Roberts and Owen, solicitors whose practices were largely made up of miners and other working-class clients, were frequently accused of being "sharp practitioners," not interested in the merits of a case but only about procuring costs.[127] Roberts and Owen were often accused of being demagogues who attempted to cheat their poor clients by stirring up conflict between employers and workers. Interestingly, Duignan, who conducted far more truck prosecu-tions than either of them, appears to have been relatively immune from such criticisms, possibly because he had a more varied practice and could not be generally considered a "poor man's attorney."[128]

No reform of the 1831 Truck Act was forthcoming in the middle of the nineteenth century.[129] Paying wages in kind continued to affect a significant number of workers in leading sectors of the British economy. For the next two decades conflict regularly erupted that pitted truck-paying employers and clas-sical liberal advocates of freedom to contract against money-paying employers, shopkeepers, trade unions, government inspectors and working-class men and women. Paying wages in goods not only gave employers an advantage over their rivals, it provided them with a powerful means to control, discipline and maintain an affordable workforce. In the mid-nineteenth century the truck sys-tem was discussed not just in terms of conflict between capital and labour but also whether working-class men and women could manage their consumption and credit relationships in a responsible and respectable manner in the absence of sumptuary control. The language of the debate over truck legislation high-lights the great importance of patterns of consumption and credit-worthiness in contemporary definitions of independence, respectability and, ultimately, political citizenship.

Notes

1 *Select Committee on the Payment of Wages* (1854), Q. 256, 258, 1053, 1377–1381, 1490–1497, 1508–1517, 1615.
2 *Select Committee on the Payment of Wages* (1854), Q. 138–139; *Birmingham Journal*, 5 Febru-ary 1848, p. 8; *Manchester Guardian*, 21 February 1844; Hilton, *The Truck System,* pp. 1, 20–22.
3 Goldsmith-Kress, Library of Economic Literature Microfilm Series: *Cases of Distress and Oppression in the Staffordshire Potteries by Labourers Wages Being Paid in Truck* (Albion Office, 1830); *Some Remarks on the Injurious Effects of the Truck System with an Appendix Consisting of Affidavits* (Albion Office, 1830); *Reflections on the Injustice and Impolicy of the Truck System* (1830), pp. 10, 12; *A Report of the Proceedings of the Anti-Truck Meeting for the Staffordshire Potteries, Held on the Pottery Race Ground on Monday 18 October 1830* (Mercury Office, 1830); *Tommy, or the Truck System, Exposed in Three Letters to the Editor of Birmingham Jour-nal* (1830); Also see: *Select Committee on the Payment of Wages* (1854) Q.81–82, 360–363; 374–377, 489–490, 505–511, 678, 1411–1417, 1747–1749; *Select Committee on the Pay-ment of Wages* (1842), Q. 8–18; House of Commons, Royal Commission on Children's Employment in the Mines and Manufactories, *First Report (Mines and Collieries) (1842),*

Parliamentary Papers, Vol. XV–XVII (380–382), pp. 159, 337; Commission of Inquiry into the Operation of the Mines Act and the State of the Population in the Mining Districts, *Report* (1852) *Parliamentary Papers,* Vol. XXI (1525), p. 432; *Merthyr Telegraph,* 12 June 1858, p. 3; *Monmouthshire Merlin,* 13 January 1844, p. 4; *Silurian,* 25 August 1838, p. 3; 1 September 1838, p. 3; *Miners' Advocate,* 2 December 1843, p. 4; *Miner and Workman's Advocate,* 15 April 1865, p. 8; *Miner,* 21 March 1863, p. 4; *Times,* 21 December 1840, p. 3, 25 August 1842, p. 6; *Wolverhampton Chronicle,* 11 May 1842, p. 3; 25 May 1842, p. 3; *Labour and the Poor in England and Wales, 1849–1851: The Letters to the Morning Chronicle from the Correspondents in the Manufacturing and Mining Districts, the Towns of Liverpool and Birmingham and the Rural Districts, Vol. II: Northumberland and Durham, Staffordshire and the Midlands,* Ed: J. Ginswick (Frank Cass and Co, Ltd, 1983), pp. 106–109; *Labour and the Poor in England and Wales, 1849–1851: The Letters to the Morning Chronicle from the Correspondents in the Manufacturing and Mining Districts, the Towns of Liverpool and Birmingham and the Rural Districts, Vol. III: The Mining and Manufacturing Districts of South Wales and North Wales,* Ed: J. Ginswick (Frank Cass and Co, Ltd, 1983), pp. 148, 153–156; Hilton, *The Truck System,* pp. 1, 4, 26–29, 40.

4 Bailey, *The Truck System,* p. 5; *Select Committee on the Payment of Wages* (1854), Q. 324; *Labour and the Poor in England and Wales,* Vol. II, p. 110; For more on Master and Servant Law in mid-nineteenth-century England, see: *Masters, Servants, and Magistrates in Britain and Empire, 1562–1955,* Eds: D. Hay and P. Craven (Chapel Hill: University of North Carolina Press, 2004); Frank, *Master and Servant Law;* R. Challinor, *Radical Lawyer in Victorian England: W.P. Roberts and the Struggle for Workers' Rights* (London: I.B. Taurus, 1990).

5 *Select Committee on the Payment of Wages* (1854), Q.83–84; Hilton, *The Truck System,* pp. 37–38.

6 *Commission of Inquiry into the Mines Act* (1852), pp. 434, 447; *Royal Commission on Children's Employment* (1842), 337–338; *Royal Commission on Children's Employment* (1843), 69–70; *Select Committee on the Payment of Wages* (1854), Q.24–32, 45–65, 68–75, 105–106, 140, 142, 148, 426, 434, 437, 441, 1396–1407–1409, 1426–1433, 1440, 1556, 1560, 1564 1600–1607, 1629–1639, 1722–1723; *Select Committee on the Payment of Wages* (1842), Q. 165–172; Commission of Inquiry into the Operation of the Mines Act, and the State of the Population of the Mining Districts, *Report* (1850), *Parliamentary Papers,* Vol. XXIII (1248), p. 22; Commission of Inquiry into the Operation of the Mines Act, and the State of the Population of the Mining Districts, *Report* (1851), *Parliamentary Papers* Vol. XXIII (1406), p. 468; *Monmouthshire Merlin,* 9 December 1843, p. 3; 13 January 1844, p. 4; Staffordshire Record Office, "Wolverhampton Anti-Truck Association" D260/M/F/5/18; *Miner,* 30 May 1863, p. 11; *Times,* 21 December 1840, p. 3; 20 April 1842, p. 14; 15 August 1842, p. 6; 1 October 1842, p. 2; 12 September 1842, p. 4; *The Merthyr and Cardiff Chronicle and South Wales Advertiser,* 19 September 1837, p. 2; *Labour and the Poor in England and Wales, Vol II,* pp. 105, 108; *Labour and the Poor in England and Wales, Vol. III,* pp. 147–156; R. Church, *History of the British Coal Industry, Vol. 3, 1830–1913* (Oxford: Clarendon Press, 1986), pp. 262–264; Hilton, *The Truck System,* pp. 10, 20–24.

7 Bailey, *The Truck System,* pp. 16–17; *Labour and the Poor in England and Wales, Vol. II,* pp. 108–109.

8 Tan, "Regulating Wages in Kind," pp. 442–458.

9 *Select Committee on the Payment of Wages* (1854), Q. 6, 8–12, 14–16, 104–105, 160–164, 273, 364, 668, 692–703, 1373–1376, 1385, 1387–1389, 1518–1525; *Miner,* 21 March 1863, p. 4; 2 May 1863, p. 3; *Select Committee on the Payment of Wages* (1842), Q. 4–6; *Royal Commission on Children's Employment* (1842), Q. 159; *Commission of Inquiry into the Mines Act* (1852), p. 435; *The Potters Examiner and Workman's Advocate,* 23 December 1843, p. 28; *Manchester Examiner,* 18 July 1846; *Manchester Courier and Lancashire General Advertiser,* 6 January 1844, p. 6; *Manchester and Salford Advertiser,* 22 January 1845, p. 8; *Birmingham Journal,* 26 August 1853, p. 8; *Commonwealth,* 17 February 1866, p. 6; *Manchester Guardian;* 25 February 1843, p. 7; 25 March 1843, p. 7; 17 June 1843; 3 January 1844; 24

January 1844; 3 February 1844; 28 February 1844; *Labour and the Poor in England and Wales, Vol. II*, 105; *Labour and the Poor in England and Wales, Vol. III*, p. 148; Hilton, *The Truck System*, pp. 10–19, 38–39; Church, *The British Coal Industry*, pp. 264, 569–570.

10 *Commonwealth*, 15 September 1866, p. 5; *Report of the Commissioners Appointed to Inquire into the Truck System, Volume I: Report, Schedules, Supplement. Vol II: Minutes of Evidence* (1871) *Parliamentary Papers*, XXXVI (c326–c327), xx; Hilton, *The Truck System*, pp. 7–8, 132; Church, *History of the British Coal Industry*, pp. 164, 264.

11 "Report on the Mining Districts 1850," Staffordshire Country Record Office, D/M/F/5/18; *Commission of Inquiry into the Mines Act* (1850), p. 22.

12 *Merthyr and Cardiff Chronicle, and South Wales Advertiser*, 19 September 1837, p. 2.

13 *Monmouthshire Merlin*, 9 December 1843, p. 4; *Times*, 31 August 1843, p. 4.

14 A. Clark, *The Struggle for the Breeches: Gender and the Making of the English Working Class* (Berkeley: University of California Press, 1995), pp. 215, 220–222, 234, 237–238; R. Shoemaker, *Gender in English Society, 1650–1850: The Emergence of Separate Spheres?* (London: Longman, 1998), pp. 198–206; R. Gray, "Languages of Factory Reform in Britain, c. 1830–1860," in P. Joyce (ed.), *The Historical Meanings of Work* (Cambridge: Cambridge University Press, 1987), pp. 150–152; W. G. Carson, "Some Instrumental and Symbolic Dimensions of the 1833 Factory Act," in R. Hood (ed.), *Crime, Criminology and Public Policy: Essays in Honor of Sir Leon Radzinowicz* (New York: Free Press, 1974), p. 121; S. Alexander, "Women's Work in Nineteenth Century London: A Study of the Years 1820–1850," in J. Mitchell and A. Oakley (eds.), *The Rights and Wrongs of Women* (London: Penguin, 1976), pp. 60–63.

15 Quote from: *Royal Commission on Children's Employment* (1843), p. Q31; This point is reiterated in: Bailey, *The Truck System*, p. 23; *Commission of Inquiry into the Operation of the Mines Act and the State of the Population in the Mining Districts, Report* (1845), *Parliamentary Papers*, Vol. XXVII (670), p. 17; *Labour and the Poor in England and Wales*, Vol. III, pp. 148, 151; *Times*, 17 March 1854, p. 8; *Select Committee on the Payment of Wages* (1854), Q. 172, 2728–2743.

16 5 & 6 Victoria, c.99 (1842) and 46 & 47 Victoria, c.31 (1883). Quote from: *Commission of Inquiry into the Mines Act* (1852), p. 434; *Select Committee on the Payment of Wages* (1854), Q. 114, 119, 123, 129; *Monmouthshire Merlin*, 17 September 1852, p. 3; *Merthyr and Cardiff Guardian*, 15 August 1846, p. 3; *Miner*, 13 March 1863, p. 4; 18 April 1863, p. 4; Hilton, *The Truck System*, p. 34; Church, *The History of the British Coal Industry*, p. 265.

17 *Select Committee on the Payment of Wages* (1854), Q. 3567–3568, 3597–3602, 3613, 3626, 4379–4381, 6110, 6302, 6365–6369; *Monmouthshire Merlin*, 2 November 1844, p. 3; From Goldsmith-Kress Library of Economic Literature Microfilm: *A Dispassionate and Succinct View of the Truck System as It Affects the Labourer, the Capitalist, the Landlord, and the State* (1830); *Advocate of the Poor, for the Security of Wages: The Universal Anti-Truck* (Derby, 1846); *Reflections on the Injustice and Impolicy . . .* (1830), 14, 16, 19, 24–25; Staffordshire Record Office, "Wolverhampton Anti-Truck Association," D260/M/F/5/18; Hilton, *The Truck System*, pp. 7–8, 16, 30.

18 *Select Committee on the Payment of Wages* (1854), Q. 91–98, 399, 495–500, 589–593, 1735–1741, 1805; *Commission of Inquiry into the Mines Act* (1852), p. 434; *South Wales Reporter*, 25 March 1837, p. 31; *Glamorgan, Monmouth, and Brecon Gazette*, 9 September 1841, p. 1; *Merthyr Telegraph*, 27 February 1858.

19 Staffordshire Record Office, "Anti-Truck Meeting at Dudley," D260/M/F/5/18; *Merthyr Telegraph and General Advertiser*, 27 February 1858, p. 3; *Select Committee on the Payment of Wages* (1854), Q. 91–97, 360, 401–402, 407–413, 495–500; *Commission of Inquiry into the Mines Act* (1852), p. 434; *Wolverhampton Chronicle*, 13 March 1850, p. 3. Bailey, *The Truck System*, pp. 19–20.

20 *Select Committee on the Payment of Wages* (1854), quote from Q. 4354. Also see Q. 4356–4358, 6018.

21 *Select Committee on the Payment of Wages* (1854), Q. 415–516, 419, 495–500, 1806–1813, 1884; *Manchester Guardian*, 10 January 1844.

22 *Select Committee on the Payment of Wages* (1854), Q. 3847–3849; *Monmouthshire Merlin*, 14 October 1843, p. 2; "Anti Truck Meeting at Dudley," Staffordshire Country Record Office, D260/M/F/5/18; *Merthyr Telegraph*, 24 April 1855, p. 2; *Cambrian*, 21 January 1837, p. 3; *Merthyr and Cardiff Chronicle*, 15 July 1837, pp. 1, 3; *Miner*, 21 March 1863; *Times*, 20 April 1842, p. 14; 11 August 1843, p. 5. Bailey, *The Truck System*, p. 21.

23 "Anti-Truck Movement!" Staffordshire Country Record Office, D260/M/F/5/18.

24 *Wolverhampton Chronicle*, 11 May 1842, p. 3.

25 *Wolverhampton Chronicle*, 1 May 1850, p. 4.

26 Bailey, *The Truck System*, p. 22.

27 *Monmouthshire Merlin*, 14 October 1843, p. 2; *Glamorgan, Monmouth, and Brecon Gazette*, 11 November 1843, p. 3.

28 *Times*, 31 August 1843, p. 4.

29 *Select Committee on the Payment of Wages* (1854), Q.99, 102, 423, 479, 514–516 1567–1572, 1653–1655, 1902–1906, 2727; *Select Committee on the Payment of Wages* (1842), Q. 19, 320–331, 2063; *Monmouthshire Merlin*, 2 March 1844, p. 3; *Silurian*, 25 August 1838, p. 3; 1 September 1838, p. 3; *Miners' Advocate*, 2 December 1843, p. 4; "Wolverhampton Anti-Truck Association," Staffordshire Record Office, D260/M/F/5/18.

30 *Commission on Inquiry into the Mines Act* (1852), p. 433; *Select Committee on the Payment of Wages* (1854), Q. 82, 1744, 1896–1901; *Select Committee on the Payment of Wages* (1842), Q. 196; Goldsmith-Kress Library of Economic Literature Microfilm: *Cases of Distress and Oppression in the Staffordshire . . .* (Burslem, 1830); *Reflections on the Injustice and Impolicy . . .* (1830), 13–14; Hilton, *The Truck System*, pp. 5, 6.

31 *Select Committee on the Payment of Wages* (1854), Q. 1410, 1573–1575, 1744, 1771–1775; *Wolverhampton Chronicle*, 25 May 1842, p. 3.

32 *Potters' Examiner and Workman's Advocate*, 23 December 1843, pp. 24–25; Hilton, *The Truck System*, p. 29; *Select Committee on the Payment of Wages* (1854), Q. 80; *Commission of Inquiry into the Mines Act* (1852), pp. 432–433.

33 *Select Committee on the Payment of Wages* (1854), Q. 1943–1946.

34 *Select Committee on the Payment of Wages* (1854), Q. 1950, 2013, 2017, 2026–2027, 2162–2163, 4249.

35 *Select Committee on the Payment of Wages* (1854), Quote from Q. 1950. Also see Q. 513–517; *Reflections on the Injustice and Impolicy . . .* (1830), pp. 10–11.

36 *Select Committee on the Payment of Wages* (1854), Q. 4249; *Times*, 15 August 1842, p. 6.

37 *Select Committee on the Payment of Wages* (1854), Q. 2913–2916; *Report of the Commissioners Appointed to Inquire into the Truck System, Volume I: Report, Schedules, Supplement. Vol II: Minutes of Evidence* (1871) *Parliamentary Papers*, XXXVI (c326–c327), xx; Curthoys, *Governments, Labour and the Law in Mid-Victorian Britain*, p. 238.

38 1 & 2 Will 4, c.37, s.6 (1831); *Select Committee on the Payment of Wages* (1854), Q. 513–517; Church, *History of the British Coal Industry*, p. 264; Hilton, *The Truck System*, pp. 5–6, 49–53.

39 This reduced the annual net profit from the shop to a mere £1,113 17*s*. Gwent Record Office, Blaenavon Co. Minute Book, D751.356. *Pontypool Free Press*, 16 July 1859, p. 1; *Pontypool Free Press*, 24 September 1859, p. 1. *Select Committee on the Payment of Wages* (1854), Q. 5079–5098; *Select Committee on the Payment of Wages* (1842), Q. 2073; *Royal Commission on Children's Employment* (1843), q336–q341; Hilton, *The Truck System*, pp. 53–54.

40 *Select Committee on the Payment of Wages* (1854), Q. 578, 638, 1088–1190, 1649; *Commission of Inquiry into the Mines Act* (1852), pp. 435–437; *Commission of Inquiry into the Mines Act* (1851), pp. 466, 468–469; *South Wales Reporter*, 18 March 1837, p. 24; 25 March 1837, p. 31; *Monmouthshire Merlin*, 14 October 1843, p. 2; Hilton, *The Truck System*, p. 29; *Some Remarks on the Injurious Effects . . .* (1830); *Advocate of the Poor, for the Security of Wages: The Universal Anti-Truck* (1846); *Tommy, or the Truck System Exposed . . .* (1829); Staffordshire Record Office, "Truck System," "Anti-Truck Meeting at Dudley," "The Truck System: Public Meeting at Bilston," D260/M/F/5/18; *Manchester Guardian*, 1 April 1843; *Times*, 1 June 1843, p. 7; *Wolverhampton Chronicle*, 11 May 1842, p. 3.

41 *Commission of Inquiry into the Mines Act* (1852), p. 435.

42 *Glamorgan, Monmouth and Brecon Gazette*, 4 November 1843, p. 3; *Wolverhampton Chronicle*, 13 March 1850, p. 4.

43 *Wolverhampton Chronicle*, 11 May 1842, p. 3; Bailey, *The Truck System*, pp. 15–16.

44 *Royal Commission on Children's Employment* (1843), Q67, Q69, Q71.

45 *Select Committee on the Payment of Wages* (1854), Q. 363; *Commission of Inquiry into the Mines Act* (1852), pp. 436–437; *Commission of Inquiry into the Mines Act* (1850), p. 23; *Times*, 23 August 1843, p. 5.

46 *Commission of Inquiry into the Mines* (1850), p. 69; *Glamorgan, Monmouth, and Brecon Gazette*, 9 September 1843, p. 1.

47 *Commission of Inquiry into the Mines Act* (1850), pp. 20–21; *Commission of Inquiry into the Mines Act* (1852), p. 437; *Cambrian*, 12 January 1837, p. 3; *Glamorgan Monmouth, and Brecon Gazette*, 9 September 1843, p. 3; Select Committee (1854), Q. 108, 148–151, 363–364, 638, 647–650, 1892, 2766–2775; *Advocate for the Poor . . . (1846); Tommy, or the Truck System Exposed . . .* (1829); Staffordshire Record Office, "Anti-Truck Meeting at Dudley," "The Truck System: Public Meeting at Bilston," D260 M/F/5/18; *Times*, 10 September 1842, p. 4; 1 June 1843, p. 7; 23 August 1843, p. 5.

48 *Commission of Inquiry into the Mines Act* (1852), pp. 437–438; *Commission of Inquiry into the Mines Act* (1850), pp. 20–21; *Times*, 10 September 1842, p. 4.

49 *Wolverhampton Chronicle*, 4 May 1842, p. 3; *Commission of Inquiry into the Mines Act* (1852), p. 438; *Commission of Inquiry into the Mines Act* (1851), p. 464; *Monmouthshire Merlin*, 14 October 1843; *Some Remarks Upon the Injurious Effects . . .* (1830); *Reflections on the Injustice and Impolicy . . .* (1830), pp. 11, 22; *A Report of the Proceedings of the Anti Truck Meeting . . .* (1830); *Commission of Inquiry into the Mines Act* (1850), p. 23.

50 *Wolverhampton Chronicle*, 3 October 1849, p. 3.

51 *Select Committee on the Payment of Wages* (1842), Q. 180–183, 282–284, 332–333, 367; *Monmouthshire Merlin*, 3 February 1844, p. 4; *Miners' Advocate*, 2 December 1843, p. 4; *Miner*, 18 April 1863, p. 5; *Times*, 20 April 1842, p. 14; 12 September 1842, p. 4; 5 July 1854, p. 10; Hilton, *The Truck System*, pp. 118–119, 121.

52 *Select Committee on the Payment of Wages* (1854), Q. 3178–3179, 5079–5098; *Royal Commission on Children's Employment* (1843), Q. 70; Morris and Williams, *The South Wales Coal Industry*, pp. 264, 267–269.

53 Hilton, *The Truck System*, p. 123.

54 1 & 2 Will 4, c.37, s.7 (1831); *Staffordshire Advertiser*, 4 May 1850, p. 7; *Select Committee on the Payment of Wages* (1854), Q. 1726–1727.

55 *Select Committee on the Payment of Wages* (1854), Q. 267–286, 303, 1729–1732, 3105–3111, 3263–3272; *Commission of Inquiry into the Mines Act* (1852), p. 443; Staffordshire Record Office, "The Truck System: Public Meeting at Bilston," D260/M/F/5/18; Hilton, *The Truck System*, p. 128; Swift, "The English Urban Magistracy and the Administration of Justice During the Early Nineteenth Century," pp. 75–92. Philips, "The Black Country Magistracy, 1835–1860," pp. 181–185; Woods, "The Borough Magistracy and the Authority Structure in the Black Country, 1858–1875."

56 Quote from: *Labour and the Poor in England and Wales, 1849–1851 . . .*, pp. 105–108; Also see: *Miners' Advocate*, 2 December 1832, p. 4; *Select Committee on the Payment of Wages* (1854), Q. 88, 247, 388, 909, 1784–1787; Staffordshire Record Office, "The Truck System: Public Meeting at Bilston," D260/M/F/5/18. *Royal Commission on Children's Employment* (1843), Q. 70; *Commission of Inquiry into the Mines Act* (1851), p. 464; *Times*, 23 August 1843, p. 5, 16 September 1842, p. 3; Morris and Williams, *The South Wales Coal Industry*, p. 269; NA HO 45/685; D. Lewis, "A Great Blessing to the People Employed: Conflicting Views of the Truck System in the Llynfi Valley, 1840–1870," *Morgannwg* 48 (2004):35–46.

57 *Wolverhampton Chronicle*, 20 March 1850, in Staffordshire Record Office D.260.M.F.5.18.

58 *Royal Commission on Children's Employment* (1843), Q. 69–70; *Times*, 24 September 1842, p. 4.

59 *Select Committee on the Payment of Wages* (1854), Q. 1311–1313; *Commission of Inquiry into the Mines Act* (1852), p. 443; Morris and Williams, *The South Wales Coal Industry*, pp. 267–271.

60 *Select Committee on the Payment of Wages* (1854), Q. 1868–1870, 1913–1916; *Commission of Inquiry into the Mines Act* (1852), p. 5; *Royal Commission on Children's Employment* (1843), Q. 71; *Commission of Inquiry into the Mines Act* (1851), p. 463; *Staffordshire Advertiser*, 31 August 1851, p. 5; Hilton, *The Truck System*, p. 123.

61 Frank, *Master and Servant Law*; Challinor, *Radical Lawyer*. For some of Roberts' victories in Truck Cases, see: Williams, *The Derbyshire Miners*, pp. 61–63; Engels, *Condition of the Working Class in England*, p. 289.

62 *Sheffield and Rotherham Intelligencer*, 18 May 1844, p. 2; 25 May 1844, p. 2; 15 June 1844, pp. 5, 8; 29 June 1844, p. 2; 6 July 1844, p. 3.

63 Morris and Williams, *The South Wales Coal Industry*, pp. 268–269; E.W. Evans, *The Miners of South Wales* (Cardiff: University of Wales Press, 1961), pp. 65, 70–71; N. Edwards, *The History of the South Wales Miners* (C. Tirling and Co, 1926). For Owen's obituary, see: *Pontypool Free Press*, 18 April 1863; 25 April 1863; 2 May 1863; 30 May 1863. For examples of Owen's involvement in labour cases, negotiating on behalf of miners, see: *Monmouthshire Merlin*, 4 March 1843, p. 3; 18 March 1843, p. 3; 3 April 1847, p. 3; 10 April 1847, p. 3; 24 April 1847, p. 4; 1 May 1847, p. 3; 8 May 1847, p. 3; 15 May 1847, p. 3; 24 May 1847, p. 3; 12 June 1847, p. 3; 14 January 1852, p. 2; 13 May 1852, p. 3; 13 May 1853, p. 5; 10 June 1853, p. 3; 24 June 1853, p. 3; *Glamorgan, Monmouth, and Brecon Gazette*, 18 March 1843, p. 3; 25 March 1843, p. 3; *Merthyr Telegraph*, 27 February 1858, p. 3; 15 May 1858, pp. 2–3; Morris and Williams, *The South Wales Coal Industry*, pp. 267–269. For some examples of Owen prosecuting truck cases: *Monmouthshire Merlin*, 5 October 1844, p. 3; 23 November 1844, p. 3; 30 November 1844, p. 3; 18 March 1853, p. 1; *Glamorgan, Monmouth and Brecon Gazette*, 16 July 1842, p. 3; *Merthyr and Cardiff Guardian*, 26 September 1846, p. 1; *Select Committee on the Payment of Wages* (1854), Q. 4724–5028.

64 This organization's purpose was to investigate the extent and nature of truck, to fund prosecutions of employers who paid their employees in goods, to assist workers who brought forward information to find new employment and to focus public attention to the evils of truck and the inadequacy of the 1831 Act. *Select Committee on the Payment of Wages* (1854), Q. 1364, 1368–1370, 1392, 1469–1472, 1658–1659; *Commission of Inquiry into the Mines Act* (1851), pp. 463, 469–474; *Commission of Inquiry into the Mines Act* (1852), p. 429; Hilton, *The Truck System*, pp. 115–129; Barnsby, *The Working Class Movement in the Black Country from 1760 to 1867*, p. 220; Staffordshire County Record Office, D260/M/F/5/18; *Staffordshire Advertiser*, 9 March 1850, p. 5; 16 March 1850, p. 5; 23 March 1850, p. 4; 1 March 1851, p. 5; 29 March 1851, p. 5; 21 June 1851, p. 5; *South Wales Reporter*, 18 March 1837, p. 24.

65 *Select Committee on the Payment of Wages* (1854), Q. 1371–1372, 1475–1477, 1526, 1530, 1645–1647.

66 *Select Committee on the Payment of Wages* (1854), Q. 1053, 1447–1450, 1531, 1532, 1550–1555, 1893–1894, 3119–3122, 3169, 3191–3195.

67 *Select Committee on the Payment of Wages* (1854), Q. 23, 252, 256, 258, 1053, 1490–1497, 1508–1517, 1615.

68 *Select Committee on the Payment of Wages* (1854), Q. 1505–1517, 1867. *Staffordshire Advertiser*, 9 February 1850, p. 5; 23 February 1850, p. 4; 9 March 1850, p. 5; 23 March 1850, p. 4; 13 April 1850, p. 4; 20 April 1850, pp. 4, 5; 4 May 1850, p. 7; 11 May 1850, p. 5; 21 December 1850, p. 5; 1 February 1851, p. 4; 1 March 1851, p. 5; 29 March 1851, p. 5; 19 April 1851, p. 5; 26 April 1851, p. 5; 10 May 1851, p. 5; 16 August 1851, p. 5; 8 November 1851, p. 5; 22 November 1851, p. 5.

69 *Select Committee on the Payment of Wages* (1854), Q. 1400–1404, 1858–1860, 1922–1923, 2906–2912, 3146; *Staffordshire Advertiser*, 20 April 1850, p. 3; 11 May 1850, p. 5; 3 August 1850, p. 5; 21 August 1850, p. 5; 19 April 1851, p. 5; 8 November 1851, p. 4.

70 *Select Committee on the Payment of Wages* (1854), Q. 23, 1380–1382, 3050–3052, 3161–3166; *Commission of Inquiry into the Mines Act* (1851), p. 463; Hilton, *The Truck System,* p. 124.

71 *Select Committee on the Payment of Wages* (1854), Q. 24–32, 45–65, 68–75, 88–89, 158–159, 165, 168, 175–183, 237–243, 252, 2266–2282, 2530, 3054–3076, 3146–3150, 3283; Commission of Inquiry into the Operation of the Mines Act (1852), pp. 430, 439–441; *Monmouthshire Merlin,* 16 July 1852, p. 4; *South Wales Reporter,* 25 March 1837, p. 31; 15 April 1837, p. 53; NA:HO 45/685; *Staffordshire Advertiser,* 26 April 1851, p. 5; *Wolverhampton Chronicle,* 18 May 1842, p. 3; Bailey, *The Truck System,* p. 17.

72 *Monmouthshire Merlin,* 23 January 1852, pp. 2–3; 27 February 1852, p. 2.

73 *Olding v. Smith,* 16 JP 601; *Select Committee on the Payment of Wages* (1854), Q. 3799–3818; *Monmouthshire Merlin,* 27 March 1852, p. 3; 14 May 1852, p. 3.

74 Bailey, *The Truck System,* pp. 11–12; *Miners' Advocate,* 2 December 1843, p. 2; *Times,* 1 October 1842, p. 2; 19 September 1850, p. 7; *Select Committee on the Payment of Wages* (1854), Q. 114–121; *Commission of Inquiry into the Mines Act* (1851), p. 467; *Commission of Inquiry into the Mines Act* (1852), pp. 435, 443–445; *Labour and the Poor in England and Wales, Vol. III,* p. 149; Hilton, *The Truck System,* pp. 31–36.

75 *Select Committee on the Payment of Wages* (1854), Q. 114–127; *Commission of Inquiry into the Mines Act* (1851), p. 467; *Times,* 19 September 1850, p. 7; *Wolverhampton Chronicle,* 18 May 1842, p. 3; Hilton, *The Truck System,* p. 125.

76 *Staffordshire Advertiser,* 9 February 1850, p. 5; 9 March 1850, p. 5; 20 April 1850, p. 5; 27 April 1850, p. 5; 4 May 1850, p. 5; 3 August 1850, p. 5; 19 April 1851, p. 5; 26 April 1851, p. 5; 22 November 1851, p. 5; *Miners' Advocate,* 27 July 1844, p. 143; Staffordshire Record Office, "The Anti Truck Movement!," "John Roby v. John Foster," D260/ M/F/5/18; *Commission of Inquiry into the Mines Act* (1851), pp. 463, 467; *Wolverhampton Chronicle,* 20 February 1840, p. 4; 13 March 1850, pp. 3, 4.

77 *Riley v. Warden* (1848); *Sharman v. Sanders* (1853); *Staffordshire Advertiser,* 15 November 1862, p. 7; *Commission of Inquiry into the Mines Act* (1851), 463; B. Napier, "The Contract of Service: The Concept and Its Application," Ph.D. diss (Cambridge University, 1975), pp. 113–114; Hilton, *The Truck System,* p. 34.

78 "Anti-Truck Movement!" "Anti-Truck Meeting at Dudley," "The Truck System: Public Meeting at Bilston," "Wolverhampton Anti-Truck Association," Staffordshire County Record Office, D260/M/F/5/18; *Advocate for the Poor . . . (1846); The Potters' Examiner and Workman's Advocate,* 23 December 1843, pp. 23–26; *Commission of Inquiry into the Mines Act* (1851), pp. 465–466; Hilton, *The Truck System,* pp. 124–126; *Select Committee on the Payment of Wages* (1854), Q. 33–35, 174; *Staffordshire Advertiser,* 21 December 1850, p. 5; NA: HO 45/685; *Labour and the Poor in England and Wales, Vol. II,* p. 105.

79 Hilton, *The Truck System,* pp. 125–127.

80 *Commission of Inquiry into the Mines Act* (1852), pp. 15–23; Hilton, *The Truck System,* p. 128.

81 *Times,* 16 March 1854.

82 "A Bill to Alter and amend the Act which prohibits the Payment of Wages in Goods, commonly called the Truck Act" (21 July 1853) *Parliamentary Papers, Vol. VII* (798), 437. Hilton, *The Truck System,* pp. 128–129.

83 *Times,* 2 March 1854, p. 8; 16 March 1854, pp. 5–6; 17 March 1854, p. 8; 23 March 1854, p. 8; "A Bill to Alter the act which prohibits the Payment of Wages in Goods, commonly called the 'Truck Act'" (21 February 1854), *Parliamentary Papers Vol. V* (21), p. 423; "A Bill to Secure the Payment of Wages without Stoppages 3 March 1853," *Parliamentary Papers* Vol. V (188), p. 341; "A Bill to Restrain Stoppages from the Payment of Wages in Hosiery Manufacture," (2 March 1854), *Parliamentary Papers Vol. V* (33), p. 429; Hilton, *The Truck System,* pp. 128–131.

84 C.W. Sutton, "Walmsley, Sir Joshua (1794–1871)," rev. Matthew Lee, *Oxford Dictionary of National Biography* (Oxford University Press, 2004); Ian D.C. Newbould, "Stanley, Edward John, Second Baron Stanley of Alderley and first baron Eddisbury (1802–1869)," *ODNB* (Oxford University Press, 2004); Matthew Cragow, "Bruce, Henry Austin, First Baron Aberdare (1815–1895)," *ODNB* (Oxford University Press, 2004).

85 *Select Committee on the Payment of Wages* (1854). This was not the first Parliamentary *Select Committee on the Payment of Wages*. Another had met 12 years earlier. The committee met between May and July 1842 and asked over 3500 questions of over 30 witnesses, though it produced no report. Many of the arguments for and against additional truck legislation are strikingly similar to those made in 1854. See: *Select Committee on the Payment of Wages* (1842). Lewis, "A Great Blessing . . ."

86 Hilton, *The Truck System,* pp. 129–130.

87 Hilton, *The Truck System,* pp. 122–131.

88 *Select Committee on the Payment of Wages* (1854), Q. 3729; *Times,* 15 July 1854, p. 7.

89 *A Dispassionate and Succinct . . .* (1830), pp. 11–12; *Times,* 15 July 1854, p. 7.

90 *A Dispassionate and Succinct . . .* (1830), p. 21; *Select Committee on the Payment of Wages* (1854), Q. 6015–6016; Hilton, *The Truck System,* pp. 56–58.

91 *Select Committee on the Payment of Wages* (1854), Q. 2170, 3501–3504, 3553, 5948; *A Dispassionate and Succinct . . .* (1830), pp. 22–24; *Times,* 20 April 1842, p. 14.

92 *Wolverhampton Chronicle,* 1 May 1850, p. 4.

93 *A Dispassionate and Succinct View of the Truck System as It Affects the Labourer, the Capitalist, the Landlord, and the State* (Birmingham, 1830), p. 8; Hilton, *The Truck System,* p. 3.

94 *Times,* 20 April 1842, p. 14; 16 March 1854, p. 6; 15 July 1854, p. 7.

95 *Select Committee on the Payment of Wages* (1854), Q. 3549.

96 *Select Committee on the Payment of Wages* (1854), Q. 2913–2916; *A Dispassionate and Succinct . . .* (1830), p. 24.

97 *Masters, Servants and Magistrates,* Chapters 1, 2, 12; Frank, *Master and Servant Law;* Bailey, *The Truck System,* p. 8; Stienmetz, "Was There a De-Juridification of Employment Relations in Britain?"; M. Steinberg, "Capitalist Development, the Labour Process, and the Law," *American Journal of Sociology* 109:2 (September 2003), pp. 445–495; Steinfeld, *Coercion, Contract, and Free Labour in the Nineteenth Century.*

98 *Select Committee on the Payment of Wages* (1854), Quote from Q. 363, also see Q. 364, 4210; *Select Committee on the Payment of Wages* (1842), Q. 337–341; *Commission of Inquiry into the Mines Act* (1852), p. 439; *Labour and the Poor in England and Wales, Vol. III,* 151; *Wolverhampton Chronicle,* 4, May 1842, p. 3; Bailey, *The Truck System,* pp. 6–7.

99 *Select Committee on the Payment of Wages* (1854) Q. 3567–3568, 3597–3602, 3626; *A Dispassionate and Succinct View . . .* (Birmingham, 1830), p. 4; Also see: *Labour and the Poor in England and Wales, Vol. II,* p. 104; *Labour and the Poor in England and Wales, Vol. III,* p. 119.

100 *Select Committee on the Payment of Wages* (1854), Quote from Q. 4381, also see: Q. 4379–4380, 6365–6369; *Monmouthshire Merlin,* 2 November 1844, p. 3.

101 *Select Committee on the Payment of Wages* (1854), Q. 3613, 6302; *Commission of Inquiry into the Mines Act* (1852), pp. 431–432.

102 *Select Committee on the Payment of Wages* (1854), Q. 6110.

103 *Royal Commission on Children's Employment* (1843).

104 *Select Committee on the Payment of Wages* (1854), Q. 3569, 3597–3611, 4250, 5811, 5813, 6038, 6092–6093, 6109, 6088–6091, 6358, 6389.

105 *Wolverhampton Chronicle,* 13 March 1850, p. 4. *Birmingham Mercury* in Staffordshire Record Office, D.260.M.F.5.18.

106 *Select Committee on the Payment of Wages* (1854) quote from Q. 3628, also see: Q. 3626–3627; *Times,* 15 July 1854, p. 7.

107 *Select Committee on the Payment of Wages* (1854), Q. 643, 2028–2037, 2091–2092, 3284, 3558–3559; Staffordshire Record Office, "Truck System," D/260/M/F/5/18.

108 *Monmouthshire Merlin,* 21 October 1843, p. 3.

109 *Times,* 20 April 1842, p. 14; 31 May 1842, p. 3; M. Flinn, *History of the British Coal Industry, Volume 2, 1700–1830, Industrial Revolution* (Oxford: Clarendon Press, 1984).

110 *Select Committee on the Payment of Wages* (1854), Q. 363–364, 1038; *Monmouthshire Merlin,* 30 September 1843, p. 3.

111 W. Hamish Fraser, *The Coming of the Mass Market 1850–1914* (London: Palgrave, 1982), p. 95.

112 *Select Committee on the Payment of Wages* (1854), Q. 2125–2132, 6071–6074; *Times*, 10 September 1842, p. 4.

113 *Select Committee on the Payment of Wages* (1854), Q. 3571–3575; *Royal Commission on Children's Employment* (1842), pp. 160–161.

114 *Select Committee on the Payment of Wages* (1854), Q. 5708–5711, 5743–5746, 5754–5767; Fraser, *The Coming of the Mass Market,* pp. 85–88; Johnson, *Saving and Spending,* p. 145; Hilton, *The Truck System*, p. 25.

115 Fraser, *The Coming of the Mass Market,* pp. 85–88; Johnson, *Saving and Spending,* p. 145.

116 Fraser, *The Coming of the Mass Market,* pp. 85–91; M. Tebbutt, *Making Ends Meet: Pawnbroking and Working Class Credit* (St. Martin's Press: 1983).

117 *Select Committee on the Payment of Wages* (1854), Q. 5733–5738. Margot Finn, *The Character of Credit: Personal Debt in English Culture 1740–1914* (Cambridge: Cambridge University Press, 2003), Part II; M. Lester, *Victorian Insolvency: Bankruptcy, Imprisonment for Debt, and Company Winding Up in Nineteenth Century England* (Oxford: Clarendon Press, 1995), pp. 118–119.

118 *Select Committee on the Payment of Wages* (1854), Q. 5746. Also see: TNA: HO 45.5248.

119 *Select Committee on the Payment of Wages* (1854), Q. 5777, 5838, 5863.

120 *Select Committee on the Payment of Wages* (1854), Q. 3652–3658.

121 *Royal Commission on Children's Employment* (1842), pp. 160–161.

122 *Wolverhampton Chronicle,* 4 May 1850, p. 4.

123 *Select Committee, on the Payment of Wages* (1854), Q. 5886; Johnson, *Saving and Spending,* pp. 146–147.

124 *Select Committee on the Payment of Wages* (1854), Q. 4254, 4257, 4338–4340; *Times*, 31 May 1842, p. 3.

125 *Select Committee on the Payment of Wages* (1854), Q. 5926–5928, 6014–6015.

126 *Select Committee on the Payment of Wages* (1854), Q. 3569, 3631–3632.

127 Frank, *Master and Servant Law*, pp. 55–59.

128 For attacks on Owen, see: *Monmouthshire Merlin,* 5 August 1843; 3 April 1847, p. 3; 10 April 1847, p. 3; 24 April 1847, p. 4; 1 May 1847, p. 3; 8 May 1847, p. 3; 15 May 1847, p. 3; 24 May 1847, p. 3; 12 June 1847, p. 4; 15 June 1847, p. 3; *Merthyr Telegraph,* 24 July 1848, p. 3; 14 August 1858, p. 3; *Glamorgan Advertiser,* 5 August 1843; *Walsall Advertiser,* 28 March 1914, p. 7; Walsall Library, Duignan travel correspondence, 48/1/32, 46–47; Duignan Travel Diaries, 48/1/1–48.

129 Hilton, *The Truck System*, pp. 131–153; T. Goriely, "Arbitrary Deductions from Pay and the Proposed Repeal of the Truck Acts," *Industrial Law Journal* 12:1 (1983):236–250; D. Howarth, "The Truck Act of 1896. Last Rights," *Cambridge Law Journal* 45:1 (1986):30–32.

2 New model unions and the effort to secure anti-truck legislation, 1863–1871

New model unions and a legislative strategy for fighting truck wages

In 1871 the TUC formed a permanent parliamentary committee to lobby Parliament. Well before this date the leaders of the largest trade unions in United Kingdom, such as Alexander MacDonald of the Miners' Association and George Howell of the Operative Bricklayers, had begun to focus upon Parliament, offering their knowledge and perspective in the hope of improving the legal and political standing of organized labour and the material conditions of workers. The leaders of many of the most prominent trade unions made a concerted effort during the 1860s and 1870s to win public acceptance and important reforms through engagement with the legislature. These union officials strove to demonstrate their respectability, moderation and political maturity to the press and both major parties. MacDonald was at the forefront of these efforts, prioritizing a parliamentary strategy for his union and hoping to prove that unions could be useful partners in production. While other union leaders had pursued similar strategies, he received more credit for his efforts than his predecessors. It appeared that he had better access to power than any previous union leader, counting mine owners, noblemen and MPs from both parties among his friends. During this period of intense and direct focus on the legislative process, trade union leaders endured grudging progress and many disappointments.

This chapter will explore the efforts of organized labour from 1863 to 1874 to convince Parliament to enact effective legislation that would end truck and deductions from wages. From the late 1860s, the leaders of the TUC advocated for legislation mandating the weekly payment of wages in the current coin of the realm, without any deductions taken by employers. Trade union leaders, particularly MacDonald, raised public awareness on this issue through public meetings, petitioning, direct lobbying, speeches, publications and presenting evidence to Parliamentary committees. These efforts led to the formation of a Parliamentary Commission in 1871, which conducted the most exhaustive study of truck to date and accepted most of the arguments made by organized labour. George Hilton, in his book *The Truck System*, misunderstands the nature and extent of the effort by organized labour to secure reform, and he misinterprets the reasons for its failure to win legislation based upon the commission's recommendations. The effort by trade unions and sympathetic MPs to obtain the facts about the truck system provides historians with important evidence of how it was experienced by men and women in a variety of trades. It also publicized these injustices with contemporaries, which might have helped in reducing the extent of the truck system. Exploring the tactics utilized by those opposed to truck also sheds light on the possibilities and limitations of organized labour's relationship with political parties and Parliament during the 1860s and 1870s.

For decades, workers in a variety of trades had articulated their grievances with the truck system, using arguments examined in the previous chapter, particularly objecting to its infringement upon their independence and the material harm it did to working-class families.[1] They also described the frustration experienced by those attempting to enforce the 1831 Act by bringing prosecutions before magistrates or sheriffs. In some cases workers bringing truck prosecutions found themselves before a hostile tribunal. In the mid-1850s, MacDonald listened with exasperation when a sheriff suggested that although truck "was unlawful it could, sometimes, be of benefit to both employers and employees." This prompted the union leader to write a series of letters explaining the injustices of the truck system and questioning whether justice would be available to miners before a bench controlled by mine owners and their friends.[2] The courts at every level often interpreted the 1831 Act strictly in terms of its scope as well as the definition of compulsion.[3] This made the Act relatively easy to evade by combining long pays with advances made technically in cash. The penalties for violations were not large enough to be a powerful deterrent, especially when compared to the considerable profits of the company store. The efforts by trade unions and anti-truck societies to end truck by utilizing the 1831 Act had at best brought about a short-term cessation of the practice.

MacDonald had long opposed the truck system in his writings and speeches, but beginning in the 1860s he directly lobbied Parliament for more effectual anti-truck legislation. In 1863 MacDonald conducted an investigation into the extent of truck and poundage in Scotland, finding that the practices "prevail to a very great extent" and published his findings in the *Glasgow Sentinel*, a newspaper in which he had a financial stake.[4] MacDonald repeatedly raised evasion of the Truck Act, organizing petitioning drives and testifying about truck before a variety of Parliamentary Select Committees. Opposition to truck was a good issue for trade union leaders because it could be expressed in liberal terms, as an unnatural restraint upon trade and the freedom of an individual to consume. It was common among respectable elites to concede that the truck system was unfair, even if many were reluctant to support legislative remedies.

In fighting for truck reform, MacDonald was agitating less for his own constituents, many of whom laboured in workplaces that had already defeated the truck system through industrial action, but for those unorganized miners who he hoped to bring into his union.[5] In April of 1868, MacDonald used his testimony before the Royal Commission to Inquire into the Organization and

Rules of Trade Unions to argue that eliminating the truck system in some regions was a beneficial service that had been performed by trade unions, and that their spread, combined with more effective legislation from Parliament, was necessary to end continued evasion of the Truck Act by Scottish mine owners and ironmasters.[6] The draft report for this Royal Commission agreed, asserting that fighting against long pays and truck were legitimate purposes for trade unions, which "would enable men as a body to decline to work for any employer who . . . adopted the truck system."[7] There had been a number of strikes led by Scottish miners and ironworkers over the issues of truck and long pay periods.[8] The problem with this interpretation is that it caused many in Parliament to argue that more stringent anti-truck legislation was unnecessary because workers could simply end truck through industrial action, ignoring the imbalance of power in many workplaces between employer and employee, as well as the state of trade union law, which made such organization difficult. Paradoxically, although strong trade unions held the key to ending truck, truck could be a powerful obstacle to organizing a workplace.[9]

Led by MacDonald, miners throughout Britain began a petitioning drive to promote a variety of reforms in Parliament related to pay, safety and working conditions.[10] The leader of the Miners' Union would later claim that trade unions spent £30,000 on lobbying and petitioning for parliamentary action against the truck system in the dozen years before the 1871 Parliamentary Commission.[11] In 1865, petitions to the House of Commons were signed by tens of thousands of miners who complained about inadequate mine safety, the failure of coroners' courts to provide justice to victims, the continued employment of women and children in mines, the lack of a uniform system of weighing miners' material and determining their pay, and that many miners were "seriously inconvenienced, and suffer great loss on account of the length of time their wages are withheld by their employers . . . thus making them dependent on truck shops for the supply of their family necessities." The petitions requested, among other things, "that a uniform system of paying wages weekly be made compulsory by Act of Parliament."[12] On 9 May 1865, Liberal MP Acton Smee Ayrton carried a motion to investigate the allegations contained in these petitions and the operation of existing mines regulation laws. The appointed Select Committee met over the next three sessions of Parliament, submitting a report in 1867.[13]

MacDonald gave testimony before the committee on two separate occasions and described how coal and iron masters evaded the 1831 Truck Act by using long pay periods combined with wage advances that were expected to be spent in the company store. He provided examples of coercion to use the company store, reporting warnings from overmen to those who did not spend sufficient amounts at the store as well as the common practice of refusing future advances to those who "sloped" the store by taking their advances elsewhere. He explained that because these stores adhered to the "letter of the law" by giving workers their advances in money they were usually beyond prosecution under the 1831 Act, but the elaborate systems of keeping track of the advance money between the office and the store, all hinted strongly at compulsion to use the Tommy shop. Employers retained just enough deniability to make compulsion difficult to prove in court.[14] He also discussed poundage, the exorbitant fees that some employers charged workers for the privilege of receiving an advance.[15] MacDonald provided the committee with a list of at least 70 different truck shops in Scotland, along with another list of employers who charged their workers poundage for wage advances. He insisted the prices at company stores were higher than at retail stores and undermined the growth of local economies.[16] Some Scottish firms, including Schotts Iron Co. and Merry and Cunninghame, paid over 45% of the wages owed in the form of advances, most of which were spent at the company stores.[17]

MacDonald was at the forefront of a group of trade union leaders who were at pains to appropriate middle-class notions of respectability and masculinity, particularly values of self-help and provident behaviour. He wanted to demonstrate their worthiness for inclusion in the political process and for partnership with employers as a necessary part of the capitalist system. Therefore, in his testimony he underscored the harmful effects that payment in truck had upon the moral habits of workers. He argued that truck impeded workers' ability to save and manage money carefully because "these stores foster the habit of improvidence, for a person is compelled to go and spend the money at the store, else he gets no money."[18] He explained the effects that truck wages had on workers, their families and wider communities, pointing out that many company stores encouraged employees to purchase alcohol: "My experience, and it is confirmed by the complaints that have reached me from the wives and children, is that the shops will willingly give drink to drunken, improvident workmen."[19] Truck undermined the ability of workers to make contributions to trade unions that provided benefits, or to friendly and burial societies. In place of these self-help institutions, truck paying mine owners sometimes took deductions from workers' wages for education and sickness clubs, over which the employees had no input.[20] MacDonald advocated the passage of new and more stringent legislation and also suggested that weekly pays would undermine both the truck systems and the dangers of credit from retail shopkeepers.[21]

The committee pressed MacDonald to explain why workers failed to use the means already at their disposal to eliminate truck, such as finding employment elsewhere or going on strike. MacDonald gave the committee several examples of Scottish miners putting down truck at specific collieries through industrial action, only to see it revived elsewhere a few years later. However, MacDonald, who was deeply committed to the avoidance of strikes and in public asserted the need for greater cooperation between employers and workers, explained:

> It would require them to be continually fighting on this question. It is a source of so great a profit to the masters that they would always be requiring to turn out on strike; that is the reason of it; and the poverty entailed by these strikes in the opinion of the men would be too great to be continually sustained by them.[22]

These strikes would bankrupt trade unions and increase hostility between employers and workers and might only bring about a short-term cessation of the truck system. MacDonald insisted that tougher legislation was necessary to help miners to secure weekly pays in the current coin of the realm without any deductions.

The mine owners and managers who discussed company stores before this committee used the same arguments they had skilfully deployed for three decades against the introduction of additional anti-truck legislation. Magistrate and ironmaster William Matthews of Staffordshire claimed that while he was opposed to truck, he equally opposed additional anti-truck legislation because "I prefer leaving the masters and men to make their own arrangements."[23] Witness after witness insisted that the 1831 Truck Act, despite its relative ineffectiveness, was an "extreme" government interference with employment contracts and that it would be unprecedented for Parliament to dictate the timing of the payment of wages, interfering with local contractual and customary practices.[24]

The other common set of arguments made against more effective anti-truck legislation were that company stores were actually beneficial to workers. Scottish mine manager John W. Orminston observed, "I think it just comes to be a question of whether it is better for these improvident classes of workmen to be dependent, in a manner, upon the masters, or for them to be dependent upon the shopkeepers." A committee member followed up by asking whether it would be better still if they were dependent upon neither.[25] Mine owners insisted that the sumptuary control provided by company stores prevented miners from drinking their wages and kept their habits regular. Mine manager Isaiah Booth argued that because miners drank heavily on payday and failed to work on the following Monday, weekly pays would mean more missed days of work. He observed of other collieries with weekly pays that "payment taking place once a week, and two thirds of the men never come to work on the Monday after that day."[26] However, John Normansell, secretary of the South Yorkshire Miners' Association, argued that the introduction of weekly payments in his district had "done away with play Mondays" and contributed to "steadier habits of working" because the payment of wages was no longer so rare as to constitute a cause for celebration.[27]

In their report, the members of the Select Committee unanimously agreed that "[t]he intention of the law against the payment of wages by truck is frequently defeated, more especially in Scotland, and that the law would require some alteration in order to render it more effectual." The committee was also in agreement that this alteration should not be mandating employers to pay wages weekly without deductions, resolving that weekly pays would cause "great inconveniences" to employers, including additional labour costs for calculating wages, as well as the more frequent "cessation of labour which unhappily too often follows the pay-day."[28] Soon after this report, inspectors of the factories informed Parliament of truck payments in glove making, knitting and other trades, increasing pressure for action.[29]

The *North British Daily Mail's* investigation into truck in Scotland

MacDonald hoped to win respectable opinion to his cause, and he succeeded in inspiring one proprietor of a newspaper to investigate his claims. In response to the miners' petitions to Parliament and their union leaders' testimony, in 1869 William Cameron and the *North British Daily Mail* (*NBDM*) conducted an investigation into violations of the Truck Act in Ayrshire and Lanarkshire, visiting dozens of individual collieries and ironworks "with a view of inquiring into the complaints which have recently been so rife against the prevalence of truck stores." The newspaper's first instalment of its report confirmed that the truck system was widespread in these districts.[30] They published their extensive findings in the issues released in June 1869 and July 1869. The report had credibility with the public because the newspaper stressed its objectivity, emphasizing that its investigators had had no direct contact with MacDonald or "the miners' friends," meaning other union leaders.[31] Many individual miners and ironworkers took great risks to provide information, and the paper took care to keep their identities secret.[32] The *NBDM* insisted that nearly all of the workers and family members that they interviewed harshly condemned the truck system.[33]

The report detailed the various disguised systems for paying workers in truck at different mines and ironworks. They all had similar features: long pay periods, with advances on wages earned but not yet paid available to employees and their families at a pay office usually right next door to the company store. The report pointed out that in addition to the long reckoning periods, the fact that employers always kept a minimum of six days wages in hand meant that it was very hard for a poor mining family to last the pay period without seeking an advance. These advances were paid in cash but with the expectation that most of the money would be spent at the company store. Failure to spend the money at the store, a practice known as "sloping the store," was treated as an act of dishonesty and was punished with reprisals.[34] The report concluded that "[i]t will be obvious that truckstering employers, if not guilty of a direct infraction of the law have contrived to set utterly at defiance with the spirit of the Act."[35] The newspaper described workplaces charging a fee of 1 shilling for every pound advanced before payday, known as poundage. A man obtaining money 10 days before payday would be paying a rate of interest of about 180% per annum for the advance of money he had already earned.[36]

The investigators judged the prices and quality of the goods provided by the company stores, which were highly variable, and in most stores the prices were higher than what local retailers charged, although there were some stores at the larger works that were competitive in terms of price and standards. However, Cameron argued that the temptation of a monopolist truck master to raise prices and lower quality would always be so overpowering that employees could not help but regard the store with doubt:

> But the temptation which it holds out to a needy or greedy and unscrupulous master to make an exorbitant and unfair profit about of his truck

store has in practice been found irresistible. Facts prove beyond a doubt that the goods provided by truck stores are both higher in price and inferior in quality to those furnished by common shops.[37]

Working families who dealt with company stores had none of the leverage that ordinary consumers had with shopkeepers who sought their patronage. In fact, the wives of miners were frequently afraid to complain about prices, quality or even being short-weighted, for fear that reprisals would find their husbands out of work.[38]

The investigators of the *NBDM* commented upon the moral and domestic impact of the truck system on mining families, finding it destroyed masculine independence and demoralized women by undermining their role in managing family consumption and budgets. Investigators commented that the patrons of one particular truck store had a "depressed, impoverished and ragged appearance," including

> an emaciated looking woman, scantily clad in dirty and ragged garments, with neither shoes nor stockings on her feet, bearing in her arms a wasted looking little child, she entered with a downcast deprecating look, and with a sigh placed her ticket on the counter.

They observed that along with her items she took "a bottle of drink (whiskey we think it was)."[39] The reports claimed that the truck system encouraged drinking among miners and their wives alike. The investigation recorded every company store that had a taproom or sold spirits, reporting stories of either men or their wives drinking large portions of their advances. *The NBDM* repeatedly condemned the employers' taprooms as "one of the very worst features of the truck system and helps to keep the workmen in continual poverty and dependence."[40]

The male workers themselves expressed that the worst part of the truck system was the loss of independence that it entailed. After interviewing some miners, the *NBDM* wrote:

> The worst of this system they said was that it pressed hardest on the married men who were compelled to be customers of their employer in nearly every department of domestic economy. They occupied his houses, subscribed to his schools, paid him for mending and sharpening their mining tools, supplied themselves with food, clothing and drink, certainly not on advantageous terms and were, they told us, reduced to a condition little better than that of slaves who work for food and raiment.[41]

As historian Alan Campbell notes, "The very existence of the stores was a constant assertion of the power of the companies in the everyday life of the colliers."[42]

The exposé cited many reasons why workers had been unable to eliminate the truck system in Lanarkshire and Ayrshire, including "employers in

Lanarkshire find truck too profitable to easily part with." Even if the company store charged competitive prices, the ability to monopolize the patronage of workers and the freedom of risk from bad debts would make it a valuable part of the mine owners' business. The investigators thought that the high salaries of the men in charge of running these stores, some as high as £1,000 p.a., far in excess of what an average retail shopkeeper earned, were highly revealing.[43] The eleven stores at the Summerlee Iron Works in Lanarkshire brought the firm annual profits of at least £20,000.[44]

The investigations also answered some of the common defences of company stores. Against the paternalist argument for keeping a company store, the newspaper editorialized:

> Perhaps the most offensive feature in the proceedings of these trucksters is the attempt to cover this unjust and injurious treatment of their workmen under the cloak of benevolence. The object of these large hearted philanthropists, forsooth, is not so much to fill their own pockets as to benefit the workman … to protect him from his own improvident habits; but as everybody knows, and the truck system most strikingly proves, monopoly and dearness, and badness too, go hand in hand, and free and open competition is the best security for fair and moderate prices.[45]

A historian of the Lanarkshire Miners Union observed "the ostensible and declared concern of the masters for their employees' welfare does appear hypocritical when considered alongside the achievement of considerable profits and a powerful instrument of industrial control from the truck system."[46]

The paper also countered the argument that the stores were for the convenience of workers in remote locations, finding that there was nearly always a number of good retail stores within a reasonable distance of the works.[47] Three years earlier MacDonald had made the same point to Parliament, "It is a gross fallacy about their being mountainous districts, and out-of-the-way districts. Wherever a demand arises, supply will at once follow. We have no mines in Scotland that cannot be reached from town in half an hour."[48]

The report concluded that although workmen could do more to end the truck system, the 1831 Act was insufficient.[49] It recommended weekly pays for miners, or if that was not possible, advances without charge, as "undue delay in the payment of wages lies at the root of the whole truck system."[50] It also recommended tougher penalties for truck and more stringent provisions to make the law more difficult to evade.[51]

The 1870–1871 Truck Commission

This investigation of the *NBDM* not only had a significant impact in Scotland but was noticed in Westminster as well. During debates on the Trade Union Bill, MP A.J. Mundella made reference to its findings, suggesting that trade unions were necessary for fighting the truck system in Scotland, which made "men …

slaves body and soul of the masters."[52] After the full series of the Report on the Truck System had its print run in the *NBDM*, it was re-published in pamphlet form and provoked a long editorial in the *Times* of London on 17 July 1869. The *Times* declared that the "Truck Act is scandalously evaded in Lanarkshire" and that

> [w]e certainly trust that the Home Secretary will think it his duty to insti-
> tute a searching investigation into the matter, and to cause the Act to be
> enforced with rigour ... and ... to take the proper steps to its amendment.
> But the surest remedy is the extinction of the long-pay system.[53]

Two days earlier, in the House of Commons, Sir David Wedderburn, MP for Lanarkshire, pressed the Home Secretary for his reaction to the reports in the *NBDM*. Home Secretary Henry Bruce replied that he had "very little doubt that there was a very wide and systematic infringement of the Truck Act in Scotland" and that he would consult with the Lord Advocate of Scotland about the proper steps to take.[54]

Despite winning only a vague promise of action from the Home Secretary, MacDonald was optimistic about the possibility of reform, reporting to a con-ference of Lanarkshire miners in August of 1869 that he sensed that the House of Commons was strongly opposed to truck system and against deductions from miners' wages. He even stated that before the previous session of Parlia-ment had ended, Sir Robert Anstruther of Fifeshire had placed on the notice paper a measure to ensure the weekly payment of miners' wages.[55] At meetings of miners' throughout Scotland, MacDonald campaigned for the mines regu-lation bill and the weekly payment of wages in the current coin of the realm without deductions.[56]

On 28 April 1870, in the House of Commons, Wedderburn communicated the disappointment that was felt in Scotland over the government's failure to act on the truck system, requesting a public inquiry into evasions of the Truck Act. Bruce, who had sat on the 1854 Select Committee that investigated the operation of the Truck Acts, doubted that an inquiry would do more than "add another Blue Book to the many we already possessed" because it would be "dif-ficult, if not impossible, to increase the stringency of the Act without interfer-ing with freedom of trade."[57]

The miners in the north, led by MacDonald, intensified their campaign of meetings and petitioning during May and June of 1870, eventually producing petitions to the House of Commons signed by at least 80,000 miners (MacDonald claimed over 103,000) complaining of evasion of the Truck Acts.[58] Armed with these petitions, on 12 July 1870, A.J. Mundella rose in the House to move for a Commission of Inquiry into the alleged violations of the Truck Acts. He spoke to the "demoralizing" moral impact of the system on families, saying it "reduced people to a state of practical serfdom" and "encouraged reckless habits of improvidence and intemperance among them." He also argued that it undermined retail shopkeepers and damaged respect for the law because so many justices of the peace, sheriffs and MPs were implicated in its practice. He also stated that truck was not only a problem in Scotland but was also practiced in Wales. Anstruther seconded the motion, observing that although the *NBDM* exposé had been in print for many months, there had not been a single public contradiction of its findings. He deplored truck because "all independence was crushed out of a man whose earnings were not his own." George Anderson of Scotland also supported the motion, suggesting an amendment to the Mines Regulation Bill to mandate weekly pays for miners, which would do more to end truck than "a hundred commissions." Home Secretary Bruce argued that the problem was less defects in the present law than "the absence of combination and energy on the part of the working men themselves in applying it." Sir Edward Colebrooke agreed, stating:

> According to the statements which have been made, [the workmen] would seem to be mere serfs and bondsmen. They had, however, entered into combinations to control the rate of wages, and in the west of Scotland almost every paper contained some report of meetings of thousands of workmen, who passed resolutions in the open day; and it was impossible to deny that a spirit of independence prevailed amongst these workmen, which might be brought to bear on these abuses.

For Colebrooke, the success of organized labour in raising awareness about the need for new anti-truck legislation was an argument as to why it was unnecessary. The Home Secretary assured Mundella that the government was "most anxious" to end the truck system but pleaded with him to withdraw his motion and allow the government to establish an inquiry "in the manner most calculated to produce the desired result." Mundella reluctantly agreed, stating his desire was to get the facts out in the most effectual manner.[59]

The *Times* was not impressed with Bruce's response to Mundella's motion and criticized him severely in a leader from 14 July 1870. It argued that the suggestion that the truck system was being evaded because of a lack of energy on the part of workmen was "a whimsical explanation" which wilfully ignored the "powerlessness of the workingman to withstand the domination of his employers." It stated that the "grave, open, and pointed" accusations of the *NBDM* should have stirred the government to action. It criticized Bruce for saying the government was "most anxious" to stop the truck system, "but anxiety which has let twelve months pass by without stirring a single stone, and now promises to spend another twelve months in pensive reflection, is not worthy of a strong government." The *Times* endorsed legislative compulsion for employers to provide advance to employees at least two-thirds of their estimated weekly earnings every week without charge in order to fight the "long pay" system and tougher penalties for violation of the Truck Act.

Under pressure from the *Times*, Mundella, Wedderburn and trade unions, on 29 July 1870, Bruce brought forward a bill establishing a Commission to investigate the prevalence of evasion of the Truck Act in England, Scotland

and Wales (but not Ireland). The commission had the power to compel witness attendance and testimony and to procure documents. It also could grant amnesty to those who testified before it.[60]

The primary commissioners under the Truck Commission Act were Charles C.S. Bowen, an English barrister, and Alexander C. Sellar, a Scottish barrister, who was the legal secretary to the lord advocate. Bowen eventually became a judge in the Queen's Bench division and later one on the Court of Appeal, while Sellar was elected to the House of Commons in 1882.[61] The investigation they ran was, in the words of Hilton, "one of the most comprehensive and intelligent social inquiries of the Victorian period."[62] The commission sat 34 times, taking testimony in Hamilton, Glasgow, Edinburgh, Cardiff, Gloucester, Prescott, Birmingham, Nottingham and three separate sittings in London. A remarkable 569 witnesses gave testimony and answered a total of 45,125 questions. They listened to testimony from a somewhat balanced range of male sources, hearing from 194 workmen, 31 of whom were brought forward at the request of employers. There were 31 different wives of workers who were interviewed by the commissioners, 4 of whom came forward at the request of the owners. Although women had a greater voice before this commission than they had enjoyed in any previous Parliamentary investigation into truck, they were still underrepresented which is odd when one considers that the "condition of women" was such a critical marker in the gendered debates over truck wages. Mine owners and mine managers represented 208 of the witnesses, and 3 different inspectors of the mines gave lengthy testimony as well. Fifty-two retail shopkeepers who competed with company stores also made their views known to the commission. The commission heard from MacDonald twice, and William Cameron of the *NBDM* shared his expertise on the subject with the commission.[63] The proceedings of the commission were often reported in trades journals, the *Glasgow Sentinel*, the *Times*, the *NBDM* and a variety of other newspapers.

MacDonald used the *Glasgow Sentinel* to publicize the popular meetings supporting truck reform and the proceedings of the Truck Commission.[64] The paper praised Bowen and Sellar but warned that previous commissions and select committees on truck had not brought needed reforms, and employers who kept company stores would use all of their influence to prevent change.[65] The paper noted the positive impact that the commission was already having by reporting that the spotlight of the investigation had pressured many truck masters in South Wales to give up truck.[66]

The commission presented its completed report to Parliament in May of 1871, and there was much in it for organized labour to be pleased about.[67] The report confirmed the existence of large amounts of "disguised truck" carried on in Wales and western Scotland as well as a surprising number of other trades. It claimed that by the lowest estimate half a million people were dependent upon works where they were either charged poundage for advances or compelled to use a company store: "That truck prevails extensively in many trades and in many parts of the kingdom is all that can safely be asserted."[68] It also stressed that, especially amongst "the best men," opposition to the truck system was nearly universal, observing "[t]he dislike of the stores among the better class of men in Scotland is strong, and undeniable."[69] It also provided evidence that Welsh and Scottish miners overwhelmingly favoured weekly pays.[70] It explained the variety of ways in which long pay periods and advances in coal and ironworks in Wales and Scotland underpinned the truck system. In all of these arrangements "the one feature common to all of them is that the workman who receives the advance is expected to become the shop's customer."[71] The report also detailed the different reprisals that were carried out against "slopers," including the refusal of future advances and dismissals.[72]

The report also addressed the issue of the price and quality of the goods available at the company stores, finding the quality variable at different locations and the prices nearly always higher.[73] Here the report made a distinction amongst employees that appeared frequently throughout its pages: the distinction between "provident" and "improvident workers." "Provident" workers were those employees who through savings and careful management could survive between the long pay periods and chose not to take advances and use the company store. The "improvident" were "the feeble and the drunkard" as well as the "timid and dependent," who were not organized and were forced to accept advances on the conditions offered by their employers. The report suggested that many witnesses testified that provident men almost never used the company store, but took their business off-premises, which was highly suggestive that the prices and quality of company stores was worse than their retailing competitors.[74] This division of workers into "provident" and "improvident" probably sat well with union leaders like MacDonald, because it mirrored how they themselves thought of the working class. However, permitting this dichotomy to stand unchallenged was a tactical mistake by organized labour. It provided opponents of reform with a rhetorical tool for arguing that legislative solutions were unnecessary. This division of the working class into dependent and independent allowed defenders of the status quo to direct attention away from the differences in power between employers and workers of *every* description.

This distinction between "provident" and "improvident" workers was also made when describing the effects of the truck system on working families. The report asserted that long pays forced many workers into credit either at a company store or with a credit-giving retailer, which in practice meant that they bought items more dearly, faced greater challenges in evaluating the consequences of their purchases and, upon falling into debt, lost their independence: "Under a long pay system the labourer must procure credit somewhere; and the necessity of living upon credit during the intervals between paydays tends to place him in the power of somebody" whether a company store, or a credit-granting shopkeeper.[75]

The report acknowledged the profitability of company stores for coal and ironmasters in Scotland and Wales. One estimate before the committee was that Welsh manufacturers benefited to the extent of around 10% of their employees gross wages from their stores, which was an important advantage over competitors who did not practice truck.[76] These company stores also had important advantages over retail stores. They were a perfectly safe investment, as employers could be certain of employee patronage, could buy in large quantities on the best terms and could avoid bad debts. Furthermore, company stores could set prices independently of the market. The report stated that company stores had unquestionably greater profits than a typical retail dealer, damaging the better shops in the area.[77]

Perhaps most importantly of all, the *Report of the Truck Commission* disputed with an official government voice many common arguments that had been used successfully in previous decades to prevent the passage of additional anti-truck legislation by Parliament. The first of these arguments was that if workers objected to truck, they already had a variety of remedies in their own hands. Rather than passing legislation that would interfere with the liberty to contract, why not suggest that workers who disliked truck not work for truck paying masters? Why have trade unions failed to use industrial action to end company stores?

The report countered the first argument by stating that there was, in fact, evidence that the very best workers, the most "provident" and "intelligent," usually refused to work for truck masters. The report stressed that there were many factors that could make it hard for a man to leave behind networks of economic and emotional support and relocate to a new job.[78] Furthermore, truck undermined the very habits of saving, self-reliance and independence that would permit a worker to leave a truck master.

The report also asserted that truck was rare in areas that had longer traditions of continuous trade union organization.[79] It asserted that truck flourished in places where "they are not organized, for trade unionism has no hold among the miners in and colliers in South Wales, nor are trade unions found to flourish side by side with truck."[80] Company stores made it hard for workers to raise the necessary funds to pay union dues or to fund prosecutions under the Truck Act.[81] In such places workers lacked the independence necessary to put down truck through industrial action. This statement by the commission about the importance of trade unions in preventing the truck system was the kind of acknowledgement of a useful role for organized labour that the leaders of the TUC had long sought. There were other reasons beyond a lack of funds why workers did not bring prosecutions under the 1831 Act. The Report argued that many feared dismissal and being blacklisted in the region if they came forward to prosecute their employers. The sheriff of Renfrew told the commission that "the main defect in the Act seems to me to consist in the want of a public prosecutor."[82]

The report also responded harshly to some of the frequently made arguments about the benefits of company-owned stores for employees. In particular, the report disputed the assertion that "the company shop removes the needy labourer from the tyranny of small hucksters" and the dangers of credit, observing that this argument "presupposes the existence of long pays and then takes credit for truck on the ground that truck will mitigate some of their evils." It also pointed out that it is a "fallacy" to assume that the choice was only between small, expensive, credit-granting retailers and the company store. If the company store's monopoly were broken up, "shops of a large size and creditable character" that charged good prices would soon move into the area, to the benefit of all inhabitants.[83]

They also challenged the argument that "short pays lead to, while the company's shop represses, improvidence and intemperance among the men." Many witnesses from works with company stores argued that on paydays miners drank heavily and squandered their wages, leading to works being idle on the following Monday. The argument in favour of truck insisted that with long pays and company stores, employers could regulate the consumption of alcohol and make sure that wives got the family wages in order to provision the home. The commissioners were sceptical of this argument, stating "employers who derive considerable profits from the monopoly can scarcely be deemed impartial witnesses on the subject of the moral advantages the monopoly secures to others." The commissioners postulated that if this were the case, the stores would be very popular with the wives of miners and that this was simply not borne out by the evidence that they collected: "Some of the bitterest opponents of the company's shop come from among the women."[84] Finally, the report argued that just "because the settlement day . . . leads, where long pays prevail, to scenes of drunkenness, [does not mean] such scenes would be multiplied proportionately by more frequent and more regular pays." It was possible that paydays were a cause for drunken celebration because they were rare.[85]

The commission recommended that Parliament amend the Truck Act to mandate weekly or quasi-weekly pays, which it argued would greatly undermine the current evasions. Even though weekly pays were not common in the coal and iron trades, and "the greater part of the objections to their practicality will be found to proceed from those who are directly or indirectly connected with the shop system," the commissioners concluded that "weekly pays in full could be carried out generally in the ironworks and collieries to which the inquiry has extended." At the very least, it suggested that employers make 90% of the gross estimated weekly wages available to the worker each week, allowing the employer at most seven lie days (days between the end of the pay period and the date when the wages were given to the employee) for calculating wages. It also recommended increasing the criminal penalties for violating the Truck Act and placing prosecutions in the hands of public officials, possibly the inspectors of mines and factories. On the question of deductions the commission was divided, acknowledging that "if truck were abandoned off-takes might furnish a new mode of deriving similar indirect profits" and that some workers objected to medical and education deductions, because they wanted to choose their own doctors or schoolmasters. The commission recommended that employees should be permitted to audit all off-takes from wages.[86] Although there was no time to act on the commission's recommendations in the current session of Parliament, on 17 August 1871, Viscount Halifax assured the Earl of Shaftsbury in the House of Lords that the government would introduce legislation based on the recommendations in the next session.[87]

The 1872 Truck Bill

The TUC was pleased with the work of the Truck Commission, which had endorsed many of organized labour's main points. Before the annual meeting of the TUC in January of 1872, A.J. Mundella proclaimed:

> That committee discharged its duties in a manner which earned for it . . . the gratitude of all the working men of this country (hear, hear). Never was a commission more fairly constituted and never had a commission more effectively performed the duties devolving upon it (cheers). Nothing was left undone that was in the power of the commission to do, and instead of passing over, as too often commissions had done, a great majority of the cases of hardship and suffering, they rooted them out and went thoroughly to the bottom of the mischief (hear, hear).[88]

MacDonald agreed that "no commission ever did its work so favourably, so fearlessly, so nobly" and proposed the following resolution:

> Congress rejoices to learn that the government intends to introduce a bill to prevent the systematic violation of the Truck Act. At the same time we feel assured that no government Act will be successful in freeing a large section of the working class from the demoralizing influence of the Truck Shop which does not enforce the payment of wages weekly in the current coin of the realm with no stoppages or deductions for any purpose whatsoever.

The motion passed, and the TUC committed itself to a Truck Bill that included weekly pays in the current coin of the realm, without any deductions.[89] Working people had convinced the Truck Commission, much of the press and many MPs with their ideas for reform. Having the better argument, however, was not the same as having the influence to move legislation through Parliament.

In February of 1872, Home Secretary Henry Austen Bruce and Undersecretary of the Home Office Henry Winterbotham introduced "A Bill to Amend the Law with respect to the Payment of Wages to Workmen in Certain Trades," a legislative proposal that exceeded the TUC's most optimistic expectations.[90] It repealed the 1831 Act and re-enacted legislation that the whole wages of any worker had to be paid in the current coin of the realm, without any deductions or any conditions on the spending of these wages. It did, however, make an exception for lodging and school fees, but it gave employees the right to have an annual audit of the education deductions carried out by two auditors of the workmen's choice. It made it a crime for a master, or a master's agents, to impose any compulsion toward a workman as to the place or manner in which he or she spent his or her wages. It was also illegal to pay wages on or adjacent to places that sold liquor or stores where goods were sold to workmen. As with the 1831 Act, a worker could recover the full monetary value of wages paid in truck as if they had never been paid. The penalty for the first offense was £10 and for a second offence £20. Enforcement was delegated to the inspectors of mines and factories in England and to the Procurators Fiscal in Scotland, who could bring cases before justices of the peace and magistrates in England, or a sheriff in Scotland. Perhaps most importantly, section six of the bill mandated that wages would accrue daily and be payable weekly, requiring employers to pay at least 90% of the estimated weekly earnings (or 70% for the first week on the job) and to make up the balance within four weeks' time. This provision would have helped many workers who had never experienced the truck system by mandating weekly pays and reducing the need for short-term credit from small retailers. The provisions of this bill would also have expanded the scope of the Truck Act by including all workers engaged in any occupations to which the Mines Regulation Acts of 1872 or the Factory and Workshop Acts of 1833, 1867 and 1871 applied.[91]

Labour leaders were very pleased with the bill, but given their experiences with other recent labour legislation, they anticipated a counterattack. An editorialist for the *Ironworkers' Journal* feared that the Home Secretary would receive protests from employers informing him that the bill "interferes with the liberty of the subject and that question should be left in the hands of employers and workmen." He warned all workers to support the Parliamentary Committee of the TUC to promote and defend the payment of wages weekly without deductions.[92] The author was right to fear a backlash against the bill, especially given the hostility some employers showed toward the idea of weekly pays before the Truck Commission. In the testimony of those associated with company stores, weekly pays were dismissed as "impracticable" to "impossible to carry out" and being a "great nuisance."[93]

In *The Truck System*, George Hilton makes the defeat of the 1872 bill sound very benign. He argues it failed because it commanded very little support and that "growing prosperity" removed any urgency for legislative action on the issue.[94] This interpretation is inconsistent with the facts. This bill, which had considerable support from organized labour and workers in Scotland and Wales and many parts of England, did not die from neglect or lack of support but was deliberately killed by employers who lobbied the Home Secretary furiously. In addition to employers who had testified against weekly pays before the commission, there was also opposition from mine owners in Northumberland and Durham, where the custom called for fortnightly pays. There were many petitions against the proposed bill from north Wales as well.[95] Mine owners worried about losing the ability to make deductions for the sharpening of tools and other equipment. MacDonald and the TUC tried to match their opponents, rallying support in the countryside by holding simultaneous meetings in Merthyr and Yorkshire, before 5,000 and 8,000 miners respectively, where motions were passed and petitions signed in favour of the Truck Bill.[96]

After a month of aggressive lobbying from employers in the coal and iron industry, Bruce and Winterbotham sought to backtrack from their commitment to workers, so they proposed to refer the bill to a committee. According to George Howell, the Truck Bill was "so good that the truck masters in the house were on the alert to insure its defeat." He and MacDonald received word on 6 March 1872 that "a movement was on foot to get the bill referred to a select committee with the object of shelving it." Together, MacDonald and Howell convinced the Home Secretary to have the bill committed after, rather than before, the second reading so "the principles of the bill are affirmed . . . before the whole bill can be recast and remodelled."[97]

On 18 March 1872 when the bill was brought up for a second reading, Winterbotham moved that it be referred to a select committee for further amendment because "we must be careful, while attempting to remedy this admitted evil, not to interfere unnecessarily with legitimate customs or with freedom to contract where the evil does not exist." He also thought that the question of deductions from wages, which had the potential to impact the customary practices in many trades, needed to be considered more carefully by the committee as well. The motion passed. MacDonald knew that the bill would either be "mutilated" with amendments or shelved altogether and was furious. George Howell later recorded,

> A consultation took place and we went to the lobby where MacDonald declared that if the bill was got rid of in any quiet sort of way, he would spend £100 to telegraph to the whole country. He was thoroughly wild and expressed himself very strongly about it. Several members began to see a storm brewing and advised quietude and moderation.[98]

MacDonald wrote to the TUC that the government bill was a "good one" that would "effectively destroy the practice of truck." However, the Home Secretary, "listening to the appeals of those in the House who are supporters of the system, and themselves opponents of the bill," had it referred to a select committee that "bears a complexion unfavourable to anything like a report that will settle firmly the questions dealt with in the bill." He told them it was his duty to "sound the alarm and urge you to take immediate action to prevent the shelving of so reasonable a bill."[99] Labour leaders were outraged by the composition of the select committee, which they continually referred to as a "secret committee" that "met behind closed doors" to purge the bill of all its favourable clauses. They were furious that the committee refused to hear or receive evidence from working men, despite repeated requests to the Home Secretary.[100] For all of their recent progress, in the debate over truck there were still limits to the access and influence of the New Model Unions in Westminster that did not apply to large mine owners and ironmasters.

The select committee produced a heavily amended bill on 6 May 1872, and three days later when the some leaders of the Parliamentary Committee of TUC saw the proofs of the bill they realized "our worst fears have been realized."[101]

The bill watered down the principles of weekly pays in the current coin of the realm without deductions. The new bill effectively removed the right to weekly pays. Furthermore, in the original government bill, the only deductions permitted were for lodging and education. In the amended bill employers were also permitted to make deductions for medical attendance, subscriptions from hospitals, fuel for work and domestic use, and "materials, tools, implements, hay, corn, provender, or victuals." Masters were allowed to make deductions for the sale of goods that they manufactured and sold to their workmen. The amendments also weakened the section that had prohibited the payment of wages on or near premises that sold liquor or goods to workmen, allowing the payment of wages near such stores provided that employer had no direct interest in the store (it was considered doubtful that receiving an exorbitant rent from the storekeeper constituted having an interest). The Parliamentary Committee of the TUC argued that these amendments created loopholes that would make the bill as ineffectual as the 1831 Act. From the perspective of labour the only improvements were the inclusion of an amendment to prohibit frame rents and the increase in the penalties under the bill for the second and third offences, which went up to a maximum of £50 and £100, respectively.[102]

The Parliamentary Committee of the TUC published a memorial to H.A. Bruce, declaring that the bill amended by the select committee was "quite inadequate to meet the existing evils." A deputation of labour representatives, including MacDonald and Howell, waited upon Bruce at the Home Office on 13 June 1872 to present their memorial and discuss the amended truck bill with him. The fact that Bruce felt it important to meet with this deputation spoke to the success of the strategies pursued by the largest amalgamated unions for gaining public acceptance, yet the ease with which the Home Secretary dismissed their concerns also demonstrated their limits. Howell argued in favour of the original bill and explaining the shortcomings of its amended counterpart. He thanked the Home Secretary for receiving them and pleaded that they were "not here to complain against the government, but to ask the government to maintain and stand by their own bill, as introduced under your own care."

MacDonald and the others "complained about the composition of the select committee, in that capital was fully represented, but no one to represent labour," as well as that the committee refused to take evidence from working men. Bruce, in his response, accidently made a point that would be picked up by many labour leaders in the months to come, which was "[n]o one regretted more than him that there were no working men on the committee, but as they *had not a single working man in the house,* the government had selected those most nearly approaching the character of workingmen's representatives." After this, the TUC demonstrated a growing interest in electing working men to the House of Commons. Bruce recounted his long history of fighting against the truck system, stating that in

> legislating upon matters of this kind there were many extreme difficulties. . . . [T]he proposals were certainly an interference with the law of the

land, with the right of one man to enter a contract with another, and it was justified on the grounds that the working men were not able to take care of themselves

but, as their presence before him demonstrated, "that was an argument that was growing weaker by the day." Paradoxically, labour's success in raising the issue of truck was used as an argument against providing legislative remedies for the problem. He compared passing the original Truck Bill to "throwing a stone at a man's head to kill a fly." Under-Secretary Winterbotham met with MacDonald, Howell and William Allen of the Amalgamated Engineers on 17 June 1872 for three hours and conceded that many of the amendments "were objectionable and ought to be struck out of the bill; others were at best doubtful and should be considered." Despite this long meeting no further action was taken to change the amended bill.

The bill was so far from the principle of weekly pays in currency with no deductions that the TUC felt was necessary for suppressing truck that they instructed the Parliamentary Committee to advise the withdrawal of the bill.[103] On 15 May, the *NBDM* questioned this decision, arguing that although the amended bill was weaker than the original measure it was a step in the right direction, with tougher penalties for violation, and workers were wrong to oppose it. MacDonald wrote to the newspaper and explained how the loopholes in the proposed measure would permit employers to continue using long pays, advances and compulsion to benefit from stores that they charged storekeepers considerable rents to keep. He explained that miners and other workers found the variety of new deductions that were permissible under the act very obnoxious. He argued that the penalties in the new bill were irrelevant as they "may be £10,000 as well as £5 if the machinery is so fitted that no conviction is likely to follow. It matters not if the penalty was transportation for life."[104]

The failure of the 1872 Truck Bill demonstrates the growth and limits of trade union power in the 1860s and 1870s. The legislative strategy and conciliatory and respectable tactics of MacDonald and other leaders did pay some dividends – labour got very close to a victory which would have improved the material conditions of working men and women. But no amount of conciliatory rhetoric could paper over some fundamental differences in ideology and economic interests between the leaders from different social classes. These differences included what constituted an unacceptable interference with the freedom to contract and the rights of employers to make arbitrary deductions from a workers' pay.

During the debate over the 1872 bill, many ironworkers suggested that only by having working-class MPs could these entrenched views of middle-class MPs be challenged and overcome.[105] In 1873 the TUC passed a resolution in support of electing working men to Parliament.[106] Howell would run unsuccessfully for Parliament in 1868, 1874 and 1881 before winning a seat in 1885. MacDonald was elected to Parliament in 1874, and one of his first questions before the House of Commons was to Home Secretary Cross asking if he would bring the Truck Bill forward in the current session. Cross said no.

Another factor in the failure of the Truck Bill was that the government had far more to fear from employers than the New Model Unions. The value of the access that the Home Secretary gave to MacDonald was greater than anything MacDonald could do for the government in 1872. In all of MacDonald's speeches in favour of truck, and in all of his petitioning demands to Parliament, he never once communicated a sense of "or else," which illuminates the limits of his strategy of winning favour with the Liberals. MacDonald had positioned his union in such a way that politically they had nowhere else to go. Slightly more comprehensive, but still disappointing, truck legislation passed in 1887, which will be discussed in the next chapter. It is not a coincidence that this was after the 1884 Reform Act, at the dawn of New Unionism and a period when there were more working-class MPs in Parliament. The TUC by that point was no longer satisfied with merely having a seat at the table.

Notes

1 Bailey, *The Truck System,* pp. 21–22; *Select Committee on the Payment of Wages* (1854), Q. 3847–3849; *Monmouthshire Merlin,* 14 October 1843, p. 2; "Anti Truck Meeting at Dudley," Staffordshire Country Record Office, D260/M/F/5/18; *Merthyr Telegraph,* 24 April 1855, p. 2; *Cambrian,* 21 January 1837, p. 3; *Merthyr and Cardiff Chronicle,* 15 July 1837, pp. 1, 3; *Miner,* 21 March 1863; *Times,* 20 April 1842, p. 14; 11 August 1843, p. 5; "Anti-Truck Movement!" Staffordshire Country Record Office, D260/M/F/5/18.

2 Wilson, *Alexander MacDonald,* pp. 80–81.

3 *Riley v. Warden and Another (1848),* 2 Exchequer Reports 59; *Sharman v. Sanders (1853)* 13 CB 166; *Ingram v. Barnes (1856–1857),* 26 LJ 82, 7 E & B QB 115.

4 Campbell, *The Lanarkshire Miners,* p. 153. Also see *The Glasgow Sentinel,* 25 July 1863; 1 August 1863.

5 *Select Committee on the Payment of Wages* (1854), Q. 2913–2916; *Report of the Commissioners Appointed to Inquire into the Truck System, Volume I: Report, Schedules, Supplement. Vol II: Minutes of Evidence* (1871) *Parliamentary Papers,* XXXVI (c326–c327), xx; Curthoys, *Governments, Labour and the Law in Mid-Victorian Britain,* p. 238.

6 *Royal Commission to Inquire into Organization and Rules of Trade Unions and Other Associations, Seventh Report, Minutes and Evidence* (1867–68), Q. 15,341–15,347; 15,375–15,376; 15,434; 15,502–15,543.

7 *Report of the Royal Commission to Inquire into the Organization and Rules of Trade Unions and Other Associations, Eleventh and Final Report* (1868–1869), pp., xxi, xli, ci.

8 Handley, *The Navvy in Scotland,* p. 201.

9 *Select Committee on the Payment of Wages* (1854), Q. 1950, 2013, 2017, 2026–2027, 2162–2163, 4249.

10 Robert Nelson Boyd, *Coal Mines Inspection: Its History and Results* (London: WH Allen and Co, 1879), pp. 160–164.

11 Campbell, *The Lanarkshire Miners,* p. 222.

12 *Select Committee to inquire into Regulation and Inspection of Mines, and Complaints in Petitions from Miners in Great Britain, Report, Proceedings, Minutes of Evidence, Appendix, Index* (1867), pp. ix–x.

13 Boyd, *Coal Mines Inspection,* pp. 162–163.

14 *Select Committee to Inquire into Regulation and Inspection of Mines, and Complaints in Petitions from Miners in Great Britain, Report, Proceedings, Minutes of Evidence, Appendix, Index* (1866), Q. 7094–7100, 7103–7118, 7132–7133, 7140.

15 *Select Committee to Inquire into Regulation and Inspection of Mines, and Complaints in Petitions from Miners . . .* (1866), Q. 8366–8371.

16 *Select Committee to Inquire into Regulation and Inspection of Mines, and Complaints in Petitions from Miners* . . . (1866), Appendix 3, p. 524. See also Q. 7089, 7124, 7125, 7139; Handley, *The Navvy in Scotland,* p. 199.
17 Handley, *The Navvy in Scotland,* pp. 200, 210.
18 *Select Committee to Inquire into Regulation and Inspection of Mines, and Complaints in Petitions from Miners* . . . (1866), Q. 7093.
19 *Select Committee to Inquire into Regulation and Inspection of Mines, and Complaints in Petitions from Miners* . . . (1866), pp. 214–217, 271–273, Q. 7088–7139, 8366–8393. Quote from 7136.
20 *Select Committee to Inquire into Regulation and Inspection of Mines, and Complaints in Petitions from Miners* . . . (1866), Q. 8384.
21 *Select Committee to Inquire into Regulation and Inspection of Mines, and Complaints in Petitions from Miners* . . . (1866), Q. 7154–7159, 8372, 8381.
22 *Select Committee to Inquire into Regulation and Inspection of Mines, and Complaints in Petitions from Miners* . . . (1866), p. 218, Q. 7153, 7160, 8381.
23 *Select Committee to Inquire into Regulation and Inspection of Mines, and Complaints in Petitions from Miners* . . . (1866), Q. 12238.
24 *Select Committee to Inquire into Regulation and Inspection of Mines, and Complaints in Petitions from Miners* . . . (1866), Q. 11242, 11244, 12297, 12303, 13682, 13710.
25 *Select Committee to Inquire into Regulation and Inspection of Mines, and Complaints in Petitions from Miners* . . . (1866), Q. 13677–13682; 13895–13861.
26 *Select Committee to Inquire into Regulation and Inspection of Mines, and Complaints in Petitions from Miners* . . . (1866), Q. 11418.
27 *Select Committee to Inquire into Regulation and Inspection of Mines, and Complaints in Petitions from Miners* . . . (1866), Q. 3682–3691. Quote from 3691.
28 *Select Committee to Inquire into Regulation and Inspection of Mines, and Complaints in Petitions from Miners* . . . (1866), pp. xx, xxii–xxiii.
29 Hilton, *The Truck System,* p. 131.
30 *NBDM,* 12 June 1869, p. 4.
31 *NBDM,* 3 July 1869, p. 3. *Glasgow Sentinel,* 17 July 1870, p. 2.
32 *NBDM,* 12 June 1869, p. 4; Handley, *The Navvy in Scotland,* pp. 203–205.
33 *NBDM,* 12 June 1869, p. 4; 10 July 1869, p. 4; 15 July 1869, p. 4; n26 June 1869, p. 4.
34 *NBDM,* 12 June 1869, p. 4; 19 June 1869, p. 4; 26 June 1869, p. 4; 3 July 1869, p. 4; 10 July 1869, p. 4.
35 *NBDM,* 15 July 1869, p. 4.
36 *NBDM,* 12 June 1869, p. 4; Handley, *The Navvy in Scotland,* p. 205.
37 *NBDM,* 3 July 1869, p. 4.
38 *NBDM,* 10 July 1869, p. 4.
39 *NBDM,* 26 June 1869, p. 4.
40 *NBDM,* Quote from 26 June 1869, p. 4.
41 *NBDM,* 3 July 1869, p. 5.
42 Campbell, *The Lanarkshire Miners,* pp. 215–216.
43 *NBDM,* 10 July 1869, p. 4; 26 June 1869, p. 4.
44 Handley, *The Navvy in Scotland.*
45 *NBDM,* 3 July 1869, p. 5.
46 Campbell, *The Lanarkshire Miners,* p. 206.
47 *NBDM,* 19 June 1869, p. 4.
48 *Select Committee to Inquire into the Regulation and Inspection of Mines and Complaints in Petitions from Miners* . . . (1867), p. 217, Q. 7147.
49 *NBDM,* 15 July 1869, p. 4.
50 *NBDM,* 3 July 1869, p. 4.
51 *NBDM,* 15 July 1869, p. 4.
52 *NBDM,* 10 July 1869, p. 4.
53 *NBDM,* 19 July 1869, p. 4.

54 *Hansard Debates,* 15 July 1869.
55 *The Ironworkers' Journal,* 1 September 1869, p. 5. Modern Records Centre, mss.36.ami.1.
56 *Glasgow Sentinel,* 16 April 1870, p. 3; 23 April 1870, p. 4.
57 *Hansard Debates,* 28 April 1870; *Times,* 14 July 1870, p. 9.
58 *Glasgow Sentinel,* 7 May 1870, p. 3; 14 May 1870, p. 3; 21 May 1870, p. 3, 28 May 1870, p. 3; 4 June 1870, p. 3, 25 June 1870, p. 3; *Hansard Debates,* 12 July 1870; Campbell, *The Lanarkshire Miners,* p. 219; *Ironworkers' Journal,* 15 February 1872, p. 4.
59 *Hansard Debates,* 12 July 1870; 17 July 1870; *Glasgow Sentinel,* 16 July 1870, p. 3.
60 "A Bill for Appointing a Commission to inquire into the Alleged Prevalence of the Truck System, and the Disregard of the Acts of Parliament prohibiting such system, and for giving such commission the powers necessary for conducting such Inquiry" (1870) *Parliamentary Papers* [252]. *Hansard Debates,* 28 July 1870, 29 July 1870.
61 A. Lentin, "Bowen, Charles Synge Christopher," *Oxford Dictionary of National Biography;* Eric Richards, "Patrick Sellar," *Oxford Dictionary of National Biography.*
62 Hilton, *The Truck System,* p. 132.
63 *Report of the Truck Commission* (1871), [c.327], p. iii.
64 *Glasgow Sentinel,* 23 July 1870, p. 3; 30 July 1870, p. 3; 6 August 1870, p. 3; 15 October 1870, p. 3.
65 *Glasgow Sentinel,* 6 August 1870, p. 3; 3 September 1870, p. 3; 10 September 1870, p. 3.
66 *Glasgow Sentinel,* 1 October 1870, p. 3; 12 November 1870, p. 3.
67 *Times,* 25 May 1871, p. 5.
68 *Report of the Truck Commission* (1871) [c.327], p. iv.
69 *Report of the Truck Commission* (1871) [c.327], p. xx. Quote from xix.
70 *Report of the Truck Commission* (1871) [c.327], p. xiv.
71 *Report of the Truck Commission* (1871) [c.327], p. vii.
72 *Report of the Truck Commission* (1871) [c.327], pp. vii, viii, xvi, xvii.
73 *Report of the Truck Commission* (1871) [c.327], pp. x, xix.
74 *Report of the Truck Commission* (1871) [c.327], p. x.
75 *Report of the Truck Commission* (1871) [c.327], p. xxii.
76 *Report of the Truck Commission* (1871) [c.327], pp. v–vi.
77 *Report of the Truck Commission* (1871) [c.327], pp. viii–ix, xxi.
78 *Report of the Truck Commission* (1871) [c.327], pp. xx.
79 Report of the Truck Commission (1871) (c326–c327), xx; M. Curthoys, *Governments, Labour and the Law,* p. 238.
80 *Report of the Truck Commission* (1871) [c.327], p. viii.
81 *Report of the Truck Commission* (1871) [c.327], pp. xiv, xviii.
82 *Report of the Truck Commission* (1871) [c.327], pp. xx, xlv, xlvii.
83 *Report of the Truck Commission* (1871) [c.327], pp. xx, xxii.
84 *Report of the Truck Commission* (1871) [c.327], p. xxiii.
85 *Report of the Truck Commission* (1871) [c.327], p. xxiv.
86 *Report of the Truck Commission* (1871) [c.327], pp. xiv, xlv–xlvii.
87 *Times,* 18 August 1871, p. 4.
88 *Ironworkers' Journal,* no. 57, 15 February 1872, p. 3.
89 *Ironworkers' Journal,* no. 57, 15 February 1872, p. 4.
90 *Ironworkers' Journal,* 1 April 1872, pp. 2–3.
91 "Master and Servant (wages). A Bill to Amend the Law with Respect to the Payment of Wages to Workmen in Certain Trades." *Parliamentary Papers* (1872) [cd. 65].
92 *Ironworkers' Journal,* 1 April 1872, pp. 4–5.
93 *Report of the Truck Commission* (1871) [c.327], pp. cii–cvii.
94 Hilton, *The Truck System,* p. 135.
95 *Hansard Debates,* 18 March 1872; *Ironworkers' Journal,* 1 June 1872, p. 7.
96 *Ironworkers' Journal,* 1 June 1872, p. 7.
97 *Times,* 14 January 1873, p. 10.
98 Wilson, *Alexander MacDonald,* p. 142.

99 *Ironworkers' Journal*, 15 April 1872, p. 2.
100 *Ironworkers Journal*, 15 July 1872, pp. 6–7.
101 *Ironworkers' Journal*, 1 June 1872, p. 1.
102 "Master and Servant (wages) A Bill [as amended by the select committee] to amend the law with respect to the payment of wages to workmen in certain trades (1872)" *Parliamentary Papers* [cd.149]; *Times*, 20 May 1872, p. 5.
103 *Times*, 14 January 1873, p. 10.
104 *Ironworkers' Journal*, 1 June 1872, p. 1.
105 *Ironworkers' Journal*, 8 May 1872.
106 *Ironworkers' Journal*, 18 January 1873.

3 Charles Bradlaugh and the 1887 Truck Act

Introduction

On 16 September 1887, the Truck Amendment Act received royal assent, giving trade unionists and anti-truck advocates a victory that they had sought for decades.[1] The new law enlarged the description of workers protected by the Truck Acts and included workers in Ireland as well.[2] It also outlawed charging workers "poundage" and slightly limited the ability of employers to profit from particular types of deductions from wages.[3] Furthermore, the 1887 Act entrusted the enforcement of the laws against truck to the inspectors of mines and factories (and the procurators fiscal in Scotland).[4] This legislation was not, however, an unqualified victory for reformers and organized labour. The demand of the TUC that employees be paid weekly without any deductions did not make it into the final bill. It did not bring any clarity to the vexatious question of the legality of employers taking deductions from workers' wages for fines, bad work, the use of materials or tools, or compulsory membership in employer-run benefit clubs. This private member's bill was intensely debated and heavily amended by many groups with conflicting agendas during its committee stage in the House of Commons. Its protections for workers were watered down further after a stand-off between the bill's supporters and the House of Lords.[5] While the TUC supported the passage of the measure, its members expressed disappointment because its content fell far short of their goals.[6] The compromises that the bill's supporters made in order to navigate it through Parliament ultimately limited its effectiveness in preventing employers from clawing back their employees' wages through a variety of shady practices.

George Hilton, in *The Truck System*, interprets the passage of the 1887 Truck Amendment Act as a surprising afterthought, asserting that in the years since the 1871 *Report of the Truck Commission* truck had ceased to be a significant social problem. He attributes renewed interest in the subject by Parliament to a period of economic downturn, which caused some in the rivet and chain trades, as well as a few isolated iron and coal masters, to encroach upon the Truck Act. He also doubted the 1887 Act's impact on reducing the payment of wages in goods because it had come "at least thirty-five years too late; the truck system had largely passed out of existence."[7] This is true only if one ignores many workers in marginal and sweated jobs and defines truck narrowly.

Historians undervalue the importance of the debate that took place in the spring and early summer of 1887 over the Truck Act. Contemporaries did not treat this legislation as superfluous, as there was aggressive lobbying and debate over its contents. Between April and July many MPs attended marathon committee sessions to argue over every clause, amendment and oftentimes word of the bill. These MPs clearly believed that this legislation had important implications for the nature of the employment relationship in Britain, as some fought to make the bill provide employees with greater control over their wages and more independence from their employers by mandating weekly pay and limiting wage deductions. In most cases, they were unsuccessful in the face of determined employer groups who worked to weaken or eliminate any far-reaching proposals that undermined their control over the workplace. Issues that were not resolved by the 1887 Truck Act were ultimately decided by the high courts in ways that were unfavourable to labour.

The debate over the Truck Amendment Act in 1887 also sheds light on other important issues of the era, including the extent of the political influence of organized labour and the TUC and the limits of what it could achieve in a Parliament dominated by two centrist parties. It provides an example of the inconsistent and conflicted efforts of Liberals and Conservatives to court working-class voters after the passage of the 1884 Reform Act, as well as the consequences of the absence of female voices before Parliament. The Tories promoted their role in the passage of the 1887 Truck Act to working-class audiences, even though they had been at great pains to deliver legislation that would only minimally interfere with the power of employers. Walking this tightrope resulted in a patchwork bill that was not adequate to the challenge of protecting workers' wages. Finally, the debate foreshadows the troubling use by the House of Lords of its veto power against progressive legislation.

The Act represented a missed opportunity for labour and had lasting significance for the working class. Although the 1887 Truck Act ultimately proved a weak weapon in the struggle against truck, fines and wage deductions, it failed for different reasons than Hilton suggests. This chapter will demonstrate that the 1887 Truck Act was limited by its compromised nature, as many of the provisions proposed in the bill were struck out, diluted or heavily amended in committee. Furthermore, the Act was little used not because employers had ceased to cheat workers by clawing back their wages in unfair ways, but because it failed to directly address the question of what deductions employers were permitted to take from workers' wages.

The continuing existence of the truck system

The suggestion that truck had ceased to be a significant social problem after the 1871 Report of Truck Commission is not correct. It is true that in the aftermath of the publicity generated by the 1870–1871 Investigation and *Report* and subsequent efforts to pass new legislation, many coal and iron companies in South Wales gradually abandoned truck. However, one of South Wales' largest companies, The Rhymney Coal and Iron Company, continued the truck system that had made it notorious in the 1871 *Report*. At the Rhymney Ironworks, employees were paid at very long intervals, sometimes ranging from seven to fourteen weeks.[8] The company permitted draws and advances on wages earned but not yet paid. It was widely understood that failure to spend advances at the company store could result in serious consequences for the employee.[9] This system was so transparently payment in truck that on 13 May 1885 the Treasury brought a prosecution on behalf of two workmen against the company for violating the 1831 Act. In each case the company was found guilty and fined 40s, a ruling which the company appealed only to have the convictions affirmed in December 1885.

Yet despite these convictions, local public meetings condemning the truck system and a memorial signed by 40 shareholders requesting that the shop be closed, the company chairman, Sir Henry Tyler, insisted upon maintaining the truck shops. Truck Act fines were trifling compared to the profitability of the shop at Rhymney, which brought the company between £6,000 and £14,000 per year in profits. In 1869, of the £200,137 of wages paid by the company, £62,723 was spent in the company store.[10]

Frustrated at the persistence of the truck system at Rhymney, MP Charles Bradlaugh pressured the government to take further action. On 15 June 1886, the Treasury once again brought charges under the 1831 Truck Act against the Company. This time the prosecution brought 14 informations and requested the maximum penalty (which for a second conviction could rise to £20) for every case. After securing a conviction and a fine of £20 with £10 and 10s in costs in the first case, the legal representatives of the Treasury agreed to withdraw the remaining cases provided the company promise to significantly modify its system of advances. It was in the company's interest to agree, for under section nine of the 1831 Truck Act, the penalties for a third violation could reach £100. The company agreed to separate the pay office from the company store and make wage advances to workers without shop tickets, implying that workers could spend the advances where they liked.[11] The company continued to keep its store open and pay wages at long intervals, but these modifications seem to have been sufficient to satisfy the courts.[12]

Other sources reveal that the company continued to exert pressure on its employees to patronize its store. In September of 1887, a group of shareholders again complained to the board of directors about the truck system.[13] In June of 1888, three shareholders in the company wrote to Home Secretary Henry Matthews to inform him that at Rhymney, "workmen are told plainly that the company finds them employment and that it is their duty to support the company by dealing at their shop."[14] A month later, Reverend W. Griffith informed the mines inspector that the truck system was "still in force . . . and the effects are most pernicious." The inspector reported to the Home Office that pressure was applied to workers to spend wage advances at the store, and in some cases advances were refused to workers who in previous pay periods had neglected to spend their wages there.[15]

Workers in Scotland continued to struggle to receive the full value of their wages. In 1886, the Chief Inspector of Factories and Workshops, Alexander Redgrave, was dispatched to Scotland to investigate the prevalence of the truck system, delivering his report to the Home Office on 22 January 1887. In his travels through the coal and ironworks of Lanarkshire and Ayrshire, he found that there were still many company-owned stores and licensed houses attached to the works. He observed that the company stores were an unfair source of competition to "less wealthy tradesmen" because they were "assured the custom of a large clientele, and had the readiest means of avoiding bad debts." Redgrave expressed hope that employers in Scotland would gradually sell their interest in company stores, converting them to cooperative associations run by the employees.[16]

Redgrave discovered that at least 17 coal and iron companies in Lanarkshire charged employees interest, or "poundage," for receiving advances on wages, in some cases as much as 1s per £1 advanced. The inspector was appalled at this practice, insisting, "such an unjust system should be made illegal by law." He identified the real problem as being the long period between paydays, forcing many families into either paying poundage or entering into credit relationships with local shopkeepers, observing that "[i]t is strongly desired by the men that the wages should be paid weekly."[17]

In addition to grievances about poundage, Redgrave also listened to the concerns that many miners expressed about the nagging deductions employers made from their wages. These grievances were significant, because increasingly when workers complained about being cheated out of part of their wages they described deductions from wages for workplace fines, faulty work, or materials, tools, heat, light or standing room instead of direct payment in goods. The legality of many of these types of deductions was an uncertain matter.[18] For example, it was a common practice in the mines of Scotland to deduct 3d per week from miners' wages for the sharpening of their tools. The inspector was able to demonstrate in his report that this sum was far in excess of what the sharpening work actually cost the employer.[19]

The miners in Scotland also commonly paid weekly 3d deductions for medical treatment. Miners complained to Redgrave that they had no influence over the selection of the medical attendant paid from their deductions. They desired to have a voice in the selection of this officer. Another common deduction was for schools, usually 2d per week, taken whether or not the employee had children. Catholic employees, who often did not use the schools to which these deductions were paid, also had to contribute. Redgrave heard complaints about other deductions from wages, as well as the concern that employees had no means of making sure that the amounts deducted were actually used for their stated purpose.[20]

Redgrave discovered that in Scotland the abuses of the truck system were a reality for many of the types of labour excluded from the 1831 Act's protections, including railway workers, fishermen and a variety of employees on large public works. He also found that women who worked knitting gloves, hose, shawls and other items were paid almost entirely in shop goods if they lived on the Orkney, Shetland or Fair Isle.[21]

Charles Bradlaugh's campaign against the truck system

Although employees in a variety of trades and regions continued to be cheated out of the full value of their wages, the issue of truck might not have received renewed national attention in the 1880s had it not been for Liberal MP Charles Bradlaugh.[22] During the 1880s he received information about violations of the Truck Act and their impact upon working-class families. In May and December 1885, and March and June 1886, he pressed the Home Secretary in the House of Commons about the prosecutions against the Rhymney Coal and Iron Company and whether the firm had reformed its practices.[23]

After pressuring the government to pursue violations of the Truck Act at Rhymney, Bradlaugh received information about systematic infringements of the Act in Scotland. He passed this information to Home Secretary Matthews and then asked him in the House of Commons on 2 September 1886 whether or not he was aware that the Truck Act was frequently violated in the mining and other industries in Scotland. In advance of the question, Matthews had dispatched Chief Inspector of the Factories and Workshops Alexander Redgrave to investigate (described earlier) and informed Bradlaugh that while he and the inspectors were unaware of widespread violations of the Truck Act, inquiries were being conducted.[24] Bradlaugh travelled to Scotland, where two days later he participated in a public meeting of miners and ironworkers at Motherwell.

In Scotland, iron, coal and steelworkers had experienced plummeting wages, which had led to conflict between the Miners' Association of Fife and Clackmannan and their employers. On 4 September 1886 between 20,000 and 40,000 people participated in a parade and mass meeting to discuss a range of proposals for fighting low wages. A large procession of people carrying banners accompanied by 17 brass and flute bands marched through the main streets and assembled at Meadowfield, a grass park on the town's eastern outskirts. The crowd assembled before three raised platforms to listen to the invited speakers and pass resolutions decrying the current low prices for coal and iron and inadequate wages for workers. They called for a law limiting the workday to eight hours and urged miners and ironworkers to unionize for their own protection. Prominent among the resolutions were "[t]hat as the evading of the Truck Act is so largely in vogue in this county we hope that energetic means will at once be taken to suppress this monstrous evil."[25]

Bradlaugh was invited to give the keynote address. As he rose to speak the platform collapsed, but he quickly recovered his composure and asked the assembled to sit on the grass so that he could address them. He denounced the truck system in Scotland and asserted that many of the deductions made from miners' wages were "dishonest." He condemned the charging poundage on advances in the strongest terms, noting "it is absolutely dishonest to

charge a man interest for loaning him his own money." He told the crowd of
his exchange with the Home Secretary two days earlier over the existence of
truck in Scotland, drawing roaring laughter from the crowd when he relayed
that Matthews did not know whether there was truck in Scotland, but everyone
could be reassured that he promised to investigate. Bradlaugh warned Matthews
that if he did not find out about these abuses by next Friday, he would present
the information to him personally in front of the House. He pledged that he
would not stop "until he had broken the truck system in Scotland" and further
stated that "[h]e knew that some employers were represented at the meeting"
and promised that "if they did not reform the system themselves, it would be
reformed for them."[26]

Donald Crawford, Liberal MP for Lanarkshire Northeast, also addressed the
meeting, telling his constituents that truck was "a disgraceful thing" and that
"he was sure . . . public opinion would condemn . . . and that the remains
of it would shortly disappear."[27] Members of the audience shared neither his
surprise at the continuing existence of truck nor his faith in public opinion,
shouting back at him "I can show you it near this place!" He stated that the
findings of the 1871 Truck Commission should have been enough to embar-
rass local employers into abandoning these practices, observing that "[h]e knew
things were a good deal better now, but he was afraid the remains of the system were still going on." Again, some listeners disagreed that the situation was
improving, one of them yelling "It's as bad yet!" Crawford denounced poundage and argued that workers who were paid fortnightly should at the very least
be permitted to draw 75% of their earnings without charge after 1 week. He
also decried the abuse of railway workers and others who were outside of the
protections of Truck Act and often compelled by contractors to accept goods
for wages. He proclaimed that "[m]en were entitled to have their wages in cash
without any deductions whatsoever."[28]

In the press coverage of the meeting, the need to end the truck system in
Lanarkshire was the agenda item that appeared to have the strongest support.
The *Motherwell Times*, heralding the meeting a "complete success," stated that
while it could not support legislating the eight hour day, agreed that the "most
stringent measures" must be applied to end the "baleful truck system." Its editorial lamented "we fear from the evidence produced that evasions of the law
are still winked at" and praised Bradlaugh for bringing the issue before the
House of Commons.[29] The *Dundee Evening Telegraph* editorialized that it "is too
obvious to be disputed" that workers should be paid weekly to prevent them
from being "fleeced unmercifully" with poundage charges.[30] The *Labour Tribune*
praised Bradlaugh for his efforts inside and outside of Parliament to expose the
"certainty that the Truck Act is largely infringed almost everywhere if not in
letter, in spirit" in Scotland.[31]

On 9 September 1886, Bradlaugh maintained the momentum with a speech
in the House of Commons proclaiming that even if the inspectors were blind to
violations of the Truck Act in Scotland, "30,000 to 40,000 workmen" attend-
ing the Motherwell demonstration were not. Bradlaugh declared that he could

prove "that the law upon this subject was, in Scotland, persistently, wilfully, and upon a wholesale scale, broken." He made reference to the abuses of the truck system made in Tiree and Shetland that had been revealed in the *Report of the Crofters Commission* from three years earlier but restricted most of his remarks to Lanarkshire and Ayrshire. Having seen pay stubs from Lanarkshire workers in mining and ironworking, he could provide information on at least 200 violations of the Truck Act. He found that many larger firms in Lanarkshire and Ayrshire combined long pay periods with exorbitant fees of poundage that were 6d per 10s advanced. Bradlaugh pointed out that this fee for a one-week loan amounted to an interest charge of 250% per annum. He accused some members of Parliament of being directly complicit, noting that "[t]here were members of the House . . . who were perfectly cognisant of the rate of interest charged, because some of them receive it."[32]

Bradlaugh asserted that poundage was not the worst of it, as in most works it was well-understood that if a miner took his advance and spent it elsewhere than the company store, he "would have to leave the works." He closed by attacking the hypocrisy of employers, some of whom had "reputations for honour and integrity," yet kept beer and whisky shops on their premises and charged men outrageous rates of interest to borrow their own money. He concluded that the 1831 Truck Act had become a "dead letter in Scotland" requiring reform.[33]

Home Secretary Matthews responded that he had spent the last five days making inquiries about the information provided by Bradlaugh but was still waiting to receive all the facts. He conceded that poundage existed in Scotland but assured Parliament that "if any efforts could tend to prevent any abuse which comes within the letter or spirit of the Truck Act, they should not be wanting in order to protect the workmen." He promised Bradlaugh that he would consult the Secretary of State for Scotland and seek the advice of the Lord Advocate to try and stimulate the activity of the Procurators Fiscal.[34]

Dr. Gavin Brown Clark, MP for Caithness, reminded the House of Commons that he had repeatedly called the attention of Parliament and the Lord Advocate to the operation of the truck system at quarries in the Highlands, in particular the Easdale Quarries, where the local Procurator Fiscal was actually an agent of the quarry's proprietor and "winked at" the violations. These quarries had been violating the Truck Act for over 50 years.[35] Workers' pay periods were three months long, and then they had to wait still another month after that to receive payment. As a result, these employees received much of their wages in advances and the employers used their control of the major local port to maintain a monopoly for their company stores, undermining the ability of other merchants to compete.[36]

As Parliament went into recess, Charles Bradlaugh journeyed to Scotland in order to collect additional information and rally support for the enforcement or reform of the laws against truck.[37] On 19 September 1886 he delivered a lecture at Albion Hall in Glasgow on the truck system in Scotland. He claimed that he was currently collecting evidence for 16 truck cases to present to the Home Secretary, including a muslin bleaching works with 300 female employees who were compelled to use a company store, a local ironworks that pressured workers to use its shop against the threat of dismissal and a shipbuilding firm that leaned on employees to patronize the pub that it kept on the grounds.[38] Bradlaugh attacked elites who were implicated in the truck system, repeating the claim that many Procurators Fiscal failed to bring prosecutions under the Truck Act because they themselves were either trucksters or their agents. He also shamed truck-paying employers for their hypocrisy, stating to loud laughter and applause, "these were good people; they subscribe to churches in the district. He would take care before he was finished with them to let it be known where their money came from." To greater laughter and cheering he related a story about a truckster who did not let the fact that he was a temperance advocate prevent him from compelling his employees to use the beer and liquor shops at his works. Bradlaugh promised "before he was finished that gentleman's right hand would know what his left is doing." He asked those assembled as well as those in the wider community to contact him about any violations of the Truck Act.[39]

Chief Inspector of the Factories Alexander Redgrave completed his report on 22 January 1887, and it was printed and presented to the Home Secretary on 7 February. Its findings, described in detail earlier, confirmed some of Bradlaugh's allegations, particularly about the extent and nature of poundage. Redgrave also uncovered some truck-related complaints that Bradlaugh had not emphasized, including what many miners and workers perceived as obnoxious deductions from their wages for the sharpening of tools, for foreign material sent up in their tubs or for education from Catholics or employees who did not have children. There was also complaints from miners about paying for medical attendance without having input into the selection of the firm's medical officer.[40]

The Chief Inspector of Factories made some recommendations to employers and others to the government. Redgrave's "matters for the consideration of employers, and which I earnestly commend to them," included transferring company stores to cooperative associations and adopting weekly pays. He also suggested that mine owners make transparent arrangements for determining the deductions, so that workmen could be sure that they were not being cheated. He thought that this "would relieve employers of much odium which attaches to the present system, and which would be really much appreciated by the workmen."

He argued for amending the Truck Act to expand its scope to cover all occupations and should explicitly apply to industries in Orkney, Shetland and the Fair Isle where the truck system was common among women performing outwork knitting and sewing for local shopkeepers. He recommended that the charging of interest or poundage upon advances of wages should be illegal and enforcement of the Truck Act be delegated to the Procurators Fiscal in Scotland. He further suggested clarifying the laws relating to deductions from wages. For example, he thought it should be legal for employers to take deductions for benefit societies, and for medical care provided that the money was paid directly to a doctor who had the confidence of the employees. He also endorsed deductions for materials, tools and gunpowder, as safety dictated that the employer should exercise control over their quality and storage. However, he also stated that workers should not be overcharged for these services.[41]

Redgrave's report was not circulated to Parliament. Later, Matthews and Under-Secretary of State for the Home Department Charles Stuart-Wortley claimed that this was due to the potential legal consequences of publishing material that alleged breaches of law.[42] While this is possible, another factor might have been that the Home Secretary and his colleagues were unsure of what action they wanted to take, if any, on the recommendations. In previous decades, truck had been a politically unrewarding topic. As recently as 1872 the government had managed to win the strong disapproval of both employers and organized labour for its handling of a bill based upon the 1871 *Report of the Truck Commission*. The demands of labour and those of employers were challenging to reconcile.

The truck bills of Charles Bradlaugh and Donald Crawford

When Parliament returned from its recess, two private members' bills were introduced into the House of Commons addressing the truck system. On 28 January 1887, Bradlaugh and five co-sponsors presented a "Bill to Amend and Extend the Law Relating to Truck," which was read for the first time. On the same day, Crawford and two co-sponsors brought their own "Bill to Amend the Law Relating to Truck," which was also read for the first time.[43] The prospects for success for either of these bills seemed very limited. The Home Secretary did not appear to have plans to introduce a bill to amend the Truck Act or even to circulate Redgrave's short report. These two private member bills were introduced by Liberals onto the very crowded agenda of a majority Conservative parliament.

Bradlaugh's bill extended the provisions of the 1831 Truck Act to cover all workers as defined in section ten of the Employers and Workmen Act of 1875, which was thought to encompass nearly all manual workers with the exception of domestic servants and agricultural labourers.[44] This would bring the protections of the 1831 Truck Act to many groups that had long suffered under the system but been outside of that law's provisions, such as railway labourers and naavies. To address the issue of long pay periods, Bradlaugh's bill proposed that whenever a pay period was longer than one week, the employee would be entitled every seven days to take an advance in cash of at least 75% of the wages earned to that point, and it would be illegal for an employer to charge any fee.[45] The bill made it illegal for employers to deduct from wages the price of goods supplied to employees or sue employees for goods supplied. Employers could not compel workers to spend their wages in particular shops or stores, either implicitly or explicitly, nor could they dismiss employees on account of where they spent their wages.[46] The responsibility for enforcing the laws against truck would be entrusted to the inspectors of mines and factories and to the procurator fiscal in Scotland.[47] This bill also addressed the truck system in Orkney, Shetland and Fair Isle with a clause stipulating that those knitting specific types of articles valued under £5 would be considered workers and had to be paid the entire price for their work in the current coin of the realm and not in goods or barter by shopkeepers.[48] Bradlaugh's bill, by mandating at least some weekly payment of wages, outlawing poundage and strengthening the language against employers compelling workers to use company stores, could disrupt many of the most egregious truck practices in Lanarkshire, Ayrshire and elsewhere, while giving workers more control over their wages. Bradlaugh's bill did not address the question of unfair deductions from wages or workplace fines.

The bill proposed by Crawford went further than Bradlaugh's proposals. Crawford also used the language of section 10 of the 1875 Employers and Workmen Act to extend the protections of the 1831 Truck Act.[49] The bill also would have enacted that employees' wages would accrue due weekly and would be payable within one week after accruing due. No interest could be charged on advances of wages earned but not yet paid.[50] The bill would have banned employers, their agents or their tenants from selling intoxicating drink, provisions or clothing to employees.[51] This would eliminate employer stores on the works and would likely be fiercely opposed by owners. Crawford believed that it was easy for employers to pressure their workers to use company stores, but hard to prove compulsion in court, so the solution was for employers to give up their stores.

An important difference between Crawford's bill and the one proposed by Bradlaugh is that the former addressed the miners' grievances related to deductions from wages. Crawford's bill proposed that no deduction could be made from an employee's wages for education except for the worker's own child or ward. It also stated that if a child attended a state-inspected school, the school fees deducted from the employee's wages would be paid directly to the director of this school. The bill included a section that permitted employees who had deductions taken from their wages for medical attendance to choose their doctor. It outlawed deductions from wages for the sharpening and repairing of tools and stated that where deductions from wages were made for the rental of housing from an employer, that employer would be required to give the employee one month's notice before an eviction.[52]

These proposals on deductions from wages were strongly endorsed by unionized workers, particularly miners. On 14 January 1887, a conference of miners meeting at Birmingham passed a resolution asserting that "[t]his conference is of opinion that the time has now arrived when all the appliances of the mines, tools, powder, light, etc. should be supplied by capital instead of labour." It was also resolved that:

> This conference, recognizing the iniquitous tenure under which many of the miners hold their houses, a tenure which allows the employers to deduct the rent from the wages of the workmen, and by the conditions of

employment evict them at will, requests the representatives of labour in Parliament to introduce a bill which should make such deductions a violation of the Truck Act.[53]

Crawford also included a clause stipulating that all sums deducted from workmen's wages were to be paid over to a person appointed by the workmen for their distribution and that appointee's wages would be paid from their deductions.[54] This clause, likely to be fiercely opposed by employers, addressed the fears of workers that employers were profiting from the deductions from their wages. Crawford's bill delegated enforcement to the inspectors of mines and factories and the procurators fiscal in Scotland.[55]

On 31 January 1887, three days after the first reading of his bill to amend the Truck Act, Bradlaugh asked the Home Secretary before the House of Commons that he share the results of his inquiries into the truck system in Scotland. Matthews responded that he would share Redgrave's report privately with Bradlaugh, but because it was confidential, and touched upon prosecutable offences, he would not lay it before the House.[56] After speaking privately with the Home Secretary, Bradlaugh persisted in his complaints about the glacial speed with which the government was moving on the specific information he supplied regarding breaches of the Truck Act in Scotland. He claimed to have written more than 25 letters to the Home Secretary with credible evidence of at least 16 different violations of the Truck Act in Scotland, some of which were "incapable of disproof." Some firms violating the Truck Act in Lanarkshire were owned by men of wealth and power, and he "submit[ed] that while the government is showing a vigorous enforcement of the law against the poor, they might take some active steps to enforce it against rich people." This statement brought loud cheers from the Liberals in the House. Bradlaugh asserted that "in the whole of the Scotch press" there were reports "that breaches of the Truck Act prevailed extensively in Lanarkshire and Ayrshire."[57] After weeks of Bradlaugh and other Liberals in the House of Commons demanding the Redgrave report be laid before the House, on 28 February 1887 it was finally presented to Parliament, increasing pressure on the government to take action.[58]

The Scottish press took particular notice of the Redgrave Report. *The Edinburgh Evening News* had a lengthy editorial in its 5 March issue, praising the findings of the chief inspector of factories and workshops but arguing that his recommendations should have gone further and banned deductions from the wages of miners. It suggested that "allowing employers the first charge on workmen's wages" meant "the reduction of workmen to the position of slaves." The article emphasized the issue of employees who lived in employer housing and had rent taken from wages, which made it very difficult to combine into a union, because the worker risked losing "not only his employment, but his home." Workers felt pressure not only to conform at work but also in their political opinions too, lest they risk an eviction. This also added another layer of employer control to their lives. These deductions were seen as a "terrible weapon of terrorism and despotism" in the hands of employers.[59] The *Falkirk*

Evening Herald also praised the report for illuminating injustices "under which miners in a number of districts in Scotland have been labouring under for a long series of years." While it was widely known in Britain that miners were suffering from reduced wages, many were unaware that "the miners have been compelled to submit to considerable deductions from their already inadequate wages, and that their employers have in many cases been making a large profit out of these deductions." The Redgrave Report confirmed the complaints that miners had been making for years about deductions for tool sharpening and "grossly unfair" charging of poundage. The editorial emphasized, "Indeed, if the fact had not been published in an official government report, it would scarcely be credible that employers would so demean themselves as to make a profit out of the scanty earnings of their workmen." It declared that "the system is a scandal" and the abolition of poundage and the adoption of weekly pays "ought to be carried out without delay." The editorial writers drew attention to the bill proposed by Bradlaugh, briefly describing its main features and declaring

> this bill ought to be supported by all interested in the prosperity of work-
> ing men, and though it will be difficult for private members to get bills
> passed this session, it is to be hoped that in justice to the miners and other
> workmen this bill may speedily become law.[60]

The reactions of the government, labour and employers to the truck bills

In early March of 1887, increased public attention on the truck system in Scotland compelled the government to decide what its stance would be toward the two private members' bills to amend the 1831 Truck Act. Home Office correspondence from early March reveals discussion about the precedents and practices of the House for handling two bills on the same topic that were both worthy of consideration. It was suggested that after a second reading the bills could go to committee where their differences could be reconciled into a single bill. Home Office officials thought one or both of the bills should be committed after its second reading, where Stuart-Wortley could assist with amending the bill and providing the government support needed to successfully navigate legislation through Parliament.[61] Many felt that there was unfinished business remaining from the recommendations of the 1871 Truck Commission Report, and the passage of a new Truck Act would allow the Tories to show the newly expanded electorate that it could effectively address working-class grievances.

On 11 March, Stuart-Wortley sent copies of both bills to the Home Secretary and Redgrave for consideration, noting that Bradlaugh's bill was currently unblocked and scheduled for its second reading in four days. Redgrave found that Crawford's bill was the "more comprehensive" of the two, dealing "with many matters which are the cause of dissatisfaction with miners." He considered that the sections of the bill on deductions "appear to meet the just complaints of the miners." In some areas, however, Redgrave thought that Crawford over-reached, asserting "I don't see the necessity of preventing a miner from dealing at his employer's stores." The Home Office officials assessing Bradlaugh's bill praised that it would extend the provisions of the Truck Act to many occupations previously uncovered, would prohibit charging interest on wage advances and would prohibit the system of barter that existed in Orkney and elsewhere. Bradlaugh's bill, in the judgement of the Home Office, "on the whole . . . is unobjectionable." Stuart-Wortley gave support to Bradlaugh, writing "tonight the bill will come on and I see no reason why we should prevent it doing so."[62] Bradlaugh's bill passed its second reading on 15 March 1887 and was scheduled for its committee stage for after Easter.[63] Bradlaugh received a private promise of assistance and support from Stuart-Wortley.

The Parliamentary Committee of the TUC also evaluated Redgrave's report and the two legislative proposals. In mid-March it issued a memo to several trades councils and societies on the truck system in mining and quarrying in Scotland. The memo began by stating that due to the persistent efforts of Bradlaugh the Home Office had conducted an investigation into the prevalence of the truck system in Scotland. It alleged that at first the government "refused to publish the report, in consequence of the serious revelations it contained," but Labour's "perseverance in demanding the report has been fully warranted by the extraordinary disclosures made." It reviewed the abuses of long pays, company stores, poundage and deductions from wages. It declared the practices revealed in the report were "an outrage to personal liberty" and thanked Bradlaugh "for bringing under public notice the kind of semi-slavery to which workers in several districts of Scotland have been subjected." Far from giving the Home Office credit for requesting the inquiry, the memo complained that "every effort has been made to keep from the public knowledge of the names of the firms that have been making unheard of profits out of the pressing necessities of the workpeople," accusing the government of throwing "the veil of secrecy over the names of the wrongdoers because they are influential and powerful people."[64]

The memo reported that two bills were pending before Parliament to amend the Truck Act, and it compared the main features of both side-by-side. Although Crawford's bill addressed the complaints about the deductions from wages to a greater degree than the proposal of Bradlaugh, the memo reported "In a rare stroke of good fortune, Mr. Bradlaugh's bill was unblocked on March 15th, and by arranging with the government to defer the committee stage until after Easter, Mr. Bradlaugh obtained a second reading unopposed." Crawford's bill was not scheduled to receive a second reading until the end of June, probably too close to the end of the session to secure passage. Because the government appeared favourable to Bradlaugh's bill, and "Mr. Bradlaugh has expressed willingness to adopt any amendments that can be shown to improve the measure," the Parliamentary Committee of the TUC recommended that organized labour urge its representatives in Parliament to assist Mr. Bradlaugh and concentrate their efforts on improving and passing his bill.[65]

Other interested parties also weighed in on the anti-truck proposals before the House of Commons. In April of 1887 the Fife and Clackmannan Coalowners' Association presented the Home Office with a memorial objecting to Crawford's Truck Amendment Bill, which it also circulated to the MPs and newspapers. The *Edinburgh Evening News* observed that "Fife and Clackmannan coal owners are leaving no stone unturned to prevent the passing of" Crawford's bill.[66] Although these objections were directed at Crawford's bill, which was unlikely to move forward in Parliament, they had relevance for the bill presented by Bradlaugh.

The mine owners asserted that passage of Crawford's bill would "cause more serious mischiefs than those which it proposes to remedy." They attacked the Redgrave Report, which they mistakenly believed had provided the foundation of Crawford's bill (his and Bradlaugh's bills were, in fact, drafted before Redgrave had submitted his report). They argued that the report had been "prepared in great haste" and was "one-sided," relying upon information provided by "miners' agents, and the secretaries of miners' associations" without obtaining information from employers. The mine owners' objections to the Crawford bill can be summarized in their statement calling it "a meddlesome interference with employers in the conduct of their business."[67] Specifically, they objected to weekly pays (or draws), questioning whether it was something miners really wanted and stating that it was "intrusive and arbitrary, and . . . will impose trouble and expense on employers." They insisted that employers and workmen should be free to set the terms of contracts of employment and that legislation mandating weekly pays would represent an "undue and petty interference in their affairs."[68]

The mine owners especially objected to the clauses related to deductions from wages that appeared in Crawford's bill. The memorial emphasized that deductions for education brought no profit to the employers, as the entirety of the money collected was given to the Treasury of the local school board so that any child of an employee could attend the local school. While workers without children and Catholic employees made contributions without receiving the benefits, "such results are incident to every union of men for mutual benefit." They claimed that the clause in the Crawford bill giving workers who had wages deducted for medial attendance the right to choose the physician was outrageous, because the clause did not provide a clear process for how this selection would take place and argued that permitting the men to select the medical advisor would cause confusion and "lower the status of the medical attendant." They objected to the bill's prohibition against deductions from wages for the sharpening of tools, calling it a "wanton and uncalled for interference between employers and employees." They disputed assertions that they overcharged miners for sharpening tools, insisting deductions "were barely sufficient to cover the cost." The clause that compelled employers who deducted wages from employees for house rent to them to give one month's notice of an eviction was described as "practically a confiscation to the workman of the employer's property." The memorial stressed that this clause had significant implications for labour disputes, because they would not be able to conveniently bring in replacement workers.[69] The Home Office received word from other large employers as well, and while most were willing to accept the prohibition of poundage and tougher restrictions on the truck system, they strenuously objected to weekly pays and any further limitation of their right to make deductions from wages.

The opinions of the Fife and Clackmannan mine owners about Crawford's bill were not shared by the men that they employed. On 14 May 1887, the board of the Fifeshire Miners' Association met at the Union Hotel to answer the objections put forth by the mine owners. The Association's Secretary, Mr. Weir, disputed the notion that the Redgrave Report was one-sided, noting that they had not disproved any of the chief inspector's findings. Weir insisted that regarding weekly pays, "the miners had always been in favor of such a system and had frequently expressed a desire for it." He accused some employers of taking more in education deductions than they handed over to school boards and argued that a smith employed at a mine "would likely not get more than half of the amount deducted for tool sharpening."[70] Whether or not employers actually derived profits from deductions, it is clear that employees believed that they did. The confusing state of the law made the limits of what employers could legally deduct from a worker's meagre wages unclear.

The board of the Fifeshire Miners' Association passed the following resolution:

> That this board views with surprise and indignation the statements made by the Fife and Clackmannan Coal Owners in their printed objections to the Truck Bill, being convinced that these statements are erroneous, inaccurate, and misleading, particularly in reference to the weekly payment of wages, deductions for sharpening tools, and tenure of miners' houses.[71]

The committee stage of the Truck Bill in the House of Commons

The Home Office, led by Undersecretary Stuart-Wortley, worked with Bradlaugh to rewrite his bill, and on 13 April new clauses were sent to the Parliamentary Counsel to be prepared as amendments to Bradlaugh's bill.[72] On 25 April Donald Crawford gave notice of his intention to amend Bradlaugh's bill to include some of the provisions of his own. The next day Henry Broadhurst, MP and member of the Parliamentary Committee of the TUC, gave notice of his intention to amend the bill to prevent deductions from wages for tools, compulsory subscriptions to employer-run benefit clubs and deductions for disciplinary fines.[73] The committee stage of this bill is important to consider because it highlights many lost opportunities for labour.

Bradlaugh's bill began its committee stage on 28 April 1887, and the first two meetings in committee revealed that the government, with the full cooperation of the bill's sponsor, intended to substantially rewrite the bill. New clauses would be debated and added to the bill to replace those that were taken out.

During the first meeting of the committee, Irish Nationalist Tim Healy argued that the bill should be amended to apply to Ireland as well. He would later get his wish. It was clear in the early part of the committee stage that clause three of the bill, which made provisions for the weekly payment of wages, was going to be complex and controversial, so its consideration was postponed until later. The approach of rewriting the bill in committee in the very early hours after midnight sat poorly with some MPs. Sir Joseph Pease complained that he struggled to understand the proceedings because "the government amendments are larger than the original bill," and many members agreed with Charles Conybeare of Cornwall that "if we are always put off until 2 in the morning, there is no hope of our getting forward on the bill."[74]

Although Stuart-Wortley and Bradlaugh had hoped to avoid controversy during the early phases of the Truck Bill, they stumbled into a lengthy debate with temperance advocates. One of the new clauses of the bill would permit servants in husbandry to contract with farmers to receive food, drink or cottages in addition to money wages for their services. Servants in husbandry were the one group for which a case could be made that truck wages were sometimes advantageous because their employers could supply them with food at cheaper prices than they could procure it on their own. The inclusion of drink in this clause was a red flag to the bull of temperance reformers.

At the urging of the Church of England Temperance Society, C.T.D. Acland of Cornwall moved to amend the proposed clause to insure that farmers could not pay their workers in alcoholic drink.[75] In many agricultural districts in England it was customary for agricultural labourers to receive a portion of their remuneration in beer or cider. This practice, which opponents sometimes referred to as "cider truck," was controversial among temperance advocates. Acland argued that being paid partially in alcoholic drink was detrimental to the health of farm labourers and introduced their children to alcohol at a young age. He complained that some farmers would not hire men who declined to accept alcohol. He also charged that in some cases farmers gave their labourers alcoholic drinks that were not of sufficient quality for them sell, passing off bad drink to the workers. This proposed amendment touched off a lengthy debate.[76]

Attorney General Sir Richard Webster stated that the government was neutral toward Acland's amendment, but he personally doubted whether agricultural labourers themselves viewed it in a favourable light. Radcliffe Cooke, who was a farmer in Herefordshire, explained that giving his agricultural labourers cider in his district was customary and that "there is no reasonable grounds for this prohibition." He complained that the amendment was introduced by men with "no experience in the wants and feelings of the agricultural classes." He reminded them that the alternative to providing cider or small beer was for the labourer to drink "miserable tea" or water, which was sometimes contaminated. He conceded that farmers usually made a small profit on the cider but insisted that this was a long-standing arrangement accepted by labourers. Murray Finch-Hatton of Lincolnshire added that "I might as well expect my threshing machine to work without oil as to expect to get an extra amount of work done . . . without a glass of beer." Major Carne Rasch of Essex was also sceptical of the amendment, asking "[t]he member does not suppose he is going to make agricultural labourers teetotallers by Act of Parliament?"[77]

Randall Cremer questioned the certainty with which many MPs insisted that agricultural labourers wanted part of their pay in alcohol, pointing out that workers were not often explicitly given a choice. He suggested an experiment in which an employer offered either a pint of beer or 3d for remuneration to see what the labourer chose, suspecting that most agricultural labourers "know better than to accept a pint of very small beer in lieu of the pence." After more debate, the division was 112 votes in favour of adding the Acland amendment to the clause and 101 votes opposed. The committee then voted to add the clause to the bill.[78]

The next time that the House of Commons considered the bill in committee was on 6 May 1887 at 1:30 a.m. Crawford proposed to amend the bill to prohibit employers, or tenants who kept shops on the employers' premises, from selling provisions, clothing or drink to employees (except in instances where the employees and employers lived in the same house). Crawford observed that despite the 1831 Truck Act, and the pressure of public opinion that was excited after 1871, employers in Scotland and elsewhere continued to keep company stores. Crawford argued that his amendment for closing these shops was necessary if truck was to be defeated because "as long as such places exist, there is a practical compulsion upon them to deal at them." He read letters from his constituents reporting that they were pressured against the threat of dismissal to deal at company stores. He insisted that forcing mine owners to sell these stores, or make them cooperatives, represented no real hardship, as "while a man is entitled to make a legitimate profit in his own trade, he is not entitled, against the will and desire of his workmen to make a second profit out of the workmen's wages."[79] Crawford's speech went so long that the House had to report progress on the bill and postpone discussion until 28 June.[80]

Although many petitions had begun to arrive in the House of Commons from trade societies in support of Bradlaugh's bill, organizations of employers warned the government and MPs about its potentially harmful effects.[81] On 10 June, the Mining Association of Great Britain, an organization of colliery proprietors and mine owners that claimed to represent over £150 million of capital and employ 500,000 workmen, sent a memorial opposing many of the clauses and proposed amendments to the Truck Bill. The principle objection of the organization was with clause three and the weekly payment of wages, which they argued went against custom and was "outside the scope of a measure dealing with truck." They insisted that it was necessary for mine owners to have at least seven days between the "measuring up day" and payday.

They also objected to Crawford's amendments, including those stipulating the prohibition of stores, the prevention of deductions from wages for the sharpening of tools, the alteration of the means of appointing the medical attendant and the extension of notice given to workmen in the case of eviction from employer housing. They protested the amendment by Henry Broadhurst of the TUC for regulating deductions from wages for benefit, sick and accident societies. While the mine owners were prepared to submit to the "most stringent legislation to protect workmen from being compelled to deal in such stores," they objected to being forced to close stores into which much "capital has been expended." They argued that the prohibition against the deduction of wages for the sharpening of tools was "an attempt to raise wages by Act of Parliament." The memorial insisted that providing workmen with houses was almost always "a most unprofitable investment" and they did not do it "for men doing no work." The Home Office also received a memorial of the Clive Shipbuilders which rejected the clause of the bill proposing weekly pays and asked to be exempted from any legislation that passed Parliament. Owners of slate mines and quarries in north Wales informed the Home Office that the enactment of weekly pays would "revolutionize the whole system of working, a system which experience has proven to be the only one compatible with the successful prosecution of the industry." In this industry it was very difficult to calculate the pay of a workman until the slate produced was sorted according to size and quality. To estimate this after one week would involve much "unnecessary labour." Other industry groups echoed these sentiments.[82]

On 7 June, Stuart-Wortley wrote to Matthews about clause three, the part of Bradlaugh's bill that would have entitled employees to a weekly advance of 75% of the wages earned without any interest or poundage charges. Representatives of the miners in Parliament "urged us to stick to the clause" but "it soon became apparent that enormous difficulties surrounded the proposals for this clause." Conservative MP William Tomlinson of Preston, who was a colliery owner and the main representative of mine owners in Parliament, informed Stuart-Wortley that they would not have allowed the bill to go forward had they known it was going to be a vehicle for regulating the length of the pay period. There were some attempts to reword this clause to make it more acceptable to employers, but in the end, the "coal owners pronounced it would be unworkable for them." For this reason "the attorney general inclines to drop altogether the attempt to regulate the period of payment." A new amended clause three, which the coal owners approved, would simply mandate that when by agreement or custom a worker was entitled to receive an advance of wages, the employer could not withhold the advance or charge poundage. Stuart-Wortley anticipated the disappointment of the bill's sponsor, writing "My own belief is that Mr. Bradlaugh will protest, but will give way rather than have his bill further delayed." He relayed to Matthews the warning that another MP gave to the undersecretary, that "great hopes have been excited . . . by the prospect of having a weekly wage clause and we shall incur great unpopularity by abandoning the attempt to pass some such clause."[83] For the second time in 15 years, the attempt to legislate the weekly payment of wages and give workers greater control over their money proved that the influence of employers was much more powerful than that of organized labour.

On 28 June, those who had hoped for a bill which would provide workers with the entirety of their wages in cash at short intervals without deductions, were disappointed, as many of their proposed amendments to Bradlaugh's bill were voted down. Some members of Parliament who had connections with the TUC had placed amendments on the order paper for the bill, including Henry Broadhurst. Broadhurst later claimed that Bradlaugh had led him to believe that the bill was unlikely to come before the House that evening, so he and his supporters left for home around 11:30 p.m. At 2 a.m. in the morning the House opened discussion on amendments to Bradlaugh's bill, beginning with those brought forward by Crawford, and including those of the absent Broadhurst as well.[84] Bradlaugh later denied that he had mislead Broadhurst.[85] The first amendment debated was Mr. Crawford's clause prohibiting employers, or tenants of employers who kept shop on their premises, from selling goods, clothes, drink or other items to their employees. Attorney General Webster objected that "this clause goes too far," and it failed by a vote of 32–109.[86]

Crawford then proposed to add a clause to the bill stipulating that where deductions were made from a worker's wages for the education of a child, and the child attended a state-inspected school chosen by the worker, the school fees of that child up to the amount of the deduction would be paid to the teacher or manager of the school. This proposal would allow parents a degree of school choice and would ensure that their deductions were used for their stated purpose. This clause was accepted by the House and added to the bill.[87]

Crawford also proposed a clause permitting employees who had wages deducted for medicine and medical attendance to select the firm's doctor. Crawford insisted that this was necessary because miners "suspected that they do not get the full benefit of the payments" from their deductions for medical care and did not always have confidence in the medical officer. The attorney general thought that this was outside the scope of a Truck Bill and described the deputations that he had received from both mine owners and the medical profession expressing strong disapproval. He emphasized that mine owners frequently subsidized the salaries of these medical attendants, so it would be unfair to deprive them of a voice in their selection. Liberal MP Charles Conybeare, however, stated that Cornish miners supported this proposal. Irish Nationalist Patrick Alexander Chance believed this clause was relevant to the issue of truck because the deductions for medical care represented payment in other than the current coin of the realm, even if it was permitted by the 1831 Act. He stated that opposition to this clause really came down to the prejudice "that the workmen are not fit to choose their own medical attendant, as other people." The amendment was defeated by the House.[88]

Crawford then moved to add a clause to the bill that would only allow deductions from wages for the sharpening of tools as part of a written contract and prohibited making acceptance of this deduction a condition of employment. He argued that these deductions were "a very heavy tax levied on workmen, and a very large profit for the masters." Bradlaugh and the attorney general both supported this clause, emphasizing that it did not prevent employers and employees from contracting to have tools sharpened but only prevented the former from automatically deducting wages for this service. This clause was added to Bradlaugh's bill.

Crawford also sought to add a clause to the bill mandating that employees who had deductions taken for house rent were entitled to one month's notice before an eviction. The attorney general found this unacceptable, as an employer would be unable to immediately evict an employee guilty of robbery, fraud or serious neglect causing injury. This proposal was voted down. Finally, Crawford moved a clause allowing workmen to appoint a person to disperse the deductions taken from their wages, to have audits to ensure that the deductions from wages were spent on their allotted purpose and to require written consent for all deductions. The attorney general informed Crawford that while he rejected most of this clause, he would be willing to add a clause to the bill allowing for an annual audit of deductions. Crawford accepted the compromise, and it was added to the bill.[89] Thanks to Crawford the bill now placed some very mild limitations upon the ability of employers to make profits from some of the deductions that they took out of the wages of employees. These clauses, however, only covered a narrow range of deductions and neglected disciplinary fines or deductions for poor workmanship, which would become important issues in the coming years.

In the early hours of the morning the amendments of Broadhurst came up for consideration, but because he and most of his colleagues had gone home for the night believing that the bill would not be considered, Randall Cremer presented them. The first was a clause making it illegal for an employer to set a condition of hiring that an employee have wages deducted for a benefit fund from which the worker would not derive any benefit from if he or she left the employment. Cremer stated that "based upon 25 years in the workshops of the metropolis" he knew of many instances where employees were compelled to make contributions to an employer benefit or accident fund, and then when they were discharged all of that money was lost, which he called "a genteel system of robbery."[90] This proposal had been on the orders paper for the bill for some time and had attracted the attention of many large benefit societies in Britain which had contacted the Home Office and MPs to explain its dangers.[91] Bradlaugh and Webster argued against this proposed clause, and it was defeated.

Broadhurst offered three controversial amendments that were important because they foreshadow the next 25 years of debate over the deductions taken from employees' wages. On behalf of Broadhurst, Cremer moved to add clauses prohibiting deductions from wages for non-wilful damage or spoilage to work and materials, disciplinary fines and lost time in excess of the value of that time at the ordinary rate of wages. Workers in many trades, but especially those in low-paying and sweated labour, were subjected to deductions from their already meagre wages for the spoilage of work that was often not their fault, or for fines for trivial offences that were far in excess of any damage done. In 1887 those suffering from these abuses did not yet have influential advocates before Parliament. For this reason, many MPs, including Bradlaugh, treated these amendments as excessive. The attorney general asserted that prohibiting deductions from wages for careless damage to materials represented "a principle . . . which we cannot possibly recognize." These amendments were decisively defeated but had they become law they might have prevented great injustices in the years to come.[92] Cremer later "complained bitterly of the treatment Mr. Bradlaugh had accorded him, and maintained that in his conduct [he was] . . . distinguished by the imperiousness of his mandate and the obsequiousness with which he obeyed the Tory Party."[93]

If organized labour was disappointed by the fate of the Broadhurst amendments, it was utterly disillusioned by the mine owner-approved clause three, which merely prohibited poundage but offered no guarantee of receiving any wages weekly. Attorney General Webster stressed how difficult the issue had been for the government, stating

> if it had been possible to introduce into this bill some clause, which would be satisfactory to both workers and employers, with respect to the compulsory payment of wages weekly, the government would have been glad to accept such a clause.

However, in the current political climate, the new clause three "seems to us as far as we can go." Bradlaugh echoed Webster's sentiments, describing how much time they had devoted to finding a workable clause three. Dr. Clark was furious, noting that the "bill will not affect the worst form of truck" because any truck bill that failed to address long pay periods would be "a farce." Conybeare also objected that his constituents of Cornwall miners demanded "that they should have something paid to them at the end of every week." He observed that "by a judicious system of compromise the whole benefit of this bill is being watered down."

Irish Parliamentary Party MP Patrick Alexander Chance made reference to a large strike that had occurred in Belfast due to employers trying to impose a system of fortnightly wages in place of weekly settlements, which the men found oppressive. His colleague in the IPP, Arthur O'Connor, stated that "the most important question in this bill is the question of dependence of the workmen upon the employer for wage advances, and with that dependence of every kind follows." If workers had weekly wages they would be able to control their money and enjoy independence from their employers and credit granting retailers.[94] The Irish members were so angry about this new clause three that when the voice vote was held they loudly forced a formal division. When the House finally divided on the question, the new clause three was added to the bill with a margin of 78 votes. Bradlaugh's bill was printed for consideration before the entire House of Commons.[95]

The Irish MPs and the weekly payment of wages

The issue of the weekly payment of wages was revived in the House of Commons by events in Ulster. On 30 April 1887, over 6,000 workers from two shipbuilding firms in Belfast went on strike after employers changed the practice of paying workers weekly to paying them fortnightly (it was suggested that this change was partially an effort to reduce absenteeism on Monday after paydays). The conflict was not about the rate of wages or hours but weekly or fortnightly pays.[96] The Reverend Dr. Hamilton, in a sermon to his Belfast congregation, while decrying the stoppage of a major local industry for a "trifling cause," argued that for workers fortnightly pays meant "men had to live on credit; credit meant debt; and debt meant loss. The man is shut out from the benefits of cash payments." He stated that the striking workers felt that "when a man had earned his week's pay, he ought to get it."[97] During a public meeting in early May, 5,000 men resolved to hold out for weekly pays and passed a motion calling upon Parliament to introduce legislation making the weekly settlement of wages compulsory.[98] After discouraging negotiations with the Belfast mayor, who was also one of the employers, the delegates for the striking workers sent a telegraph to Thomas Sexton, a MP from Belfast, requesting that he amend Bradlaugh's bill to mandate the weekly payment of wages.[99] At the end of May, the employers offered to accept the weekly payment of wages if the "Scottish Truck Bill" became law.[100] By 17 June 1887, the men terminated the strike, securing only a vague promise from their employers that they would give "their best consideration" to the weekly payment of wages.[101]

On 30 June Sexton took up the cause in Parliament, bringing forth a petition from the workers and asking whether the government would make the weekly payment of wages for workers in Ireland part of the Truck Bill. Home Secretary Matthews claimed that "[p]ersonally, I am in favour of weekly or fortnightly payment of wages where workmen are paid according to time," but given the difficulty in writing an acceptable clause on this point, he could not commit to its inclusion. Sexton asked the next day whether the clause could be added to the bill if he secured the support of all Irish MPs. Matthews made no promises but stated that an agreement among all the Irish MPs would "carry great weight."[102]

On 12 July, the bill came before the House and Sexton offered an amendment adding a clause stating that in Ireland where an employee's wages were calculated by time, those wages should be paid weekly. Sexton described the recent strike in Belfast and stated that he had advised the workers to return to work and petition Parliament for redress. The Home-Ruler noted that nearly all of the MPs from Ireland were in agreement with this clause and "you should consider the wishes of Irish members in this respect and give them the same effect as they would have if we had a Parliament of our own." Bradlaugh and the attorney general both stated that the amendment was outside the purpose of the Truck Bill, but they would not oppose it if supported by nearly all of the MPs from Ireland. Tomlinson stated that if weekly wages were made mandatory by an Act of Parliament in any part of the country, there should first be an investigation the implications of such a proposal. After much debate, the House voted to add the clause to the bill.[103]

On 15 June the House considered amendments to Bradlaugh's bill, a number of which were slightly different versions of amendments that had been considered during the committee stage. At the urging of Bradlaugh and the government, nearly all of them were defeated. One exception came at 1:55 a.m., when Dr. Clark of Caithness rose and once again took up the cause of the employees in Scottish quarries who were paid at intervals of three months or longer and frequently forced into accepting truck wages. He proposed a clause to the bill that would require employees in Scottish quarries be paid at least fortnightly. Bradlaugh, familiar with the injustices faced by these workers, informed the House that he would not oppose adding this clause and the House agreed.[104]

On 18 July the bill received its third reading, but many friends of organized labour, especially Cremer, were not in a celebratory mood. Cremer lamented "the imperfect character of the bill" which "left underdressed many grievances from which thousands of workmen still suffered." He was particularly disappointed with the failure of the bill to more tightly regulate deductions from wages and give workers greater control and choice in the dispersal of funds taken from their pay packets. The bill passed its third reading and moved to the House of Lords.[105]

Stand-off with the House of Lords

Lord MacNaughten introduced the bill into the House of Lords on 4 August, and on 8 August the Lords introduced a number of hostile amendments. Even though the bill's supporters had already compromised on clause three, which stated that in trades where it was contracted or customary to permit advances on wages, the employer could not refuse to grant them or charge poundage, this clause still went too far for the Duke of Argyll, who considered it "very inexpedient and very violent in its interference between employers and workmen." He insisted that it had "nothing to do with the subject of truck" and carried a motion to strike the clause from the bill. Similarly, other Lords demanded the removal of clauses four and five, which allowed for weekly pays for Irish workers and fortnightly ones for miners in Scottish slate quarries. The Lords thought these an unacceptable interference with freedom to contract and observed that it was illogical and unfair that these trades and regions should be given special treatment. Also struck from the bill was the clause aimed at curbing truck in Shetland and the Scottish highlands by preventing barter between shopkeepers and their outworker employees. The Lords removed the prohibition against employers dismissing workers over where the latter chose to spend their wages. Bradlaugh publicly warned the House of Lords that their amendments to the bill were unacceptable.[106]

On 19 August, the House of Commons considered its response to the Lords' changes to the bill. Bradlaugh urged the House to disagree with most of the Lords' amendments, especially the changes to the clause prohibiting poundage and the elimination of the clauses mandating weekly pay in Ireland and fortnightly pay for Scottish workers in slate quarries and protecting outworkers in particular trades from being made to accept barter from shopkeepers.

The attorney general, however, seemed to agree with the House of Lords that these clauses "had nothing to do with the object of the bill." Crawford insisted that long pays "lay at the root of truck." Many others in the House of Commons found these clauses relevant to the question of truck, observing that both the 1871 Truck Commission and the Redgrave Report endorsed weekly pays because "truck cannot be effectively prevented except by the abolition of long pays." The House also held firm to the barter prohibition aimed at outworkers in the Scottish highlands.[107]

Both Bradlaugh and the Duke of Argyll took their cases to the public. Argyll wrote a letter in *The Scotsman* on 19 August that was widely reprinted in Scottish newspapers. He wrote that he abhorred the truck system and believed it is the duty of the legislature to assist workers in receiving their wages in the current coin of the realm. However, the bill pending before the House of Lords contained clauses that had nothing to do with the truck system. Many of these clauses were "quite novel, and founded on no intelligent principle." The clause preventing shopkeepers from bartering with those engaged in cottage industry in specific trades went too far and would harm many of the poor women who traded materials made in their cottages with shopkeeper/employers who provided them with tea or sugar or other items. He stated "It may be that in Shetland . . . the poor get very small returns for their industry. But they will get still less if this kind of market is closed to them."[108]

Bradlaugh responded with a lecture in Glasgow entitled "The Duke of Argyll and the Truck Bill." Bradlaugh complained that the House of Lords had removed "nearly all the material clauses" from the bill. He described how each of the clauses struck out by the House of Lords was important to the prevention of abuses by employers that cheated workers out of their wages. Bradlaugh defended the clause preventing barter as a way of payment for outworkers arguing that these practices had been complained about for over 200 years, referencing the specific recommendations of the 1871 *Report of the Truck Commission,* the 1884 Crofters' Commission, as well as Redgrave's investigation in 1887. He quoted the Redgrave Report, which recommended that in Orkney, Shetland and the Fair Isle "it would be a good thing if this mode of trading could be found to be illegal and finally stopped." He noted that the clause was supported by both the late and current Lord Advocate in Scotland and had the support of the region's sheriffs. He closed by stating that he intended to hold firm after making a great many concessions and compromises to get the bill through the House of Commons, insisting that "much as he would regret to lose the bill, which he considered of great importance to the working class, he should refuse to allow it to pass into law if the barter clause is struck out."[109]

On 7 September the House of Lords conceded agreement with most of the House of Commons' clauses of the bill but insisted on striking out weekly pays for Ireland and fortnightly pays in Scottish slate quarries, arguing that

> the obligation to pay wages at different periods in different parts of the United Kingdom is undesirable, and . . . provisions for regulating the

periods when wages should be paid are not strictly germane to a bill to amend and extend the law relating to truck.[110]

The *Edinburgh Evening News* called the Lords' actions "a wanton exercise of power" and lamented that the government was not doing more to convince them to accept the Commons' position. It accused the government of being "exceedingly shifty, and it is suspected that they have been influenced by two or three Tory magnates in Belfast." The paper feared that "the bill is now in great danger of being lost."[111] *Reynolds Newspaper* argued that the Lords' amendments were "prompted by grasping, greedy self-interest" because many of the Lords had financial interests in mines, quarries and railways, the industries where truck was often practiced. It accused the House of Lords of deliberately thwarting legislation that would "make the working classes over the whole United Kingdom-not a portion of it merely-more independent of their employers" because "the Lords have no interest in or sympathy with the masses." It warned the House of Lords that "the constitution of this country has outgrown them."[112] The TUC passed a motion condemning the behaviour of the House of Lords in deleting these desired clauses.[113]

On 9 September, despite strong urging from both the TUC and the Irish MPs that the House of Commons hold its ground in this dispute, Bradlaugh joined the government and conceded the loss of clauses four and five to pass the remaining bill into law, saying "even as it stands, the bill is a most valuable bill and I dare not risk its loss."[114] The House of Commons agreed, and the Truck Amendment Act received Royal Assent on 16 September 1887.

Reactions to the 1887 Truck Act

Despite its shortcomings, the 1887 Truck Act was considered by many to be one of the more important achievements of an otherwise disappointing session of Parliament. The legislative session of 1887 was not an overly productive one, and the mainstream press highlighted the Truck Act as one of its few success stories. The *Dundee Courier* argued that the passage of the Truck Act "will make more stringent the laws against dishonesty and overreaching between employers and their subordinates and the workmen under them."[115] Indeed, in meetings with constituents in the months after the end of the session, both Liberals and Conservatives alike claimed credit for the Act.[116] Members of the East Hunslet Conservative Association were told that the Truck Act was "strong evidence of the interest taken by the Conservative government in working people" and of their "earnest desire to remove the grievances of working men."[117] The Conservative Solicitor General Edward Clarke told a meeting that the Truck Act was an example of legislation pushed by the Conservatives for the benefit of the working classes. Attorney General Richard Webster echoed these sentiments at another constituency meeting.[118]

Shepherding the Truck Act through Parliament greatly enhanced the reputation of Bradlaugh outside of trade union circles.[119] The *Leeds Times* wrote of the 1887 Parliamentary Session, "it has passed fewer bills than usual, and the only private member who has carried any measure of importance being Mr. Bradlaugh with his Truck Act."[120] The *Liverpool Mercury* commented

> the name of Mr. Bradlaugh readily occurs as that of the individual who has most improved his position in the past six months. In his conduct of the Truck Act the member for Northampton has shown an unsuspected power of self-restraint, and shines as an opportunist among radicals.[121]

The TUC was more reserved in its reaction to the new Truck Act, announcing that the organization was "glad" that the measure had passed. However, the Parliamentary Committee felt obliged to explain to members that because the bill was practically a government bill, "no amendments of private members, unless favoured by the government, had any chance of being incorporated into the Act." Cremer gave an account to the TUC of what he felt was underhanded dealing in considering labour amendments to the measure on 28 June at 2 a.m., when most of the supporters of these amendments were not present. Later, at the 1887 annual meeting of the TUC at Swansea, a motion was made to express thanks and appreciation by the Congress to Bradlaugh for introducing and shepherding the Truck Bill through Parliament that passed only after much debate.[122] The TUC also passed resolutions urging the Parliamentary Committee to continue pursuing legislation mandating the weekly payment of wages and prohibiting deductions from wages for employer-run benefit societies.[123] In addition to the TUC, there were others who expressed a wish that the Act had been more far-reaching. Crawford told constituents in Lanarkshire that while he was pleased that some of his amendments became part of the new Truck Act, the new law was "not so complete as it might be." Randall Cremer also remarked in a speech that he

> would have preferred the question embodied in the truck bill to have remained open for another session rather than it should have been dealt with and settled in the unsatisfactory way it was in the Truck Act of Mr. Bradlaugh.[124]

Testing the 1887 Truck Act

In December of 1887 an abstract of the Truck Acts was sent to inspectors of mines and factories which described the terms, procedures and penalties of the Truck Acts. It explained the deductions from wages that were explicitly legal under the Truck Acts, but did not address the question of whether deductions for bad work, disciplinary fines, tools and materials, or for benefit clubs were legal.[125] The 1887 Truck Act proved to be an unsatisfactory tool for helping workers to secure the full value of their wages. It failed to explicitly address many questions related to deductions from wages and left inspectors uncertain about their ability to act against widespread abuses. Bradlaugh believed that the

Factory Inspectorate showed a lack of vigour in its enforcement of the new act and used his platform in Parliament to draw the attention to alleged violations.[126] Even when the government prosecuted cases under the Act, the results were often disappointing due to resistance from magistrates, and even high court justices. The passage of the 1884 Summary Justice Act provided magistrates with the discretion to inflict lower fines on guilty parties, a discretion that magistrates, who often had connections with the guilty employers, exercised.[127] Sometimes the government invested considerable time and expense to secure a conviction under the Truck Act that resulted only in negligible penalties. Furthermore, Bradlaugh, and to some extent the law officers of the Crown, had a much more expansive interpretation of the provisions of the 1887 Truck Act than local magistrates or high court judges. As workers complained more frequently about deductions from their wages, Bradlaugh and the Home Office sought to test the legal proposition that these exactions were illegal under the existing Truck Acts. It was a test that the Acts would fail.

After the passage of the 1887 Truck Act, Bradlaugh received information from different parts of the country about offences, which he passed to the Home Office and inspectors, pushing them to bring the new legislation into force. In April and May of 1888, Bradlaugh asked in the Commons about reported violations of the Truck Acts in Belfast, Armagh, Rhymney and Bristol. After inspectors investigated the first two allegations, they found that these were cases where employers had "unwittingly" violated the Truck Act because they had been unaware of the recently passed legislation and were voluntarily coming into compliance. In the case of the Rhymney Iron Company, a persistent violator of the 1831 Truck Act, the Home Secretary reported that there was not a "complete breach of the Act" but the Company was negotiating with its men over disagreements related to their store system, and he hoped that "all differences will be healed."[128] The Home Secretary was mistaken on this point, as no such negotiations were taking place and very serious violations of the Truck Acts were continuing to occur at Rhymney.[129]

Bradlaugh reported that the Bristol firm C.J. King and Sons were charging their stevedores a "tax" of 1d per 1s on wage advances known as "subs" (short for "subsistence money") in direct contravention of the 1887 Truck Act. The allegations were initially made to Factory Inspector W.H. Johnston, who was uncertain whether he was authorized to interfere in a matter outside of factories and workshops. Bradlaugh pressed Home Secretary Matthews, and the Home Office instructed the inspector that the 1887 Truck Act permitted him to investigate, so the inspector prepared a case to be tried before magistrates in June of 1888. After the summons was issued to the employer, he posted notices informing all employees that no further advances on wages would be given to anyone, which the inspector interpreted as a further violation of section three of the 1887 Act. Although section three of the Act made it illegal for an employer to refuse to grant advances of wages in instances where contracts or custom entitled workers to them, the action taken by the employer in this case highlights the vulnerability of employees in many trades and explains why many would prefer to submit to injustices that cheated them out of a small portion of their wages than risk the potentially greater consequences that could result from the attention of inspectors.

During the hearing the defendants contested that the stevedores enjoyed a customary entitlement to an advance of wages, but the magistrates ruled that the prosecution had proved that there was a custom dating back at least 25 years allowing advances on wages. However, the magistrates, who communicated throughout the hearing that they did not find this a serious offence, ruled "we convict, but this being the first case under so recent a statute, we make the penalty a nominal fine of 10s" rather than the minimum fine of £5 under the 1887 Truck Act. The magistrates also refused to grant costs.

The inspectors tried three more cases against C.J. King and Sons in October of 1888 and won £1 and costs in one case and £2 and costs in another. In January of 1889, the Home Office decided that given the improbability of substantial penalties being imposed by the magistrates, no further proceedings would be taken. In the meantime, the firm had dismissed any employees who had expressed objection to the "tax" on "subs" and had been compelled to pay only nominal fines after expensive government prosecutions. This was not an encouraging use of the 1887 Truck Act. Although the firm was compelled to change its practices and abandon charging workers fees for receiving advances, several employees had lost their livelihoods.[130]

The dangers for workers in cooperating with inspectors to bring prosecutions under the Truck Acts was an issue that the Home Office and the Treasury solicitor wrestled with between July and October 1888 when deciding whether to bring charges against the Rhymney Coal and Iron Company in Wales. The Inspector of the Mines concluded that the company pressured its workmen to spend their wages at the company store, but a prosecution would cost any man testifying his employment, home and ability to find work in the region. The inspector and the Home Office discussed the possibility of compensating witnesses who came forward. By the end of July 1888, the discussion had gotten as far as suggesting that a maximum of £350 could be set aside for the testimony of six witnesses, but in October of 1888 the Treasury solicitor wrote to the Home Secretary expressing his discomfort with the principle of compensating witnesses, and the case temporarily fell apart.[131]

In July of 1888, Bradlaugh was informed of a brickmaker and publican named Henry Haynes from Alperton, Middlesex. For the 15 years Haynes had been paying his employees' wages in one shilling checks instead of currency. He employed enough brickmakers that some local shopkeepers accepted the script. Although the checks had the nominal value of 1s each, they only had the purchasing power of 11d. When shopkeepers collected 20 of these checks they would sell them back to Haynes at a discount of 5–20% of the face value. However, the majority of these checks were used to purchase beer in Haynes' public house. Bradlaugh forwarded this information to Chief Inspector Redgrave, who dispatched Inspector Edward Gould to build a case against Haynes, and by the end of July he had collected at least eight witnesses. By early August, however, the case fell apart. As with so many other truck cases, a number of the possible witnesses against Haynes were reluctant to continue, as they occupied his cottages and thus were fearful of losing both their employment and their homes.

In December of 1888 the men once again petitioned Bradlaugh, and he informed the Home Secretary that he considered Haynes' offences "so great and flagrant" that unless they were prosecuted he would raise the matter in the House of Commons. The Home Office corresponded with local inspectors who described the great difficulty in getting witnesses to come forward, noting

> I quite feel that it is most important to obtain penalties whenever practicable, but if the result of the proceedings is that workmen who give evidence lose their employment, I don't quite see how we benefit those for whose protection these Acts were passed.[132]

On 20 December 1888, Bradlaugh asked the Home Secretary in the House of Commons why no prosecution had taken place. Matthews replied that there was not yet a good possibility of success, but that he had directed the inspector to "keep a careful watch."[133] Although the inspectors were unable to make a case, Haynes was frightened enough by the government's increased interest in his business that in January of 1889 he called in all of the script that he had issued and ceased to pay his workers in checks.[134]

Bradlaugh was not content to let the matter rest here, and on 30 April 1889 during a debate over funding for the Home Office and subordinate departments criticized the Home Secretary and the Factory Inspectorate for its lack of effort enforcing the 1887 Truck Act. He challenged the factory inspectors, many of whom he felt were too old to do their jobs, and were covering territories too large to supervise effectively. He also denounced corrupt magistrates and the Home Secretary himself, complaining that he had put undeniable evidence of violations of the 1887 Act directly in his hands. He complained that "if inspectors were old and incapable, and employers unscrupulous, men would be so demoralized that the whole statute would become a dead letter." Matthews and Stuart-Wortley tried to explain the challenges faced by inspectors in collecting evidence, and they stressed that in many cases merely investigating the matter had been sufficient to compel employers to change their practices.[135]

On 29 May 1889, at Edgware Petty Sessions, Inspector Gould brought charges against Haynes for paying three brickmakers in his employ in goods. On 24 April, John Watts and two fellow brick makers were drinking in Haynes' public house and had consumed 3s 10d worth of alcohol. Haynes said to the men "You have had some beer and port wine . . . I'll sub you 4s to pay for it." Haynes took 4s out of his pocket and passed it to Watt, who then passed the money back to Haynes, who returned 2d change. Haynes then crossed off the entries for drink from his account book. The next day when the men received their wages, 4s had been deducted from Watt's pay for an "advance." The prosecution argued that the 4s was not an advance in actual cash and had only been given with the understanding that it must be immediately be given back for the drink, and thus was a clumsy attempt to disguise a transaction of payment in goods (or drink). The prosecution cited the case of *Wilson v. Cookson (1863)* which was precisely on point. The magistrates, however, ruled that Watt had been given an advance in money, which he had the power to use anywhere he chose. They dismissed the case, and the Treasury solicitor asked for a case stated.[136]

The case was heard by Justices Coleridge and Bowen on 29 November 1889, and both judges ruled that it was a clear violation of the Truck Acts. Coleridge stated "This is without doubt an attempt to evade the Truck Acts. If such a transaction as this were to be permitted, these statutes might as well be repealed at once." They ordered the case to be sent back to the magistrates, who in January of 1890 convicted Haynes and fined him £5 12s and costs. Half of the fine was given to Watt, who was no longer employed by Haynes.[137] This case did result in an employer abandoning some highly exploitative practices under the truck system. However, the year-and-a-half-long struggle revealed the limitations of the 1887 Truck Act for prosecuting even relatively straightforward instances of the payment of wages in goods. The inspectors found it a great challenge to convince witnesses to risk their livelihoods and provide evidence. Furthermore, the case shows how local magistrates were determined to interpret the Truck Acts in a way most favourable to the employer. The government was put to considerable time and expense to end the payment of wages in goods in a single workplace.

In addition to the challenges of using the 1887 Act to prosecute straightforward instances of the payment of wages in goods or the charging of fees for advances, Bradlaugh began to pressure the Home Office to apply this legislation to the more vexed question of deductions from wages for workplace fines and materials and services not listed in sections 23 and 24 of the 1831 Truck Act. On 29 May 1888, some employees of the Bristol firm Derham and Sons, boot manufacturers, complained that their employers deducted from workers' weekly wages for the rental of a workbench and for gas. Bradlaugh believed that these deductions were "clearly illegal," but in fact, the legal question was not a simple one.[138] Bradlaugh believed that section three of the 1831 Truck Act, which enacted that

> the entire amount of the wages earned or payable to any artificer . . . in respect of any labour by him done . . . shall be actually paid . . . in the current coin of this realm and not otherwise,

meant an employer taking deductions for any items not authorized in sections 23 and 24 of the 1831 Act, including disciplinary fines, represented a failure to pay the entire amount of wages due to the worker in the current coin of the realm.[139]

This was doubtful in light of the ruling of the high courts in the precedent of *Archer v. James and another (1862)*. In that case a framework knitter attempted to use the 1831 Truck Act to recover deductions that employers took from his wages for frame rents, fire, gas, winding and some occasional small fines. The Court of Queen's Bench ruled that these deductions were not the payment of wages otherwise than in the current coin of the realm but were the means of determining the amount of wages owed to the employee, meaning that only the net wages owed after deductions had to be paid in money. This interpretation was appealed to the Exchequer Chamber where it was affirmed when the judges split in a three-to-three vote. In his decision, Baron Bramwell revealed his scepticism of the 1831 Truck Act in general noting that it "interferes with that freedom of contract and conduct which is universally recognized as of the greatest benefit," and it enabled a worker who might have been treated fairly when receiving a payment in goods to go to court and claim wages a second time. Bramwell reminded the court to keep sight of the purpose of the Truck Act, insisting "it is necessary to see what are the mischiefs of what is called the truck system" that this legislation was intended to prevent. Bramwell thought that there were three: that an employer might promise fair wages in goods and then provide a worker with inferior ones, that the employer might promise fair wages in money and then provide goods of a lesser value or the employer might supply goods beyond the wages of a worker to get him into debt and then have an injurious degree of control. Bramwell argued that the deductions taken from the wages in this case "is not within any of the mischiefs I have specified." Bramwell's ruling in this case would be often quoted in future setbacks for the Truck Acts.[140] In addition to *Archer v. James (1862)*, the 1871 *Report of the Truck Commission* also expressed doubt that section three of the 1831 Truck Act outlawed deductions from wages not explicitly sanctioned by the Act. This report was especially relevant because one of its principle authors, Charles Bowen, was currently sitting as a Lord Justice of Appeal and in a position to potentially determine these questions in the future.[141]

In July of 1888, the Home Office had adopted the position that deductions from wages for disciplinary fines at least were unaffected by the Truck Acts. Permanent Under-Secretary of State for the Home Office, Godfrey Lushington, argued,

> deductions from wages by way of fines on a working person can hardly be considered 'truck.' There is no notion in such a fine of supplying any article in place of the money wage but it is meant to be a simple penalty for alleged breach of contract on the part of the working person.

Stuart-Wortley thought that the urgency with which organized labour had attempted to amend the 1887 Truck Bill to outlaw disciplinary fines was clear evidence that there was nothing in the existing law to prohibit them.[142] The Home Secretary agreed and on 25 July 1888 instructed, "I think the Inspectors may be told that fines for negligence or misconduct are not within the provisions of the Act."[143] Despite this, many continued to believe that deductions from wages not explicitly sanctioned by the 1831 Truck Act, including those for disciplinary fines, were illegal.

In terms of the specifically alleged infractions at Derham and Sons, the Home Office and Chief Factory Inspector Redgrave discussed whether a workbench could be considered a "tool or implement" or whether gas in this context was to be considered "fuel," making them deductions specifically permitted by the Truck Acts. However, there was the larger question of whether deductions not expressly permitted by the Truck Acts were actually illegal, and here the Home Office was doubtful and decided that this case was not worth pursuing.[144] Bradlaugh continued to argue in the House of Commons that it should be prosecuted.

The legality of deductions from wages for workplace fines, bad work and materials remained uncertain in many minds, and in June and July of 1888 the issue received renewed consideration as a result of the famous labour dispute between Messrs. Bryant and May, match manufacturers, and their 1400 female employees. On 15 June 1888, the Fabian Society resolved to boycott matches made by the firm on account of the appallingly low wages paid to its workers when compared to the large dividends paid to its shareholders. On 23 June 1888 Annie Besant directed public attention to the plight of the workers at this firm, publishing "White Slavery in London" in her journal *The Link: A Journal for the Servants of Man*, in which she described the long hours, terrible wages and degrading treatment endured by the firm's female employees. She also highlighted that the already low wages of the matchmakers were further reduced by fines and deductions from their pay. Workers were fined for talking, leaving untidy workbenches or tardiness in amounts that were far in excess of any damage such offences did to their employers.[145] Bryant and May disputed the claims in Besant's piece and attempted to discover which of their employees had cooperated with the author. Despite the uncertain legal status of workplace fines and deductions from wages under the Truck Acts, a factory inspector made inquiries with the management of the firm. Shortly after the inspector's visit, the firm announced that it would no longer inflict fines on its employees.[146] On 7 July, Besant celebrated

> the Factory Inspector has visited Messrs. Bryant and May's factory, and the system of fines is put an end to. In this case, as at Woolwich, Mr. Bradlaugh's Truck Act is proving an invaluable weapon against the petty oppressors of the poor, and the wisdom of the provision which throws the duty of enforcing it on the Factory Inspectors being proved.[147]

In November of 1888, Bradlaugh again raised the question of workplace fines and deductions under the Truck Acts in the House of Commons.[148] In addition to the case of Derham and Sons, bootmakers and their deductions for workbench and gas, Bradlaugh had been disturbed by the ruling of a Marlborough Street Magistrate on 31 October 1888 in a case where a mother was helping her son recover wages owed to him. Messrs. Model and Company, cabinet makers, had employed Willie Grant, aged 13, for several months and had failed to pay some of the wages he was owed and had made a number of deductions from his wages, including 1s 4d for fines. The magistrate, Mr. Hannay, dismissed Grant's claim for 1s 4d that had been taken from him for fines, stating that he "failed to see anything illegal in the imposition of fines," but he did order the payment of 2s in unpaid wages and 1s for costs for some of the other deductions taken from his wages without a contract permitting them.[149] Bradlaugh was bothered enough by the magistrate's statement that on 9 November 1888 he asked the attorney general whether under section three of the 1831 Truck Act deductions from wages for fines were illegal and whether he would direct the inspector of factories to take action accordingly. The attorney general stated that no decision had been made generally, and he did not believe that this was an instance for interference by the inspector.[150] Bradlaugh followed up with questions in the House of Commons on 12 and 13 November, in which he pointed out that many factory inspectors were refusing to make prosecutions under the Truck Act for deductions from wages on account of fines. The Home Secretary stated his own belief was that as long as there was a contract that provided for fines and deductions from wages, such exactions were not illegal, but he promised to consult the opinion law officers of the Crown on this point.[151] Chief Inspector of the Mines had also written to the Home Secretary many times to get clarification as to whether deductions from wages for items not explicitly permitted by section 23 of the 1831 Truck Act were legal.[152]

As a result, in late November 1888, the Home Secretary put a case to the law officers of the Crown, asking them four questions: (1) Were the deductions taken by Derham and Sons from the wages of their workpeople for the rental of a workbench legal? (2) Were the deductions taken by Derham and Sons for gas legal? (3) Broadly speaking, were deductions from wages which were not explicitly prohibited by the Truck Acts legal? (4) Were deductions from wages for fines for misconduct prohibited by the Truck Acts? The Home Office explained to the law officers that the deductions for workbench or gas fit imperfectly with the deductions permitted by sections 23 and 24 of the 1831 Truck Act but "there remains to be decided the general question whether the Truck Acts forbid all deductions that they do not expressly authorize." The Home Office appeared to doubt very much that this was the case, and directed the attention of the law officers to *Chawner v. Cummings (1846)* and *Archer v. James (1862)*.[153] On the question of deductions from wages for workplace fines, the current Home Office position was that "they do not seem at all in the nature of truck." In the 1875 case of *Willis v. Thorp*, the high court judges held that a framework knitter was unable to recover 3s 9d deducted from his wages for fines under section three of the 1874 Hosiery Manufacture (Wages) Act. This section, which primarily banned deductions from wages for frame rents, also required that the entire wages owed to an employee be paid in the current coin of the realm, using similar language to section three of the 1831 Truck Act.[154] The Home Office reasoned that if the courts ruled that the deduction for fines was not a failure to pay the full amount of wages owed in the current coin the realm under the Hosiery Act, it was not be under the 1831 Truck Act either.[155] After contextualizing these four questions, the Home Office requested the legal opinion of the attorney general and the solicitor general.

On 7 December 1888, Attorney General Richard Webster and Solicitor General Edward Clarke provided their surprising answer to the Home Office. They acknowledged that the "questions submitted to us raise many difficulties, and it is not without doubt that we have arrived at the opinion" because the "Truck Acts are not clear" and the "decisions given by the courts . . . by no means lessen the difficulty." They stated that with regard to the first two questions, because the deductions taken by Derham and Sons did not appear to be the means of arriving at the wages owed, both the deductions for the rent of workbench and gas were illegal. The law officers further stated that they considered no deductions from wages to be legal except for those explicitly mentioned in sections 23 and 24 of the 1831 Truck Act and Section eight of the 1887 Truck Act. Finally, they also asserted the opinion that deductions from wages on account of fines for misconduct were also illegal.[156]

The Home Office appeared to be surprised by the far-reaching nature of the law officers' opinion. On 10 December Lushington wrote that while he had no objections to informing the inspectors of the law officers' opinion, he worried that implementing their ruling that deductions for disciplinary fines were illegal under the Truck Acts could have "most serious consequences." Many establishments in the United Kingdom administered fines for various forms of misconduct in the workplace, and if inspectors enforced this prohibition "we shall not be long before we have a hornet's nest about us." He expressed doubt about the law officers' interpretation, as there was nothing in the recently passed 1887 Truck Act, or its debates, to suggest a prohibition on fines had even been seriously considered. He warned that

> to carry out the opinion therefore would be to introduce innovation and to put upon the Act of 1831 a construction which has not hitherto been adopted. General instructions on this point ought not to be issued without very great consideration.[157]

Home Secretary Matthews interpreted the ruling as still permitting some disciplinary fines, when they could be treated as the "means of arriving at wages earned." For example, if an employee was contracted to earn a certain amount of wages per week, provided he or she arrived at work every day on time at 6 a.m., but then arrived an hour late at 7 a.m. one day, the amount of wages owed would obviously be less. However, there had to be a relationship between the time lost and the amount of the deduction. Under this interpretation, deduction of a day's wage for the loss of ten minutes would be illegal. The Home Secretary wrote back to Lushington that

> I think that we must raise these points for decision by selecting typical cases for prosecution, and when the courts have adjudicated . . . instructions

can be issued by way of circular [to the Inspectors]. Meanwhile, let the Chief Inspector see the L.O.C. and have instructions to select cases for prosecution.[158]

The opinion of the law officers of the Crown on the legality of disciplinary fines became public in early December when Bradlaugh asked the attorney general in the Commons to communicate the conclusions the law officers had reached. Attorney General Webster informed him that "deductions from wages as fines other than as the stoppage of unearned wages was illegal."[159] This statement had the potential to be disruptive to many regimes of labour discipline practiced throughout the United Kingdom. Within days of the attorney general's answer in the House, the owner of Selsby and Co., manufacturers in Glasgow, wrote to the Home Office to request clarification. He asked if fines could be legal if employees signed a contract permitting them to be deducted from their wages. The Home Office replied that deductions from fines other than as the stoppage of unearned wages were illegal.[160]

Redgrave v. Kelly (1889)

In January and February 1889 an effort was underway to locate suitable test cases against employers deducting disciplinary fines from their employees' wages. One case considered had been brought to the attention of the Home Office by Bradlaugh in December of 1888. Bradlaugh shared information about the fines inflicted upon employees of Whiteley's Department Store in London. Whiteley's had published a list of over 176 transgressions for which shop assistants could be fined, including for such offences as wearing colours, gossiping, loitering, standing too close together, making unnecessary noise or taking off one's coat if one was a male employee. In case the employer had forgotten any possible infractions, offence #176 on the list inflicted a fine of 6d for "any mistake not before mentioned."[161] Bradlaugh considered that "the bulk of these deductions are clearly illegal" but thought that Thomas Whiteley should be contacted personally instead of prosecuted in the first instance because he "possibly misapprehended the law."[162] The Home Office considered it as a possible test case, but it became a lower priority because of doubts as to whether the Truck Acts applied to the employees at Whiteley's and because upon further investigation it was discovered that the fines were not deducted from the wages of employees, which were paid in full. When the accumulated quantity of an employee's fines reached a certain level, he or she was asked to pay them. The Home Office determined that Whiteley's employees were covered by the Truck Acts and strongly suspected that Whiteley's arrangement for paying fines might violate the provision of the Truck Act that made it illegal for employers to determine the manner in which wages were expended, but declined to pursue it.[163]

The Home Office, the Inspectorate and the Treasury solicitor also gave some consideration to pursuing a test case against T. Wright and Son Iron Mill in Wolverhampton, which fined six employees 5s each for fighting, or bringing a prosecution against the Cleveland Iron Company, which fined Richard Evans 12s 6d for allowing the furnaces to stand one night, which caused the company some financial loss. Ultimately, the case that determined the legality of fines under the Truck Acts would be a prosecution against the London confectioners Française and Company.[164]

On 28 February 1889, the Home Office determined that the most suitable test case for the question of the legality of deducting fines from wages under the Truck Acts was that of two young girls who were employed at Française and Company in London, owned by Joseph Kelly. In the first week of February, Kelly fined Louisa Donovan 2d for spoiling a paste brush and for badly wrapping goods manufactured by the company. The following Saturday, Donovan, who would normally have received 3s, was only paid 2s 10d. During the same week, another young female employee, Anne Lewis, had 2d deducted from her wages for spoiling a tray of work and for "being impudent." On that same Saturday, Lewis received only 3s 10d of wages, when her normal weekly pay would have been 4s. The Chief Factory Inspector Redgrave contended that the employer's set-off from the girls' wages represented a violation of section three of the 1831 Truck Act by failing to pay "the entire amount of the wages earned . . . in the current coin of the realm."[165]

The case was heard on 8 April 1889 at Southwark Police Court before magistrate Wyndham Slade. Mr. Mead, representing Inspector Kelly, stated that under the Truck Act, these deductions from wages were illegal and that the "wages ought to be paid in full, leaving the option of paying the fine to the employer" after those full wages were received.[166] Slade dismissed both summons without hearing from the respondents, later writing "I decided that the setting off the fines as aforesaid was not a payment at all, and therefore could not be 'a payment otherwise than in the current coin of the realm,' or an illegal payment." The deduction from wages for fines was not a payment of wages in goods but was a non-payment of wages, and therefore outside of the Truck Acts. Mead applied to the magistrate to have a case stated for the Court of Queen's Bench. The next day, Lushington wrote that "until this case has been adjudicated upon it is useless to prosecute Messrs. Whiteley or anyone else for deducting fines."[167]

On 16 May 1889, in the Queen's Bench Division, Justices Grantham and Matthew heard the case of *Redgrave v. Kelly*. Mr. Danckwerts represented the government, and he presented his arguments without any opposing counsel present. He argued that Kelly, by deducting wages for fines "for some trifling offence," had violated the Truck Acts by failing to pay the entire wages owed in the current coin of the realm.[168] He reminded the justices that "[a] fine for impudence or spoiling goods is capable of great abuse, and this it was the intention of the legislature to prevent."[169] The 1831 Truck Act enacted that the entire wages owed must be paid in currency. Because the Act listed specific items for which deductions from wages could be taken by employers, it was

> very strong to show that the primary intention of the legislature was that the worker should get the whole of his money without any deductions

whatsoever. Now the nature of the deduction sought to be made is called a fine, but in truth it is a deduction or otherwise compensation to the employer for spoilt work.[170]

Danckwerts also supported his argument with *Smith v. Walton* (1877) where an employee who spoilt work was given the damaged item and had the value deducted from his wages, and the courts held that this was a violation of the Truck Acts. Judge Matthews did not find the case analogous because in *Smith v. Walton* "an equivalent of some sort was alleged to be given for the balance of wages withheld." Matthews contended that for Danckwerts to make this argument work he would have to demonstrate the employer paid the girls in the goods that they spoiled, which did not fit with the facts.[171] He stated

> in all the cases which have been held to come within the act there had been some supposed equivalent given to the workman instead of his wages – that is, there were attempts to pay wages by goods. Here there was more non-payment of wages in consequence of the deduction of fines.[172]

Matthews asserted that the amount of wages that the employer withheld did not represent payment of wages in goods, but simply the non-payment of wages. He asked Danckwerts if the employer refusing to pay any wages at all would also fall under the Truck Acts. Matthews quoted Baron Bramwell's statement from *Archer v. James (1862)* about the purpose of the Truck Acts, insisting that they existed to prevent the payment of wages in goods, and that was not what had happened in this case. He ruled:

> Really the case is so plain and so clear that one is almost ashamed to give any reasons for the decision. It is only necessary to look at the Act of Parliament and to see it to hold that non-payment of wages by an employer is not yet subject to any Act which involves the penalties imposed by the Truck Act; The appeal therefore must be dismissed.[173]

Justice Grantham agreed.

On the basis of this decision, the interpretation by the law officers of the Crown issued the previous December could hardly have been less correct. Home Secretary Matthews was particularly concerned about the potentially far-reaching nature of the verdict which appeared de facto to legalize deductions from wages for nearly anything except for goods sold by the employer to the employee. In almost any other type of a prosecution for an illegal deduction under the Truck Acts, an employer could argue that the deductions were the means of calculating the wages owed, bringing the employer within the protection of *Archer v. James (1862)* or that the amount deducted was the non-payment of wages, supported by *Redgrave v. Kelly (1889)*. Section 23 of the 1831 Act contained the provision that deductions from wages could not be taken by employers in the absence of a written contract permitting them, but Matthews thought that the *Redgrave* ruling made this a "dead letter," because the employer could simply claim that deductions not agreed to by contract were a non-payment of wages and outside the Truck Acts. He on 29 May 1889, he wrote, "The question can hardly be allowed to rest here. Either the case should be taken to the court of appeal, or an action for the amount of the deductions should be brought, or both." He also requested the law officer of the Crown for their advice on the best course of action.[174]

The immediate impact of *Redgrave v. Kelly* can be seen in the failure to convict the Bristol firm Derham and Sons, boot manufacturers. Factory inspectors had been investigating their taking deductions from the wages of employees for shop rent and gas, which were sometimes taken even when employees were not using gas. The Treasury solicitor wrote to Lushington to inform him that the deductions for gas and shop rent appeared to be very similar to those ruled legal in *Archer v. James (1862)*, and

> it did not, therefore, appear to me that a conviction was likely to be obtained unless the present case could be distinguished from that above mentioned and it could be shown that deductions were made in respect of gas for periods during which no gas whatsoever was used.

He suggested that one possible way of proceeding would be to arrange for some employees to not use gas during the next pay period and then take out summons under the Truck Act on their behalf against the employer for not paying the entire wages owed in currency. This way the employer could not argue that the deductions were the means of arriving at the wages owed. The Treasury solicitor was still not optimistic, but Home Secretary Matthews pointed out that the employer was taking these deductions in the absence of a written contract, and gas was not one of the deductions authorized by section 23 of the 1831 Truck Act, and "neither of these points depends on whether gas has been used or not. Direct a prosecution." The case was tried before Bristol magistrates on 13 June 1889. The magistrates, citing *Redgrave v. Kelly (1889)*, ruled the amounts deducted from the wages of the employees did not represent a payment of wages in goods outlawed by the Truck Acts, but merely a short payment, "for which the worker could sue civilly" under the Master and Servant Acts.[175]

Attorney General Webster and Solicitor General Clarke, responding to the request of the Home Secretary to advise whether the government should pursue further legal action or introduce new legislation, stood by their erroneous legal opinion of December 1888 to a surprising degree. They conceded that

> the case of *Redgrave v. Kelly (1889)* was scarcely arguable as the prosecution could only be supported on the ground that the non-payment of wages was the same thing as the payment of such portion in goods or instead of money.

However, they still insisted that the only deductions from wages which were legal were those mentioned in sections 23 and 24 of the 1831 Truck Act, which must be subject to a contract in writing between the employer and employee. They argued that if an employer took deductions, an employee could pursue the employer in civil court to recover unpaid wages under the Master and Servant Acts and the employer would not be able to defend himself by arguing that the unpaid amount was a set-off from those wages because these deductions would be illegal. They continued to assert that "although the matter is by no means free from doubt," deductions for fines in excess of the actual amount of damage sustained by an employer through the misconduct of an employee could be recovered by the worker through the Master and Servant Acts.[176] There was nothing in the *Redgrave v. Kelly (1889)* ruling to support this interpretation, and in fact it rested entirely upon a reading of the Truck Acts that all deductions from wages not explicitly permitted by them were illegal, which had been repeatedly rejected by the higher courts. In fact, the law officers of the Crown later came to interpret *Redgrave v. Kelly (1889)* to mean, "all fines, therefore, of every sort are legal, whether for bad work, or disobedience, or misconduct, or in respect of any act whatsoever."[177]

One can hardly fault Justices Matthews and Grantham for their ruling in *Redgrave v. Kelly*, as it is clear in the Parliamentary debate over the 1887 Truck Act that the legislature did not intend for that Act to outlaw deductions from wages for fines, damaged or poor work, or for tools or materials provided by employers. In fact, every attempt to amend the 1887 bill to explicitly outlaw deductions from wages for fines, damaged work, contributions to employer-run benefit societies or most materials had failed. Bradlaugh thought that section three of the 1831 Act could be interpreted as making deductions from wages not explicitly sanctioned by the Truck Acts illegal, and this was a belief shared by most labour leaders. However, there was very little reason to think that the courts agreed with this interpretation, and cases like *Archer v. James (1862)* pointed very strongly in the opposite direction. The compromises that were required in order to get the 1887 Truck Act through Parliament made it a "patchwork upon an already existing patchwork, and made the law very difficult to understand" for those attempting to enforce it.[178] For this reason the debates over the 1887 Truck Act represented a lost opportunity for workers. The provisions of the 1887 Act were inadequate to protect the most vulnerable workers from being cheated by their employers out of the full value of their wages. Unfair and excessive deductions from wages and workplace fines were a growing grievance for many workers, particularly female employees in marginalized or sweated trades. As had so often been the case, it was the workers in the most precarious and least unionized trades that felt the greatest impact of these dishonest practices. Workers in sweated trades and female outworkers continued to have their meagre wages clawed back. In 1887 they did not have a powerful enough presence to lobby Parliament for greater legal protections. It was not until the appointment of active and committed female factory inspectors and the interventions of female labour organizations that these abuses were exposed to the public and greater efforts made to end them.

Notes

1 *Hansard Parliamentary Debates online, House of Commons,* 16 September 1887.
2 50 & 51 Victoria, c. 46, s.2, 18. The 1887 Act extended its provisions and those of the 1831 Act to all those who fell within the jurisdiction of section 10 of the 1875 Employers and Workmen Act, which stated

> does not include a domestic or menial servant, but save as aforesaid, means any person who, being a labourer, servant in husbandry, journeyman, artificer, handicraftsman, miner, or otherwise engaged in manual labour, whether under the age of twenty-one years or above that age, has entered into or works under a contract with an employer, whether the contract be made before or after the passing of this Act, be express or implied, oral or in writing, and be a contract of service or a contract personally to execute any work or labour.

3 50 & 51 Victoria, c. 46, s.3, 7, 8, 9.
4 50 & 51 Victoria, c. 46, s.13.
5 *Hansard Parliamentary Debates Online, House of Commons,* 8 September 1887, 9 September 1887; *Hansard Parliamentary Debates Online, House of Lords,* 8 August 1887; 15 August 1887; *Times,* 19 August 1887; *Edinburgh Evening News,* 8 September 1887; *Yorkshire Post,* 10 August 1887; 8 September 1887; 9 September 1887; 10 September 1887; *Reynolds Newspaper,* 18 September 1887; *Bury Free Press,* 17 September 1887; *Evening Telegraph,* 25 August 1887; *Lords Amendments to the Truck Bill* (1887), Parliamentary Papers online [cd.377]; *Lords Reasons for Insisting on Certain Amendments and Their Consequential Amendments to the Bill* (1887), Parliamentary Papers online [cd. 389].
6 *Edinburgh Evening News,* 12 September 1887; *Report of the Twentieth Annual Trades Union Congress* (Swansea, 1887), p. 14.
7 Hilton, *The Truck System,* pp. 140–145, quote on 145.
8 *Report of the Commissioners Appointed to Inquire into the Truck System, Together with the Minutes of Evidence, Vol. 1* (London, 1871). Parliamentary Papers, [c.326, 327]; Thomas Jones, *Rhymney Memories* (Newton: The Welsh Outlook Press, 1938), p. 105.
9 *Western Mail,* 14 May 1885; *Weekly Mail,* 16 May 1885; *Cardiff Times,* 16 May 1885; *Northeastern Daily Gazette,* 11 March 1886.
10 *Northeastern Daily Gazette,* 11 March 1886; *Northampton Mercury,* 13 March 1886; *Western Mail,* 18 May 1885; *Western Mail,* 16 May 1886; *Hansard Parliamentary Debates online, House of Commons,* 11 March 1886; *Report of the Commissioners . . . Into the Truck System* (1871), Abstract of Evidence, pp. 52–54; Jones, *Rhymney Memories,* pp. 114–115; TNA, HO 45 9789 B3899; Hilton, *The Truck System,* p. 12.
11 *Western Mail,* 16 June 1886; *Cardiff Times,* 19 June 1886; 30 April 1887; *Weekly Mail,* 19 June 1886; Jones, *Rhymney Memories,* p. 115; 1 & 2 William IV, c. 37, s.9; *Hansard Parliamentary Debates online, House of Commons,* 17 June 1886.
12 *Western Mail,* 12 November 1886.
13 *Cardiff Times,* 3 September 1887.
14 TNA, HO 45 9789 B3899.
15 TNA, HO 45 9789 B3899.
16 *Report of Alexander Redgrave, Esq., C.B., H.M. Chief Inspector of Factories, Upon the Truck System in Scotland* (January 1887), 4, 6. HO 45/9768.
17 *Report of Alexander Redgrave . . .,* 8. HO 45/9768.
18 Section 3 of the 1831 Truck Act states "that the entire amount of wages earned by or payable to any artificer . . . shall be actually paid to such artificer in the current coin of this realm and not otherwise." Some interpreted this to mean that aside from the deductions allowed by sections 23 and 24 of the 1831 Act for tools, medicine, fuel and rent, employers had to pay the entirety of wages owing in cash without deductions for fines or other items. However, in the cases of *Archer v. James and Another (1862),* 31 L.J. 153 and *Chawner v. Cummings (1846),* 8 Q.B. 311 seemed to indicate otherwise. Despite this,

many, including apparently Charles Bradlaugh continued to believe that the Truck Act made fines illegal.

19 *Report of Alexander Redgrave . . .*, 9–11. TNA, HO 45/9768.

20 *Report of Alexander Redgrave . . .*, pp. 9, 12.

21 *Report of Alexander Redgrave . . .*, pp. 17–19.

22 Walter Arnstein, *The Bradlaugh Case: A Study in late Victorian Opinion and Politics* (Oxford: Oxford University Press, 1965).

23 For the personal relationship between Bradlaugh and the Director of the Rhymney Coal and Iron Co, see: Hypatia Bradlaugh Bonner, *Charles Bradlaugh: His Life and Work* (London: T. Fisher Unwin, 1894), pp. 238, 308, 369; *Hansard Parliamentary Debates online, House of Commons*, 11 March 1886, 17 June 1886.

24 *Hansard Parliamentary Debates Online, House of Commons*, 2 September 1886; *Edinburgh Evening News*, 17 September 1886.

25 *Fife Herald*, 8 September 1886; *Northampton Mercury*, 11 September 1886; *Glasgow Evening Herald*, 6 September 1886; *Motherwell Times*, 11 September 1886; *Dundee Advertiser*, 6 September 1886; *Edinburgh Evening News*, 6 September 1886; *Glasgow Observer*, 11 September 1886.

26 *Fife Herald*, 8 September 1886; *Northampton Mercury*, 11 September 1886; *Glasgow Evening Herald*, 6 September 1886; *Motherwell Times*, 11 September 1886; *Dundee Advertiser*, 6 September 1886; *Edinburgh Evening News*, 6 September 1886; *Glasgow Observer*, 11 September 1886.

27 Roy Jenkins, "Dilke, Sir Charles Wentworth, Second Baronet (1843–1911)." *Oxford Dictionary of National Biography Online* (Original Version 23 September 2004. Online Version 24 May 2008).

28 *Glasgow Evening Herald*, 6 September 1886.

29 *Motherwell Times*, 11 September 1886.

30 *Dundee Evening Telegraph*, 7 September 1886.

31 *Labour Tribune*, 18 September 1886.

32 *Hansard Parliamentary Debates, House of Commons, Online*, 9 September 1886.

33 *Hansard Parliamentary Debates, House of Commons, Online*, 9 September 1886.

34 *Hansard Parliamentary Debates, House of Commons*, 9 September 1886. *Edinburgh Evening News*, 10 September 1886.

35 *Hansard Parliamentary Debates, House of Commons*, 9 September 1886. *Edinburgh Evening News*, 10 September 1886; *Hansard Parliamentary Debates online, House of Commons*, 20 August 1886.

36 *Hansard Parliamentary Debates, House of Commons*, 9 September 1886. *Edinburgh Evening News*, 10 September 1886.

37 *Motherwell Times*, 11 September 1886.

38 *Glasgow Herald*, 20 September 1886; *Edinburgh Evening News*, 20 September 1886; *Dundee Telegraph*, 21 September 1886.

39 *Glasgow Herald*, 20 September 1886; *Edinburgh Evening News*, 20 September 1886; *Dundee Telegraph*, 21 September 1886.

40 *Report of Alexander Redgrave, Esq., C.B., H.M. Chief Inspector of Factories Upon the Truck System in Scotland.* TNA HO 45.9768.

41 *Report of Alexander Redgrave, Esq., C.B., H.M. Chief Inspector of Factories Upon the Truck System in Scotland.* TNA HO 45.9768.

42 *Hansard Parliamentary Debates Online, House of Commons*, 31 January 1887; 14 February 1887; 22 February 1887.

43 *Hansard Parliamentary Debates Online, House of Commons*, 28 January 1887; "A Bill to Amend and Extend the Law Relating to Truck." *House of Commons Parliamentary Papers online*, 1887 [cd.109]; "A Bill to Amend the Law Relating to Truck." *House of Commons Parliamentary Papers* 1887 [cd.21]. The co-sponsors of Charles Bradlaugh's bill [Bill 109] included the following Liberal MPs: Cornelius Warmington of Monmouthshire, colliery owner John Ellis, Arthur Williams of Glamorganshire, and Mr. Esslemont of Aberdeen.

Bradlaugh's bill also had one Conservative co-sponsor, Howard Vincent of Sheffield. The Co-Sponsors of Donald Crawford's bill [Bill 21] were Liberals Stephen Mason of Lanarkshire and Edmund Robertson of Dundee.

44 "A Bill to Amend and Extend the Law Relating to Truck." *House of Commons Parliamentary Papers online,* 1887 (109), s.2.
45 "A Bill to Amend and Extend the Law Relating to Truck." *House of Commons Parliamentary Papers online,* 1887 (109), s.3.
46 "A Bill to Amend and Extend the Law Relating to Truck." *House of Commons Parliamentary Papers online,* 1887 (109), s.4–7.
47 "A Bill to Amend and Extend the Law Relating to Truck." *House of Commons Parliamentary Papers online,* 1887 (109), s.8–9.
48 "A Bill to Amend and Extend the Law Relating to Truck." *House of Commons Parliamentary Papers online,* 1887 (109), s.10–11.
49 "A Bill to Amend the Law Relating to Truck." *House of Commons Parliamentary Papers* 1887 (21), s.21. In addition to excluding domestic servants and servants in husbandry, he also placed "seamen or apprentice to the sea service" outside the reach of his bill.
50 "A Bill to Amend the Law Relating to Truck." *House of Commons Parliamentary Papers* 1887 (21), s.4–5.
51 "A Bill to Amend the Law Relating to Truck." *House of Commons Parliamentary Papers* 1887 (21), s.6.
52 "A Bill to Amend the Law Relating to Truck." *House of Commons Parliamentary Papers* 1887 (21), s.7–10.
53 *Times,* 14 January 1887.
54 "A Bill to Amend the Law Relating to Truck." *House of Commons Parliamentary Papers* 1887 (21), s.11.
55 "A Bill to Amend the Law Relating to Truck." *House of Commons Parliamentary Papers* 1887 (21), s.12, 16, 17.
56 *Hansard Parliamentary Debates online, House of Commons,* 31 January 1887.
57 *Supplement to the Northampton Mercury,* 5 February 1887; *Reynolds's Newspaper,* 6 February 1887.
58 TNA HO 45/9768; *Hansard Parliamentary Debates online, House of Commons,* 14 February 1887; 22 February 1887; *Times,* 23 February 1887.
59 *Edinburgh Evening News,* 5 March 1887.
60 *Falkirk Evening Herald,* 9 March 1887. Also see: *Times,* 7 March 1887.
61 TNA HO 45 9773 B1261.
62 TNA HO 45/9773/B1261.
63 *Times,* 16 March 1887.
64 "The Truck System in Mining, Quarrying, and other Industries in Scotland," *The Parliamentary Committee of the Trades Union Congress* (March 1887), London Metropolitan University Archives, TUC Publications, HD 6661.
65 "The Truck System in Mining, Quarrying, and other Industries in Scotland," *The Parliamentary Committee of the Trades Union Congress* (March 1887), London Metropolitan University Archives, TUC Publications, HD 6661.
66 *Edinburgh Evening News,* 5 March 1887.
67 TNA, HO 45 9773 B1261.
68 TNA, HO 45 9773 B1261.
69 TNA, HO 45 9773 B1261.
70 *Dunfermline Press,* 21 May 1887; *Glasgow Herald,* 16 May 1887.
71 *Dunfermline Press,* 21 May 1887; *Glasgow Herald,* 16 May 1887.
72 TNA HO 45/9773/b1261.
73 TNA HO 45/9773/b1261.
74 *Hansard Parliamentary Debates online, House of Commons,* 28 April 1887; 2 May 1887; 3 May 1887; *Times,* 3 May 1887.
75 TNA HO 45/9773/B1261.

76 *Hansard Parliamentary Debates online, House of Commons,* 3 May 1887; 5 May 1887; *Times,* 6 May 1887.

77 *Hansard Parliamentary Debates online, House of Commons,* 5 May 1887; *Times,* 6 May 1887.

78 *Hansard Parliamentary Debates online, House of Commons,* 5 May 1887; *Times,* 6 May 1887.

79 *Hansard Parliamentary Debates online, House of Commons,* 6 May 1887.

80 The bill was again considered on 13 May at 2:50 a.m., but debate was postponed. *Hansard Parliamentary Debates online, House of Commons,* 13 May 1887.

81 *Times,* 23 April 1887; 3 May 1887.

82 TNA HO 45/9773/B1261.

83 TNA HO 45/9773/B1261.

84 *Times,* 12 September 1887; *Edinburgh Evening News,* 12 September 1887.

85 *Hansard Parliamentary Debates online, House of Commons,* 12 September 1887.

86 *Hansard Parliamentary Debates online, House of Commons,* 28 June 1887; *Times,* 29 June 1887.

87 *Hansard Parliamentary Debates online, House of Commons,* 28 June 1887; *Times,* 29 June 1887.

88 *Hansard Parliamentary Debates online, House of Commons,* 28 June 1887; *Times,* 29 June 1887.

89 *Hansard Parliamentary Debates online, House of Commons,* 28 June 1887; *Times,* 29 June 1887.

90 *Hansard Parliamentary Debates online, House of Commons,* 28 June 1887; *Times,* 29 June 1887.

91 TNA HO 45/9773/B1261; *Yorkshire Post,* 10 June 1887; *Sheffield Daily Telegraph,* 10 June 1887.

92 *Hansard Parliamentary Debates online, House of Commons,* 28 June 1887; *Times,* 29 June 1887.

93 *Times,* 12 September 1887.

94 *Hansard Parliamentary Debates online, House of Commons,* 28 June 1887; *Times,* 29 June 1887.

95 *Hansard Parliamentary Debates online, House of Commons,* 28 June 1887; *Times,* 29 June 1887.

96 *Dundee Courier,* 23 April 1887; *Sheffield Daily Telegraph,* 30 April 1887; *London Daily News,* 30 April 1887; *Belfast News-Letter,* 9 May 1887.

97 *Belfast News-Letter,* 9 May 1887.

98 *Sunderland Daily Echo,* 6 May 1887; *Gloucestershire Echo,* 6 May 1887.

99 *Edinburgh Evening News,* 18 May 1887.

100 *Falkirk Herald,* 1 June 1887.

101 *Sunderland Daily Echo,* 17 June 1887.

102 *Hansard Parliamentary Debates online, House of Commons,* 30 June 1887, 1 July 1887; *Times,* 2 July 1887.

103 *Hansard Parliamentary Debates online, House of Commons,* 12 July 1887; *Times,* 13 July 1887.

104 *Hansard Parliamentary Debates online, House of Commons,* 15 July 1887.

105 *Hansard Parliamentary Debates online, House of Commons,* 18 July 1887; *Times,* 19 July 1887.

106 *Hansard Parliamentary Debates online, House of Lords,* 8 August 1887; 15 August 1887; *Times,* 5 August 1887; 16 August 1887; "Lords Amendments to the Truck Bill," *Parliamentary Papers online,* 15 August 1887 (377); *Yorkshire Post,* 10 August 1887.

107 *Times,* 20 August 1887.

108 *Shetland Times,* 3 September 1887.

109 *Edinburgh Evening News,* 29 August 1887; *Evening Telegraph,* 25 August 1887; *Northampton Mercury,* 3 September 1887.

110 "Truck Bill. Lords reasons for insisting on certain amendments and their consequential amendment to the bill." *Parliamentary Papers online,* 9 September 1887 (389); *Yorkshire Post,* 10 September 1887; *Edinburgh Evening News,* 8 September 1887.

111 *Edinburgh Evening News,* 8 September 1887.

112 *Reynolds Newspaper,* 18 September 1887.
113 *Pall Mall Gazette,* 9 September 1887; *London Evening Standard,* 9 September 1887.
114 *Hansard Parliamentary Debate online, House of Commons,* 8 September 1887; 9 September 1887; *Yorkshire Post,* 9 September 1887. Irish MPs did not give up on attempting to secure the weekly payment of wages for Irish workers. In early 1888 Mr. De Cobain of Belfast introduced such a bill, but it failed to get its second reading. *Hansard Parliamentary Debates online, House of Commons,* 10 April 1888.
115 *Dundee Courier,* 17 September 1887.
116 *Essex Newsman,* 11 October 1887; *Exeter Daily Gazette,* 26 September 1887; *Dundee Courier,* 28 September 1887.
117 *Yorkshire Post,* 28 September 1887.
118 *Isle of Wight Observer,* 22 October 1887; *Manchester Courier,* 5 October 1887.
119 *Northeastern Daily Gazette,* 6 September 1887; *Pall Mall Gazette,* 29 October 1887.
120 *Leeds Times,* 17 September 1887.
121 *Liverpool Mercury,* 24 September 1887.
122 *Report of the Trades Union Congress,* 1887, pp. 14, 21, 29, 46.
123 *Times,* 12 September 1887.
124 *Hackney Express and Shoreditch Observer,* 8 October 1887; *Motherwell Times,* 15 October 1887.
125 TNA HO 45 9778 B2165.
126 TNA HO 45 9792 B4772.
127 47 & 48 Victoria, c.43.
128 *Hansard Parliamentary Debates Online, House of Commons,* 17 April 1888; 30 April 1888; 1 May 1888; 10 May 1888; 14 May 1888; 4 June 1888; HO 45 9789 3899.
129 TNA HO 45 9789 3899.
130 TNA HO 45 9789 b3912; *Hansard Parliamentary Debates Online, House of Commons,* 4 June 1888.
131 TNA HO 45 9789 3899.
132 TNA HO 45 9792 b4772; TNA HO 45 9778 B2165.
133 *Hansard Parliamentary Debates Online, House of Commons,* 20 December 1888.
134 TNA HO 45 9792 b4772; TNA HO 45 9778 B2165.
135 TNA HO 45 9792 B4772; *Hansard Parliamentary Debates Online, House of Commons,* 2 May 1889.
136 Under the Summary Jurisdiction Acts, 20 & 21 Victoria, c.43 (1848) and 42 & 43 Victoria, c.49 (1884).
137 *Law Journal Reports New Series,* Vol. 49, pp. 9–10; TNA HO 45 9792 B4772.
138 TNA HO 45 9789 B3912.
139 1 & 2 William IV, c.37, s.3.
140 *Archer v. James (1862), 31 L.J. 153.*
141 *Report of the Truck Commission* (1871), p. XLVI; TNA HO 45 9893 B17716.
142 TNA HO 45 9893 B17716; TNA HO 45 9778 b2165.
143 TNA HO 45 9893 B17716.
144 TNA HO 45 9789 b3912.
145 *The Link: A Journal for the Servants of Man,* 23 June 1888.
146 *Pall Mall Gazette,* 4 July 1888; *The Link: A Journal for the Servants of Man,* 7 July 1888.
147 *The Link: A Journal for the Servants of Man,* 7 July 1888. *Times,* 7 July 1888; *Hansard Parliamentary Debates Online, House of Commons,* 6 July 1888.
148 TNA HO 45 9789 B3912; HO 45 9893 B17716.
149 *Times,* 1 November 1888.
150 *Times,* 10 November 1888.
151 *Hansard Parliamentary Debates Online, House of Commons,* 12 November 1888; 13 November 1888.
152 TNA HO 45 9778 B2165.
153 TNA HO 45 9789 B3912; HO 45 9893 B17716; HO 45 9778 B2165; *Archer v. James (1862),* 31 LJQB 153; 15 LJQB 161.

154 TNA HO 45 9789 B3912; HO 45 9893 B17716; HO 45 9778 B2165; *Willis v. Thorp (1875)*, 10 LRQB 383.
155 TNA HO 45 9789 B3912; HO 45 9893 B17716; HO 45 9778 B2165.
156 HO 45 9789 b3912; HO 45 9893 B17716.
157 TNA HO 45 9789 B3912.
158 TNA HO 45 9789 B3912.
159 *Hansard Parliamentary Debates Online, House of Commons,* 7 December 1888; TNA HO 45 9798 b3912.
160 TNA HO 45 9789 B3912.
161 TNA HO 45 9802 B5581.
162 TNA HO 45 9802 B5581.
163 TNA HO 45 9802 B5581.
164 TNA HO 45 9789 B3912.
165 TNA HO 45 9789 B3912; HO 45 9893 b17716; 37 *The Weekly Reporter* 543; *The London Evening Standard* 10 April 1889.
166 *The London Evening Standard* 10 April 1889.
167 TNA HO 45 9789 B3912; HO 45 9893 b17716; 37 *The Weekly Reporter* 543; *The London Evening Standard* 10 April 1889.
168 TNA HO 45 9893 b17716; 37 *The Weekly Reporter* 543–544.
169 *The Weekly Reporter* 543–544.
170 TNA HO 45 9893 b17716.
171 TNA HO 45 9893 b17716; 37 *The Weekly Reporter* 543–544.
172 *Times,* 18 May 1889; TNA HO 45 9789 B3912.
173 TNA HO 45 9893 b17716.
174 TNA HO 45 9789 B3912; HO 45 9893 B17716.
175 TNA HO 45 9789 B3912.
176 TNA HO 45 9789 B3912; HO 45 9893 B17716.
177 TNA HO 45 9893 B17716.
178 TNA HO 45 9893 B17716.

4 Fines, deductions from wages and the passage of the 1896 Truck Act

Introduction

High court cases such as *Redgrave v. Kelly (1889)* and *Archer v. James (1862)* appeared to place deductions from wages for fines or materials and services supplied by the employer outside of the scope of the Truck Acts, but individuals in management, labour and government continued to express uncertainty. Those administering the law showed striking differences of opinion as to whether deductions not explicitly permitted by the Truck Acts were lawful. In the early 1890s this controversy manifested in court cases that challenged the legality of deductions from wages for contributions to employer-run benefit clubs. By late 1894, the rulings of the high courts caused Home Office officials to doubt whether there were any legal limits at all on the employers' ability to make deductions from wages under the Truck Acts. Factory inspectors, especially newly appointed female factory inspectors who were given a special mandate to enforce the Factory and Truck Acts among female sweated workers, began to report cases where workers had excessive portions of their low wages clawed back by unfair fines and deductions for spoiled work. Their reports increased the pressure upon the government to clarify what deductions employers were permitted to take.

An important obstacle to reform was that historically truck legislation had been politically unrewarding for governments. Employers were opposed to any interference with their ability to discipline workers and exercise control over the workplace and were predisposed to resist the imposition of any new regulatory burdens. Workers in strongly unionized trades were less likely to be subjected to fines or deductions for spoiled work, and many had informal mechanisms for adjudicating disputes over these matters. The deductions taken from unionized workers' wages for materials were carefully negotiated with employers causing workers in these trades to believe, incorrectly, that under the Truck Acts deductions from wages for fines were already illegal. They perceived that any legislation that failed to explicitly abolish fines and deductions was a step backward. This left few options for compromise legislation. First the Liberal government in 1895 and then the Conservative government the following year pursued a middle course between the demands of labour and capital, seeking to regulate fines and deductions by making them more transparent and less excessive. The result was the 1896 Truck Act, which was unpopular with both employers and workers. However, for all its flaws, the 1896 Truck Act did result in a reduction in the amount of fines and deductions taken from British workers.

Deductions from wages for shop clubs and *Hewlett v. Allen (1892)*

In 1892 a high court ruling in the case of *Hewlett v. Allen and Sons* created confusion among employers, workers, magistrates and government inspectors about the legality of deductions from wages under the Truck Acts. The case was specifically about whether it was legal under the Truck Acts for employers to take deductions for contributions to employer-run sick, benefit or accident clubs that their workers were required to join as a condition of employment. The ruling, however, appeared to have much broader implications for the ability of employers to take set-offs from wages.

This issue had arisen periodically in discussions about the Truck Acts. In 1871, *The Report of the Truck Commission* briefly considered the question, which it merged with the larger question of deductions from wages for medical attendance and education. The commissioners concluded that despite some complaints, these deductions were beneficial and argued that "[n]o satisfactory case on the evidence has been made out for their abolition."[1] In 1887, Alexander Redgrave, in his report on the truck system in Scotland, supported regulation of deductions from wages for education and medical attendance but felt that the deductions for employer-controlled benefit and sick funds was "an arrangement greatly for the benefit of the men. It insures the subscriptions being kept up, and provided the men know exactly the principle and conditions of the society, I consider such deductions should be legal."[2] For many policy makers, compulsory membership in benefit societies run by employers provided workers with safeguards against misfortune and encouraged values of thrift and self-help.

However, the TUC objected to these deductions and unsuccessfully attempted to amend the 1887 Truck Act to prevent employers from making them a condition of employment. One concern was that given the precarious nature of employment, it was possible to lose one's job before ever making a claim on the fund to which one had regularly paid dues.[3] Furthermore, employer-run clubs varied considerably in terms of the transparency of their rules and expenditures.[4] Some employer funds had clear rules and were managed with openness and worker participation, while others were opaque and arbitrarily administered. Workers sometimes suspected that they were not receiving the full value of these exactions or that employers were using them for their own benefit.

Additionally, employer-run benefit funds competed for scarce employee contributions with friendly societies, sick and accident clubs run by the working class. They also offered benefits that overlapped with those provided by larger New Model Unions. An employer providing a club could be using it to undermine union organizing. Compulsory deductions for contributions to these funds embodied many of the objections that had been made against the truck system. It was an unfair source of competition, and it violated the notion that workers, as autonomous people, should be free to spend their wages as they chose, independently of their employers' control. They should have the ability to choose which friendly societies, accident clubs or trade unions suited their needs. They should be free to take the risk, even if it was a bad choice, of not joining any at all.

Section 24 of the 1831 Truck Act explicitly permitted employers to make advances and take set-offs from their employees' wages for contributions to friendly societies, savings or for "relief of sickness." Making membership in these clubs a condition of employment appeared to violate section six of the 1887 Truck Act and section two of the 1831 Truck Act, which prohibited employers from dictating to workers how they were to spend their wages.[5] In most instances of complaints about deductions for benefit societies, as long as there was a written contract between the employers and the employees, the inspectors chose not to interfere.

In 1891 the legality of these deductions was challenged in *Lamb v. the Great Northern Railway Company*. The plaintiff was a porter and guard employed by the Great Northern Railway Company between August of 1876 and June of 1890. As a condition of his employment he signed a contract permitting the company to deduct weekly contributions to the Northern Railway Sick and Funeral Allowance Club, which was run by the company. The club provided medical attendance, sickness benefits and death and funeral benefits. After leaving the company, Lamb brought suit against the company in the Doncaster County Court for £2 7s 8d, the amount deducted from his wages for contributions since September of 1887, when the 1887 Truck Act came into effect. He argued that section six of the 1887 Act made it illegal for his employer to make it a condition of employment where he spent his wages. To contemporaries, this suit was dishonest because Lamb had already benefitted from greater claims on the fund than he had paid in contributions. The hearing revealed that between September 1887 and June of 1890, the fund had paid Lamb 8s for medical attendance as well as an additional 2 guineas for doctors to care for his pregnant wife.

The county court judge ruled for the defendants, finding that section six of the 1887 Truck Act was overruled by section 23 of the 1831 Truck Act, which permitted employers to take deductions from wages for medical care and medicine as part of a written contract. The case was appealed, and on 7 April 1891 Justices Grantham and Smith upheld the ruling of the county court. Grantham stated that "section 23 of the Act of William IV overrides everything in this Act [the 1887 Truck Act], and the present case is within the exception." Justice Smith dismissed the argument that because the fund covered more than medical attendance it did not fall within the exception of section 23 by stating that

> as to this I need only say that the whole of the plaintiff's contributions, and more too, were paid to the doctors for medical attendance upon the

plaintiff and his wife, and he cannot now turn round and attempt to take advantage of the old Truck Act.

Smith added some dicta which went to the question of whether the Truck Acts forbade all deductions that they did not explicitly sanction, observing "the legislature seems undoubtedly to have started by making all drawbacks illegal, but there were some they did not wish to make illegal, so they legalized them by section 23."[6] Although the case upheld the legality of deductions taken for a sick club, it seemed to cast doubt upon the validity of other deductions under the Truck Acts.

In 1892, a similar case, *Hewlett v. Allen and Sons*, was heard by the Supreme Court of the Judicature, and it added to the uncertainty, less for its ruling than for the reasoning used to reach the verdict. Between August of 1886 and June of 1891, Louisa Hewlett was in the employment of F. Allen and Sons, confectioners. When she was hired she became a member, like all employees of the firm, of the Amicable Griffins Sick and Benefit Society, run by the employer. Employees made contributions to the fund in proportion to their wages, which for Hewlett meant a weekly contribution of 2 1/2d. The fund provided the employee with access to a doctor, and in the event of sickness or accident would pay Hewlett 4s 6d per week. In the event of her death it would deliver £3 3s to her beneficiary. Upon leaving the firm the employee would receive 3s, provided that no claims had been made during the previous 12 months.[7]

Hewlett had never made a claim against the fund, and after leaving Allen and Sons, she sued the firm at county court for £1 13s 7d, the amount deducted from her wages for the sick club. Her counsel argued that the deductions taken from her wages violated both section two of the 1831 Truck Act and section six of the 1887 Truck Act, which stated that any employment contract dictating how the worker must spend his or her wages was void. She also based her claim upon section three of the 1831 Act, which stated that an employer must pay the entirety of the wages owed to the employee in the current coin of the realm. She testified that although she had 2 ½d deducted from her wages every week, she never saw a doctor or received a sickness benefit. The only benefit that she received was the 3s bonus paid upon her dismissal. The counsel for the defendants called no witnesses but argued that the deductions were part of a written agreement that was legal under section 23 of the 1831 Truck Act, which permitted deductions from wages for medicine and medical attendance. To support this claim, they cited *Lamb v. Great Northern Railway Company (1891)*. After some discussion between the plaintiff and the judge, the plaintiff withdrew 6s 9d of her claim, the amount which represented the contributions for the doctor and the 3s bonus she was paid from the fund upon her dismissal. Therefore, the remaining deductions for the club were for purposes not permitted by section 23 of the 1831 Act. The judge awarded her £1 6s 10d and costs, on the grounds that this amount represented deductions that were not permissible under the Truck Acts.[8]

The case was appealed to the Divisional Court, where it was heard before Justices Day and Charles on 6 May 1892. Justice Day noted the high stakes of the case to the defendant, because if the ruling were upheld "it may be one of many actions which may be brought against them involving to them a very considerable amount of money." Day ruled that the controlling case in this instance was *Lamb v. Great Northern Railway Company (1891)*, where the court found that section 23 of the 1831 Truck Act allowed employers to make deductions for medicine and medical attendance under a written contract. He asserted that although the club at Allen and Sons provided death and funeral benefits, "it is substantially a sick club which is formed for medical aid and assistance" bringing it within section 23. He stated that it made no difference that Hewlett had made no claims upon the fund for medical attention. During the term of employment if she had ever had the misfortune of being ill, she would have been entitled to draw a benefit from the club. The ruling of the county court judge was reversed and the case was then appealed to the Supreme Court of the Judicature.[9]

The case was heard again on 10 August 1892, and one of the judges was Charles Bowen, who was quite familiar with the law of Truck, having been instrumental in writing the 1871 *Report of the Truck Commission*. Bowen upheld the ruling of the Divisional Court, but for very different reasons than Justices Charles and Day. By saying much more than was required, Bowen destabilized the interpretation of the Truck Acts until the House of Lords took up this case in 1894. Bowen ruled that the contract between the employer and the employee was illegal because it provided wages otherwise than in the current coin of the realm and possibly because it directed how and where an employee was to spend wages. He went further:

> It is clear, to begin with, that the contract between the defendants and the plaintiff that these deductions should be made was an illegal one. It may well fall within section 2 of the Act of 1831 and section 6 of the Act of 1887 . . . [but] it appears to us still to be illegal under section 1 as being a contract that wages shall be paid otherwise than in the current coin. No justification can therefore be found in the signed contract for anything done under it. The plaintiff has not actually received her entire wages in the current coin of the realm.[10]

The judge dismissed the suggestion that section 23 of the 1831 Act, which permitted deductions from wages for medical care or medical attendance, was applicable in this case, as the contributions to the doctor were struck out at county court, and the other objects of the fund, including death and funeral benefits, were not sanctioned by section 23.

Despite deciding that the contract between Hewlett and her employers was void, Bowen ruled that Hewlett could not recover her unpaid wages. He made the remarkable statement that although the contract between the employer and employee had been illegal, the payments that were made to the sick and benefit club were not. Justice Bowen ruled that if an employer paid wages in the current coin of the realm to a third party authorized by the employee to receive them, then it was the same as paying the employee. Bowen argued that there was a distinction between the penal and civil aspects of the Truck Acts. While the employer in this case did not have a defence against the criminal charge of making an illegal contract with an employee and failing to pay the entirety of wages owed in the current coin, in a civil case the employer had a defence against the employee attempting to recover the wages. Oddly, the defence was one that the employer's counsel did not think to make, but Bowen insisted that

> we should not allow justice to be defeated upon a mere defect of pleading, and the matter in the Court of Appeal must be treated as if all facts had properly been pleaded which are undisputed facts in the case.

Bowen put forward that the contract for deducting wages from Hewlett for the fund was illegal, but she had long acquiesced to making contributions from her wages. Therefore, the payments to the fund were legal, and she could not recover them under the Truck Acts. The justice ruled,

> It could not be right that a workman should sanction the handing over of his contributions to a fund created for his own benefit and the benefit of others, and years afterwards recall his contributions. Such a gift, or contribution, would be irrevocable.

He continued,

> We do not think that she can, years afterwards, complain of what has been done with her knowledge and with her tacit consent. The Truck Act has been broken, but she has precluded herself, by her long acquiescence in the payment to the fund of her contributions, from now recalling them.[11]

By assenting to the valid payments from an illegal contract, the plaintiff lost her claims under the Truck Acts. Although Allen and Sons won the verdict they could hardly be satisfied with the ruling because in addition to having their contracts with their employees declared illegal, Bowen refused to grant them costs. Bowen ruled,

> As we are not satisfied that the actions of the defendants in respect of this fund has been consistent with the provisions of the Truck Act, we think that, although the plaintiff's civil claim against the defendants fails, there ought to be no costs in this appeal.[12]

Bowen believed that the Truck Acts made it illegal to make it a condition of employment for a worker to agree to have wages deducted for dues to a benefit club, but also thought it was unfair for Hewlett to have enjoyed the protection the club offered and then sue to recover her contributions. Bowen's ruling was clever, stating that the contract deducting wages for contributions for an employer-controlled sickness club violated the Truck Acts but preventing a stampede of claims against employers running similar clubs by asserting that employee acquiescence barred them from recovering these payments. Bowen, however, said more than was necessary to make his ruling. In going beyond barring the claim for acquiescence, he suggested that the contract violated section two of the 1831 Truck Act because it directed how employees were to spend their wages and hinted that there was a violation of sections one and three of the same Act because the entire amount of wages owed had not paid in the current coin. If this interpretation of his ruling held, it would appear to overturn *Redgrave v. Kelly (1889)*, and thus for a time left many uncertain about the legality of different types of deductions from wages under the Truck Acts.[13] This confusion contributed to a growing desire for an amendment of the Truck Acts to clarify the law.

Interpreting and applying *Hewlett v. Allen (1892)*

Adding to the uncertainty created by the high courts was that fact that September of 1892 was a period of transition for both the Home Office and the Factory Inspectorate. A Liberal government had just come to power, with Herbert Asquith assuming the position of Home Secretary and Herbert Gladstone becoming the Undersecretary of State for the Home Department. There was also a new Acting Chief Inspector of Factories and Workshops, Richard Sprague-Oram, who served in that position between 1893 and 1896. Employers and inspectors were uncertain as to how this new leadership planned to apply the recent ruling.

Less than a month after the Bowen's ruling, James Fuller, a boot manufacturer in Braintree, wrote a letter to Factory Inspector H.J. Cameron asking about the implications of that case for his own benefit club, claiming his employees requested him to deduct weekly contributions from their wages so that their subscriptions would stay up-to-date. His son administered the club and was paid a salary from the dues paid by the workers. He asked Cameron "Am I, or rather my son, legally entitled to do them this favour?" Fuller also informed the inspector that at his works there was a code of rules and workers were fined for transgressions with the proceeds going toward the club. The boot manufacturer insisted that

> I am by no means the only manufacturer in this county who is doing that and I should think the law would surely recognize the importance of a master being able to control his men in some way if they are unruly.[14]

While Inspector Cameron was addressing the concerns of Mr. Fuller, another factory inspector, Mr. Bowers, requested guidance from the Home Office after receiving complaints about two sick clubs in Reading run by Messrs. Huntly and Palmer, biscuit manufacturers, and Messrs Limited, Timber Importers. In both instances employee membership in the clubs, which provided medical attendance and benefits in the event of sickness or injury, were required, and deductions were taken from workers' wages and put toward the funds. Bowers informed the employers that deducting the subscriptions from wages violated the Truck Acts, so the firm would need the workers to instead pay their dues independently of receiving their wages. Huntley and Palmer asked whether they would be in compliance with the Truck Acts if each employee signed a request to the employer to take deductions for the fund. The employers emphasized the "extreme difficulty of successfully carrying out any other plan than that of deducting subscriptions from wages." In the Home Office, Godfrey Lushington, who felt that these sick clubs were beneficial to employees, insisted "it is manifest that the Acts, if they are to be strictly construed, require amending" though Gladstone thought that "if the law is altered I think it should be done only after careful inquiry and examination" because of the complexity of the issues.[15]

Inspector Cameron, uncertain of the position of his new superiors, forwarded the letter from Fuller to Richard Sprague-Oram, Acting Chief Inspector. Cameron informed him that under his predecessor, Chief Inspector Redgrave, deductions from wages at the request of workers for sick funds were permitted provided they were part of a written agreement and subject to annual audits. He also noted that after the high court ruling in the case of *Redgrave v. Kelly (1889)* it had been the policy of the Factory Inspectorate to not interfere in cases of workplace fines. Sprague-Oram forwarded these communications to the Home Office but expressed a different opinion from his predecessor. He felt that under the 1831 Truck Act, deductions for benefit clubs were illegal, as they fell outside of the deductions permitted by section 23 of that Act. Payments to the club should be made by the workpeople themselves and not deducted from their wages, which needed to be paid in full. Ignoring *Redgrave v. Kelly (1889)*, he also thought that deductions from wages for workplace fines were illegal as "there being nothing in the Truck Acts to warrant such deductions."[16]

On 10 October 1892, the Home Office, in order to get a clear sense of the implications of *Hewlett v. Allen (1892)*, submitted the case to the law officers of the Crown for an opinion. Attorney General Sir Charles Russell and Solicitor General Sir John Rigby responded on 15 November 1892. With the ruling *Hewlett v. Allen (1892)* in mind, they wrote that an employer taking deductions from an employee's wages for contributions to a sick club as part of a written contract between the two parties would offend against the Truck Act. However, if the arrangement took the form of a revocable authority to pay part of his or her wages to the club given by the worker to the employer each pay period, then the employer would be protected from any actions on the grounds of employee acquiescence. Approving the deduction week after week meant the employee acquiesced to the payment and therefore, according to *Hewlett v. Allen (1892)*, unable to sue under the Truck Acts. The law officers believed that codes of rules enforced by fines deducted from workers' wages were illegal under the Truck Acts but warned the Home Office and the Inspectorate about the dangers of giving employers interpretations of potentially difficult points of law which they had little authority to decide. They wrote,

> We would suggest to the Home Secretary to consider whether it is within the functions of the Inspectors, or indeed the Home Secretary, to advice employers as to the law. Neither the Home Secretary nor the Law Officers have any authority to declare what is the law, and we suggest that this should be made clear in any communication.

While it was true that the prevailing interpretation of the law by the Home Office and the Inspectorate was no guide to how the courts at different levels would rule, it was still relevant to employers and workers because it determined when Inspectors would choose to intervene. The law officers were aware of the peculiarity of a contract to make deductions from wages for a sick and benefit club being void, but the set-offs becoming legal through acquiescence if employees authorized them week-to-week, noting "the recent case of Hewlett v. Allen leaves the law in a condition not entirely satisfactory."[17] This tentative opinion was sent to Fuller, Huntley and Palmer and guided the policy of the Inspectorate with respect to deductions for benefit clubs for the next few years.

The introduction of the female factory inspectorate

The enforcement of the laws against truck transformed significantly in April of 1893 with the appointment of the first two "Lady Inspectors," May Abraham and Mary Paterson. These female inspectors had the mandate to enforce the Factory Acts as well as the Truck Acts, focusing upon the conditions of low-paid women workers in sweated industries who had not been given adequate attention by the male factory inspectorate. Additional factory inspectors Lucy Deane and Adelaide Anderson were appointed in 1894, and Rose Squire joined the inspectorate in 1895. On the eve of the Great War, the number of female factory inspectors had risen to 21.[18] In 1896, female factory inspectors were grouped into a separate branch of the Factory Department with May Abraham appointed Chief Lady Inspector, a position that she held until her retirement in 1897. Adelaide Anderson succeeded her in the post.[19]

In January of 1893 Herbert Asquith announced his intention to appoint female factory inspectors at a meeting of the National Liberal Federation, providing a qualified victory for some feminists and female trade unionists.[20] As early as the 1870s, Emma Paterson of the Women's Protective and Provident League, which evolved into the Women's Trade Union League, argued for the appointment of working-class women to the position of factory inspector, as these women had practical knowledge of the conditions experienced by female workers in sweated trades.[21] The groups agitating for the appointment of female inspectors with special jurisdiction had to overcome the disagreement of some feminists who opposed labour legislation that treated women workers differently than men, as they feared that they might reduce female employment opportunities or devalue women workers.[22] The TUC passed resolutions in support of the appointment of female factory inspectors every year after 1878, though its Parliamentary Committee does not appear to have lobbied very hard on this issue.[23] Emma Paterson passed away in 1886, but her work was carried forward by Emilia Dilke, who did not share Paterson's belief that the inspectors should be from the working class, feeling that only middle class women possessed the professionalism, tact and standing to gain the ear of employers.[24] Dilke's views prevailed with Home Secretary Asquith.

By the 1890s there was a significant pool of experienced and qualified women to appoint. Paterson and Abraham had served as assistant commissioners on the Royal Commission on Labour between 1891 and 1893, and many other women had participated in social investigations and campaigns against sweated labour, acquiring expertise on these issues.[25] Government investigations made it clear that male factory inspectors had a blind spot to abuses and violations of the Factory Acts involving female workers, and Adelaide Anderson herself noted, "women inspectors were necessary if certain evils were to be redressed and rules enforced in places where women were employed."[26] Witnesses before the Royal Commission on Labour testified that despite the fact that many female sweated labourers worked in appalling conditions, they represented almost none of the complaints made to male factory inspectors.[27]

In the late 1880s Charles Bradlaugh complained in the House of Commons about the male factory inspectors' lack of vigour in enforcing the laws against truck. No such complaint could be made against the female factory inspectors, who were noteworthy for their persistent efforts to enforce the Factory Acts and Truck Acts. Desmond Greer and James Nicolson observed that the appointment of female inspectors "brought about a change of emphasis" and might have "encouraged their male counterparts to greater activity" as well.[28] Many of the women appointed as female factory inspectors had activist, public health or philanthropic backgrounds, which caused them to view their work as a moral imperative.[29] Some of the female factory inspectors had experience as officers and organizers in the WTUL, some had served on the Royal Commission on Labour and some had worked on anti-sweating campaigns, which gave them strong sympathy with the working poor and a commitment to improving the terms under which women worked. These inspectors were in constant contact with labour-friendly politicians, feminists and female trade union leaders, to whom they provided "unpublished statistics, examples of gross breaches of factory legislation, and cases of industrial disease."[30] These connections, and the perceived novelty of female factory inspectors, meant that their activities were well covered in the press, which drew attention to many of the abuses suffered by female sweated workers.

The hardships of workplace fines, and deductions from wages for damaged work, were most pervasive, and most outrageously abused, in workplaces where there was a high proportion of non-unionized and low-paid female and child labour. In the decades before World War I, female factory inspectors were on the front lines of the enforcement of the Truck Acts. Their discussions and negotiations with employers caused many to voluntarily abandon exploitative deductions. The prosecutions that the female factory inspectors initiated resulted in much of the case law that defined the Truck Acts and through their investigations, reports and testimony they produced and disseminated expert knowledge about the hardships endured by sweated labour. This knowledge contributed to the political pressure for further reform of the Truck Acts.

Confusion about the legality of deductions from wages under the Truck Acts, 1893–1896

Employers, workers, magistrates and inspectors continued to demonstrate uncertainty and striking differences of opinion about the applicability of the Truck Acts to various deductions from wages, and during the 1890s the Home Office and the courts did not provide consistent guidance. Workers complained to inspectors about deductions from their wages for disciplinary fines, damaged work, tools and materials, and even heat, light and standing room, which they believed represented a failure to pay the entire wages owed in the current coin of the realm. In these areas of uncertainty, the male factory inspectorate often declined to act unless strongly pressed by their superiors, and this left them open to public criticism from organized labour, the press and royal commissions. In instances when inspectors enforced the Truck Acts to stop employers for taking deductions from wages, the employers went over their head and complained to the Home Office. By 1894, legislation was required to clarify the legality of different deductions under the Truck Acts.

In August of 1893, a Branch of the Amalgamated Association of Weavers complained about deductions taken from weavers' wages at W.E. Wood Brothers, Birch Mill near Heywood. The weavers had previously fetched their own weft and carried their finished pieces to the warehouse, but the employers had recently put in a tramline and employed an individual perform these tasks for them. The employers stopped a 1/2d each week out of every weaver's wages to pay this new employee's salary. The union inquired to the Home Office whether this was a violation of the Truck Acts. The Home Office dispatched Factory Inspector James Pearson to investigate, and the manager agreed to suspend the deductions when informed the arrangement violated the Truck Acts.[31]

However, on 1 September the union again contacted the Home Office over a notice posted at W.E. Wood Brothers Mill stating that a collection for the tram service would be made on Saturday. Inspector Pearson was dispatched and found that the firm circumvented the Truck Acts by paying wages in full on Friday, and then on Saturday making a collection for the payment of the wages of the worker who ran the tram service. The firm informed Pearson that in the future they would make it a condition of employment that workers contribute a ½d every Saturday for these wages. Pearson observed that on the first Saturday the collection was made about half the weavers paid and half refused, but the firm did not dismiss the workers who refused.[32] Because the men were paid their full wages in the current coin of the realm, and no weaver had been fired for refusing to contribute, Chief Inspector Sprague-Oram did not believe that they could interfere. However, it was clear that in the future weavers employed at that workplace would be pressured to pay an expense that should be borne by the employer.

Deductions for tools, materials, heat, light and the space necessary for work was a grievance shared by many descriptions of workers. Cutlery and edge tool workers represented by the Table Blade Grinders Association in Sheffield complained about excessive deductions from their wages for wheel rent, which was 7s per man per week and charged to them 51 weeks a year, regardless of whether or not work was available. They often paid an additional 3s 6d for other materials necessary for their work. Through the TUC they sought a legal opinion as to whether these deductions were legal under the Truck Acts and were disappointed with the answer. In September of 1892 and September of 1894, the TUC passed resolutions demanding reform of the Truck Acts to prohibit deductions for materials and standing room, resolving that "This conference is of the opinion that employers should provide conveniences and material for the execution of their work; that no deductions from wages nor charges be made to workmen for workroom, motive power, tools, workings stuffs, etc." The Sheffield union sent this resolution to the Home Secretary in January 1895.[33]

Another deduction that concerned workers in many trades was fines for tardiness. In September 1893 weavers from Heywood appealed to the Home Office to enforce the Truck Acts, objecting to the Derby Mills Spinning and Manufacturing Company fining weavers at a rate of 1d for every three minutes they were late.[34] This fine was far in excess of the weavers' rate of pay and possibly contrary to the Truck Acts. In October of 1893 there was a similar complaint from a group of apprentices in Brighton who were excessively fined for tardiness.[35] The Home Office decided in both cases "deductions for being late have been considered as unearned wages, and therefore not in violation of the Truck Acts." Workers thought this unfair because employers were not simply withholding wages not earned during the period they were not at work but also took additional wages as well. Both the law officers of the previous and current governments were in agreement that while it was illegal under the Truck Acts to deduct fines for misconduct from wages, fines for being late were simply the means of arriving at the wages earned.[36]

Lushington thought that the issue might be more complex in light of Justice Bowen's ruling in *Hewlett v. Allen and Sons (1892)*. Lushington interpreted Bowen's ruling to mean all wages owed had to be paid in full in the current coin without any deductions, unless they were expressly authorized by the Truck Acts. A worker who arrived late to work would not have earned a full day's wages, so the fine could be considered simply arriving at the wages owed, which would be legal according to the precedents of *Archer v. James (1862)* and *Redgrave v. Kelly (1889)*. However, Lushington, thought that if the fine was greatly in excess of the actual loss that the employer sustained by the tardiness it might be illegal under the Truck Acts. In the case of Derby Mills, Lushington thought the fines were reasonable and the Inspectors should not interfere.[37]

Deductions from wages for damaged or defective work were also highly vexatious. Employers often charged workers considerable amounts for mistakes resulting in products that could not be sold. In early December 1893 Factory Inspector May Abraham reported to the Home Office that on her tour of linen mills and factories in Ireland she discovered "infringements of the Truck Act were almost universal." She found that employers made deductions from the wages of young women for needles, thread, steam power and light, as well as for the use of waterproof aprons to protect them from wet spinning. She was particularly appalled at the deductions from workers' wages for mistakes or errors in production, observing "deductions for damage were in some cases calculated much in excess of the actual injury done to the goods" and far out or proportion to the workers' wages. Abraham informed her superiors that after explaining to the manufacturers that their practices were illegal under the Truck Acts, she secured a promise from them to abandon these deductions.[38] However, the Flax Spinners and Power Loom Linen Manufacturers Association of Ireland wrote to Home Secretary Asquith to express their "surprise" at Abraham's interpretation of the law and to demand the legal precedent upon which Inspector Abraham's assertion was based. The manufacturers "are totally at a loss to see how a substitute can be found to counteract the tendency to carelessness and inattention which will always be found amongst operatives." The only alternative would be to dismiss workers. Lushington drew the manufacturers' attention to *Hewlett v. Allen and Sons (1892)*.[39]

Two weeks later, the Home Office was contacted by the South Scotland Chamber of Commerce (SSCC). In October of 1893, Factory Inspector Mary Paterson informed tweed manufacturers Messrs. George Roberts and Company of Selkirk that taking deductions from weavers' wages for allegedly spoiled work was contrary to the Truck Acts. The company replied that these deductions had long been part of the trade and insisted that they prevented employees from working carelessly. The SSCC argued that this interpretation of the Truck Acts was unfair because in order to earn full wages, an employee must perform perfect work. If an employee produced work that was not perfect, it was reasonable for an employer to deduct from the worker's wages. Like the manufacturers in Ireland, the representative of the SSCC stressed that if this interpretation of the Truck Acts held, then the only option for disciplining workers was dismissal.[40]

Several in the Home Office thought that the interpretation offered by the SSCC "sounds like a plausible contention." Lushington wrote that the current state of the law

> appears unsatisfactory: and an early opportunity should I think be taken to put the law on a proper footing. In the meantime it should not be enforced in cases where it is evident that no unfair advantage is being taken of the workmen.

The problem was, however, that Inspectors Abraham and Paterson had demonstrated that unfair advantage *most certainly was* being taken.[41]

On 29 December 1893, Chief Inspector Sprague-Oram after being repeatedly instructed not to pursue cases under the Truck Acts where employers too deductions from wages for power, light, tools and materials expressed his frustration with the current state of the law. Sprague-Oram wrote,

> The Truck Act appears to have embarrassed judges and law officers as well as inspectors and as a trifling amendment in a clause would render it clear as to what deductions are legal, I submit that such an amendment to the law is worthy of consideration.

Lushington wrote back to the chief inspector that no proceedings should be taken until the law was in a more clear state.[42]

Sprague-Oram wrote back a week later to reiterate the difficulties inspectors faced when enforcing the Truck Acts. On 3 January 1894, Inspector J.A. Hill applied to an assistant stipendiary magistrate for a summons against J. Lodge of Leeds for violating the Truck Acts. In mid-December 1893 Hill had visited Lodge's factory, and heard of a case where yarn with different qualities of wool had been mixed together, and the mistake was not discovered until after the cloth was dyed. Although it was not certain who had made the error, Lodge deducted half of the value of fixing the cloth from the wages of a male spinner, who immediately quit, and the other half from the wages of the spinner's two young female assistants. One of the assistants also quit, but Emily Ramsden stayed and had 5s 9d taken from her pay, leaving her with fortnightly wages of only 2s 9d. Hill informed Lodge that these deductions were illegal, and Lodge replied that he would remit the deduction to Ramsden, but if he did, she would be fired. This prompted Hill to prosecute Lodge for not paying the entire wages owed in the current coin. However, the assistant stipendiary refused to grant the summons, stating that the deductions did not come under the Truck Acts. The chief inspector was disappointed and requested that the Home Office make the magistrate explain himself. He also dispatched Inspector Abraham to conduct a full investigation of the factory searching for any violations and requested that "these cases be brought under the special notice of Mr. Asquith. As I before submitted, I think the Truck Act should be amended." Lushington wrote to him that no further action should be taken until the law officers gave their opinion on these legal issues.[43]

On 5 January 1894, the Home Office presented the law officers of the Crown with the question of the legality of deductions from wages for damaged or spoiled work under the Truck Acts, referring them to previous opinions of the law officers related to the legality of different types of deductions under the Truck Acts.[44] On 22 January 1894, the law officers responded that while deducting a disciplinary fine from wages as a punishment for ruining work would be illegal, a deduction from wages that did not exceed the amount by which the value of the service or work had been reduced by spoilage would be legal because it could be considered the means of arriving at the correct amount of wages earned.[45] After receiving this advice from the law officers, the Home Office discouraged interference by inspectors in cases where employers deducted wages for damaged goods, but Lushington thought that this was unsatisfactory, and noted "the whole matter requires to be made clear by legislation."[46]

In March of 1894, the Leeds Tailoresses' Union passed a resolution requesting an amendment to Truck Acts to outlaw employers charging workers for power, tools or materials.[47] The president of this union presented the resolution to Inspector Abraham, who forwarded it to Sprague-Oram. She informed her boss that during the previous summer she had visited Leeds and found many employers deducting the costs of needles and thread and other materials from the wages of employees at a cost 50% greater than retail price. Abraham convinced most of the Leeds employers to abandon the deductions, but the vice president of the Tailoresses' Union informed her that some firms now simply sold them to employees separately and if a worker purchased materials from outside the firm, she was dismissed. Abraham requested a test case.

She reminded the chief inspector that through the threat of legal action she had persuaded employers in London, Belfast, Bristol and Oxford to abandon exploitative deductions. She stressed that often workers were given no explanation for the deductions that were taken from their wages, and in many cases they were being cheated.[48] Sprague-Oram wrote to the Home Office and asked for permission to inform employers that deductions from wages for needles, thread and other materials were illegal under the Truck Acts, and if necessary, prosecute a test case. He hoped that action in these matters would not be postponed until the passage of a new Truck Act, which he prophetically thought "may not pass for two more years."[49] The Home Office rejected this course of action but did promise that the truck question was under special consideration by the Home Secretary.[50]

At the end of April and early May 1894, the case of *Hewlett v. Allen and Sons* was heard by the House of Lords, where Lord Chancellor Herschell upheld Lord Bowen's ruling while diminishing much of Bowen's dicta. Herschell, like Lord Bramwell in the case of *Archer v. James (1862)*, brought the emphasis back to what he perceived as the original legislative intent of the Truck Acts. He interpreted the purpose of those Acts were to prevent employers from placing their workers at a disadvantage by paying their wages in goods rather than money, or to prevent workers from receiving something other than the agreed upon remuneration. He thought that did not happen in this case, because a payment by the employer to someone authorized by the employee to receive it was the same as paying that employee. Her acquiescence of these payments barred her claim, and Herschell stated "I can find nothing in the Truck Acts ... to prevent the employer when sued relying on the fact of such payments [to the sick club] as a discharge of his obligations toward his employee." He thought that taking deductions to pay subscriptions to a sick or benefit society "obviously would not be in the slightest degree within the mischief against which the statute was directed." Lord Watson and Lord Morris agreed and went further to argue that Hewlett's contract of employment, with its stipulation that she had to join the sick club and have dues deducted from her wages, was legal under the Truck Acts.[51]

In October of 1894 Herbert Asquith told a public meeting in Fife of his intention to amend the Truck Acts, informing the audience that they needed to be extended in scope and amended to prevent employers for making deductions from wages for tools or materials in excess of their cost. Under the current law an employer was "practically enabled to deprive workmen or women of an appreciable amount of the wages to which they are entitled." He promised to "bring a bill which will close up the meshes of the law and make such abuses impossible."[52]

The Home Office continued to field queries from inspectors of mines and factories about the limits, if any, on employers taking deductions from wages. In most instances, the Home Office instructed the inspectors not to interfere. In October of 1894, Inspector W.H. Johnston reported to Sprague-Oram that Greenwich shirt manufacturers Messrs. McBride and Co. every week made the following deductions from employees' wages: 3d for cotton, 1d for needle, 1d for shuttle and 2d for gas. Employees also had to consent to have 2d deducted for the purchase of a book upon which pay and deductions were recorded. Sprague-Oram requested permission from the Home Office to instruct the employer that this was not legal. Lushington replied that inspectors should not interfere unless there was an actual payment in goods, noting "The law is in a very perplexed condition at present and when it is amended it is quite likely as not that deductions like this will be allowed as similar deductions are allowed in mines."[53]

However, the many miners found deductions for materials increasingly objectionable. After receiving complaints from miners in north Wales in November 1894, Mines Inspector Hall asked Lushington whether it was legal for employer to profit from deductions for items such as oil, explosives or tools. Mine owners in north Wales purchased these items wholesale and then charged the miners retail prices for them. For example, in one colliery, miners were charged 10d per quart of oil that employers purchased for 1s 9d per gallon, giving the later a 1s 7d per gallon profit from this deduction. Lushington wrote that the legality of this deduction had not been settled the courts but "it is difficult to see why employers should not be entitled to a reasonable profit" and he urged inspectors not to interfere unless "the price appears extortionate or unfair."[54] A week later Hall wrote to Lushington, relaying the complaints from Lancashire miners whose employers were making a significant profit on detonators paid for from deductions from wages. He asked if it was illegal for employers to deduct more than the "real and true" value of the materials it supplied. Lushington replied that "it is not expedient to pursue this matter further."[55] Until an amending Truck Act passed Parliament to clarify the legality of deductions from wages, the Home Office would discourage inspectors of the mines and factories from interfering.[56]

Asquith's 1895 bill to amend the Truck Acts

By January of 1895, Home Secretary Asquith was preparing to clarify the laws relating to deductions from wages. Henry Hardinge Cunynghame, the legal assistant of the Home Office, produced a memorandum on the current state to the Truck Acts. He argued that as the law presently stood it was illegal to pay wages in goods, but deductions from wages for contributions to benefit societies, tools, machinery, materials, light or heat, and fines caused by lateness, misconduct or damaged work were legal.[57] He described the complaints that had been received by inspectors about the Truck Acts. Many workers were outside of the reach of existing legislation, including shop assistants. Others felt that disciplinary fines were unfair. Cunynghame thought that some fines were probably necessary, but "it is manifestly unjust and likely to cause irritation that the employer should be judge in his own cause, more especially when the fine goes into his own pocket." Another grievance was that deductions taken for materials or the use of tools often "are in excess of their true value." He argued that options available for reform were to repeal and redraft the truck laws, pass legislation forbidding all deductions or enact a law that would prohibit deductions that were not reasonable. He thought that the first option was not practical, the second might "dislocate trade," leaving the third as the best option. He argued in favour of requiring all deductions to be a part of a signed contract between the employer and employee, and be fair and reasonable in their amounts. He also thought that employees should be given receipts for all deductions, itemizing the deduction and amount charged.[58]

On 7 January 1895, Asquith produced a Home Office Note in response to the Cunynghame memorandum. Asquith stated that while the laws prohibiting truck were clear "as regards truck in the strict sense," they were "full of obscurity and doubt as regards such questions as deductions from wages for materials, tools, lighting; for fines of all kinds; and for contributions to sick and accident clubs." He complained that *Hewlett v. Allen and Sons* "with its luxuriant crop of dicta, has not made matters more plain." While he would have liked to have repealed all existing Truck Acts and then create a new law that had greater clarity, "we must be content with a less ambitious procedure." Asquith had decided on a short amending Act based upon Cunynghame's recommendations.[59] Nine days later, a trade union deputation waited upon the Home Secretary and urged him to go further and prohibit all deductions from wages "under any pretence whatever." A representative from the Boot and Shoe Operatives National Union complained of men being "charged as much as 2s a week for standing in an employer's workshop to do the employer's work."[60] Asquith was not prepared to go this far, and put the draftsmen to work on a more modest reform measure.

On 1 March 1895, Asquith introduced a one-page bill to amend the Truck Acts. It stated that deductions from wages for fines, damaged work, materials, tools, machinery, standing room, light, heat or other items were illegal unless certain conditions were met. One was that they had to be part of a signed contract between the employer and employee. Also, the deductions or charges had to be "reasonable having regard to all circumstances of the case." The bill also stated that the employer had to provide the worker with the written particulars of each deduction, showing the nature and amounts deducted. The Act would be enforced by the inspectors of mines and factories.[61]

Asquith informed the House that his bill was intended to meet the grievances of workers because he was satisfied that some of the deductions made by employers "did impose hardships very near extortion." He was not prepared to make all deductions illegal but wanted to ensure that deductions had to be part of a contract signed by a worker, and that there would be fairness and transparency for every deduction made. He explained the meaning of "reasonable" in the act as follows:

> if a poor woman employed in needlework were obliged to pay an employer for needles and thread at higher prices than those at which they could be bought at a retail shop in the neighbourhood, their cases might at once be brought before a magistrate, and it would be held that the charges were unreasonable and therefore illegal.[62]

The Home Secretary's bill lacked strong backing from either employers or workers. Most trade unions favoured the complete abolition of fines and deductions from wages and objected to fines and deductions being legal as part of written contract because they believed that employers would make such a contract a condition of entering employment. They also did not share the Home Secretary's confidence that magistrates would interpret "reasonable" in a way that was favourable to their interests. Other labour advocates who continued to believe that fines and deductions were already illegal under the 1831 Act thought that Asquith's proposal might legalize fines and deductions. Even those who recognized the legality of fines due to *Redgrave v. Kelly (1889)* worried that this legislation might legitimize them with statutory sanction, thus making them more common. On the other hand, most employers disliked the notion of any additional regulations interfering with their authority to discipline workers or take deductions.

Many different groups wrote to the Home Office with suggestions for amendment to the Truck Bill. The Hull Branch of the National Shop Assistants' Union requested that their description of employment be included within the new legislation. Shop assistants suffered from heavy fines for violation of shop rules, and others who were part of the "living-in" system received part of their remuneration in the form of room and board, which many in the Home Office thought "amount to truck." While the government thought that it would be desirable to afford some protections to the shop assistants, it was feared that this would be too great an innovation to enact without having a full inquiry. There was also the question of how to enforce the Act for shop assistants. Would this responsibility be added to the already thinly stretched Factory Inspectorate or would the shop assistants be left to enforce the Act on their own?[63]

On 20 March 1895 Sprague-Oram forwarded a copy of the rules from R & F Keane, Metal founders in Waterford, to the Home Office after that firm had asked the inspectorate about the legality of deducting fines from wages. Upon entering employment workers had to sign a list of rules that the chief inspector thought were "somewhat drastic and that it is worthy of consideration whether the question of their legality should be submitted to the Law Officers." These fines included deductions for whistling, shouting or "unnecessary noise," as well as a 6d penalty for preparing to leave before the bell had rung. Workers agreed to be fined double time for any hours that they were absent without permission. Spoilt work would result in a deduction from the workers' wages of the cost of the material and the time spent working on it.[64] Herbert Gladstone was optimistic that "this case will be partially met by the Truck Bill" but agreed that the workers' lack of recourse in the face of these fines "is bad – no one should be judge in his own case."[65] The Home Office recommended to the company that it eliminate or modify some of the offences in its rulebook.[66]

On 25 March a deputation of female trade union leaders associated with the Women's Industrial Council met with Home Secretary Asquith and Sydney Buxton to request that the Truck Bill be amended to better protect women workers. The women, led by Clementina Black, described the hardships women workers suffered from arbitrary fines and deductions for string, tea and other materials. Asquith, who was called away before all the women had been given an opportunity to speak, agreed with them that a more comprehensive Truck Act would be desirable, but given the late stage in the session there was not enough time. He insisted that it would not be possible to completely prohibit all deductions from wages, as that would "dislocate trade in general." Buxton told the women that many of the unfair deductions that they complained of would be covered by the new bill requiring deductions be "reasonable."[67]

On the 21 June 1895 the divided Liberal Government resigned after losing a supply vote, and the Conservative Party called and won an election in July, and in consequence, Asquith's Truck Bill died. Sir Matthew White Ridley became the new Home Secretary, and shortly after assuming office, he received notice from Sir Charles Dilke of his intention to ask him before the House of Commons whether the government would inquire into the practice of fining workers and making deductions from wages. On 2 September in the House of Commons Home Secretary Ridley assured the Liberal MP that he intended to give the question "full consideration . . . both with regard to the possibility of legislation and the lines upon which legislation is desirable."[68] Indeed, the Home Office began reviewing returns from the inspectors of factories detailing the types of deductions taken from workers' wages in different industries.[69]

The 1896 Truck Act

Ridley's answer to Dilke's question caused unions to lobby the Home Secretary for legislation that would end deductions from wages. On 9 September 1895, at the annual meeting of the TUC, a motion passed instructing the Parliamentary Committee to urge the government to introduce legislation to prohibit deductions from wages, and at the same meeting representatives of the WTUL secured a motion to draw the government's attention to

> the urgent necessity of amending the Truck Act, so as to make it a real protection for workpeople by abolishing all deductions or charges for house rent, work room, conveniences, including motive power, light, tools, or for anything whatever.[70]

On 21 September 1895, the National Union of Shop Assistants, Warehousemen and Clerks wrote to Ridley hoping that he would initiate legislation to prohibit deductions from the wages of workers, particularly "the evil practice of fining employees" and extend the Truck Acts to include shop assistants, warehousemen and clerks. The union described the extensive rulebooks of many establishments that made it so "in a vast number of cases fines are so numerous that it is almost impossible to evade them, and as a consequence, the weekly earnings of shop assistants are seriously curtailed." They doubted whether the practice of fining workers "materially effects discipline," as some of the better run establishments did not fine at all.[71] In September, the Home Office also received requests to prohibit the extensive codes of fines used by Silk Mercers and Drapers in the West End.[72]

By the end of September 1895, Henry Cunynghame produced another *Memorandum on the Amendment of the Law Relating to the Truck Acts, with Appendices*. It was a detailed history of legislative action to prevent truck, including all of the relevant statutes and case law. He also observed that legislating upon this topic was politically hazardous:

> No subject seems to present such difficulties as this. The law is very uncertain, so hardly anyone knows what it is. If a legislator refuses to take up the Truck question he is accused of apathy, if he takes any line short of prohibition of all deductions whatever, he is attacked by the unions. If he proposes total prohibition of deductions, he is met not only by the opposition of employers, but by the opposition of large benefit societies, . . . I am unable to suggest any form of change which will not be strongly opposed in some quarters.[73]

On 13 November 1895, the Home Secretary met with a deputation from the TUC to discuss some of the resolutions passed at the previous annual meeting. The Home Secretary was pressed on deductions from wages for materials and fines, which "in some cases poor girls had . . . inflicted upon them in a shameful way."[74] Ridley conceded that the law was in a very "uncertain" and "unsatisfactory" state. He promised those assembled that "I am giving the subject my best attention." He understood that most of his audience favoured abolishing all deductions, but he thought that "the method proposed by my predecessor was in itself reasonable." While he could make no promises of legislation, "as great as the difficulties are, I have not given up all hope."[75]

By the end of 1895 Ridley and the Home Office were working to acquire a complete understanding of the state of the laws against truck as they applied to fines and workplace deductions. On 20 January 1896 the Home Office once again sought the opinion of the law officers of the Crown with a view to amending the Truck Acts.[76] They asked the Attorney General and the Solicitor General five questions. Were agreements for fines between employers and workmen invalid or offences under the Truck Acts? Was it an offence under the Truck Acts to deduct fines from wages? Could workmen who had deductions taken from their wages by agreement recover those deductions in civil proceedings? Did it legally matter whether fines and deductions were reasonable or unreasonable, or were in excess of the damage done by the employee? Was there any legal distinction under the Truck Acts between fines deducted for absence or lateness, poor workmanship or disciplinary offences?[77]

Solicitor General Robert Finlay was emphatic that the Truck Acts did not interfere with deductions from wages for fines or poor workmanship. He argued that a contract between an employer and an employee that contained provisions for deductions for disciplinary fines or poor workmanship was not directing how a worker was to spend his or her wages but was establishing that if the worker was guilty of certain acts or omissions those wages would not be earned. He did not think that workers could recover these deductions via civil proceedings under the Truck Acts. It made no difference whether the fines and deductions were reasonable or unreasonable or were in excess of the damage caused to the employer, as long as they were consistent with the contract. He also argued that there was no distinction under the Truck Acts between deductions for fines for lateness, poor work or breaches of discipline. Attorney General Richard Webster, who often asserted that deductions from wages not explicitly authorized by sections 23 and 24 of the 1831 Truck Act or section eight of the 1887 Truck Act were illegal, stated that "I concur with considerable hesitation in the above opinion." While he continued to think that there was "fair ground" to believe that his former interpretation was correct, he conceded that "I feel considerable doubt whether such a connotation would ultimately be supported" by the courts. He concluded that "I think legislation is required."[78]

Under growing pressure from Sir Charles Dilke and other Liberals, Ridley and the Home Office were already preparing legislation, though they had no intention of going as far as Dilke, who favoured the abolition of all fines.[79] The inspectors of mines and factories had been instructed to collect information about workplace rules and fines and deductions taken from the wages of workers in a variety of trades. The Solicitor General produced a set of recommendations for reform, and a Home Office committee reported on the most expedient form such legislation should take for passage in the current session of Parliament.[80]

May Abraham reported to the chief inspector that in Northern Ireland she had received numerous complaints from workers about heavy deductions from wages imposed for spoiled work, often in excess of the damage done. This was especially galling to employees because it was frequently not their fault but rather the result of the actions of other workers or the use of poor materials. There was little opportunity for workers to contest these penalties because the particulars of the deductions were not supplied, and they were usually not made until long after the work had left his or her hands. Workers in Northern Ireland often were charged at a higher-than-retail cost for thread, needles and other materials, which were deducted from their wages. The first female factory inspector also reported the oppressive nature of disciplinary fines, which were imposed upon women for laughing, talking, "answering the foreman," sitting at the wrong table or entering through the incorrect door. At one workplace, employees could be fined 2s 6d for "failure to report any breach of rules by another worker." At that workplace a stool was broken after a young woman stood on it to open a window. The foreman was unable to discover which employee had broken the stool, so he fined every female employee 2s 6d for not reporting the breach of the rules. The stool, which cost 1s, yielded £12 9s for the employer.[81] Factory Inspector Gerald Snape confirmed Abraham's findings in Belfast, reporting that workers were not given the particulars of the deductions taken from their wages and often at the end of the week they had little idea what was owed to them. Snape, however, did not believe that deductions for damaged work were excessive relative to the loss to the employer because the materials that weavers worked with were so valuable.[82]

Abraham also took up the cause of shop assistants, reporting that they were subjected to very heavy fines which they found difficult to resist. Abraham observed that in lower end shops, especially drapers' shops, it was "almost universal" to fine shop assistants for the failure to sell goods. If a product that a customer wanted was out of stock, a shop assistant could be fined if he or she failed to sell the customer a substitute. If shop assistants made an error on a bill, not only were they charged for the amount of the error, but had an additional fine deducted from their wages. Many shop assistants also were provided food and accommodation by the employer as part of the "living-in" system, which was considered part of their pay. They complained about the poor quality of the food provided by employers. Abraham doubted whether shop assistants came within the scope of the Truck Acts and was certain that they were beyond the jurisdiction of factory inspectors but suggested that extending these protections in any amending Act.[83]

The Home Office Committee, after examining the memoranda of Cunynghame, the opinions of the law officers of the Crown, the solicitor general's suggestions for reform and the reports of the inspectors of mines and factories, reached the conclusion that the branch of Truck law concerning deductions from wages "is in urgent need of a clearer definition and amendment." The report stated that the current state of the law was such that

> grave doubt whether any deductions from wages, however unreasonable, could in ordinary cases be brought within the penal provisions of the Truck Acts and there are in most cases great, if not insuperable difficulties in recovering the amount of unreasonable deductions by civil proceedings.

As a result of court decisions the Home Office had for some time discouraged inspectors from intervening in cases of fines and deductions that many once thought were illegal. Indeed, the persistence of the belief that fines and deductions from wages were illegal under the Truck Acts, despite a number of court rulings to the contrary, was itself an important reason to amend the law. The committee observed "the law indeed has been popularly supposed to be much more stringent than, on being really tested, it has proved to be."[84]

There was overwhelming evidence that "the most unreasonable fines are enforced with impunity." The reports of female Factory Inspectors Lucy Deane and May Abraham had demonstrated in "cases where trade organization is weak and workers consequently helpless, especially in the case of women and girls, there is a need of greater protection against extortion in the form of unreasonable deductions." An amendment to the Truck Acts was necessary because

> in this, as in so many other social questions, the justification and even necessity of the interference of law with the freedom of contract is to be found in the failure of all other means to make the inferior class of employers conform to the standard which is voluntarily adopted by the better class.[85]

On 20 April 1896, Ridley introduced a bill to amend the Truck Acts, informing the House of Commons that his intent was to deal with "the extreme uncertainty of the present law" by defining the conditions under which deductions could be made from the wages of workers.[86] It was similar to Asquith's bill, except that it separated the three issues of workplace fines, deductions for damaged work and charges for materials and tools. The proposal was narrowly focused and steered clear of more difficult questions, such as deductions for benefit clubs, so Ridley thought "the bill was not controversial, and he hoped that it might be the means of improving and clearing the law."

The bill stated that an employer could only deduct fines from the wages of workers if it was part of a written contract signed by the worker that clearly specified the acts and omissions for which a worker could be fined and the amounts taken. Furthermore, an employer could only fine for acts and omissions that were likely to cause hindrance to the business and the amount of the fine had to be "fair and reasonable having regard to all circumstances of the case." Employers could only make deductions for bad or negligent work if they were part of a signed written contract with the worker, and the amount deducted could not exceed the actual or estimated loss to the employer. The amount taken also had to be "fair and reasonable having regard to all circumstances of the case," and an employer had to provide written particulars to the worker for every deduction. Deductions for tools, materials, light, heat or standing room were subject to the same conditions: there had to be a written contract, the deductions could not exceed the actual cost to the employer, the amounts of the deductions had to be "fair and reasonable having regard to all circumstances of the case," and the employer had to provide the worker with written particulars. Enforcement of this Act was given to inspectors of the mines and factories, who had the power to prosecute violators before magistrates for a maximum penalty of 40 shillings per offence. There was also a civil procedure that allowed a worker to go before a magistrate and recover amounts illegally deducted from his or her wages. Liberal Richard Haldane asked if the bill would apply to shop assistants, and Ridley stated that it would not because their inclusion would delay the passage of this bill.[87]

The labour movement, as well as some Liberal Members of Parliament, were in favour of eliminating fines and deductions from wages altogether. On 4 May 1896, when the bill was read for a second time, Dilke declared that "he was an advocate of the complete abolition of fines and deductions" and hoped that the Standing Committee would be able to amend the bill. Dilke also desired to amend the bill to include shop assistants who "suffered as much as, perhaps, on the whole more than did workmen from the practice of fines and deductions." Shop workers, who experienced fines that were "so vexations as virtually to amount to a system of slavery," deserved relief from Parliament. Liberal Thomas Lough thought that the bill "seemed to permit, rather than prevent, fines and deductions for damaged goods and materials." Many MPs agreed. Liberal MP and retailer H.E. Kearly argued that he had once relied upon a system of fines to enforce discipline and had since abandoned it, finding that "the former system was bad. He was in favour of the abolition of fines altogether."[88] Other MPs observed that many of the phrases in the bill that were open to wide differences in interpretation, such as "fair and reasonable" or "interruption or hindrance to his business."

Some Conservatives defended workplace fines as necessary, including shipbuilder Col. J.M. Denny, who argued that if fines were abolished "there was no way of maintaining discipline unless dismissal were resorted to." Sir James Fergusson asked if there were no fines "what would they do with workpeople who came late in the morning?" W.E.M. Tomlinson insisted that, "the plan of levying small fines had worked well" in maintaining discipline in the mines. Ridley thought that the total abolition of fines and deductions was neither possible nor desirable, but this bill strengthened the protections against ones that were arbitrary or unreasonable. Ridley reassured MPs about the vagueness of some of the key phrases in the bill, as "one or two decisions by the Courts of law would settle the meaning." Given the history of the high courts' interpretation of the Truck Acts, this was precisely what organized labour feared. The bill passed its second reading and then went to the Standing Committee on Trade of the House of Commons.[89]

Groups outside of Parliament expressed disappointment at the failure of the government to abolish fines and deductions from wages. Two days after the introduction of the Truck Bill, The General Committee of National Union of Women Workers passed a resolution that it was "useless for the prevention of the grievances in connection with the deductions and fines made by employers from the wages of their workers" and petitioned that the government amend it so it would be "an effective protection to the worker."[90] These sentiments were echoed by the Manchester and Salford District Women's Council.[91] The Sheffield Table Blade Grinders' Association complained that the bill did not compel employers to "provide the convenience and materials necessary for the execution of their work" and might not prevent the fees for grindery and power.[92] The National Union of Boot and Shoe Operatives had similar objections to the bill, observing that for deductions from wages for machine rent and the use of materials, the bill very much "leaves us where we are." The General Secretary of the organization complained to the Home Secretary that even if the bill passed "women have still to pay for machine rent and steam power to work at the employer's own machine."[93]

Of all the complaints made by workers about the bill, none frustrated the Government as much as the assertion, stated by the Yorkshire Textile Workers Federation, that it "legalizes fines instead of abolishing them altogether."[94] Organized labour objected to the fact that the bill recognized fines and deductions for spoiled work as being legal and regulated them rather than declaring them illegal. The Government's response was always to emphasize that these fines and deductions were *already legal* under the current law, and this bill would at least impose some conditions that employers would have to meet when making them. The Chairman of the Preston Trades Council told an assembly of workers that "the bill would legalize fines" and they would be "better off without it." He complained that some workers in Preston laboured under heavy fines because "employers did not like to give 20s for 20s worth of work" and the bill would not prevent this because "it was not worth the paper it was written on." The workers had little faith in the clause stipulating that the amount of fines be "fair and reasonable" as their experience with the courts told them that "the employer was the only judge of the reasonableness of the fine."[95] The assertion that the 1896 Truck Act "legalized workplace fines," would be persistently made by labour leaders for many years to come.

The Standing Committee on Trade in the House of Commons took up the bill on 19 May 1896 and made some important changes. Home Secretary Ridley won an amendment to the bill that when an employer imposed a fine, he would have to provide the worker with written particulars of the act or omission for which the deduction was made. More far reaching, Ridley, perhaps under pressure from Dilke and H.J. Tennant, also added a subsection to section one on workplace fines that "this section shall apply to the case of a shop assistant in like manner as it applies to the case of a workman," which for the first time brought this class of workers within the scope of the Truck Acts. Conservative MP Charles Renshaw secured an amendment that made it acceptable for an employer to substitute a printed notice listing rules for fines and deductions affixed at the factory entrance or pithead, for a written contract. Renshaw also moved to amend clause three, which dealt with deductions for tools, materials, heat, light and standing room. As it stood, this clause proposed that deductions for materials, the use of tools or machinery, standing room, light heat or "any other thing" could not exceed the actual or estimated cost to the employer and had to be "fair and reasonable" having regard to all circumstances.

Renshaw felt that this was too restrictive and proposed to remove it, as he and others worried that this "might have the effect of preventing fair and reasonable arrangements being made between employer and workman." Attorney General Webster intervened and proposed compromise language requiring deductions for materials and tools to not exceed the cost to the employer and be "fair and reasonable," while deductions for the use of machinery, light, heat or "any other thing" the employer could charge "a fair and reasonable rent or allowance having regard to all circumstances of the case." This compromise language was accepted.[96] Dilke was unsuccessful in his attempt to amend the bill to regulate deductions from wages for payment to employer-run benefit societies.[97]

Employers who opposed the Truck Bill on the grounds that it would interfere with their businesses were aided by the fact that workers in well-organized trades, or those in occupations where fines were less common, also objected to the bill, though for much different reasons. Strongly unionized trades were capable of contesting unfair fines and deductions and feared that this bill would make that more difficult by normalizing and giving legislative endorsement to them. On 3 June a deputation consisting of a number of Lib-Lab politicians representing the National Miners' Federation waited upon the Home Secretary and expressed their opposition to the Truck Bill, which many worried "would seriously interfere with the mining industry." Benjamin Pickard, a Lib-Lab MP representing a Yorkshire district with a high proportion of coal miners, asserted that they "could certainly prefer to have no new bill." Charles Fenwick, a Trade Union Leader and MP, worried that the bill would weaken the ability of organized labour to negotiate over fines and deductions because

> the coal owner might set forth the list of offences for which deductions might be made and post them on the pit-head, and that would be sufficient justification for making deductions other than those agreed upon at present by employers and workmen.

He also thought the term "fair and reasonable" would have to be expensively litigated and would be interpreted in a way unfavourable to workers.[98]

The fact that many Lancashire textile workers opposed the bill because it did not abolish fines and deductions helped Stockport MP George Whiteley, who was the partner in a Blackburn cotton firm, argue that the cotton weaving-industry should be entirely exempt from the bill. The Northern Counties Amalgamated Association of Weavers, representing between 140,000 and 150,000 operatives, objected to the fact that the bill did not abolish fines and deductions and demanded the bill be withdrawn or their industry be made exempt. These petitions, combined with the letters of the manufacturers, greatly strengthened Whiteley's position in the House.[99] In fact, he threatened to bring a motion to postpone consideration on the bill for three months, unless the government exempted his industry. The business of the Parliamentary session, and the fact that neither capital nor labour was very enthusiastic about this bill, made it appear unlikely to pass.[100]

On 27 July 1896, when the Standing Committee on Trade met to consider the bill, Whiteley withdrew his motion to postpone consideration of the measure because the Home Secretary agreed to amend the bill so that it "met with the wishes of the cotton trade." The Home Secretary proposed to introduce a ninth clause to the bill that enabled the Home Secretary, should he find that the protections of the Act are not necessary for workers employed in a particular trade or business, either generally or within a specific region, to grant an exemption from the provisions of the Act for those engaged in that trade. The amendment also stated that the Home Secretary could amend or revoke such an exemption at any time. Every order for an exemption would have to be laid before both Houses of Parliament, and if either House objected, the exemption would be annulled. Dilke objected to the clause because he believed it was a misunderstanding about the current state of the law that divided textile workers in Lancashire, noting "he had received resolutions from Lancashire affirming that this bill would legalize fines and deductions. As a matter of fact, there were no fines or deductions made legal by this bill which are not legal now." Over Dilke's objections the Committee voted to add the clause to the bill.[101] It is unclear whether Whiteley secured an advance promise from the Home Secretary that his industry would be exempt from the bill's provisions, but out of the many applications that came to the Home Secretary for exemptions after the passage of this bill, the only one that was granted was to the Cotton Weavers of Lancashire, Cheshire, Derby and the West Riding of Yorkshire.[102]

Harold Tennant then proposed an amending clause that would extend the jurisdiction of factory inspectors under the 1887 Truck Act to enforce its provisions in laundries and where work was given out by the occupiers of a factory or workshop, or by subcontractors. This clause was added to the bill, and it is important to note that there was a clear legislative intent that outworkers be covered by the protections of the Truck Acts.[103] This is especially important to keep in mind in light of some of the high court cases described in the next chapter.

As the House of Commons went through the clauses to approve them, MP Philip Stanhope of Burnley objected to the ability of an employer to substitute a printed notice of fines for a signed contract. He argued that these operatives objected to an employer being able to simply impose these fines through a printed notice when what they really wanted was the abolition of fines altogether. Whiteley encouraged the House to see this measure in "a practical light," asserting that it would not be possible to secure written contracts with every employee in a workplace. He also stressed the importance of fines and deductions for employers in his trade:

> So far as regarded the cotton trade it ought to be borne in mind that a good deal of the work in the cotton weaving sheds was educational. Children entered the sheds just as they left school, and they had to learn the business, and they did so at the expense of the master. Fines and deductions for bad work were some return to the master for the work that was spoiled by the children while they were learning.

Whiteley's remarks caused derisive laughter in the House. Jonathan Samuel, a Liberal MP from Stockton-on-Tees, explained that from 1831 to 1889 among labourers "the common impression in the country was that fines were illegal," an impression which was upset by *Redgrave v. Kelly (1889)*. Rather than making fines illegal, as labourers across the country wanted, "the employer was empowered by the bill, by simply enumerating the causes of fines to impose any fines he likes on his workmen."[104]

The issue of the posted notice being equal to a written contract continued to be controversial. Conservative MP Lionel Holland, the son of an aristocrat, complained that the clause

> was intended that the mere fixing of a notice should bind the workman to all provisions contained in it, even though they had never come to his knowledge. In other words he was bound by a contract which was not a contract, but a mere fiction of Parliament.

Holland's objections were brushed aside. However, in section six of the bill, Reginald McKenna and Attorney General Webster secured amendments to ensure that all employees received copies of the contract or notice at the time of its creation and that they could obtain a copy at any time free of charge.

Radical Liberal Edward Pickersgill won an amendment to the bill requiring employers to keep a register of deductions, which would record the amount and the nature of all fines imposed on employees. This register had to be available at all times for inspection by the inspectors of the mines and factories. Pickersgill noted that before 1889,

> it was at least doubtful whether fining was not illegal, and since then the practice of fining had occupied a very uncertain and ill-assured position. Now, by the Bill, they were going not only to legalize, but to regularize the practice of fining, and . . . raise the practice of fining to a position which it had never yet occupied on the statute-book.

He argued that a register would provide a safeguard for employees, while at the same time allowing Parliament to collect evidence about the nature and extent of workplace fines. Other MPs agreed that such a register might act as a disincentive for frivolous fines and also demonstrate with evidence that such exactions were not necessary. It became a part of the bill, which then passed its third reading.[105] The bill passed in the House of Lords and received Royal Assent on 14 August 1896.

Reactions to the 1896 Act

In the months after the passage of the 1896 Truck Act unionized workers and some politicians bitterly complained that the legislation "legalized fines" by giving them statutory sanction for the first time. They also expressed objection to the so-called "placard clauses," which they claimed permitted employers to unilaterally impose long codes of rules and fines simply posting a notice in the factory. To some workers this appeared to be the case because in January of 1897 (when the Act came into effect) new lists of fineable offences were posted upon the walls of many workplaces where fines had not been common before, causing workers to associate the employers' ability to fine them with the new Act. In November of 1896, Jonathan Samuel, an MP and former Mayor of Stockton-upon-Tees, told a meeting that "the Truck Act of the past session in a definitive manner legalized fines for the first time." Because the employer posting fines on a publicly posted placard was a legal substitute for securing a signed written agreement with the employee under the Act, Samuel argued "the employer had it all his way and could put what he thought proper on the notice."[106] These arguments were frequently repeated during the following year. Surprised Conservatives defensively argued that there were no fines or deductions from wages that were legal under the 1896 Truck Act that had not been legal before, and in fact, many vague and unreasonable fines that had been legal prior to the Act's passage were now prohibited. The government countered these misapprehensions by publishing a memorandum intended for inspectors of the mines and factories that explained the terms of the Truck Acts. It was laid before the House of Commons and published in the *Times*.[107] The challenge for Conservatives was that while the Act was disliked by labour, many employers considered it a burdensome regulatory interference. Employers' associations in a variety of industries worked with trade unions to flood the Home Office with requests to be exempted from the provisions of the Truck Act by the discretion granted to the Home Secretary under section nine.

In November of 1896 a deputation from the TUC waited upon the Home Secretary and the Chief Inspector of Factories and Workshops to discuss recently passed labour legislation, including the Truck Act. Boot maker W.B. Horninghe attacked what he perceived as the "root cause of the objections of the workers" to the 1896 Truck Act, which was that it had failed to make fines and deductions from wages illegal. He argued making fines legal if they were part of a written contract or a posted notice was no protection at all because employers and workers were not equal parties when entering into contracts. In particular, the workers who were most vulnerable to fines and deductions had very little, if any, input into the terms of their employment. He observed "it is said that men and women voluntarily enter into these conditions – that there is no compulsion – there is none but starvation." He stressed that the uncertain meaning of Act's provisions that all fines and deductions had to be "fair and reasonable having regard to all circumstances of the case" was a doubtful protection given the hostility of the courts toward labour, and "we ask that we shall not be compelled as a trade union to spend £2–3,000 to put the law into action." He hoped for the abolition of fines and deductions because "what we desire is to prevent workers being absolutely robbed of the wages they earn." Home Secretary Ridley responded that he "never pretended that I had it in contemplation under the Act of last session to abolish all fines and deductions," and indeed, he thought many were necessary. He answered that the Act imposed conditions for fines and deductions that protected workers with transparency and the requirement that all exactions made be "fair and reasonable." Ridley and Hornighe were speaking past one another largely because they understood the contract of employment differently. Ridley thought that by forcing employers to clearly state the nature and amount of fines and deductions from wages, workers could make an informed choice about whether or not to accept employment under these terms. Hornighe knew that the workers most likely to experience fines had to accept employment on whatever terms offered.[108]

It is possible that Hornighe and other trade union leaders underestimated the ability of workers to stand up for themselves. In January of 1897 to comply with the new Truck Act many linen manufacturers in Belfast and the surrounding areas began posting placards containing lists of fineable offences and the amounts to be deducted for each violation. In response, as many as 10,000 workers, mostly women, went on strike and held demonstrations protesting the new rules.[109] These workers were supported by Dilke, who wrote to the Secretary of the Belfast United Trades Council declaring that the heavy fines listed on the new placards, at the very least, violated the spirit of the new Truck Act.[110] The employers submitted a modified list of fines to the Ulster Conciliation Board, but the workers rejected this list. Finally, the employers submitted a third list of fines, which were greatly reduced in both the number of offences and the level of fines. The workers accepted this list and won an important victory.[111] Inspired by the stand taken by these workers, a number of other weavers and spinners in the textile trades in Northern Ireland also went on strike in the following months and were able to win similar reductions in the number of offences and the amounts of fines posted on the new placards.[112] At the Island Spinning Company in Lisburn outraged workers actually tore the notices off the walls as they went out on strike.[113] There was additional conflict in Armagh, where employers sought to evade the terms of the 1896 Truck Act by abandoning fines in favour of a "bonus system." Under this system, workers' wages were reduced by as much as 50%, but "if the work is well done" they would receive a bonus that would bring their pay up to its old levels.[114]

In an editorial in the *Pall Mall Gazette*, these strikes were used as examples of the beneficial effects of the 1896 Truck Act. The author argued that before the Act, "the old rules gave employers the power to fine to an enormous extent" because arbitrary fines could be decided by foremen or forewomen on the spur-of-the-moment. Once there was transparency in the rules and penalties, workers could negotiate, and in some cases strike, over their contents, which would then be certain and fixed. The requirement that the employer post all fineable offences meant that an employer who wanted to look respectable in the community would feel pressure to make sure that offences and their penalties looked reasonable on paper, reducing the likelihood of frivolous or excessive fines. He reported that "there are several instances of employers in Lancashire mills who have preferred abolishing fines to putting up the placard."[115] Dilke, who continued to favour the abolition of fines and deductions, nonetheless argued in a speech at Victoria Hall in Hanley that although the new Truck Act was not perfect, it would do much good for workers, particularly shop assistants. He also drew attention to the fact that many large firms had responded to the new legislation by agreeing to abolish workplace fines rather than bother with the requirements of complying with the new Act.[116] Factory Inspector Lucy Deane also found this to be the case, reporting that in 1897 and 1898 she had enjoyed

> the cordial cooperation of some large firms in carrying out the fresh regulations necessitated by the Truck Act. In some cases the questions, after receiving thoughtful consideration, has been solved by the total abolition of the fining system and the substitution of a more reasonable form of discipline.[117]

The 1896 Act had the potential in some trades to cause changes that were favourable to workers. For example, in February of 1896, 2000 chain makers in Staffordshire went on strike because they insisted that under the new Truck Act the excessive deduction employers took from them for providing "blast" was illegal.[118] Despite these gains from the Act, the more pervasive view among workers was than the 1896 Truck Act had "legalized fines." Trades councils in many parts of Britain passed resolutions condemning the new law and made requests to MPs that they support Henry Broadhurst's proposal to repeal the 1896 Act and abolish fines and deductions. John Toyn, president of the Cleveland Miners Association, addressed the Stockton and Thornby Trades Council, calling the Truck Act "a disgrace to a body of gentlemen sitting as legislators" because it "had legalized fines" and could be put into force by the mere posting of a placard.[119] In February 1897 "A Bill to Amend the Truck Acts" was introduced into the House of Commons by Broadhurst and four other MPs. It not only proposed to repeal the 1896 Act but also to make it illegal to form a contract between employer and employee, including shop assistants, for any deductions or payments for fines, damaged work or materials. It did not advance in the House of Commons.[120] This bill had the support of the London Trades Council, which passed resolutions condemning the 1896 Act and pledged all its resources to promote Broadhurst's measure.[121] Robert Hopper, Secretary to the Hartlepool Trade Council, addressed his organization calling the 1896 Truck Act "the most disgraceful ever put on the statute book" and blamed it for at least six recent strikes. His colleague Mr. Allen added the familiar if incorrect refrain that, "the Truck Act had made fines legal." The meeting passed a resolution against the Act and another to write to MPs J. Richardson and Sir Henry Havelock-Allen demanding that they support Broadhurst's bill.[122] Richardson wrote back to the trades council, expressing frustration that "you entirely misunderstand the purport of the Act." Havelock-Allen wrote a similar response, complaining

> it is a great pity that instead of studying the bill for yourself you and your friends should take for granted the assertions of agitators on the radical

side, who are endeavouring to misrepresent the operation of this bill for their own party purposes.

He promised "this is a bill enacted entirely in the interests of the wage earning classes."[123]

Many Conservative MPs appeared to be surprised by the degree to which it was necessary to defend the 1896 Truck Act against the attacks of working people, and this began to manifest in a series of by-elections. In early February 1897, the Conservatives lost a by-election seat in Walthamstow (London) to a Lib-Lab candidate, and nearly lost another in Romford (London). Many attributed these electoral struggles to the reactions of workers toward the new placards of fines going up in workplaces as a result of the 1896 Truck Act. The Conservatives discovered that the Truck Act was "an incredible irritant upon the very persons whose welfare they were intended to serve."[124] One observer noted that in Walthamstow, the Conservative candidate lost the votes of large numbers of railway workers because "the Unionist Party allowed themselves to make legal a system of fines." Shortly before the election the Great Eastern Railway had put up a large list of fineable offences with penalties ranging from 5s to 20s. The editorialist believed that "the said notices caused more bad blood against the Great Eastern Railway Company and the Conservative Party generally than a thousand professional agitators could do."[125] At a by-election in Yorkshire, the *Times* complained that "trade union agitators have played the truck card for all its worth."[126]

In a by-election at Cherstsey, Surrey, the Conservatives were put on the defensive because "considerable use has been made by Liberal speakers of the Truck Act."[127] This argument was particularly effective with "the railway workers, who are greatly incensed at that measure. It is generally believed that the contest will be close."[128] Lord Wakeworth addressed a large crowd at Woking, Surrey, and insisted that

> as to the Truck Act, there had been more misrepresentation and misunderstanding about it than possibly about any Act which had been passed in recent years by the government. The Act was passed not in the interests of the employers, but in the interests of the working classes.

At the same meeting, Jesse Collings, the Parliamentary Secretary to the Home Office, explained the provisions of the new Act in great detail, and promised "that it protected hundreds of thousands of men, women and children from fines and deductions from their wages who had never been protected before."[129] He denounced the demagoguery of "radical agitators" spreading falsehoods about an Act that benefitted wage earners.[130] The Conservatives were able to hold Cherstsey, but it required an unusual effort to overcome the discontent caused by the Truck Act.

An editorialist from the *North Devon Gazette* reported that "The government has not earned the credit that it expected — and perhaps deserved — over its

Truck Act last session." The writer connected worker outrage over the Act with the posting of placards in workplaces and agitators' misleading rhetoric about the legislation, writing

> the unsophisticated British workman connects the imposition of the fine with the Act and is angry with the government (vide the Walthamstow election) and again consequently, the radical orator, in his numerous references to the Act, is not hasty to remove the British workman's impression.[131]

The *Hartlepool Northern Daily Mail* editorialized that "no surprise can be felt at the curious spectacle of Conservative candidates – some of whom have since become Conservative members – promising to vote for the repeal of the Act."[132] The *Pall Mall Gazette* complained that "few expedients in party warfare have been more impudent than the attempt of the radical party to make use of the Conservative Truck Act of 1896 as an election weapon in 1897." In the by-elections in 1897,

> the radicals are carefully fostering the idea that the lists of fines which employers may levy, or may attempt to levy upon their workmen are lists of new fines – fines legalized or called into existence by the Truck Act of 1896.

The article stressed that while the notices were new, the ability to levy fines was not.[133] Whether the radicals were engaged in unfair tactics is debatable, but what is clear is that the 1896 Truck Act was unpopular enough with working people that it was exploited as an election issue.

Shortly after these by-elections, the *Times* described the new instructions from the Home Office to the inspectors of factories and mines, observing that "[i]t is evident that very strange misconceptions exist with respect to the effect of the new Truck Act, and that political capital is being made out of the ignorance of working men on this subject." The author noted that no longer could foremen deduct arbitrary amounts from the wages of workers for fines or damaged work, insisting "workmen are the gainers by these changes." The author was incredulous that Broadhurst had introduced a bill to abolish all fines and deductions for bad or negligent work, calling the ability to damage the property of an employer and not pay for it a "strange class privilege." The author treated receiving one's full wages undiminished by fines or deductions as a privilege, "A few years ago the representatives of workmen in the House of Commons was 'give us equality;' 'abolish privileges.' Today their demand is 'Give us privileges; abolish equality.'" The article praised the efforts of the Factory Inspectorate in enforcing the Truck Acts for having "prevented a great deal of petty tyranny and extortion."[134]

Workers could be forgiven for believing that the 1896 Truck Act had "legalized" fines, because in workplaces across the United Kingdom notices listing fineable offences began going up on the walls. The *Londoner* complained "the new year had scarcely dawned when there appeared upon all our local railway stations an extraordinary placard." The article reprinted much of the long list of fines and stated

> the explanation for these preposterous fines and deductions just now is to be found in the reactionary truck act of the Tory Government . . . this declares that if an employer sticks up a notice that he intends to levy certain fines such notice becomes part of the workman's agreement.

The result of this new law was "thousands of tyrannical fines."[135] Railway companies worked to produce notices that would bring them into compliance with the new Act and sought the advice of MPs Herbert Asquith and Charles Cripps. These lists of fines angered railway workers, because they grouped together a series of broadly defined offences and then listed the maximum fine that the railway could impose for such an offence, retaining the discretion to impose a lesser fine.[136] The outcry from the employees, as well as questions from MPs to the Home Secretary in the House of Commons, brought these placards to the notice of the Home Office. On 23 February 1897, the Home Secretary was asked in the House if he was aware that "several of the large railway companies and some of the printing trades have posted up in their works long lists of new additional fines to be taken from their employees' wages, to which fines the workmen object." The Home Secretary assured the House that these notices did not contain new fines, but to comply with the Act the railways posted the terms of fines that they were formally entitled to inflict. He thought that the publication of these fines might attract criticism and pressure the employer to abolish some of them.[137]

The Home Secretary, however, sought the opinion of the law officers of the Crown as to the legality of the placards posted by the railway companies. The law officers reported that under the 1896 Truck Act the specific amount of the fine, or at least the precise particulars by which such amount could be ascertained, had to be printed. A range of possible fines, or a maximum, for an offence was not specific enough. Mr. Digby of the Home Office informed the railway managers the vague placards that had been widely deployed in the railway industry were not in compliance with the 1896 Truck Act because "for the fine to be good the fine must be certain." On behalf of the Home Secretary he "would suggest that the company should lose no time in withdrawing their lists of fines."[138] The Northeastern Railway Company and the locomotive department of the London and Northwestern Railway Company, decided to abolish fines even before the Home Office letter was sent out on 5 March 1897. The Southeastern and South Western Railway Companies abolished fines shortly after receiving the memorandum.[139] The manager for the London, Brighton and South Coast Railway wrote after receiving the Home Office letter that despite having fined 707 men a total of £61 during the previous year, "I do not think we shall be under any disadvantage by the abolition of fines." The Great Northern Railway's manager also thought "I see no great difficulty in doing away with fines altogether" though he preferred the transition to be gradual.[140] Many of these companies experimented with reprimands, or for accumulated offences, suspension. By January of 1897, the Chair of the Amalgamated Society of Railway Servants grudgingly conceded that the 1896 Truck Act "had some good and some bad qualities."[141] Even though railway workers remained hostile to the 1896 Act for failing to abolish fines, there is reason to think that the legislation contributed to some companies abolishing workplace fines, and others reducing their penalties and making the offences more precise.

In April of 1897 the Wigan District Trades Council published a pamphlet written by Stephen Walsh, a leader in the Lancashire and Cheshire Miners' Federation. In 1906 Walsh would be elected to Parliament for the Labour Party. Walsh opened with the hyperbole that few of the labour laws passed in the reign of Queen Victoria "have been the subject of such angry controversy" or "have evoked such discordant opinions" as the 1896 Truck Act. He argued that this Act went against the spirit and the letter of all previously passed legislation on the subject. Walsh argued the widely held, but incorrect, belief that the 1896 Act had "legalized" fines and deductions. In his analysis of the 1831 and 1887 Truck Acts Walsh ignored the case law that defined them and instead focused upon their text. He adopted the interpretation of the 1831 Act that only those deductions it explicitly permitted in section 23, and were part of a written contract between the employer and worker, was permitted. He conceded that

> we do not for one moment contend that the aforesaid Act has been administered in the spirit in which it was constructed; indeed, it is perfectly well known that it has been violated times out of number, but the intention of the legislation was perfectly clear, viz, to secure the full and undiminished wage to the workers, subject to no deductions except those to which they had of their free will consented.

If one considers cases like *Archer v. James (1862)*, *Redgrave v. Kelly (1889)* and the ruling in the House of Lords in *Hewlett v. Allen (1894)*, then these statements are clearly incorrect, but they were widely believed in the labour movement. Walsh objected to the 1896 Act because he perceived that it gave employers taking fines and deductions from their workers legislative endorsement. He contended that the Act "established a system of fines made easy," giving the employer "practically a free hand in those cases where the workers are disorganized." He also argued that the provision that employers post printed notices of fines "is of itself an inducement and incentive to unscrupulous employers to make the list as large as possible . . . and since the Act, a host of frivolous, but fineable, offences have sprung into existence." He described a recent notice where workers could be fined 2s 6d for throwing orange peels upon the floor, or 1s for taking too long on an errand, or a whopping 5s for coming to work without proper rest. With deductions for damaged work, the employer would be the "judge in the first instance," and it would be very difficult and risky under the Act for the worker to challenge the deduction in the courts and attempt to recover the lost wages.[142]

Employers were not enthusiastic about the 1896 Act either, and many complained about the burdens of contracting with individual workmen or compiling a notice that complied with the terms of the Act. In some cases employers worked alongside trade unions to attempt to secure exemptions from the Act under Section nine. Because the only grounds on which the secretary of state for the Home Department would grant an exemption from the Act was that it was unnecessary for the protection of workpeople, industries that applied for an exemption would in practice require the cooperation of trade unions or at least significant numbers of workers in the trade. The only exemption granted by the Home Secretary was to the cotton weaving industry in Lancashire, Cheshire, Derbyshire and the West Riding of Yorkshire.[143]

The applications to the Home Office for exemptions confirm a number of important points about deductions from wages for fines or damage to materials. One point is that the protections of the 1896 Truck Act were much less necessary for workers in organized trades. Quite frequently workers in trades with strong trade unions had over time developed formal mechanisms for contesting unfair fines or deductions which were simply not available to workers in sweated or marginal trades. For example, the Midland Iron and Steel Wages Board represented 75 firms from Staffordshire, Worcestershire and Shropshire, or about 90–95% of the iron and steel works in those counties. It had been in existence for six years and was composed of equal representation of employees and employers. This board provided a subcommittee of masters and men that could adjudicate appeals from representatives at various works contesting fines or deductions for spoiled work. The Board argued that the 1896 Act would not only be inconvenient but would be much more divisive than the current procedure. Similarly, the Board of Conciliation and Arbitration for the Manufacture of Iron and Steel in the North of England had existed for 28 years, representing firms on the Tees, Wear and Tyne. It had similar mechanisms for adjudicating and resolving disputes about the fairness of fines and deductions and argued that the Act would be worse for all parties than what presently existed. Furthermore, having inspectors or magistrates make judgements about what was "fair and reasonable" would always be inferior to the decisions of "practical men" with experience in the trade. For this reason they asked to be exempt from the 1896 Act. Their appeal for an exemption was rejected.[144] In trades with strong union representation, nagging fines and deductions were less common than in sweated trades. When the Stockton District Committee of the Amalgamated Society of Engineers applied for an exemption from the terms of the Act, Chief Factory Inspector Whitelegge had a lengthy discussion with G.H. Barnes of the Engineers in which the later asserted that "he believed that fines were illegal until the new Act gave them a conditional legality." A frustrated Whitelegge attempted to correct Barnes' misperception.[145]

In cases where workers were less organized, employers sometimes made use of workers' ignorance of the law in order to win support for exemption requests. For example, the Northern Ireland shirt and collar trade, an industry where workers very much needed the protections of the new Truck Act, sent the Home Office a petition of both employers and employees requesting an exemption from the Act. Factory Inspector Deane was dispatched to Northern Ireland to investigate further. She found that the petition of the workers was "valueless as an expression of their desires." It had been signed by only 4,308 of the 12,281 workers employed by the firms it claimed to represent. She found that the method of collecting signatures was to give the petition to foremen or forewomen in the various workplaces who then collected signatures in their departments. While she could not prove explicit compulsion to sign the petition, the implicit pressure was obvious, and she found that "extremely few" of the workers whose names were on the petition could to explain its contents to her. Some foremen and forewomen simply told workers to sign the petition if they "are satisfied with things as they are."[146] Deane's investigation revealed that this misrepresentation was especially important because of the widespread infringements of the Truck Act in this industry in Northern Ireland. She found that in outlying districts workers faced heavy deductions relative to their wages for damaged work. In one case a young woman who earned 1s 3d per dozen shirts made, mixed up a pattern and had £1 4s deducted from her wages, an amount so large that it had to be taken in instalments over several paydays. Deane also found deductions from wages for materials that were in violation of the 1896 Truck Act.[147]

The 1896 Truck Act met with a harsh reaction from both employers and workers, and it was an imperfect instrument for protecting wages. The government, in return for creating rules about the conditions under which employers could fine workers gave fining statutory legitimacy. However, for all its flaws, a dedicated Factory Inspectorate, especially the female factory inspectorate, used the Act as leverage to negotiate and cajole employers to reduce or eliminate fines and workplace deductions. They brought prosecutions for violations of the Act, which generated publicity about the petty oppressions faced by sweated workers. Factory inspectors, through their investigations, prosecutions, reports, letters, speeches and testimony before Parliament about the operation and flaws of truck legislation generated a body of expert knowledge that enabled them and their allies in the labour movement to agitate for new laws that would greatly reduce or eliminate workplace fines and deductions. That will be the subject of the next chapter.

Notes

1 *Report of the Commissioners Appointed to Inquire into the Truck System, Vol. I: Report, Schedules, Supplement* (1871). *Parliamentary Papers* XXXVI (C326-C327), xlv.
2 *Report of Alexander Redgrave Esq., C.B., H.M. Chief Inspector of Factories, Upon the Truck System in Scotland* (January 1887), p. 12, TNA HO 45/9768.
3 "The Truck System in the Mining, Quarrying, and other Industries in Scotland," *The Parliamentary Committee of the Trades Union Congress* (March 1887), London Metropolitan University Archives, TUC Publications, HD 6661; *Hansard Parliamentary Debates Online, House of Commons*, 28 June 1887; *Times*, 29 June 1887.
4 50 & 51 Victoria, c.46, s.9.

5 1 & 2 William IV, c.37, s.2, 24; 50 & 51 Victoria, c.46, s.6.

6 *Lamb v. Great Northern Railway Company (1891)*, 2 Q.B.D. 281.

7 *Times*, 11 August 1892; TNA HO 45 9778 B2165; *Hewlett v. Allen (1892)*, 56 J.P. 822.

8 *Times*, 11 August 1892; Folio 38, TNA HO 45 9778 B2165; *Hewlett v. Allen (1892)*, 56 J.P. 822; *Lamb v. Great Northern Railway Co. (1891)*, 2 Q.B.D. 281.

9 *Times*, 11 August 1892; HO 45 9778 B2165; *Hewlett v. Allen (1892)*, 56 J.P. 822; *Lamb v. Great Northern Railway Co. (1891)*, 2 Q.B.D. 281; *Nottingham Evening Post*, 7 May 1892; *Worcester Chronicle*, 14 May 1892; *Preston Chronicle and Lancashire Advertiser* 14 May 1892; *Glasgow Herald*, 18 May 1892; *Western Gazette*, 13 May 1892.

10 *Hewlett v. Allen (1892)*, 2 Q.B.D. 662; *Times*, 11 August 1892; Folio 38, HO 45 9778 B2165.

11 *Hewlett v. Allen (1892)*, 2 Q.B.D. 662; *Times*, 11 August 1892; Folio 38, HO 45 9778 B2165.

12 *Hewlett v. Allen (1892)*, 2 Q.B.D. 662.

13 TNA HO 45 9893 b17716; HO 45 9778 b2165.

14 TNA HO 45 9893 b17716; HO 45 9778 b2165.

15 TNA HO 45 9893 b17716; HO 45 9778 b2165.

16 TNA HO 45 9893 b17716; HO 45 9778 b2165.

17 TNA HO 45 9893 b17716; HO 45 9778 b2165.

18 Adelaide Mary Anderson, *Women in the Factory: An Administrative Adventure, 1893 to 1921* (London: John Murray, 1922), pp. 10, 14; Mary Drake McFeely, "The Lady Inspectors: Women at Work, 1893–1921," *History Today* 36 (1986):49.

19 Hilda Martindale, *Women Servants of the State, 1870–1938: A History of Women in the Civil Service* (London: George Allen and Unwin, 1938), pp. 51, 57. May Abraham retired because of her marriage to H.J. Tennant and birth of her first child, after which she became May Tennant.

20 Anderson, *Women in the Factory*, pp. 2, 6–10; Helen Jones, "Women Health Workers: The Case of the First Women Factory Inspectors in Britain," *Social History of Medicine* 1 (1988):167–171; McFeely, "The Lady Inspectors: Women at Work, 1893–1921," pp. 48–49; Ruth Livesey, "The Politics of Work: Feminism, Professionalisation and Women Inspectors of Factories and Workshops," *Women's History Review* 13:2 (2004):233–236, 245; Desmond Greer and James Nicholson, *The Factory Acts in Ireland, 1802–1914* (Dublin: Four Courts Press, 2003), p. 200.

21 Anderson, *Women in the Factory*, pp. 6–7; Jones, "Women Health Workers: The Case of the First Women Factory Inspectors in Britain," p. 167; Livesey, "The Politics of Work: Feminism, Professionalisation and Women Inspectors of Factories and Workshops," pp. 233, 243; Martindale, *Women Servants of the State, 1870–1938*, p. 51.

22 Rosemary Feurer, "The Meaning of 'Sisterhood': The British Women's Movement and Protective Labour Legislation, 1870–1900," *Victorian Studies* 31:2 (1988):235–236.

23 Anderson, *Women in the Factory*, p. 7; Jones, "Women Health Workers: The Case of the First Women Factory Inspectors in Britain," pp. 167–168.

24 McFeely, "The Lady Inspectors: Women at Work, 1893–1921," p. 48; Livesey, "The Politics of Work: Feminism, Professionalisation and Women Inspectors of Factories and Workshops," pp. 236, 243.

25 Livesey, "The Politics of Work: Feminism, Professionalisation and Women Inspectors of Factories and Workshops," p. 233; Jones, "Women Health Workers: The Case of the First Women Factory Inspectors in Britain," pp. 169–171.

26 Anderson, *Women in the Factory*, p. 6; Martindale, *Women Servants of the State, 1870–1938*, p. 53.

27 Anderson, *Women in the Factory*, p. 3. Helen Jones argues that the cause of appointing female factory inspectors was also assisted by the retirement of Chief Factory Inspector Alexander Redgrave, who had long been hostile to the idea. Jones, "Women Health Workers: The Case of the First Women Factory Inspectors in Britain," pp. 169–170.

28 Greer and Nicholson, *The Factory Acts in Ireland, 1802–1914*, p. 200; Livesey, "The Politics of Work: Feminism, Professionalisation and Women Inspectors of Factories and Workshops," pp. 248–249.

29 Livesey, "The Politics of Work: Feminism, Professionalisation and Women Inspectors of Factories and Workshops," p. 248.

30 Livesey, "The Politics of Work: Feminism, Professionalisation and Women Inspectors of Factories and Workshops," p. 239; McFeely, "The Lady Inspectors: Women at Work, 1893–1921," p. 49.

31 John W. Ogden to Home Secretary, 11 August 1893; R. Kay to Factory Inspector James Pearson, 18 August 1893, Folio 55, TNA HO 45 9778 B2165.

32 James Pearson to R.E. Sprague-Oram, 7 September 1893, Folio 57, TNA HO 45 9778 B2165.

33 *Times,* 12 September 1892. Folio 4, 26 February 1895, TNA HO 45 9893 b17716.

34 John Ogden to Home Office, 2 September 1893, Folio 58, TNA HO 45 9778 B2165.

35 Albert W. Goble to Home Office, 21 October 1893, Folio 61, TNA HO 45 9778 B2165.

36 Home Office Note. Folio 58, TNA HO 45 9778 B2165.

37 Home Office Note, Godfrey Lushington, 21 September 1893, Folio 58, TNA HO 45 9778 B2165.

38 May Abraham to H.M. Chief Inspector of Factories, 9 December 1893, Folio 64, TNA HO 45 9778 B2165.

39 Flax Spinners and Power Loom Linen Manufacturers Association of Ireland to Herbert Asquith, 9 December 1893, and Godfrey Lushington Home Office Note, Folio 64, TNA HO 45 9778 B2165.

40 South Scotland Chamber of Commerce to Home Secretary Asquith, 15 December 1893, Folio 66. TNA HO 45 9778 B2165.

41 Home Office Notes, Folio 66, TNA HO 45 9778 B2165.

42 *Times,* 12 September 1892; 6 September 1894; Sprague-Oram to Lushington, 29 December 1893, Folio 68, TNA HO 45 9778 b2165.

43 J.A. Hill to Sprague-Oram, 3 January 1894, Sprague-Oram to Godfrey Lushington, 5 January 1894, Folio 69, TNA HO 45 9778 B2165.

44 Case for the Law Officers of the Crown, Folio 66, TNA HO 45 9778 B2165.

45 Case for the Law Officers of the Crown, Folio 66, TNA HO 45 9778 B2165.

46 Home Office Note, folio 72, 23 January 1894, Home Office Note, Folio 73, 24 February 1894, TNA HO 45 9778 B2165.

47 Resolution of the Leeds Tailoresses Union, 16 March 1894, Folio 77, TNA HO 45 B9778 B2165.

48 Factory Inspector May Abraham to Chief Factory Inspector Sprague-Oram, 22 March 1894, Folio 77, TNA HO 45 B9778 B2165.

49 Chief Factory Inspector Sprague-Oram to Sir Godfrey Lushington, 22 March 1894, Folio 77, TNA HO 45 B9778 B2165.

50 Home Office Note, 27 March 1894, 14 November 1894, Folio 77, TNA HO 45 B9778 B2165.

51 *Hewlett v. Allen and Sons (1894),* App. Cas. 383; *Times,* 8 May 1894.

52 *Times,* 26 October 1894.

53 Home Office Note, 19 October 1894; W.H. Johnston to R.E. Sprague-Oram, 17 October 1894, Folio 86, TNA HO 45 9778 B2165.

54 Home Office Note, 14 November 1894; Henry Hall to Godfrey Lushington, 14 November 1894, Folio 87, TNA HO 45 9778 B2165.

55 Henry Hall to Godfrey Lushington, 21 November 1894; Home Office Note, 4 December 1894, Folio 91, TNA HO 45 9778 B2165.

56 For a similar exchange, see: Charles Foster to Herbert Asquith, 3 December 1894, Folio 91, TNA HO 45 9778 B2165.

57 Memorandum on the Amendment of the Law Relating to Truck, Folio 1, TNA HO 45 9873 B17716.
58 Amendment of the Truck Acts: Minute by the Secretary of State, 7 January 1894, Folio 1, TNA HO 45 9893 B17716.
59 Amendment of the Truck Acts: Minute by the Secretary of State, 7 January 1894, Folio 1, TNA HO 45 9893 B17716.
60 *Times,* 17 January 1895.
61 A Bill to Amend the Truck Acts, *Parliamentary Papers* (Bill 154).
62 *Hansard Parliamentary Debates Online, House of Commons,* 1 March 1895.
63 Folio 8, 8 March 1895, TNA HO 45 9893 17716.
64 Sprague-Oram to Undersecretary of State for the Home Department, 20 March 1895, Folio 92, TNA HO 45 9778 B2165.
65 Home Office Note, 1 April 1895, folio 93, TNA HO 45 9778 B2165.
66 Folio 97. TNA HO 45 9778 B2165.
67 *Times,* 13 March 1895.
68 *Times,* 3 September 1895; *Hansard Parliamentary Debates Online, House of Commons,* 2 September 1896; Folio 95 TNA HO 45 9778 B2165.
69 Folio 98 TNA HO 45 9778 B2165.
70 *Times,* 9 September 1895.
71 National Union of Shop Assistants, Warehousemen, and Clerks to Sir Matthew White Ridley, 21 September 1894, Folio 101, TNA HO 9779 B2165.
72 Albert Biggs to Sir M.W. Ridley, 3 September 1895, Folio 99, TNA HO 45 9778 B2165; Albert Biggs to Sir M.W. Ridley, 15 September 1895, Folio 100, HO 45 9778 B2165.
73 *Memorandum on the Amendment of the Law Relating to Truck, with Appendices.* TNA HO 45 9798 17716.
74 *Times,* 14 November 1895; TNA LAB 14 34.
75 *Times,* 14 November 1895; TNA LAB 14 34.
76 Truck Acts, 20 January 1896, Folio 105, TNA HO 45 9779 B2165.
77 Truck Acts, 20 January 1896, Folio 105, TNA HO 45 9779 B2165.
78 Truck Acts, Opinion, 12 February 1896, Folio 109, HO 45 9779 B2165.
79 *Hansard Parliamentary Debates Online, The House of Commons,* 14 February 1896. Home Office Note, 18 February 1896, Folio 110, HO 45 9779 B2165.
80 Folio 1, 26 March 1896, TNA HO 45 9908 B20863.
81 Folio 118, TNA HO 45 9779 B2165.
82 Folio 119 TNA HO 45 9779 B2165.
83 Folio 118, TNA HO 45 9779 B2165. Also see: *The Solicitor General's Suggestions for a Bill to Amend the Truck Acts,* Folio 1, TNA HO 45 9908 B2063.
84 *Amendment of the Truck Acts: Copy of the Report of the Committee,* Folio 1, TNA HO 45 9908 B2063.
85 *Amendment of the Truck Acts: Copy of the Report of the Committee,* Folio 1, TNA HO 45 9908 B2063.
86 *Hansard Parliamentary Debates Online House of Commons,* 20 April 1896; Bill 184, Folio 4, TNA HO 45 9908 B20863; *Amendment of the Truck Acts: Copy of the Report of the Committee,* Folio 1, TNA HO 45 9908 B2063.
87 *Hansard Parliamentary Debates Online House of Commons,* 20 April 1896; TNA Bill 184, Folio 4, HO 45 9908 B20863.
88 *Hansard Parliamentary Debates Online, House of Commons,* 4 May 1896.
89 *Hansard Parliamentary Debates Online, House of Commons,* 4 May 1896.
90 Folio 132 TNA HO 45 9779 B2165.
91 Manchester and Salford District Women's Council to Home Office, 15 may 1896, Folio 12, TNA HO 45 9908 B20863.
92 Folio 11, TNA HO 45 9908 B20863.
93 William Inskep to Sir Matthew White Ridley, 9 June 1896, Folio 25; William Inskep to Henry Cunynghame, 13 June 1896, Folio 27, TNA HO 45 9908 B20863.

94 Folio 31, TNA HO 45 9908 b20863.
95 *Preston Herald*, 6 June 1896, HO 45 9908 B20863.
96 *Times*, 12 May 1896; 20 May 1896.
97 *Times*, 22 May 1896.
98 *Times*, 4 June 1896.
99 *Manchester Courier*, 8 June 1896, Folio 26, TNA HO 45 9908 B20863; *Hansard Parliamentary Debates Online, House of Commons*, 27 July 1896.
100 *Hansard Parliamentary Debates Online, House of Commons*, 15 June 1896, 15 July 1896, 20 July 1896, 21 July 1896.
101 *Hansard Parliamentary Debates Online, House of Commons*, 27 July 1896.
102 TNA HO 45 9918 B22738, A, C, F, E, D, G.
103 *Hansard Parliamentary Debates Online, House of Commons*, 27 July 1896.
104 *Hansard Parliamentary Debates Online, House of Commons*, 27 July 1896.
105 *Hansard Parliamentary Debates Online, House of Commons*, 30 July 1896.
106 *Northeast Daily Gazette*, 24 November 1896.
107 *Times*, 12 February 1897.
108 *Notes from the Deputation of the Trades Union Congress Parliamentary Committee*, 18 November 1896, TNA LAB 14 34.
109 *Ballymena Observer*, 22 January 1897; *Pall Mall Gazette*, 16 February 1897; *Derby Daily Telegraph*, 21 January 1897; *Edinburgh Evening News*, 23 January 1897; *Dundee Courier* 21 January 1897; *The Star*, 2 February 1897.
110 *The South Wales Echo*, 1 February 1897; 2 February 1897.
111 *Pall Mall Gazette*, 16 February 1897; *Hartlepool Northern Daily Mail*, 2 February 1897; *South Wales Echo*, 2 February 1897.
112 *Hull Daily Mail*, 2 March 1897; *Daily Gazette for Middlesbrough*, 2 March 1897; *Edinburgh Evening News*, 25 February 1897; 2 March 1897 *South Wales Echo*, 23 February 1897; *Lancashire Evening Post*, 2 March 1897; *Dundee Evening Telegraph*, 2 March 1897; *Times*, 23 January 1897; 4 March 1897.
113 *Dundee Observer*, 24 February 1897; *South Wales Echo*, 23 February 1897; *Times*, 23 January 1897; 4 March 1897.
114 *South Wales Echo*, 2 February 1897.
115 *Pall Mall Gazette*, 16 February 1897.
116 *Dundee Courier*, 19 November 1896.
117 *Factories and Workshops: Annual Report of the Chief Inspector of Factories and Workshops for the Year 1898, Part II: Reports* (1900), Parliamentary Papers [cd.27], p. 184.
118 *Morning Post*, 2 February 1897.
119 *Hartlepool Northern Daily Mail and South Durham Herald*, 20 March 1897. Similar demands came from the Wigan Trades and Labour Council.
120 *A Bill to Amend the Truck Acts*, 3 February 1897, Parliamentary Papers [Bill 115].
121 *Londoner*, 19 February 1897, p. 6. Nineteenth Century Collections Online. Web 15 January 2015.
122 *Hartlepool Northern Daily Mail and South Durham Herald*, 5 March 1897.
123 *Hartlepool Northern Daily Mail and South Durham Herald*, 15 March 1897.
124 *Hull Daily Mail*, 5 February 1897.
125 *London Evening Standard*, 6 February 1897.
126 *Times*, 11 January 1897.
127 *Edinburgh Evening News*, 16 February 1897; *Shields Daily Gazette*, 18 February 1897.
128 *St. James Gazette*, 12 February 1897.
129 *Times*, 17 February 1896.
130 *St. James Gazette*, 17 February 1897.
131 *North Devon Gazette*, 6 April 1897.
132 *Hartlepool Northern Daily Mail and South Durham Herald*, 16 March 1897.
133 *Pall Mall Gazette*, 15 February 1897.
134 *Times*, 22 February 1897.

135 *Londoner,* 8 January 1897, p. 6. Nineteenth Century Collections Online. Web 15 January 2015.
136 TNA, RAIL 783 82.
137 *Times,* 24 Feb 1897.
138 TNA RAIL 783 82; *Edinburgh Evening News,* 20 March 1897.
139 *Daily Gazette for Middlesbrough,* 15 February 1897; *Reading Mercury,* 13 March 1897.
140 TNA RAIL 783 82.
141 *Times,* 6 January 1897.
142 The Wigan District Trades and Labour Council, *The Labourer and the Truck Act, 1896.* London Metropolitan University Archives, TUC Papers, HD 4928 1897.
143 *Manchester Courier and Lancashire General Advertiser,* 16 December 1896; *Lancashire Evening Post,* 16 December 1896, 8 March 1897; *Times,* 15 December 1897.
144 TNA HO 45 9919 b22738I.
145 TNA HO 45 9918 b22738e. Also see, Folio 7, HO 45 9919 B22738H.
146 TNA HO 45 9918 b22738g; Also see Kevin J. James, "Outwork, Truck and the Lady Inspector: Lucy Deane in Londonderry and Donegal, 1897," in Francis Devine, Fintan Lane and Niamh Puirseil (eds.), *Essays in Irish Labour History: A Festschrift for Elizabeth and John W. Boyle* (Dublin: Irish Academic Press, 2008), pp. 110–111.
147 TNA HO 45 9918 b22738g; Also see Kevin J. James, "Outwork, Truck and the Lady Inspector: Lucy Deane in Londonderry and Donegal, 1897," pp. 110–111.

5 The factory inspectorate and the enforcement of the Truck Acts, 1896–1906

Introduction

The 1896 Truck Act came into effect in January of 1897, and it was the duty of the inspectors of the factories and mines to ensure compliance with its provisions. Chief Inspector of Factories Arthur Whitelegge estimated that the new law impacted at least 250,000 factories, workshops and laundries and over five million workers within the jurisdiction of the Factory Inspectorate.[1] This is to say nothing of miners under the jurisdiction for Inspectors of the Mines or employees in railways and retail shops, who were also covered by the 1896 Act but were not within the jurisdiction of an inspectorate. The female factory inspectorate was more publicly prominent than their male counterparts in enforcing the new law. This was partially because the trades in which deductions from wages for fines, materials and damaged work were most commonly abused were those that employed large numbers of non-unionized, female and juvenile labour. It is also noteworthy that by the late-1890s, nearly all of the violations of the 1831 and 1887 Truck Acts for paying wages in goods involved female outworkers in remote locations, which also fell to female factory inspectors to prosecute.[2] Female and juvenile labour needed the protection of a government inspectorate to fight truck and unfair fines and deductions because they were less likely to benefit from the advocacy of trade unions. In contrast, in 1899 Inspector Wolfe in Birmingham reported that "taking the district all through I think that the Truck Acts are well observed. This may be due to the number of trade union men employed whose officials certainly keep a sharp eye on any malpractices." Other factory inspectors made similar remarks.[3]

The Inspectorate, both male and female, pursued multiple strategies for using the 1896 Truck Act to reduce the levels of fines and deductions experienced by workers. The most common and successful means by which the Inspectorate reduced deductions from the wages of workers was by meeting with employers and using their official status and knowledge to instruct them on the terms of the Act, informing them when their workplace policies were in violation of the law. They sometimes went further by suggesting that employers reduce or eliminate workplace fines and deductions for damaged work, using the example of the well-run modern firms that had abandoned these methods of discipline.

The Factory Inspectorate played a significant role in promoting the belief that efficient managements made little use of workplace fines and deductions from wages.

When employers did not respond to the official warnings about violations of the Act, inspectors initiated prosecutions before magistrates. This was a more costly, time-consuming and risky method of proceeding. Inspectors themselves conducted most of the prosecutions at the local level, but employers were almost always represented by attorneys, who pounced upon technical errors in form and took advantage of the biases of magistrates.[4] The magistrates were often employers of labour themselves, sometimes in the same trade as the defendants, and it was common for them to dislike truck legislation. The factory inspectors secured convictions in 75.5% of the cases that they prosecuted under the Truck Acts between 1897 and 1906, but this conviction rate was considered disappointing because it was lower than the rate under the Factory Acts.[5]

On the positive side, a successful prosecution compelled an employer to alter exploitative policies and deterred others. The reporting of prosecutions also raised public awareness about the injustices inflicted upon marginal, and frequently invisible, workers. Conversely, a defeat in court could undermine the effectiveness of the Act by giving legal endorsement to questionable actions by employers. Furthermore, prosecutions were not always in the best interests of employees, because hearings often required inspectors to reveal which workers had cooperated with them, exposing informants to dismissal.[6] Indeed, when Inspector May Abraham resigned from the Inspectorate, she started the Law Indemnity Fund to assist workers who had lost their employment for cooperating with the Factory Inspectorate.[7]

The stakes of prosecutions grew when parties initiated appeal to the higher courts, which could result in precedents that defined the terms or scope of the Truck Acts. In the history of the case law over the Truck Acts, the higher courts consistently interpreted this body of legislation narrowly. The Home Office was often reluctant to permit inspectors to initiate test cases to define the many vague and uncertain terms that appeared in the 1896 Truck Act, such as "fair and reasonable having regard to all circumstances of the case." Between 1899 and 1910, the work of the female factory inspectorate resulted in five appeals to the higher courts that weakened the effectiveness of the 1896 Act.

Another means by which inspectors assisted in reducing fines and deductions was through the dissemination of their expert knowledge about the experiences of sweated workers and the effects of unfair practices in paying wages. They communicated this knowledge through their annual reports, published articles and testimony before Parliament, much of which was reprinted in the mainstream press. As Chief Lady Inspector Adelaide Anderson later wrote, "The published reports of the Women Factory Inspectors down to 1914 remain an historical record of the depredations on their wages that women suffered and of the pitiful smallness of their average earnings."[8] Female factory inspectors communicated regularly with labour leaders, anti-sweating advocates and politicians. These labour leaders, particularly Gertrude Tuckwell and Clementina

Black, reported violations of the law to the inspectors, while the inspectors sent back information and case studies that were useful to activists.[9]

The advocacy of female factory inspectors was sometimes controversial. On 8 July 1901, Manchester MP William Galloway asked the Home Secretary in the House of Commons

> whether he is aware that His Majesty's lady inspectors of factories and workshops, by lectures, the writing of pamphlets, and advice, take an active part in the work of a body called the Industrial Law Committee, with which is connected a scheme termed the Industrial Law Indemnity Fund, established for the purpose of giving payment to certain informants under the Factory Acts and Truck Acts?

The Home Secretary replied that these activities were consistent with the duties of inspectors, as one of their responsibilities was making the law known to the public. He corrected Galloway, stating that the purpose of the Law Indemnity Fund was not "giving payment to certain informants" but rather helping those who were fired from their jobs for giving evidence in court.[10]

The information generated by the Factory Inspectorate helped advocates for reform to make better-supported arguments. Newspaper reports of the inspectors enforcing the Truck Acts publicized abuses and demonstrated that disciplinary fines and deductions for damaged work, which oppressed the poorest workers, were not necessary for maintaining discipline in well-managed workplaces. In 1906 the government appointed a Departmental Committee to investigate the operation of the 1896 Truck Act and to consider whether or not fines and deductions from wages should be prohibited. The contributions of the inspectors to this committee were considerable, and they inspired reform campaigns to improve the wages of the poorest workers. This chapter will explore the operation and enforcement of the Truck Acts between 1896 and 1914, focusing upon the efforts of factory inspectors, labour leaders, activists and politicians to eliminate truck and reduce the amount of fines, deductions for damaged work and charges for materials that were taken from the wages of manual workers.

Instructing and advising employers about the 1896 Truck Act

Whether on routine visits to factories and workshops or responding to specific complaints, when factory inspectors discovered infractions of the Truck Acts, they almost always first warned employers, giving them the opportunity to comply with the Act.[11] Inspector Anderson explained in 1906 that Truck Act prosecutions "are avoided if we can avoid them, if we can get results without them, as a rule."[12] Instead, "advice, instruction and warning form the larger, and in many ways, the most important, part of our work."[13]

Immediately following the passage of the 1896 Truck Act, inspectors explained its terms to employers and corrected their misinterpretations of its requirements. The official status of the factory inspectors, combined with the support that they had from the Home Office, gave them authority in declaring what fines, or deductions for materials or spoiled work, in posted notices, met the Act's "fair and reasonable" standard. Factory Inspector Rose Squire wrote in her memoirs that when the 1896 Truck Act

> came into force in January, 1897, we women inspectors soon found our hands full in applying it to many cases of hardship brought to our notice. At first the Act was widely misunderstood. Employers thought that they had only to post up a list of the fines and deductions to make them legal, and the workers seeing the lists thought the Act made their position worse. Our first task was to scrutinise their lists and explain that only if the fines and charges conformed to certain conditions would they be legal. . . . Much improvement was effected by persuasion and advice.[14]

Inspector Mary Paterson reported at the end of 1898 that "No more interesting work is among the duties of H.M. Inspectors than the administration of the Truck Acts. This year, as in 1897, it had to be largely giving instructions, securing the removal of objectionable notices of deductions, etc."[15] The vagueness of the Act's terms could strengthen the ability to the factory inspectors to negotiate lower levels of fines and deductions, because employers were not yet sure how the Act would be interpreted by magistrates and the higher courts, and it could be expensive and embarrassing to find out. Whitelegge testified that "it is a very common practice for the employers to come to the inspectors . . . asking advice as to lists of fines and deductions under the 1896 Act." Inspectors challenged objectionable rules or fines, and employers were "often quite ready to receive advice."[16]

Most employers preferred to have a non-confrontational relationship with the Inspectorate and the Home Office, which sometimes enabled inspectors to negotiate reduction in the number and levels of fines and deductions beyond the requirements of the Act. Chief Inspector Whitelegge testified that while Inspectors had conducted 94 truck prosecutions in the first two years of the 1896 Act's existence, he was pleased to report that "much has been affected without recourse to legal proceedings."[17] Between 1898 and 1906, Inspector Lewis of Swansea regularly examined copies of all the contracts and notices issued in his district under the 1896 Act, "and any terms thereof which, in my opinion, were not fair and reasonable, I have had the employers alter, in accordance with the terms of the Act."[18] Inspector Shinner of Norwich reported that while some prosecutions under the 1896 Truck Act had been necessary in 1900, "in most cases it has been sufficient to point out the unreasonableness" of the fines to the employer to bring about a change in policy.[19] Inspectors repeatedly reported success in remonstrating with employers and convincing them to lower or eliminate fines and deductions.[20] Inspector Redgrave stated that his experience of enforcing the Truck Act in the Bristol area was that "in most cases, indeed, I think in almost all, where we have remonstrated and pointed out what should be done, we have arrived at a result satisfactory to the workpeople concerned."[21]

In 1911, Inspectors Anderson and Martindale visited an Irish linen-weaving factory and discovered that every pay period at least two-thirds of the employees had had their wages reduced by an average of nearly 9d from excessive fines. The inspectors met with the owners and recommended better methods of training and supervision and threatened legal proceedings if the situation did not improve. As a result, the percentage of workers in the factory who were fined in subsequent pay periods fell to under 7%. In another weaving shed in the area, at least one-third of all workers faced weekly reductions in wages due to faults in the material they produced, but Martindale and Anderson convinced the employers to refund these deductions.[22]

In 1906 Inspector Squire testified that many times she had found employers' deductions from wages for damaged work to be unreasonable and convinced them to refund them without resorting to a prosecution.[23] Likewise, in 1901 Inspector Gerald Snape reported that in cases "where, in my opinion, money has been deducted illegally, it has been my practice to interview the occupier and get the money returned, and I have contented myself with reporting each case, but not submitting a prosecution."[24] Inspector Redgrave praised the instances where Inspectors convinced employers to change their policies and refund deductions to workers without resorting to prosecutions because

> practical justice is done to an aggrieved person at the very smallest expense all around. We save the man being put in the very awkward position by bringing him up as a chief witness against his employer; and if the employer were fined the workman wold probably get nothing at all, whereas, in the cases I have mentioned, he gets back his money.[25]

Sometimes factory inspectors had discussions with groups of employers in the same trade or region, convincing them to comply with the Act by adopting a uniform set of rules that reduced or streamlined fines and deductions from wages. Anderson wrote in 1905 that "there is a certain advantage to workers when a uniform contract is adopted in a town or trade" because it provided workers with fewer deductions from their wages and also with greater certainty and transparency.[26] The "best" firms were often anxious to reach industry-wide agreements that would prevent them from being undercut by less reputable employers who used deductions from wages to lower labour costs. In 1900, Inspector Paterson convinced an entire district of textile manufacturers in Scotland to come together and create a general contract with uniform rules that reduced the amount of fines and deductions experienced by workers. Paterson noted that the new contracts "replaced a set of contracts of the most primitive and unreasonable type."[27] She had similar success with the National Association of Launderers in 1905.[28] In 1898, Commander Smith, an Inspector in Sheffield, negotiated with the legal representatives of the Master Silversmiths to work out the meaning of "reasonable" deductions for material such as sand, oil, tools, and power.[29]

There were a number of cases where the inspectors convinced employers to abandon fines and deductions altogether.[30] In her memoirs, Anderson wrote that

> [i]n numerous instances where, after careful investigation in a factory by the Inspector of the whole effects of the fining system, the matter was once fully brought to the knowledge of the head of a firm, voluntary abolition of the system followed. Where it was abandoned in favour of better methods of discipline, return to the system was unknown.[31]

In 1901, Inspector Squire was pleased to report that "firms notorious for their long lists of disciplinary fines and the frequent infliction of penalties have in numerous cases abolished fines altogether, and others have reduced them to a few inflicted only for serious acts of insubordination."[32]

When arguing in favour of the elimination of fines, inspectors often made reference to the well-run workplaces that maintained exceptional discipline without the use of fines. As female factory inspector A. Tracey noted, "that fines are not a necessary part of factory discipline is exemplified by the many well conducted places which have never resorted to this disciplinary measure, and the others which have abandoned it."[33] Factory inspectors repeatedly reported that in workplaces that had proper training and supervision, disciplinary fines were unnecessary.[34] Clementina Black agreed, writing, "I think it is always the mark of a bad employer to have too much fining; it is the mark of a mismanaged factory."[35] The Factory Inspectorate played a significant role in spreading information in the public discourse that only incompetently managed firms required fines to maintain discipline.

Squire also stressed to employers that fining workers actually contributed to poor workplace discipline, arguing,

> It is probable that the system of fining itself creates the need which it supplies. Where fines are attached to breaking rules, an employee, it seems, feels that a certain amount of lawlessness or carelessness can be bought for small sums.

In contrast, "where no fining exists, each worker knows that her situation depends on obedience and good behaviour."[36] Inspector Deane similarly testified that workers had told her that being fined did not make them feel the need to reform their behaviour to keep their job but rather that "I have paid for it, I am squared with him."[37] This point was raised by many labour leaders.[38]

Squire assured factory owners that "where the employer has allowed himself to be persuaded to abolish fines, his verdict, after a trial, has so far always been favourable."[39] Every time that a large workplace agreed to abandon fining workers, Inspectors used that example to convince others to follow. In 1900, Squire convinced one of the largest laundries in the United Kingdom, which had previously maintained discipline with "innumerable fines . . . for every conceivable neglect or default," to abolish fines and deductions. The new manager was thoroughly pleased with discipline and punctuality under a non-fining regime.[40] For the next two decades, factory inspectors continued to emphasize that "in all such cases where such fines have been abolished, discipline has been improved thereby, instead of deteriorating."[41] Inspectors, such as Inspector McCaghey of Bradford, observed that employers who used fines as a means of discipline often lost the competition for quality workers: "it is significant that firms who get a reputation for fining, always have the largest number of looms standing for want of weavers."[42] In 1906, another factory inspector from Bradford reported that

> [c]uriously enough, the best firms where employment is good, and who have quite a command of labour, seldom, or never, inflict any fines whatever, and state that they are not needed; whilst others, even where labour is scarce, make a general practice of fines, and allege it would be impossible to conduct their business without doing so.[43]

The passage of the 1896 Truck Act encouraged some firms to abolish fines and deductions because it increased the bureaucratic burden of imposing them.[44] Under the terms of the Act, fines and deductions had to be part of a contract or posted notice that specifically described each deduction and its amount. Employers had to record these deductions in a register that was regularly inspected by inspectors and supply written particulars to the fined workers. In 1898, Factory Inspector Jackson of Walsall reported that "I am pleased to say that many employers, when they found that deductions were illegal without a written and signed agreement or notice exhibited, decided to discontinue to make deductions."[45] In 1901, reflecting upon the first five years of the operation of the Truck Act, Inspector Squire stated that "the very fact that each matter for fining must be subject to a definite notice, that the particulars of each sum obtained from the employee must be recorded, and a receipt rendered for the amount, places a check upon the fining system."[46]

Some respectable factory owners were embarrassed to post notices of fines and abandoned fining workers. Inspector Garvie, describing the Act's requirements of a posted notice of fines and deductions, observed that in the Halifax area "[a]mong the better class of works one would think such provisions would have very little effect, but indeed they have, for very many masters, sooner than publish a notice relating to fines, have quite abolished fines."[47] Inspector Lewis reported that his regular inspection of the registers of fines and deductions in his district was "a very salutary check upon the tendency which prevails in certain works to aggravate trivial offences, and impose fines and deductions out of all proportion to the . . . delinquency."[48] Simply knowing that they were being watched made many employers behave better.[49]

Inspectors also had discussions with employers about the legality of deductions for materials under the 1896 Truck Act. Section three of the 1896 Truck Act stated that employers could not charge workers for the "use or supply of materials, tools or machinery, standing room, light, heat, or in respect of any other thing to be done or provided by the employer in relation to the work or labour of the workman unless" it was part of a written contract or a notice, the sum deducted from the wages did not exceed the actual or estimated cost of the item or service provided, and the deduction was "a fair and reasonable rent or charge."[50] Inspectors were sometimes able to use section three to convince employers to lower or abandon deductions for materials. In 1903, Inspector Paterson reported:

> I have investigated numerous complaints of heavy deductions for materials to be used in work, needles, cotton, silk, power, etc. The custom of making these must always, I believe, be a source of complaint, and in the matter of power especially, where it is not possible to arrive at an exact charge. . . . With much investigating and discussion I have succeeded in some cases in having the charges reduced and I am hoping that . . . many employers will adopt the system (an equally common one) of making no such charge.[51]

Although in many parts of the country these deductions were gradually disappearing because of pressure from organized labour and changing industry standards, some employers continued to insist they were necessary to prevent waste and fraud.[52] Anderson and other inspectors disagreed, believing that better supervision and training could be just as effective in preventing waste.[53]

The annual reports of the factory inspectors are filled with descriptions of Inspectors negotiating the reduction or elimination of charges for materials, heat, light, gas, or services without recourse to prosecutions.[54] In 1898, Inspector Deane found that a laundry was making deductions for gas used in heating irons at a rate that was well in excess of the cost to the employer. She instructed the employer to reduce the deductions, and he complied.[55] In 1906, Inspector Snape convinced many large boot manufacturers in Bristol to reduce deductions for "grindery" and supplies, which had been much higher than the real cost.[56] In 1906, Inspector W.J. Law of Manchester found that machinists in a factory had 4d per week deducted from their wages for power, even though the weekly wages of employees varied from 4s a week to 28s. The inspector wrote that "on remonstrating to the occupier that a graduated charge would be more equitable, he readily adopted the system."[57] When a Birmingham inspector found that workers were having deductions taken from their wages for "sanitary conveniences" he had "a remonstrance with the occupier to put matters right."[58] In her memoirs Anderson describes how it was not uncommon for employers to deduct sums from the wages of female employees to pay another worker to clean the factory. Even worse, in the many instances the employer deducted more money from the employees than he paid to the worker who cleaned the factory, turning a tidy profit.[59]

Female workers, who were less likely to benefit from trade unions, appeared to suffer disproportionately from these deductions. Inspector Jackson reported that in his region "the worst of all these deductions is that they are almost always from women workers only, the men who receive at least double the wages of the women do not a pay anything."[60] In 1905, Inspector Ireland found that at a firm in Norwich female employees were charged 50% more than their male counterparts for "standing room," even though male employees earned triple the wages. The inspector demanded an explanation from the employer, who replied that "the men would kick against any greater reduction, but the women submitted." At the insistence of the inspector, the level of the deduction made from women's wages was immediately lowered to the same level as the men.[61] Inspector Vines intervened in a case where an employer deducted 7d from every female employee earning over 4s per week for providing a cup of tea per day. When the inspector asked the employer about this arrangement, he countered that "this system of tidy service was an assistance in the formation of good manners and refinement." Vines was unmoved and the employer agreed to reduce the deduction.[62] In her memoirs, Rose Squire wrote that

> [a]s the provisions of the Act became well known the women and girls in clothing factories became very careful in their scrutiny of any fresh contracts requiring them to pay for their sewing cotton. The employees from different firms would come to my office to ask whether in regard to such and such prices it would be right that they should sign a contract submitted to them. In most cases the charges proposed needed reduction.

When 15 women were dismissed from a factory for refusing to sign a contract that contained excessive deductions for materials, they approached Squire. The Inspector called upon the employer and informed him that his charges for cotton and needles were greater than their cost. To avoid prosecution the employer agreed to lower the charges and reinstate the women.[63]

The reports of the factory inspectors repeatedly asserted that charging workers for supplies and heat, light, and standing room was a holdover from an earlier age and not something practiced by advanced, modern firms. In Walsall, Inspector Jackson scrutinized deductions for materials described in notices and contracts, and by 1900 he was able to inform his superiors that it had "resulted in many manufacturers giving up the practice of deducting for 'shop room' and gas, and it is not likely that once having been given up, these deductions will again be reimposed."[64] By 1901, Inspector Wright of Nottingham treated deducting the cost of materials from workers' wages as a badly outdated practice, observing, "I regret to say that the 50 years behind the time system of employing persons and deducting from their wages for needles, thread, machine hire, oil, etc., is still carried out in some few factories in this district."[65] In the same year, Inspector Squire asserted that "I find . . . the charges for materials, tools (including needles), room, power, gas, etc., either gone altogether or reduced to their lowest figure."[66] By 1905, many inspectors reported that the practice of charging workers for shop room and materials "is gradually dying out."[67]

Squire complained about the limitations of the 1896 Truck Act for dealing with the injustice of deductions taken from wages for materials that went into work. While the provisions of section three helped to prevent fraud through gross over-charging, it did not change the fact that in some trades workers were charged for materials that went into the product that the employer then sold for a profit. Squire observed that regardless of posted notices,

> [T]he piece work price for which she toils includes the cost of these, and only what remains when this is paid is the reward of labour. The majority of piece workers . . . do not realize this, and are not able to estimate the piece work prices offered them in their actual value.

This meant that these workers experienced "disappointment and vexation when week after week deductions of from two to five shillings are made from wages of between five and fifteen shillings."[68]

While discussions with employers could result in employees keeping more of their wages, there were limits to the ability of inspectors to convince employers to reduce "unreasonable" deductions when the employer was determined to evade the Truck Acts. In some contentious cases, the intervention of the inspector could actually leave the employees worse off. In the fall of 1897, Inspector Squire investigated complaints from workers about heavy deductions for damaged work at Messrs. Black and Co., worsted spinners of Bradford. The firms to which Black and Co. supplied worsted yarn sometimes weeks after the delivery sent the work back with a claim for compensation due to defects in the yarn. Black and Co. would then deduct the entire amount of compensation demanded by the clients from the female spinners, even though the defects were not always their fault. These deductions could represent between one and two weeks' wages, which was taken from their pay in weekly instalments of 6d until the amount was repaid. In a particular case, five women had experienced very large deductions from their wages for damaged work.[69] Inspector Squire felt that these deductions were not "fair and reasonable having regard to all circumstances of the case." She argued that the "circumstances of the case" that had to be considered were the smallness of the wages earned by the spinners, their young age, the risk of faulty work, the time that elapsed between the damage and the deduction, and the custom of other firms in the region.[70] Squire investigated the trade in Bradford and found that no other firms fined for bad work.[71]

Because Messrs. Black and Co. had failed to give the five women receipts for the deductions at the time they were taken, they had undeniably violated the law and could be prosecuted under the Act. Using this leverage, Squire convinced the firm to refund the entire amount of the deductions taken from the women. However, Black then gave each of the girls who had deductions refunded a written notice that each of their wages would be reduced by 6d per week going forward. He privately informed Inspector Squire that "he will do this to recoup his loss without being troubled by the Truck Act, adding that if any further bother is made he will dismiss the girls."[72]

Squire further investigated the firm for grounds upon which a prosecution could be based, but she had to meet with female employees in their homes rather than the factory; she wrote to Inspector Anderson:

> I abstained from visiting the factory and questioning the girls there, as I was afraid lest they should suffer still further in consequence, being told that any person whom I addressed in the mill was to be cross questioned by the employer.[73]

After consulting with the Treasury solicitor it was determined that an action under the Truck Act against Black would be unlikely to succeed, and the Home Office feared that "an unsuccessful prosecution would only serve to advertise this method of evading the Act."[74] The strongest argument against making workplace fines illegal was that employers would simply reduce wages, suspend workers, or fire them for frivolous mistakes for which they previously would have been fined. Inspector Deane thought that "this method of evading the law is, however, a striking illustration of the helplessness of the work woman in the matter of the conditions imposed on her in her (so-called) 'free' contract with her employers."[75]

Organized labour had been certain that the passage of the 1896 Truck Act would contribute to an increase in the number and level of deductions from wages by normalizing them through weak regulations. There is an abundance of evidence, however, to suggest that in a large number of workplaces, the opposite occurred. Employers who were desirous of having a positive relationship with the Factory Inspectorate and the Home Office quite often voluntarily adopted new rules and procedures, and, in fact, many went further than the law required and abolished these deductions altogether. Firms that followed this second path increased the stigma upon employers who continued to deduct from the low wages of employees. The work of inspectors convincing employers to make less use of disciplinary measures that took from workers' wages led to a change in public norms. Within ten years of the passage of the 1896 Truck Act, there were a large number of men and women who felt that the government should prohibit employers from taking any deductions, and still more who felt that at the very least it should be even more strictly regulated. The 1896 Truck Act is sometimes described as a failure because when prosecuting offenders inspectors experienced high-profile defeats before magistrates and the high courts. However, the greatest victories achieved under the 1896 Truck Act were those that were won outside of the courtroom.

Prosecutions under the Truck Acts, 1896–1906

Often, factory inspectors were required to prosecute employers who had either ignored warnings or so flagrantly violated the law that it was necessary to set an example. The majority of prosecutions at the local level were conducted by the factory inspectors themselves before justices of the peace, magistrates or sheriffs.[76] This was sometimes challenging because few factory inspectors had formal legal training, and employers often hired attorneys to defend themselves. Some inspectors found that the complexity of the Truck Acts, and the often-confusing case law that defined their terms and scope, increased the difficulty of prosecutions.[77] Chief Inspector Whitelegge defended the abilities of factory inspectors as prosecutors, noting that through experience they developed expert knowledge of the Truck Acts, the relevant case law and their operation in practice. He testified that "the inspector being in constant touch with the Acts, becomes familiar with every detail that is likely to arise in discussion."[78] Despite having had no previous legal training, during her first year, Factory Inspector Abraham conducted 80 prosecutions under the Factory and Truck Acts and enjoyed a high rate of success.[79]

Most factory inspectors lacked formal legal training, but so did most justices of the peace, magistrates and sheriffs. Because so much of the inspectors' work involved the Truck Acts, their knowledge of this body of law was often superior to that of the magistrates. In her memoirs, Squire complained that when prosecuting under the Truck Acts

> my task was not in these cases made lighter by the fact that so often they had to be argued before a provincial bench of justices of the peace unversed in legal subtleties and sometimes with an undisguised bias in favour of the defendant or of the practices under discussion.[80]

Many magistrates were of the opinion that cheating workers out of their wages was not a serious offence.[81] Inspector Shinner of Norwich complained that when prosecuting truck cases "the word 'technical' is a favourite one with defending solicitors pleading for small fines. It alternates with or is in addition to the word 'trivial' and the alliteration is no doubt attractive – it is especially liable to be pleaded in truck cases."[82] The perception that violations of the Truck Act were not deliberate harms done to workers but rather a failure to keep up with technical regulatory burdens often led to magistrates using their discretion to impose small penalties, which lessened the deterrent impact of the conviction.[83] Anderson complained that "much will be achieved, however, when local magistrates have learned that conviction and penalties must follow on every case proved in court of infringement of the law against truck."[84]

Another difficulty faced by factory inspectors when bringing prosecutions was that the language in the 1896 Truck Act was maddeningly vague. It contained a number of undefined phrases, most notably "fair and reasonable having regard to all circumstances of the case." Whitelegge stated that while his inspectors won around 75% of the cases brought under the 1896 Act, "the number of cases we lost is considerable, and much larger than the proportion under the Factory Acts." This was because

> the Truck Acts, so far at least as the cases we take into court are concerned, deal largely with matters of opinion as to whether a given charge . . . is

reasonable in all the circumstances of the case, and what circumstances should be taken into account.[85]

Inspectors won 97–98% of the prosecutions that they brought under the various Factory Acts, so the rate of success that they had under the 1896 Truck Act was disappointing.[86] The average penalties for convictions under the Truck Acts were lower than those under the Factory Acts as well.[87]

When female factory inspectors conducted prosecutions before magistrates it attracted attention from contemporaries. Although women had acted on their own behalf in British courts for centuries, it was unusual for a woman to conduct an official prosecution on behalf of the state. The press sometimes treated female factory inspectors in the courtroom as a curiosity and expressed surprise at their success in the courtroom. Anderson, in her memoirs, quoted a "typical press comment" on a prosecution by a female factory inspector, which read,

> A small sensation was caused in Police Court when for the first time a lady advocate appeared. . . . She made her statement with such clearness and ease as any more accustomed advocate, and as the facts and laws were alike indisputable, conviction necessarily followed.[88]

The complexity of the law, the employers' use of attorneys, the hostility of the magistracy to the Truck Acts and sexism sometimes combined to make these prosecutions challenging for female factory inspectors. On 1 May 1900, Inspector Paterson brought four charges under the Truck Acts against Henry Reid and Sons of Dunfermline, Scotland, for paying part of their workers' wages in table napkins and linen cloth. In preparing the informations (the formal charges) for the case, she used a template that was originally created for violations of the Factory and Workshop Acts, but she had not sufficiently altered this template; the attorney for the defendants objected to the error in form, and the case was dismissed. On 19 May 1900, Paterson came back to the sheriff with new informations against the same defendant, but once again it was dismissed upon technical grounds. During the hearing, the Sheriff Gillespi scolded Paterson for bringing the case without first having had a discussion with the employer: "He would say to Miss Paterson that she should bear in mind that the Home Office contemplated that there should be a friendly remonstrance in the first instance, and she had not asked for any explanation."[89] Paterson assured the Sheriff that she was acting with the full authority of the Chief Inspector of Factories and the Home Office. After delivering his ruling, the Sheriff announced that

> it was really not fair on the part of the Law Officers of the Crown to make Miss Paterson fight their battles. He thought the case was one of great importance, and the Lord Advocate or some other official ought to revise the complaint.

Inspector Paterson fired back that "she had had to do with a great many more cases under the Truck Acts. Only once had the Lord Advocate appeared for her, and he lost the case in the high court which she had won in the Sheriff Court." Chief Inspector Whitelegge was not amused with Gillespi, and he wrote to the Home Office about the possibility of a third prosecution of the firm. He expressed irritation that Paterson had been "harassed by hostile and occasionally unfair criticism" from the Sheriff and insisted, "It is not to be understood ... that employers are allowed to disregard the Acts until an inspector has first discovered the irregularity and warned the offender in every case."[90] The Home Office corresponded with the Lord Advocate, who advised against a third prosecution.

A female factory inspector prosecuting a case under the Truck Acts was also criticized in Ireland in 1904. Inspector Squire charged the Greenmount Spinning Company with deducting fines for lateness from the wages of Mary Cooney and Catherine Travers without having a written contract or a posted notice authorizing them. Irish nationalist and King's Counsel Timothy Healy represented the defence. He told the magistrate that "[t]he Great Home Office sent over their Lady Inspector to prosecute the firm. It was too absurd. It was an example of the English method of Government in Ireland." Healy raised no legal issues during the hearing and in fact conceded that there had been "a technical breach of the regulations." Yet he objected to Squire's lack of legal training, arguing,

> [U]nder ordinary circumstances they might expect to have the Attorney General represent in such a case. However ably this lady from the Home Office construed their rules, they were entitled to have such a case conducted not only by a lady who knew the Factory Acts, but by a person who knew the law and legal procedure.

Why Healy felt the need for a prosecuting attorney is unclear, because the firm had very obviously violated the statute. The magistrate agreed with Healy, stating that it would be "a great advantage to the lady inspector, and to them all, if the Home Office provided proper legal assistance."[91]

The cases prosecuted by the Factory Inspectorate under the Truck Acts between 1896 and 1906 provide important insight into the hardships experienced by workers from the continued existence of the payment of wages in goods, as well as excessive deductions from wages for disciplinary fines, damaged work and materials. They also illuminate the complex relationship between workers, unions, the regulatory state, and different levels of the law. The prosecutions that inspectors brought under the Truck Acts, even unsuccessful ones, could have a very large impact on the conditions of work and the take-home pay of workers. The investigations into these cases were reprinted in annual factory reports, were recounted in testimony before Parliamentary Committees and were part of a growing body of expert knowledge about the injustices experienced by sweated workers. The cases taken up by inspectors were widely reported in the press and highlighted the ways in which marginal

workers were cheated out of their wages and the inadequacy of existing legislation to protect them. The reports of these cases were seized by labour leaders
and anti-sweating advocates to generate momentum for new legislation to protect vulnerable workers in the years just before World War I.

Prosecutions under the Truck Acts: the payment of wages in goods and *Squire v. Sweeney and Sons (1900)*

The prosecutions of the factory inspectors under the Truck Acts after 1896
demonstrate that truck was not extinct in Great Britain. As Anderson noted
in 1898, "It is interesting to note that the duty of enforcing the new Truck
Act, during the routine work, has resulted in bringing under our notice the
gross infringement of the older Truck Acts."[92] Female members of the Factory
Inspectorate discovered that many low-paid female outworkers in Northern
Ireland, Somerset, Cornwall and elsewhere were paid wages in goods.[93] From
1897, the female factory inspectorate worked to stop employers in County
Donegal, Ireland, paying the wages of female outworkers in tea, sugar and groceries. At the centre of this effort was a nine-month investigation and prosecution of John Sweeney and Sons for violations of the Truck Acts.[94] This struggle
required seven sittings before local magistrates, as well as three trips to the Irish
Queen's Bench Division, and resulted in a damaging precedent for the Truck
Acts in Ireland. Sweeney and the other local elites in the Dungloe area fought
this prosecution with great determination. Squire wrote of the case: "Every
artifice which the Irishman's wit could devise was employed to prolong and
complicate the legal process, and to avoid conviction."[95]

This prosecution by the Factory Inspectorate challenged a number of long-
standing practices and hierarchies in the region. Many of the most powerful
men in this remote locality were implicated in truck, and the enforcement of
the Truck Acts undermined their economic interests. Local elites claimed that
the enforcement of these laws potentially undermined the economic development of the county, and they used their power in the magistrates' courts and
the economy to resist the Inspectorate.[96] There was also a nationalist dynamic
to the resistance, as English factory inspectors were enforcing a law passed by
the Westminster Parliament that had not applied to Ireland until 1887. This
prosecution also upset gender hierarchies. The employees paid in goods were
women, who were expected to be untroublesome and deferential, and their
case was taken up by a female factory inspector, who challenged male employers. The language of local employers and magistrates reveals that they were
clearly uncomfortable with the authority and confidence of the factory inspectors. Inspector Whitelegge praised Inspector Squire in his annual report for
withstanding an unprecedented level of obstruction from local elites, noting,
"[N]othing could exceed the courage and ability displayed by the Lady Inspector in circumstances of altogether exceptional difficulty."[97]

In 1897 Inspector Anderson travelled to Ardara in Donegal to investigate
reports of women being paid wages in "inferior goods" and was surprised by

the prevalence of the truck system, reporting, "A fortnight's residence as a private individual in the country enabled me, beyond my expectations, to gauge the extent and deep rooted character of the system of payment in kind."[98] In northwest Ireland many poor families relied upon credit extended by shopkeepers in order to survive. These shopkeepers, or "gombeen men," also acted as agents for larger Belfast, Londonderry, or Glasgow firms, providing work to local women to do in their homes. This work might include knitting wool into socks or stockings or embroidering linen handkerchiefs or clothing. The shopkeepers were paid very low commissions for these items by the larger firms so it was essential to keep labour costs low. As a result, the women workers were paid almost entirely in goods.[99]

The inspectors found that though "bitter were the complaints [that] . . . reached the government on the peasants' behalf, . . . they themselves were so terrified of the employers," who might deny them credit at the shops or future employment.[100] Inspector Deane later remembered: "Women were terrified; they told me of things but I could not easily get them to give evidence against any particular contractor."[101] The fear of reprisals from the shopkeepers was understandable, because in rural districts they were powerful men who were not afraid of the Inspectors:

> The manifest sense of security . . . on the part of the law breakers – who by their shops, their inns, and their proprietorship of the cars, represent the wealth and carrying power of the local community, and by their connections through marriage with the priests' and the magistrates' families, and in some cases even their positions as magistrates themselves, represent the order of the community –was almost warranted by the difficulty of the task of bringing home the offences.[102]

Inspector Squire complained that

> the Government was aware of this state of things and desired to enforce the Truck Acts in the district, but the people were so terrorized by the great men of the district in whose power they were that no sufficient evidence could be obtained on which to base prosecution.[103]

Factory Inspectors Lucy Deane and Mary Paterson were dispatched to Ireland, with Paterson going undercover to gather evidence, and in December of 1897, with the cooperation of some of the outworkers, they successfully prosecuted one of the shopkeepers, Mary Boyle, on four counts of violating the Truck Acts. She was fined £40. As many had feared, the workers who had assisted the Inspectors lost their employment, and it was only through the Factory Inspectorate and its allies that were they able to obtain financial assistance and new jobs.[104]

After receiving further reports of truck in Donegal, Squire was sent to investigate, and if necessary, initiate additional prosecutions. Squire had to gather evidence from workers but worried that "the reluctance of the Irish peasantry to accept the assistance of an official of the government to free them from oppression, and their dread of being stigmatized as an informer by their neighbours, makes it impossible to obtain any information." Squire determined that the best way for her to gather evidence was to go undercover, because "they are, however, quite ready to talk freely of their grievances and troubles to a sympathetic English visitor."[105] Squire arrived in Dungloe in September 1899, and for three weeks she resided in a hotel posing as an English tourist, talking to workers and gathering evidence of violations of the Truck Acts.[106] In her memoirs she claimed that the local fishermen "out of their own imagination" spread the rumour that she was an author doing research about the area for a novel.[107] Squire bicycled through the countryside and met with women "who were always ceaselessly knitting." She confirmed that "[t]here was no doubt about it, the whole district seethed with discontent at the truck system and groaned under the tyranny of the gombeen man."[108]

Squire discovered multiple offenders against the Truck Acts but identified the firm of Sweeney and Sons of Burtonport and Dungloe as a persistent violator.[109] In prosecuting this firm, Squire was challenging one of the area's powerful families. John Sweeney, the owner of the firm, was a county councillor, and his father James was a local magistrate. Sweeney and Sons were grocers and publicans but also contracted with larger Belfast firms to deliver knitted hosiery and socks. They distributed this work to women who completed it in their homes and were paid largely in groceries, frequently tea.[110] Squire found that "in all cases they received as payment tea and other groceries. No money passed at all, and they could not obtain money." She also argued that the tea was of poor quality and overpriced.[111] Squire prosecuted Sweeney and Sons for paying a female outworker who knit woollen socks with a ticket that was then used to purchase groceries in their shop in October 1899. Sweeney denied that the worker had been compelled to use his store and claimed that the people of the area were being "harassed" by Squire. Local elites opposed this Truck Act prosecution, believing that these employers were doing a service by providing work in a poor district.[112]

A local magistrate, Anthony O'Donnell, attempted to dissuade Squire from prosecuting the shopkeepers. Squire refused, but a persistent O'Donnell stormed into the room where she was meeting with witnesses and demanded to hear their stories. Squire wrote that

> as the girls were terrified and became hysterical, I went out, calling to the girls to follow me, but as they attempted to do so he sprang up, put his arm across the doorway and flung the girls back into the room, shouting at me "You go to hell," and slammed the door in my face,

leaving the witnesses alone in the room with the magistrate. Squire had the landlord of the hotel assist her in re-entering the room and ejecting the magistrate, who was "continuing a flow of objectionable language." Squire found the "trembling girls . . . promptly all took back their promise to appear as witnesses."[113] She complained to her superiors, and the Lord Chancellor demanded an explanation from the magistrate, but despite the fact that Squire had the support of both the Home Secretary and the Chief Inspector of Factories, O'Donnell was not disciplined by the Lord Chancellor and continued to act as one of the magistrates presiding over the Truck prosecutions.[114] As a practical matter, it was extremely difficult to discipline a magistrate for even egregiously bad behaviour.[115] It would be very difficult to imagine O'Donnell behaving in such a manner with a male factory inspector.

On 14 November 1899, when Squire prosecuted Sweeney and Sons at Dungloe Petty Sessions, Sweeney's solicitor objected to the summons because it listed John Sweeney as the defendant rather than all the members the firm.[116] The Bench ruled in favour of the defendant, so Squire and Deane went to Sweeney's premises to obtain the necessary information to write a correct summons. Sweeney ordered her to leave in an "angry and abusive manner." Sweeney later testified that when confronted by the women, "I did not consider from the arrogant tone they took up that I was going to make them any wiser" and told them to leave.[117] It is doubtful that Sweeney would have been as troubled by the "tone" of a male inspector. As a result, Squire charged Sweeney with obstructing a factory inspector, and the case was heard before the Dungloe magistrates on 12 December 1899.[118] The magistrates dismissed the obstruction charge by ruling that the 1878 Factory and Workshop Act only provided the Inspector right of access to the place where the employees received their work, and therefore Sweeney had been within his rights to prevent her entry to another part of his premises. Squire demanded a case for the Queen's Bench Division, which came to be known as *Squire v. Sweeney (no. 1) (1900)*. The court ruled that the magistrates' interpretation of the Factory Act was incorrect, sending the case back to the magistrates, who defiantly found Sweeney not guilty of obstruction on other grounds.[119]

Finally, in March 1900, the truck case against Sweeney was tried again, and this time the Crown sent counsel to conduct the case. The Lord Lieutenant sent two resident magistrates to sit with the seven local justices in the hope of ensuring a fair hearing. They were still at a disadvantage because four of the local justices of the peace were fellow shopkeepers and gombeen men, and one was Sweeney's nephew. After a very disorderly and contentious hearing, the magistrates dismissed the charges by a vote of 6–3, with the two magistrates sent by the Lord Lieutenant forcefully dissenting.[120] Squire applied to have a case stated for the higher courts, but the magistrates refused to grant it, compelling the government to obtain a peremptory writ of mandamus to force the magistrates to state a case for the Court of Queen's Bench in Dublin. Even at this point, the magistrates were unable to comply with the court's order because they could not reach agreement on the contents of the case to send to the high court. In June of 1900, an order for attachment against six magistrates was obtained, giving them a week to demonstrate why they should not be held in contempt of court. Finally, a case was presented by the clerk of Petty Sessions.[121]

These proceedings put the local magistrates to much personal expense, which was not reimbursed.[122]

In June 1900, the Queen's Bench Division in Dublin heard the case, known as *Squire v. Sweeney (no. 2) (1900)*, and that court delivered a ruling which severely limited the scope of the Truck Acts in Ireland. The court ruled that the female outworker in this case was not a workman or artificer within the meaning of the 1831 and 1887 Truck Acts and was therefore outside of their protections. Section two of the 1887 Truck Act stated that its provisions and those of the 1831 Truck Act covered all workmen as defined by section ten of the 1875 Employers and Workmen Act, which stated that 'workman'

> means any person who, being a labourer, servant in husbandry, journeyman, artificer, handicraftman, miner, or otherwise engaged in manual labour, whether under the age of 21 or above that age, has entered into or works under a contract with an employer, whether the contract be made before or after the passing of this Act, be express or implied, oral or in writing, and *be a contract of service or a contract to personally execute any work or labour.* (my italics)[123]

The italicized portion of that section was decisive in this case. The court ruled that because the outworker who had taken the work to perform in her home was not contractually obligated *to personally* perform the work, she was not a workman. The contract would have been fulfilled if she had done all of the work herself or if she had paid others to assist in its completion. The nature of the contract did not require her to "personally execute any work or labour," and therefore she was not a workman.[124] This case not only led to the dismissal of the charges against Sweeney and Sons but due to the persistence of T.D. Sullivan, the MP from Donegal, it also resulted in the remission of the fines imposed on four other employers who had been convicted for paying outworkers in goods.[125]

More importantly, the ruling placed most outworkers in Ireland beyond the protections of the Truck Acts. Anderson, in her annual report, observed that outworkers in Ireland could still be protected under the Truck Acts if they were able to negotiate contracts that expressly stated that they were to personally perform the work, "but our reports abundantly show that the peasant women in congested districts of Ireland are not in position to impose their will upon any would-be employers."[126] Women in this line of work did not haggle over the conditions of employment but took what was available on the terms offered.

The inspectorate expressed "deep regret" for the peasant women of Donegal because the ruling "terminated for them (until the law is amended) the possibility of obtaining, by legal process on their behalf, redress of their grievances." The "immense disappointment" felt by the government at the ruling was mitigated by that belief that it only applied to Ireland. This ruling excluded from the scope of the Truck Acts those workers who were most in need of its protections. The ruling was also a disappointment because from the debates in Parliament during the 1880s and 1890s the legislature clearly intended to include outworkers within the provisions of the 1887 and 1896 Truck Acts.[127]

This case highlights the dangers for inspectors in pursuing cases to the high courts, which had always been at great pains to restrict the terms of the Truck Acts. The inspectors consoled themselves by arguing that the publicity generated by the long campaign against truck in the region might "enlist the sympathies of the better section of public opinion" and "arouse some organized effort in their midst."[128] This seemed doubtful.[129] Among those in the "better section of public opinion" were the leaders of the large Belfast firms that gave work to the shopkeepers who then hired the Donegal outworkers. Inspector Deane complained that for some of these large firms it was a "matter for incessant self-congratulations . . . that they have . . . given employment to thousands of peasant women in distant parts of the country," but this was "unaccompanied by a sense of responsibility." The "little agents" who received the work from the larger firms could not easily profit from their low commissions, "and the truck system naturally followed." If truck could not be stopped by the courts, Deane hoped it might be ended from public pressure applied to the large firms who were the beneficiaries of this exploitative system. She reported that "special care was also directed in bringing prominently before the 'head firms' in the large manufacturing towns in the north and west of Ireland, the grave responsibility which they had incurred in this matter."[130] Deane testified that as a result of the effort against truck in Donegal, some of the large firms in Londonderry and Belfast "gave strict injunctions to their agents" to pay all female outworkers in money. She even stated that one firm refused to give work to agents who kept truck shops and offered a higher commission so that they could profit without truck.[131]

However, by 1903 Inspector Squire reported that the progress made in County Donegal since the prosecutions was limited. She found that

> some agents evidently really do pay in coin, which is carried away when the money is needed by the workers, but the majority expect, if they do not require, the workers to leave the amount in the agent's shop, either towards settling the account, or in purchase there and then of goods.[132]

In 1907, Inspector Harriet Martindale visited Ireland and reported that "we found no evidence in support of the statement that the Truck Acts are being complied with in Donegal." She stated that the gombeen men had become more subtle in their methods but still paid outworkers in truck.[133] In 1913, factory inspectors reported that of the 138 agents in the Belfast area who distributed to outworkers, more than half were shopkeepers who paid employees in disguised truck. A local woman said that "workers who ask for money cannot get work, or can only get badly paid work."[134]

Magistrates throughout the North of Ireland continued to show that they did not think that violations of the Truck Act were very serious. In 1908, Inspector H.E. Brothers brought four charges under the 1887 Truck Act against merchant and millowner David Patton, who had ignored repeated warnings. At Monaghan Petty Sessions it became clear that Patton was guilty but the magistrates expressed conflicted feelings. The magistrates "wanted to let the public know ... it was an illegal practice to do what Mr. Patton, and what every merchant all over the north of Ireland probably, was doing," but the offence carried a minimum penalty on each count of £5, which they felt was excessive for such a "trivial breach of law." At the suggestion of the Inspector, the magistrates penalized Patton £5 and costs on the first count but only made him pay the costs for the other summons.[135]

Despite the ruling in *Squire v. Sweeney (no. 2) (1900)*, it was widely understood that outworkers in England, Scotland and Wales were still protected by the Truck Acts.[136] This was confirmed in the fall of 1900 by Inspector Squire's successful prosecutions in Cornwall and Somerset, which were similar to the Donegal cases. In Somerset, large glove manufacturers gave out quantities of work to subcontractors known as "bag women," who kept shops and gave work sewing gloves together to the outworkers residing in nearby villages. The commission paid to the bag women by the manufacturer was so low that their only means of profiting was to pay the workers in groceries or drapery. Squire secured a conviction in Somerset and informed her superiors that "gradually the truck system of payment which was almost universal in this industry is being driven out, and probably the convictions obtained this autumn against one of the agents, or bagwoman, has been its deathblow."[137]

In Cornwall, the wives of fishermen were sometimes paid in goods by local drapers to knit fishermen's Guernsey frocks.[138] Inspector Squire prosecuted some of the Cornwall drapers for paying in truck and reported

> in every case taken a conviction was obtained, and it is hoped a lesson was learnt by the tradesmen of the West of England that the homeworker has the same right as any other wage earner to handle the whole of her wages in cash.

This successful prosecution signalled to Anderson that the impact of *Squire v. Sweeney (no. 2) (1900)* would be limited to Ireland, because "the magistrates were unanimous in holding that the law, as it had hitherto been interpreted, must continue to protect these outworkers."[139]

Payment of wages in goods continued with little interference from the law in the shawl-knitting trade in the Shetland Islands and the Harris Tweed trade in the Hebrides. Factory Inspector Archibald Newlands, stationed in Edinburgh, testified before the Departmental Committee on the Truck Acts in 1906 about the persistence of the truck in these remote locations. A high proportion of women in the Shetland Islands were engaged in hand knitting and sold their products to merchants who paid them entirely in non-perishable goods.[140] Truck had been widespread in Shetland throughout the eighteenth and nineteenth centuries, and section ten of the 1887 Truck Act had been intended to bring the exchanges between merchants and hand-knitters within the reach of the law. In the Shetland Islands women knitted woollen shawls and then travelled to Lerwick or Scalloway, where merchants paid for them by allowing the knitter to select goods. These goods were marked up 20% higher than the normal cash price charged to other customers.[141] In 1900, Newlands reported that the merchant "never under any circumstances pays for such work other than in the goods he sells in the shop."[142] In 1900, Newlands issued a warning to all of the merchants on the islands, and he believed that the following year there was a "decided diminution of truck" and that "the experience we have is that insisting on cash payment did not injure the trade."[143] In the summer of 1902, Newlands initiated a Truck Act prosecution against William Pole of Lerwick. Despite the fact that section ten of the 1887 Truck Act was specifically intended to combat the truck system in the Shetland Islands, this was the first truck prosecution there in over a decade. Pole pled guilty and was fined, and Newlands reported a "considerable improvement" in 1903 and 1904, but the old practices returned.[144]

In 1905, Inspector Anderson visited the Shetland Islands, and she estimated that 90% of the women there were engaged in spinning or knitting of wool, who were paid in truck by merchants. Anderson observed that

> there is a good deal of dissatisfaction; all the knitters would prefer to receive money, but the market for hand-knitted goods has been bad for two or three years and the people are so deeply in debt, that they acquiesce in the present system.[145]

May Tennant wrote to the Lord Advocate in 1906, urging him to enforce the law in the Shetland Islands and referring him to the Law Indemnity Fund should any witnesses suffer for giving testimony.[146] In June of 1908, Sinclair Johnson of the Shetland Hosiery Company was convicted and fined £2 and costs for paying women in truck and he defended himself as simply conforming to the "use and custom of the trade."[147] The editors of the *Scotsman* complained about the inspectors' vigour in truck prosecutions in the Shetland Islands. They worried that these convictions caused "the trade in knitted goods to be practically at a standstill." They acknowledged that a minority of knitters wanted to be paid in cash, but among the majority "there is a strong feeling . . . that the government should be petitioned to repeal the Truck Act." The truck system in Shetland was so deeply ingrained that the writers defended the shopkeepers, stating,

> [I]t is unreasonable to expect them to accumulate piles of unsaleable hosiery goods and pay ready cash and stand mutely by and see the money go into the till of the opposition shop across the way, or be sent to the emporiums in the south for goods.[148]

Inspector Newlands also reported that between 60% and 75% of the Harris Tweed Trade in the Hebrides was paid for in truck.[149] The laws against truck were not enforced on these outer islands partially due to their remote location, a lack of concern on the part of local officials and, as pointed out by Inspector Brown of Inverness in 1906, because it was doubtful that section ten of the 1887 Truck Act applied in the majority of cases. That section was limited to sales under £5, but the average length of a web of tweed was 40 yards at 2s 9d per yard, which would add up to £5 10s and put the transaction beyond the Act's provisions.[150] However, a larger factor was the lack of cooperation from the knitters themselves.[151] Despite the fact that many complained about the truck system they often had sympathy with the merchants. Newlands described:

> [T]hose merchants year in and year out have assisted them considerably. In the case of a bad harvest or a bad fishing, or illness, or anything of that sort, the merchant you usually find has given unlimited credit during the illness; they do not look at the business side of the thing, and see that he is very well paid for it, but they say to themselves: "he is a very decent man, he has been very kind to us" and they do not see any hardship in their paying under those circumstances 3 1/2d instead of 2 3/4d. They allow their sentimental regard for the man to overlook the mere business nature of his transactions.[152]

During the years after 1896, most of the energy and focus of factory inspectors in enforcing the Truck Acts was directed toward the enforcement of the 1896 Act and the regulation of deductions from wages for fines, damaged work and materials. Yet into the twentieth century there remained unfinished business related to the payment of wages in goods. By the end of the nineteenth century it was no longer coal miners or ironworkers who suffered from being paid their wages in truck at a company store but instead female outworkers in remote locations in Ireland, Scotland and Cornwall.

Prosecutions for deductions from wages for damaged work under the 1896 Truck Act

The factory inspectors faced many challenges when enforcing the second section of the 1896 Truck Act. This section stated that in order for an employer to make a deduction from a worker's wages for bad work or damage or injury to materials, three conditions had to be met. The deduction had to be part of a signed contract between the employer and the employee or part of a notice affixed in the workplace. The deduction could not exceed the actual or estimated damage. Finally, it had to be "fair and reasonable having regard to all circumstances of the case."[153] In the mass-produced clothing trade there were large numbers of women employed and paid by the piece. The barely subsistence wages of these women were often reduced further by deductions for allegedly spoilt work. In some workplaces, if a worker damaged or failed to complete work properly, an employer would not only refuse to pay the piece rate but also insist that the employee pay the value of the damaged item, an amount that was almost always vastly in excess of the employee's wages.[154] Deductions for damage were sometimes so large that employers took the amount from workers' wages in instalments spread across many pay periods.[155]

Some employers mitigated the deduction taken from an employee's wages for spoiling work by allowing the worker to have the damaged item. However, these products were of little use to the employee and were difficult to sell.[156] Inspector Tracey described the hardship this posed for workers, writing:

> Of what use can a gross of collar tops be to any worker. . .? Broken Biscuits, soiled or damaged garments have their uses no doubt, but it is not on such articles as these that a girl or even a woman wishes to spend her scanty earnings.[157]

Inspector Squire testified that the worker could recoup some losses by raffling the damaged garment to her co-workers, observing that in many cases "they were not sold at all and were cut up by degrees for the children; or they would be produced to me years after from where they had been put aside." For women compelled to purchase khaki suits that they had damaged during the Boer War, "they could not get rid of those at all because the men would not wear them even in the fields, so that . . . was a dead loss."[158]

These forced purchases of damaged goods were aggressively prosecuted by inspectors because they had the strong appearance of the payment of wages in goods. Prosecutions for the compulsory purchase of damaged goods were often successful because of the precedent set in the case of *Smith v. Walton (1877)*, where the Court of Common Pleas ruled this type of transaction to be a violation of the 1831 Truck Act.[159] In that case a young power loom weaver had twice delivered pieces of cloth to his employer that had "floats" in the side of them and were deemed unusable. When the weaver, Smith, collected his wages he was informed that he would not be paid the 18s 8½d owed for the pieces but could have the damaged cloth instead. He at first refused to take the cloth but at the urging of the Weavers' Trade Union he accepted it, so that they could initiate a test case to determine whether this constituted a payment of wages in goods. The County Court dismissed the case, ruling that this type of transaction was not what the 1831 Truck Act had been intended to prohibit, but when the case was appealed to the Court of Common Pleas the judges ruled that part of Smith's wages had been paid in damaged cloth, which was a violation.[160] The precedent set by this case led to the peculiarity that under the 1896 Truck Act as long as the terms of section two were complied with it was possible to take deductions from an employee's wages for damaged work, but if the employer then gave the spoiled item to the employee, it could be prosecuted as a violation of the 1831 Truck Act as payment of wages in goods.

Inspectors prosecuted a number of cases where employers compelled workers to purchase goods that they had damaged.[161] In 1905 Squire initiated prosecutions of employers in Leeds for the forced purchase of damaged garments. The stipendiary magistrate "severely censured the employers," and Squire and other inspectors publicized these convictions, which they "hoped stamped out this practice" in Leeds.[162] In 1906, inspectors prosecuted a number of similar cases which helped to publicize that compelling employees to purchase damaged products was illegal.[163] However, as late as 1913, a Nottingham firm was prosecuted by Factory Inspector E.R. Eatock for forcing a woman to purchase a blouse that she had stained in the course of her work. In their defence, the firm insisted that young women liked purchasing damaged blouses because they were cheaper than those in the stores. The magistrate was unmoved by these arguments and fined the firm 20s and costs.[164]

In clothing factories workers sometimes reduced the loss from deductions for bad work by "raffling" damaged items. In some cases the workers themselves organized these raffles as a type of mutual assistance, but it was more legally dubious when employers arranged the raffle.[165] Raffles organized by the employer resulted in a deduction from each worker's wages in return for a ticket for a weekly raffle in which damaged goods were won. The fund helped employees who had damaged goods by spreading the risk around to all of the workers.[166] In 1910, Squire summoned a Manchester firm for violating the 1831 and 1896 Truck Acts for telling a female employee who had spoiled six skirts that she would have to buy them or raffle them away to the other employees. The worker held a raffle and used the proceeds to pay her employer 7s 6d. The magistrate fined them £3 and costs. The *Times* used this case to editorialize against raffles, stating

> so much has been said by employers recently (and justly so) of the perniciousness of gambling and bookmaking in mills and workshops, that we think the semblance of such an evil, even in the mild form or raffling off spoiled work, should be discouraged.[167]

Inspector Paterson urged the Inspectorate to discourage raffles; he said,

> I think it tends to make workers careless in their work; to make foremen and their employers careless about training good workers and indifferent to fairness when they assess the damage which is not to be paid for by the worker, probably young and inexperienced, who actually did it, but is to be levied from as many workers as the number of pennies they collect.[168]

Deductions from wages for damaged work were often arbitrary and unfair. In some trades, work passed through many hands and processes before its completion, and it was not easy to detect at which stage the work was spoiled.[169] Squire explained this by using the example of the pen trade, where each pen passed through 16 or 17 processes before completion, and defects might not be identified until late in the process.[170] Anderson observed that in the collar-making trade it was common "at a late stage [for] the worker [to declare] that the damage is not due to her fault; that the injury was traceable to some earlier process; that she could not turn the work good."[171] Work could also be spoiled because of problems with the machinery or inferior quality materials provided by the employer. The open-ended language of the 1896 Truck Act, which allowed employers to hold workers accountable for "acts or omissions" resulting in damage, gave employers a wide latitude to take deductions, whether it had been caused by real negligence or not.[172]

In April of 1903, Inspector Squire brought charges against the Belfast firm of McBride and Williams for violating section two of the 1896 Truck Act by taking deductions from two women and one girl for damaged work that were not fair or reasonable. The first case involved Maggie Saunders, who had worked at the firm for two-and-a-half years as a hemstitcher and was paid by the piece. During a normal week she earned between 12s and 15s. She had been given a type of stitching that she had never done before and made an error that resulted in the soiling of four dozen handkerchiefs. Her employers deducted 5s from her wages. In opening the first case, Squire reminded the magistrates that when deciding what was "fair and reasonable" some of the circumstances to consider included the "age and experience of the worker, the culpability of the worker, and the amount of wages which she would earn on the week." The firm, represented by counsel, established that the handkerchiefs had been soiled because of an error by Saunders and called owners and managers from rival firms to testify that the amount of the deduction was only about half of the value of the damage to the handkerchiefs. The magistrates dismissed the charge.

The next case was that of 47-year-old Mary Gray, who was also a hemstitcher and normally earned 9d for every *twelve* dozen handkerchiefs that she passed through a machine. Her employers deducted 1s 5 ½d for an error that had soiled *four* dozen handkerchiefs. Gray insisted that the damage had not been caused by her, but the defendants called the forewoman to establish that Gray caused the damage and witnesses from other firms confirmed the value of the damage. Squire thought that "there was no evidence at all that the soil was occasioned by the worker" and that the sum deducted was outrageously large. The magistrates agreed with the defendants that Gray was responsible and dismissed this case as well.

The most controversial of the three cases involved 14-year-old Rebecca Watson, who at the time of her error had just begun learning hemstitching. She was able to earn 2s 10d during a normal week but because she spoiled three dozen handkerchiefs she was fined 8 ½d. The magistrates were less comfortable with this deduction, questioning the appropriateness of taking such a large deduction for spoiled work from a learner. The ruling magistrate stated that while he was not prepared to say that the fine was unreasonable, "he did not think they showed that amount of caution they ought to have done." He dismissed the case, but, to penalize the firm, he refused the defendant's application for costs, which in this case might have been larger than the fines under the Truck Acts.[173]

In 1904, Inspector Squire prosecuted a firm in Leeds where some female machinists worked making trousers. The employer discovered that one pair of trousers that they produced had a hole in it, while another had an oil spot. The employer was unable to determine which of the three machinists had made the errors, so he deducted 1s 2d from the wages of each employee. The magistrate convicted the employer, not because of the arbitrary act of fining multiple workers without proof that they had caused the damage but on the grounds that the notice posted in the factory was insufficient under the 1896 Act.[174] This was not the only case of its kind.[175]

In non-unionized trades it was nearly impossible for an employee to contest or dispute the judgement of the foreman or forewoman as to either the blame or the amount of damage. Inspector J.A. Redgrave observed that although in unionized trades there was sometimes an informal committee of senior workers and management who examined defective work and agreed on a proper deduction, in most instances "the amount of the loss is generally fixed by one party": the employer. Tuckwell thought that employers often inflated their estimates of the losses from damaged work, stating

> that of course frequently happens . . . these deductions either from home work or from the lower skilled factory work do not represent the damage done; in a great majority of cases they represent a payment into the employer's pocket over and above the damage done.[176]

Labour leaders and inspectors thought that it was unfair that the employer could assess fault and the amount of damage without recourse to an independent authority. Many female inspectors thought that the employer should have to sue in the courts to recover the damage, so that at least a fair assessment of the damage could be made.[177]

Relative to the paltry piece rates earned by sweated workers, the deductions from their wages for any mistake made with valuable materials could be extraordinarily high.[178] In most cases, when magistrates determined whether fines or deductions were "fair and reasonable," the wages of the worker were considered much less relevant than the cost of the damage.[179] In 1898 Inspector Squire reported on the plight of workers employed in an India rubber factory, who had to trim the outer edge of tires with scissors. For every *dozen* tires trimmed the employee earned 1 ½d, but for every *single* tire that was cut unevenly the worker had 1d deducted from his or her wages.[180] There are numerous examples of inspectors prosecuting employers for taking deductions for spoiled work that were very large relative to the wages of employees.[181]

In 1902 Inspector Squire investigated a wholesale tailoring factory in Bristol that employed additional outworkers to meet orders. Women employed as finishers on men's trousers were paid between 3d and 5d per pair. If an employee called the passer judged the trousers to be damaged, for example stained with grease or improperly sewn, the finisher could have between 3s and 5s deducted from her wages. Women working on men's coats were paid 6d to 8d per coat, but if they made a mistake on the pattern they could lose the staggering sum of between 18s and £1 5s from their wages.

Squire brought a case before Bristol magistrates, testing whether these types of deductions for damaged work were "fair and reasonable." For Squire a "fair and reasonable" deduction considered the age and experience of the worker, the clarity of the employer's instructions, the level of the training and supervision, the quality of the materials provided, the nature and degree of the employee's error, and, most importantly, the size of the worker's wage. For the Bristol magistrates who dismissed the case, all that needed to be evaluated was the loss to the employer.

After the magistrates dismissed the case, the Home Office contacted the firm, which in the face of public pressure voluntarily agreed to change the level of its fines for damage.[182] The factory inspectors held this case up as an example of the value that could come from even unsuccessful prosecutions, by shining a spotlight on unsavoury employment practices. Whitelegge later testified: "Even when prosecutions have failed we have found beneficial results to follow."[183] Anderson agreed that "[s]ometimes with the mere publicity bringing out these heavy deductions and fines, the public is so much against it that the abuses get rectified. It was so in a group of Bristol cases."[184] The Bristol cases were not the only instances where a prosecution failed, but because of the negative publicity generated by the case, the employer voluntarily changed policies to come into conformity with the view of the inspectorate.[185]

Oftentimes, in order to successfully prosecute an employer for taking large deductions for damaged work, Squire had to use other grounds than "fair and reasonable." When it was possible to secure a prosecution under the 1896 Truck Act on other grounds, such as the lack of a posted notice or the failure to give the employee the full written particulars of the deduction, the Home Office directed inspectors to proceed that way. Inspector Anderson stated that

> we have to bring a great many cases into court which appear as purely technical, that is, failure to make a contract when a fine has been deducted, when really what we mind is the fact that an unreasonable fine has been deducted from the worker's wages.[186]

In January 1899, the Inspectorate prosecuted Messrs. John Mitchell and Co., collar manufacturers, for deducting £1 each from the wages of Emily Haywood and another woman for damaging four dozen collars that they were stitching. The amount was deducted from their wages in 2s weekly instalments, but the employers did not have a written contract with the women, nor did they post a notice that would allow them to take deductions for damage. As a result, the magistrate convicted the employer, fining him 40s and 6s for costs for each count.[187] Similarly, Inspector C.F. Wright prosecuted the Yorkshire Copper Works Company on six counts of deducting 5s from the wages of six workers for damage done to the property of the company. The company had not posted a notice or secured a written contract with the workers and was compelled to pay fines and costs and change its workplace policies.[188]

Inspector Snape described the difficulty in determining the reasonableness of a fine, because of the enormous gulf between the value of workers' wages and the value of the materials with which they worked. He wrote that a deduction for damage

> would appear exorbitant in proportion to the amount of wages but not of work, for when one has to consider the value of the material that is being woven, the fine imposed might not by any means recompense the employer for the damaged done.[189]

In 1899, Inspector Tracey, while describing workers being charged for damaged work in amounts that had to be deducted from their wages in instalments stretching over many weeks, complained that "under present circumstances there is practically no limit to the risk that an employee runs, the wages being in no way commensurate with the liability. The need of setting some limit to a worker's liability, even for her own carelessness, does seem worthy of attention."[190] Inspector Squire in her reports strongly emphasized "the need for some clearer definition of the meaning of 'fair and reasonable,'" and suggested that "the workers' wages seem to be the proper basis on which to form a judgement about what amount is fair and reasonable to deduct."[191] In 1908, the majority report of the Departmental Committee on the Truck Acts lamented that when determining the meaning of "fair and reasonable having regard to all circumstances of the case" there was a clear

> tendency on the part of the magistrates in deciding cases to treat the loss to the employer as the test of the deduction that might be properly made.... In other words, what was intended by the legislature as a maximum limit only, has been treated as the standard to be ordinarily adopted.[192]

Squire frequently argued that the level of training and supervision provided by the employer had to be part of "all the circumstances of the case." She successfully prosecuted a firm for compelling a young woman to purchase 12 pairs of male trousers that she had incorrectly sewn at a price of £3. She had sewn the hip pockets at the wrong angle, but Squire proved that she had not been given a pattern, had no previous experience with this type of work and had been provided with minimal training. Squire argued that deductions for damaged work incentivized bad practices by employers because "it was easier and cheaper to throw the burden of purchase upon the worker than to spend money on training or on supervisors to look after the workers or the machinery or tools."[193]

Because of the difficulty in defining the phrase "fair and reasonable," the Home Office was reluctant to encourage test cases on this question. At every level, cases challenging the fairness and reasonableness of the deduction were hard to win. In March 1898, Inspector Squire responded to worker complaints about two weaving firms in Keighley, Yorkshire: Messrs. Merrall and Sons and Messrs. Haggas and Sons. These firms had taken very large deductions from workers for damaged work without posting a notice or supplying them with written particulars. Squire gave repeated warnings to both firms, so she requested permission to bring prosecutions. Inspector Anderson wrote to Chief Factory Inspector Whitelegge about the possibility of using one of the prosecutions as a potential test case for defining "fair and reasonable," insisting that the level of the employee's wages should be taken into account when determining if a deduction was reasonable. She asked whether the Home Office could supply a maximum proportion of wages that might constitute a reasonable deduction. Anderson wrote,

> [I]n the absence of any decision on this question we have been practically unable to control the proportionately large sums deducted from workers' earnings in respect of damages which might conceivably involve workers in debt exceeding the amount of weeks or months of their earnings.[194]

Anderson, who had written articles comparing the laws against truck, fines and deductions in different European countries, noted that in Germany the maximum deduction from wages for fines or damaged work permitted was one half of the daily wage, unless the worker's act endangered another worker.[195]

The Home Office recommended that prosecutions against the firms proceed on the grounds of their having failed to affix a notice and supply the employees with the written particulars. Home Office Officials stressed the difficulty in determining a maximum proportion of the wages that could be deducted for bad work, using a hypothetical example. They imagined a worker who was paid ½d for every shirt he or she made and that the wholesale price of each shirt was 3s. If through carelessness the worker damaged the shirt and was fined 1s, this might be reasonable even though it was 24 times greater than the piece rate for the shirt, because it was still only one-third of the shirt's value to the employer. Inspector Squire brought ten cases against Messrs. Merrall and Sons, and the magistrates inflicted a fine of 2s 6d in every case but only granted costs in a single case because they felt that Squire had brought more cases than was necessary for making her point.[196]

The conservative approach of the Home Office, however, could not guarantee that there would not be a damaging precedent limiting the protections provided by the Truck Acts. In lace factories in Nottingham, after the lace was removed from the machines, it was taken to women known as "clippers," who would remove extra threads. These clippers laboured in their home, paid by the piece, and could take in work from many firms. In June of 1904, Squire found that the Midland Lace Company had made deductions from the wages of two women who worked as clippers for damaging pieces of lace without having a contract or a posted notice. On 13 June 1904, Annie Lizzie Flinders (a policeman's widow), whose only connection to the firm was as a clipper, had

6d deducted from her wages for having damaged some lace. Ten days later, Amy Lamb, who worked in the factory during the day but in the evenings brought home lace for her and her daughter to clip together, was fined 6d for damaging a piece. Squire prosecuted the Midland Lace Company before two justices of the peace.[197]

The firm admitted the facts of the case but argued that the two women were outside of the protections of the 1896 Truck Act because they were not workmen or artificers. This was the same argument used in the Irish case of *Squire v. Sweeney (no. 2) (1900)*, which the Home Office had considered and incorrectly decided as not applicable in England. As in that previous case, the attorneys relied upon the case of *Ingram v. Barnes (1856–57)*, in which the Court of Common Pleas ruled that "a man is not an artificer within the Act unless the employer has by the contract the right to require his *personal* work and labour in return for wages."[198] Although both women personally performed the labour of lace clipping (though one had the help of her daughter), there was nothing in their agreement with the firm that required them to perform the labour personally. They could have taken the lace and then hired others to do the work. The justices of the peace agreed with this argument and dismissed the case. Squire requested a case for the high courts, and it was heard by the Court of the King's Bench in April of 1905.

Lord Chief Justice Kennedy and Justice Ridley heard the case and based upon the wording of section ten of the 1875 Employer and Workmen Act and the precedent of *Ingram v. Barnes (1856–57)* agreed that "a workman with the protection of the Truck Acts must be a person absolutely bound by the terms of the contract to work by his own hands in the performance of it."[199] Kennedy recognized that however correct his ruling was as a matter of law, it was entirely unsatisfactory as a matter of policy. He ruled that

> we must therefore dismiss the appeal. We do so with some reluctance, having regard to the facts disclosed in this case as to the nature of the employment and the position of the women clippers, who . . . are evidently, as a class, wage-earning manual labourers and not contractors in the ordinary sense.

He added: "we venture to express the hope that some amendment of the law may be made so as to extend the protection of the Truck Acts to a class of workpeople practically indistinguishable from those already within its provisions."[200]

The ruling of *Squire v. Midland Lace Company (1905)* was a setback for those fighting to secure for workers in marginal trades the full value of their wages. Inspector Edwards considered the decision "disastrous."[201] Whitelegge thought that the court's "position is the more regretted because we had had a considerable amount of success in securing improved treatment of outworkers under the Truck Acts."[202] Squire argued that the Truck Acts had been especially important to outworkers because they were "a great army, taking the lowest pay, suffering the heaviest charges on material and 'damages.' There is no cooperation among them, no one to voice their needs." Squire felt that the female factory inspectors had been that voice:

> [M]uch time has been spent for many years in enforcing the Truck Acts among outworkers, both as regard payment in money instead of goods, and fines and deductions, and some of the worst abuses, and saddest cases of injustice and fraud have been brought to light and remedied in the course of these enquiries and successful prosecutions.

The victories won for outworkers "have been the means of reforming the practice of whole districts."[203] A year later, Squire testified that "in the numerous cases of hardship and complaints made to me by outworkers since that case" she now had to first ascertain whether there was a contract that specified that the outworker was to do the work personally, and in most instances, "I failed to find it."[204] Anderson insisted that "the ordinary outworker wants protection even more than the in worker, whether she is working with the help of her husband or somebody else at home, or whether she is working herself."[205]

The inspectors and many Home Office officials were sceptical about whether an employer should be entitled to the wholesale value of the item damaged by the worker. Cunynghame explained the difference between the mere non-payment of wages that had not been properly earned and charging the employee for damages, by using the example of a woman who had contracted with an employer to make 100 rosettes. If she spoiled 1, it was perfectly reasonable for the employer to only pay her for 99,

> [b]ut the moment that such deductions go beyond the value of the actual wages earned – if for instance you begin to make a deduction for the spoiling of one out of 100 rosettes bigger than the mere deduction of the one-hundredth part of the wages ... you are coming to something in the nature of damages.

He was doubtful whether employers should be permitted to be prosecutor, judge and jury in instances where workers being charged damages for spoiled their work. He and much of the Factory Inspectorate thought that they should have to exercise the civil remedies provided by the courts.[206]

Inspector Paterson argued that deductions for damaged work had no value as a deterrent to sloppy work, because "the worker does not put any better work into her work because she thinks she is going to be fined." Because of the size of these deductions relative to the wage, "the worker feels it keenly, having done work with which no fault has been found for six months, that one oversight even, should be the cause of a fine."[207] Inspector Deane reported that the management of a Worcestershire china factory abandoned deductions for damaged work, explaining to her that

> fining only frightens those who are nervous and does no good. If they are careful workers and they make a few accidental mistakes we will try to

make them better; if they are not careful workers it is not worth our while to keep them at all.[208]

Some inspectors raised the question of whether employers who took deductions for damaged work had properly trained their workers. Inspector Deane expressed surprise that "in spite of the girls being so young, in spite of their being so ill-trained, in spite of their working so fast, they yet do really so little damage. It is extraordinary; I am astonished at it." She thought that

> [t]his kind of damage is so natural under the circumstances that it should be regarded as a risk incidental to the advantage of employing cheaper (incompetent) labour, or working at great pressure and should be dealt with otherwise than by fines or deductions.[209]

Deane felt that if a worker damaged a product wilfully or through gross negligence, the employer should be able to sue the employee but not automatically make a deduction.[210] Whitelegge agreed, stating that "if an employer chooses to employ, let us say, children or unskilled hands, or casual hands, at low wages, he must expect more risk of damage to goods as a consequence of the system upon which he works."[211] These sentiments were often repeated.[212]

Some employers insisted that they needed to be able to deduct from workers' wages for damaged work in order to prevent carelessness and the waste, but the prosecutions brought by the factory inspectors brought negative publicity to the practice, even when the employer prevailed in court. The Inspectorate produced examples of hardship and unfairness imposed upon the lowest paid, and these cases built support for the argument that if deductions were to be permitted at all, they should be capped at a proportion of the employees' wages. In the cases of juvenile workers, many insisted that they not be permitted at all.

Prosecutions for deductions for materials, power, standing room and mess halls

When factory inspectors discovered deductions from workers' wages for materials, tools, light, heat, gas or "standing room" that they thought were unreasonable, or in excess of their actual cost to the employer, they usually warned the employer to conform to section three of the 1896 Truck Act. As more employers abandoned these types of charges the accepted custom in trades gradually transformed to the expectation that employers would supply materials at their expense. This strategy of remonstrating with employers was preferable to inspectors because prosecutions under section three were not easy to win in court. From the perspective of factory inspectors, the meaning of "fair and reasonable" charges for materials or services was just as vexatious to determine as it was for damaged work. Workers and trade unionists felt that deductions from wages for motive power were unreasonable in any amount. Herbert Withey of the Amalgamated Union of Clothiers Operatives described a firm that deducted ½d per every shilling earned by its female employees for the power that drove the machinery. The firm employed 200 women earning an average of 10s a week, so Withey calculated that "they will pay for the building in a month. Stopping money for power is the worst thing in the trade."[213] Factory inspectors were uncertain how much an employer could fairly charge for materials, heat, light, tools or power. In 1901, the Midlands Division of Factory Inspectors reported that "we are confronted by the survival of old fashioned arrangements" for deducting wages for light and power and "we are left with the awkward problem as to when and how an unreasonable charge has been made." The only way to know for certain whether the charge met the standard of "unfair and unreasonable" was to test the question in a court.[214] Furthermore, it was not a simple matter to determine the true cost of materials supplied by an employer to an individual employee, particularly items such as gas or heat.[215]

Because these prosecutions were uncertain, wherever possible, inspectors prosecuted deductions from wages for materials not based upon the fairness or reasonableness of the charge but instead on grounds that the employer had failed to make them part of a written contract or a posted notice. Redgrave noted that testing "reasonableness" before the courts was quite risky, as "the court before which the case is brought is the actual arbiter as to what is reasonable or unreasonable. We may have our opinions, but we can only verify them by the court being on our side with respect to that."[216] The courts tended to give deference to the employer on the reasonableness of deductions. For example, in 1906, factory inspectors won a conviction under the 1896 Act against the owner of a factory where skirts were made. Women employed at a machine with three needles earned 18s 10d each pay period but were charged 7s for cotton and needles. Even though these deductions represented over one-third of the women's wages and appeared to be "unreasonable," the inspector chose to prosecute on the more certain ground that they were not part of a written contract or a posted notice.[217] Inspector Lewis prosecuted an employer who deducted the cost of boiling water in the mess room from workers' wages without announcing it in a contract or posted notice. It was far too risky to try and prosecute on the grounds that charging workers for such a service was not "fair and reasonable."[218] Inspector Saunders in 1911 prosecuted a Kingswood firm three times for deducting wages from its female workers for the maintenance of sewing machines, a charge that he thought was unreasonable. He finally succeeded by prosecuting the firm because it had not secured a contract with the employees to deduct these fees.[219] There are many other examples of inspectors prosecuting technical violations when they wished to prosecute for deductions that were not "fair and reasonable."[220]

Prosecutions under the 1896 Act demonstrated the difficulty in finding the "real or estimated cost" of materials deducted from the wages of workers. In 1904 Inspector Owner prosecuted a Bristol bootmaker who made deductions from the wages of female employees for the costs of "machines, room, thread and for work done by another worker." One woman, whose gross wages were 14s 6d a week, only received the sum of 9s 9d after these deductions. The inspector believed that this woman was charged more for these materials and services than they cost the employer, a violation of the 1896 Act. Before the bench of magistrates, Owner forced the employer to concede during cross-examination that

> the amount for running the machine included prime cost, repairs, driving, depreciations, light, rent, rates, taxes, in fact all his charges. He thought it fair to make the worker pay those amounts rather than charge them to the cost of production.

The bench dismissed the charges, ruling that the deductions were reasonable and in the most technical sense did not exceed the estimated cost to the employer, but they thought that the behaviour of the defendant was dubious enough that they penalized him by refusing to grant costs.[221]

In court, the burden of proof for demonstrating that employers were overcharging for materials and services was entirely upon the inspector.[222] Inspector Squire found that

> the difficulty is really to find (the overcharge) out. The employer may or may not produce his invoices or any particulars. I have been refused these particulars and the retail price at which one can buy these materials is not always a guide.[223]

This was especially true for charges for light, heat or gas where the costs to the employer might be variable. It was possible to investigate and prove what an employer paid for these services for the factory as a whole but to determine the fair price for each individual employee was much more complex. Was it legal to charge a piece worker a fixed rate for heat, light or gas when their usage might vary? At Messrs. Wername in Stoke, both piece workers and those paid by the day were charged 6d per burner per week for light. In 1911, Inspector Parkes was confident that this represented more than the actual cost even though it was very difficult to ascertain because "the need for lighting varies day to day and depends upon so many circumstances that it will probably be impossible to arrive at an exact – and at the same time practical – method of charges."[224] Inspector Redgrave testified that it was common for an employer to set the level of a deduction from workers' wages to pay for items, such as needles or gas, and over time the cost of the item to the employer might fall without any alteration in the deduction. However, if the price of the item rose, the deduction would immediately be adjusted upward.[225]

In 1907 Inspector Vines identified a china factory, Wileman & Co. in Fenton, Staffordshire, as a workplace where employees were overcharged for the consumption of gas. Employees' consumption of gas was variable but the deduction from their wages for its use was a fixed amount. Some weeks workers were charged more than the actual cost to the employer for their gas consumption. Vines forwarded the information related to this case to Anderson and

Whitelegge to evaluate whether a test case should be initiated. The owner of the firm was politically well connected and enlisted the assistance of MP John Ward, who on 21 December 1907 wrote to the Home Secretary on behalf of his constituent explaining that the china industry in Staffordshire had long practiced a custom where employees supplied their own candles for light and in some workplaces this had held over to modern times, though light was now supplied by gas. He wrote to the Home Secretary: "We are bound to assume that the object of the Home Office, and our factory inspectors is to secure due observance of the law, not a mere humiliation by the public imposition of penalties." In early January 1908, the firm agreed to conform to Inspector Vines' views and change its deductions. The Office of the Chief Inspector recommended that Vines explain to the employer on the deductions for heat, light or gas: "This Department regards all such charges or deductions as unreasonable; further that such charges are in the present day not common in other trades or in other districts."[226]

The Inspectorate avoided prosecutions for unreasonable or excessive deductions for heat and light. For this reason the chief inspector suggested in February of 1912 that

> I think it better to exhaust every effort to induce the firm to abandon the charges before considering the instituting of proceedings which, at the best, can only result in fixing upon the workers such a charge as the court considers are reasonable.[227]

There is much anecdotal evidence to suggest that inspectors were successful in discouraging charges for materials and gas, heat, light and power and that over time these became less common. Undoubtedly, the reports of factory inspectors and the publicity given to their testimony before the Departmental Committee on the Truck Acts contributed to the idea that such charges were anachronistic. As Inspector Paterson noted in 1904, "I do not think this practice grows, and the number of factories where no such deduction is made is large."[228] By 1922, Anderson described deductions for material, heat and light in her memoirs, writing, "Deductions for motive power, used in the manufacturing process, were often found in our earlier years of inspection, but they had already begun to die out, and I think, have long since done so generally."[229] Five years later, in her own memoirs, Squire agreed, writing, "It would now be generally conceded that it rests with the factory occupier to provide at his expense all things necessary for the performance of the work, including room, machinery, heat, light and the materials to be used."[230]

There were other troublesome deductions taken from the wages of workers that were outside of the protections of the 1896 Truck Act. These included deductions from wages for food prepared and consumed on the premises. Section 23 of the 1831 Truck Act allowed such deductions provided that they were part of a written contract with the employee, but there was no requirement that the deductions be "fair and reasonable" or that they not be more than the cost to the employer. Inspector Deane thought it was "an excellent thing" when employers provided mess halls and made food available to the workers but found that there were some cases of abuse. In 1898 Deane investigated a firm that made tinned provisions and had a rule that no worker was permitted to leave the premises during the working day, even during meal times. This compelled workers to use the mess hall, and as a condition of employment these workers signed an agreement allowing the firm to deduct from their wages for food that "was valued by the firm at a sum manifestly in excess of the possible cost to them." When some female employees attempted a work stoppage over the quality of the food, the firm fired six ringleaders for "insubordination" and the protest collapsed. Because of the existence of a written agreement, Deane was helpless to intervene beyond describing the circumstances in her annual report.[231] This was not an isolated case.[232]

In August 1905, the Home Office sent out a circular requesting factory inspectors to enquire into the charges made for provisions and mess rooms and discover the extent of abuse. Most inspectors reported back that the deductions made for food consumed on premises were reasonable and workers were satisfied.[233] There were a few instances where inspectors found the charges excessive and after a remonstrance with the employer the deductions were reduced.[234] Inspector Pringle of Manchester thought the arrangement of factory mess halls to be mutually beneficial because employers were assured a prompt return to work after meal times and workers were provided with hot food and water at a reasonable rate.[235] Squire found that in the factories she investigated it was not an unpopular deduction as long as workers perceived that they got their money's worth.[236]

Not only was it difficult to secure prosecutions of employers for making unreasonable fines and deductions for materials, heat, light, gas, "standing room" or food, the Inspectorate also failed to prevent employers from taking deductions from workers to pay for services that employers were required by law to provide. Factory Inspector Owner discovered that S.R. Hooper, a manufacturer of walking sticks and umbrellas, every fortnight paid each of his 30 workers their entire wages in cash but also gave each a slip of paper with an amount written on it that was the equivalent of 2d per each £1 of wages. The employee was expected to give the amount written on the slip back to the cashier. Hooper used this money to pay the insurance premiums necessary to cover his statutory liability under the 1897 Workmen Compensation Act. As unfair as this was to his workers, it was even worse because Hooper's insurance premiums cost him 8s per £100 of wages he paid, yet the amount he received back from his employees was 16s 8d per £100 of wages. Owner prosecuted Hooper for violating section three of the 1831 Truck Act in March 1903. The Gloucester justices of the peace who heard the case thought that while it was entirely possible that Hooper had violated section three of the 1896 Truck Act by taking a deduction that exceeded the actual or estimated cost of the item provided, he did not violate section three of the 1831 Truck Act because it was not a payment of wages in goods.

Owner had a case stated for the higher courts, and the appeal was heard in the King's Bench Division on 7 July 1903. The judges unanimously agreed with the justices of the peace. The lord chief justice noted the distasteful behaviour of the employer, ruling that "whether the respondent was entitled [to] act as he did or not, it could not be said that he violated section 3 of the Truck Act, 1831 by making payment of wages otherwise than in cash. . . . [T]he appeal must be dismissed."[237] This case was disappointing to the Inspectorate because Hooper was not the only employer who was taking money from his employees to meet statutory obligations toward workers.[238]

Deductions for materials, tools, heat, light and standing room were often holdovers from an era when workers had greater independence from employers and more control in the production process. By the end of the nineteenth century, this relationship had changed dramatically and as waged employees it made little sense for them to be required to supply materials that went into the product that the employer was going to sell. The 1896 Truck Act could not prevent this, but it could be used to compel greater transparency in these charges and reduce the ability of employers to profit from them. Between 1896 and 1906, factory inspectors had much greater success remonstrating with employers to abandon these charges than they did in prosecuting them under the 1896 Act.

Prosecutions for illegal fines under the 1896 Truck Act

Section one of the 1896 Truck Act required that fines in the workplace be considered legal only if they were part of a signed contract or a notice affixed in the workplace. This contract or notice had to list the specific acts or omissions for which a worker could be fined, as well as information to enable the employee to ascertain the amount of the fine. Employers could only fine workers for acts or omissions which were likely to cause hindrance to the business, and such fines had to be "fair and reasonable having regard to all circumstances of the case."[239] Female factory inspectors initiated a number of prosecutions under this section because women in sweated and non-unionized trades suffered disproportionately from unfair disciplinary fines. One of the conclusions reached by the Departmental Committee on the Truck Acts in 1908 was that fining remained prevalent among workers in sweated trades and "the worst cases occur where workers are not in any union."[240] Squire wrote that at the time of her appointment as factory inspector the practice of fining workers had "grown to such dimensions as to have become an intolerable burden, especially in the case of women and girls earning low wages."[241]

Disciplinary fines for the late arrival at work were common and they were often excessive relative to the wages earned by the employees. In 1899, Inspector Paterson initiated a prosecution against Clark and Co., hosiery manufacturers in Scotland, who had posted a notice stipulating that employees would be fined for being late according to the following scale: The penalty for arriving up to 5 minutes late for work was 1/2d. The penalty for arriving between 5 and 10 minutes late was 1d. A worker who was between 10 and 20 minutes late was to be fined 2d, and one who was more than 20 minutes late would lose a half-day's wage. Paterson charged the firm with levelling fines that were not fair and reasonable upon four young women who were paid by the piece. Three of the women had arrived at 8:30 a.m., rather than the normal 7 a.m. start time but between 8 a.m. and 8:30 a.m. was breakfast, so the employer had only lost an hour of their work. These employees each earned on average between 7s and 12s during a normal week, and the fines that were imposed upon the four of them ranged from 7½d to 1s 4½d. Paterson also argued that the fines were unreasonable because of mitigating circumstances. Two of the women had been ill and one was tending to a sick mother. Furthermore, as the women were piece workers, the loss to the employer for an hour of their work was minimal. The sheriff in this case separated his ruling from his personal feelings. He ruled that the purpose of heavy fines was to act as a deterrent against late arrival to work, which inconvenienced the employer and other workers. He dismissed the charges, ruling, "I cannot condemn as unfair and unreasonable the fines which were imposed in these particular cases." However, he stated that his personal opinion was that the fine of a half-day's wage for being 20 minutes late was too high, and "I think the respondents should amend that part of the scale."[242] Paterson complained that this case demonstrated the need to reform the Truck Acts, reporting "if the principle of such fining is to continue legalized, some definition is wanted which will make the worker's position a clearer one." She added that she was "constantly in receipt of such complaints, but in which I find myself quite powerless, and as a rule, only after considerable 'higgling,' to secure some sort of compromise."[243]

In June of 1903, Inspector Owner had more success against a Bristol firm that took excessive deductions from the wages of a female weaver missing a day of work. The weaver was paid by the piece and was normally capable of earning 2s 6d for a day's work. She was a married woman who sometimes struggled with punctuality because of the domestic demands of her household. Owner's attention was drawn to the fact that she missed the day after the Easter holiday, and, in addition to not earning any wages for the day she was absent, she was fined another day's wages as well. Owner brought this case and four other similar ones before a magistrate and secured convictions, setting the employer back £3 and costs.[244]

Inspector T.O. Edwards of the Southampton district had a mixed record of success in prosecuting employers for taking excessive fines for lateness. At a dressmaking firm where women were paid by the piece, the firm fined women 2d for being up to a half hour late. One dressmaker whose weekly wages averaged 2s 9d per week and another less experienced one who earned 2s 2d a week were late a total of 40 minutes and 33 minutes during the week. The employers deducted 2d from each of their wages. Edwards noted that charging the women 2d for a half hour would mean that the time was worth 4d per hour. Assuming a 52-hour work week, this would mean the weekly value of their time was over 17s per week, when the two women were paid just over 2 shillings per week. The value of these women's time to the employer was worth very little when it came to paying wages but became quite expensive when assessing the damage caused by their unpunctuality. Edwards convinced a magistrate of the unreasonableness of these fines.[245]

Inspector Anderson described a failed prosecution from 1911 of Russell and Woolven, down quilt manufacturers from South London, where an employee who earned 6s a week during a normal week was fined 5d for being 5 minutes late. The magistrate did not find it excessive that the employer had fined the employee over four hours' wages for the loss of 5 minutes, considering it "fair and reasonable." The case generated enough outrage that Lord Henry Cavendish-Bentinck questioned the Home Secretary about it in the House of Commons. A year later, in another South London factory, Anderson discovered that of the 500 employees in the factory, more than 276 had been fined for tardiness amounts ranging from 4d to 8d per pay packet, and the firm took back as much as £156 of their workers' wages each year from late fines.[246] Inspector Edwards prosecuted a different firm that fined more than 1/3 of its 30 employees every week, most for lateness. In the first six months of the year, the firm had collected over 250 fines from its workers.[247]

Disciplinary late fines were large relative to the wages that women could earn. Tuckwell was able to provide examples of women who lost 20–25% of their weekly wages to fines. She observed that "the amount of the fines seems extremely in excess of any disorganization which could be caused by one girl being late."[248] Herbert Withey of the Amalgamated Union of Clothiers complained of the "exorbitant fines that are imposed upon workpeople for going in late. I am especially thinking of girls who are not paid more than 4s or 5s a week."[249] In some firms, these fines were regular enough that women pooled their resources together for mutual assistance. In 1905, Inspector Vines found that in a large factory 50 women had started their own fine club, in which each woman, depending upon her wages, would contribute 1/2d or 1d a week to the fund. This fund was then used to pay any fines inflicted by the employer.[250] Squire argued that late fines were especially unjust when one considered "all circumstances of the case" because "rarely was the reason found to be mere carelessness or laziness. Generally some difficulty in means of transport from home to factory was the cause, or children or a sick husband to be seen to."[251]

Inspector Tracey insisted that not only was the level of these fines unjust, but they were ineffective as a deterrent to unpunctuality. She wrote, "The fine for late attendance is one that is oftenest inflicted, and though usually it is out of proportion to the earnings of the girls, its very frequence demonstrates the little real effect it has in compelling punctuality."[252] Five years later, Tracey reiterated that "the fine has had no affect whatever upon them; and so as a disciplinary measure it has failed."[253]

It was difficult to enforce the provision that fines had to be "fair and reasonable." Magistrates often interpreted this phrase in a way most favourable to employers while also adopting an expansive understanding of the acts or omissions that were likely to hinder an employer's business. Inspectors had the best chance in securing convictions for fines under the 1896 Truck Act in instances where employers failed to post a notice, give the fined worker written particulars or record the fine in the register. Employers complained that these were "technical" violations of the Act, but Whitelegge responded that

> if an employer chooses to carry on his business on lines of fines and deductions which other employers do not find necessary, I hardly think that he is entitled to much sympathy if he is called upon to do a little book-keeping.[254]

In 1901, Squire responded to complaints about a corset-making factory in Bristol where an employer had posted a notice informing the employees that "all workers shall observe good order and decorum while in the factory, and shall not do anything which may interfere with the proper and orderly conduct of business thereof or of any department thereof." The penalty for violating this vague rule was a fine of 6d. The employers had imposed numerous fines under this rule for speaking, laughing and even sneezing. The workers, mostly female, were unsure what specific acts constituted a failure to "observe good order and decorum" and "were at the mercy of their respective overseers."[255]

Squire prosecuted this firm for fining corset sewers for singing and dancing. The employees were given an hour for dinner and were permitted to take their meal in the workroom because there was no meal room on the premises. During the dinner hour, the young women sang songs and danced. No foreperson was present, but a clerk witnessed the dancing and reported the matter to the employer, who fined the women 6d each under the "good order and decorum" rule. Cunynghame considered it "a most cruel and improper fine" and an "illustrating case of a thoroughly bad fine."[256] With the support of the Home Office, Squire brought two charges against the firm, arguing that section one of the 1896 Truck Act had been violated in two ways. The rule did not specify the acts or omissions for which the employees could be fined, because the rule requiring the maintenance of "good order and decorum" was too vague. Workers could never fully be certain whether their actions violated this rule because it depended upon the interpretation of the foreperson. Whitelegge agreed that the rule under which these women were fined "appears to me singularly lacking in definition."[257] Anderson felt that under such a vague rule the foreman or forewoman would have nearly "absolute authority" to fine for anything deemed to fall short of good order.[258] She insisted that enforcing such rules on poorly paid workers was unfair because "[t]he payment, speaking generally for women and girls, is a subsistence wage, and it is of the utmost importance that they should not have deductions made unless it be for actions which they know they can avoid."[259] The requirement in the 1896 Truck Act that fines be part of a written contract with the employee, or be posted in the workplace, was intended so that fines would not be arbitrary. This transparency allowed workers to understand precisely the actions for which they would be held to account. A rule requiring "good order and decorum" was too subjective to provide such clarity. In fact, Helen Robbins, one of the female workers fined, insisted that she had never been told that it was wrong to dance and sing during the dinner hour.[260] Squire also charged the firm on the grounds that the fine imposed violated section one of the 1896 Truck Act because "the innocent and natural amusement of the girls during a time when no work was going on could not cause damage or loss to the employer or interruption or hindrance to his business."

Counsel for the defence argued that the rule was specific enough, and the employer could not be expected to anticipate every precise act or omission that could possibly harm the business. The employer was permitted to generalize in the contracts and notices. They also argued that dancing kicked up dust, and dust could potentially damage machinery and materials. The magistrates agreed with the defence and dismissed the charges. Squire requested a case stated for the higher courts, and, in May 1901 the case, known as *Squire v. Bayer and Co. (1901)*, was heard by the Court of King's Bench.

In *Squire v. Bayer and Co. (1901)* the Lord Chief Justice Alverstone reluctantly ruled that "[t]his case is not free from difficulty, but I cannot see my way to hold the decision of the Justices wrong."[261] He found that "it would be going too far to say that the language of the rule is necessarily too general," because

> while it does not specify the particular acts and omissions . . . I think that it is sufficient compliance with the requirements of the Truck Act, 1896 to say that a fine may be inflicted if the employee does not observe good order and decorum in the factory.

He also rejected the argument that the employee had done nothing which might hinder the business of the employer, noting that in the room where the offense had occurred there was "much valuable machinery and materials," which might have been damaged.[262]

Squire put a positive interpretation upon a significant setback for regulating the fines taken from workers' wages. She argued that the case had produced some benefit even though the government had lost because the behaviour of the corset manufacturers was widely condemned in the press and amongst other employers, who "reformed their own methods to conform to the official view which had been set out in the legal proceedings."[263] She also thought that this setback from the high courts could "demonstrate the need for amendment of the Truck Act if the workers are to have the benefit these statutes were designed to provide."[264] Anderson agreed that despite the defeat in the high courts, "it is of greatest advantage to have the wholesome light of public opinion let in."[265] The outcome of this case was continually referenced in the press as the supreme example of the petty tyranny of workplace fines, with one editor asking readers of the ruling, "Can you imagine anything meaner?"[266]

While this case did result in bad publicity for the firm and drew public and political attention to the abuse of workplace fines, it also resulted in a number of unscrupulous employers adopting vague rules stating that workers must maintain "good order and decorum." Anderson acknowledged that "[w]e found . . . afterwards that the advertisement thus given to that vague form of contract led to its being adopted in other factories."[267] Even Squire conceded that "[s]ince the case of Bayer . . . the contract that was the subject of that case has been reprinted and placed in a number of factories and pointed out to me as being the only rule that now had absolute sanction."[268] Workers, particularly female workers, could be fined under the "good order and decorum" rule for offences that appeared unlikely to cause serious harm or hindrance to an employer's business.[269] Clementina Black provided a Parliamentary Committee with examples of women being fined for laughing, noisiness, talking, reading, wearing hair curlers, meddling with tools or using bad language. The amounts of such fines ranged from 3d to 1s.[270] In one case five girls were fined 3d each for laughing when a co-worker fell off a stool.[271] Squire heard complaints about women who were fined under the "good order and decorum" rule for singing, sneezing, wearing hair curlers or "cheeking the foreman."[272] In another case a young girl was fined 6d for putting a spider down next to another girl. Employees in a needle-making factory were fined 3d for throwing tea leaves down the drain. A West End dress maker fined female employees if they came down the stairs in pairs.[273] In a Belfast factory, maintaining "good order and decorum" meant banning all political discussion, with a rule that "[a]ny person using party expressions or wearing any colours calculated to annoy others shall be liable to a fine not exceeding 2/6."[274]

Inspector T.O. Edwards did, however, convict an employer who fined a woman for being more than 5 minutes in the lavatory and also won a conviction against an employer who had fined some corset makers 6d for laughing during mealtime. In 1905, Edwards convicted a laundry firm for fining women who were wearing hair curlers. The firm had not made the fine part of a written contract or posted notice, and he argued that "it would not be fair and reasonable because whenever women factory workers were employed near machinery the Factory Inspectors always strongly urged the fastening up of hair."[275] Despite Edwards' victories in court, such convictions were never certain. In 1906, he was unable to win a prosecution against an employer who fined two female bottle washers for laughing while at work.[276]

While factory inspectors were not always able to win convictions against employers who fined workers for frivolous offences, they fared better in the court of public opinion. A significant proportion of the press, politicians and even employers came to accept the idea, so long promoted by factory inspectors, that modern and well-run workplaces did not require fines to maintain discipline.[277] The *Birmingham Post* commented that "[w]hen girls are fined for sneezing, or wearing hair curlers, or going downstairs in couples, it can only be said that the machinery of discipline must be contemptibly inefficient to need such weapons."[278] Squire questioned a foreman who fined a girl for sneezing, testifying that he "seemed to think it was the only way of enforcing his authority to inflict a fine of 6d."[279]

The ability to fine workers for something as subjective as the maintenance of "good order and decorum" gave power and discretion to foremen or forewomen. Tuckwell found that "[t]hat power is recklessly used very often."[280] Black argued that foremen and forewomen did not always apply the rules in a consistent or predictable way. For example, in one factory, workers could be fined for talking, but "the girls say it depends on the temper of the foreman. That is a fine which will sometimes not be imposed and other times will be imposed very severely."[281] This made it difficult for an employee to avoid being fined, because what was allowed on one day might be a fineable offence on another. Such discretionary powers could also contribute to abuse and harassment in the workplace.[282]

The imposition of fines for good order and decorum reflected different expectations for male and female behaviour in the workplace. The firm of Messrs. Alfred Meakin, Ltd., earthenware manufacturers from Tunstall deducted a whopping 10s from the wages of Emma Harrison as a fine for using bad language. Inspector Shuster prosecuted the firm for failing to provide written particulars of the fine. The defendants had a contradictory defence. On the one hand, they argued that "the language used by the woman, on this occasion was particularly bad, while filthy songs were also sung. It is difficult to get respectable young women to work with them on account of filthy language used." The director testified that he had received complaints from the parents of girls working with Harrison, and while he "did not pretend to be pious" he was "determined to put down bad language at the firm." At the same time the defence argued that the deduction was not a fine, even though it was recorded in the register as a fine and five officers from the firm admitted to the inspector that the fine was for bad language. Despite clear evidence that the deduction was a fine and that the firm had failed to give Harrison written particulars, the magistrate thought that "this was a case in which he ought not to convict."[283] Male workers were not often fined for the use of bad language. An editorialist for *The Common Cause* complained that

> I have never found men fined to anything like the extent to which women are fined. I have never found men fined . . . for looking out of the window, or 2d for every time they laughed, nor have I found they were fined for unpunctuality when doing piecework. . . . These fines and many more are what women only have to bear.[284]

In the experience of the factory inspectors not only were disciplinary fines abusive and unfair, but just like fines for unpunctuality, they were unnecessary and ineffective. Anderson testified about many workplaces that abandoned the fining system and saw discipline improve.[285] Squire echoed these sentiments, insisting that disciplinary fines were unnecessary, because "if a foreman or forewoman knows his or her business there is no need whatever for a disciplinary fine."[286] She supported this assertion with evidence of large factories in Birmingham and Bristol, in fields ranging from tailoring, corset manufacture and chocolate making, which had abandoned fines and seen no deterioration in discipline.[287] When asked how it was possible to maintain good order in the factory without fines, Squire replied,

[T]he same good discipline would be maintained as is now maintained in large works where there is never any fine, but where it is understood clearly by the other workers that no insubordination will be tolerated. The manager and the foreman control the girls by influence and other means.[288]

She and many other inspectors believed that workers rose to the level of expectations for keeping their jobs. When asked whether the abolition of fines would lead to more dismissals of workers, a representative of railway workers argued that fining and dismissal were not alternatives. He observed that employers who used workplace fines were just as quick to dismiss workers for breaches of discipline.[289] Because employers required the labour of experienced workers, the threshold of misconduct for which they would be prepared to fire an employee would always be significantly higher than that for which they would impose a fine. Many believed that dismissals would not rise but rather employers would have to find new means of coping with petty violations.

Fines and "living in" for shop assistants

Shop assistants in retail stores were heavily fined and poorly protected by existing legislation. Section one of the 1896 Truck Act explicitly applied to shop assistants, but it required their personal initiative for the law to be enforced because no inspectors had jurisdiction over retail shops.[290] As a result, many retail stores adopted large codes of fines which strained the definition of "fair and reasonable," and others did not bother complying with the Act by keeping a register of fines. Stephen Fox and Mrs. J.R. MacDonald complained in an article for *Women's Industrial News* that the 1896 Truck Act "remains a dead letter in respect to the protection of shop assistants from unreasonable deductions and fines." This was regrettable because "fines now form a monstrous feature in shop employment" and "shop assistants, whether male or female, rarely belong to any trade organization, and are therefore singularly ill-equipped to resist petty tyranny." They called upon the government to establish a shop inspectorate.[291]

In some cases, unions, such as the National Amalgamated Union of Shop Assistants, Warehousemen and Clerks (NAUSAWC), took up the cause of shop assistants who experienced unfair fines. The Union sometimes wrote to the employer and got the fine returned. In other cases the Union had to hire a solicitor and threaten to prosecute. In one case, the starting time for shop assistants was 8:30, but the employer asked an assistant to come at 8:15; he arrived at 8:18 and was fined. Before the case was called to court the employer refunded the fine. When the union threatened to take cases to court, the employer would usually return the fine before it could be tried.[292] The problem was that this union, the largest body of organized shop assistants, represented only 22,000 members spread across the entire United Kingdom. Their assistant secretary, Margaret Bondfield, conceded that they were no substitute for the power of a government inspectorate.[293]

In 1898, the *Daily Chronicle* produced a series of articles describing the excessive regime of fines that many shop assistants laboured under. A shop in Holloway had a code of 75 rules, including fines of 3d for gossiping, standing in groups, "lounging about in an unbusinesslike manner," bringing a newspaper to the shop or failing to return supplies promptly to their proper places. A shop assistant failing to address the customer by the correct name could be fined 2s 6d. The 75th and last rule on the list stated that

> if anything is done, or permitted to be done, by an assistant, contrary to the interests of the firm, which is not specified in the foregoing rules, the offender will be subject to a fine not exceeding 2s 6d at the discretion of the firm or their representatives.

The author of the article joked, "[I]t appears . . . that by the time the firm got to rule 75 they thought better of it, and enacted a sort of omnibus fine." This shop was not the only one to have as its last rule an open-ended, catch-all offense.[294] The Holloway store's code of rules was not unique in terms of its considerable length either. *The Daily Chronicle* found a West End shop with 72 rules, a Knightsbridge store with 123 rules, a shop in Piccadilly Circus that had 198 rules and a shop in South London that had a code of 136 rules.[295]

The Daily Chronicle also described fines listed in London shops, including 6d for speaking to a customer without a coat on, 3d for wearing soiled collars or cuffs, 1s for standing on a chair, 2d for exceeding mealtimes or 6d for failing to introduce each customer to at least two articles.[296] Fines for unpunctuality were also common, with one shop fining workers who were less than five minutes late 3d, 5 to ten minutes late 4d, 10 to 30 minutes late 6d and over a half-hour late 1s.[297] If shop assistants made errors in billing, or had short tills, it was not uncommon for them to not only have to make up the difference out of their own pockets but to be fined additional amounts for the errors.[298] The author wrote that for a shop assistant to avoid having his or her wages clawed back "there must be no mistakes."[299] The editorial pointed out the arbitrary power, or "Star Chamber Jurisdiction," exercised by the shop walker, "a kind of walking magistrate" in the store with authority over the shop assistants, for whom "the infliction of fines is no small part of his duties."[300] The employees had no opportunity to appeal the shop walkers' decisions.[301]

The article in *The Daily Chronicle* attracted the attention of a Lib-Lab MP Samuel Woods, the former secretary of the Parliamentary Committee of the TUC and vice president of the Miners' Federation of Great Britain. On 25 March 1898, Woods asked the Home Secretary if he had read about the fines described in *The Daily Chronicle* and whether he thought that they were legal under the Truck Act. He also asked about the possibility of an inquiry to explore the abolition of fines.[302] The matter was discussed in the Home Office, and the Home Secretary replied that only a court of summary justice could determine whether or not they were legal and it was up to shop workers themselves to bring such case.[303] This answer was not satisfactory to shop assistants. On 31 March 1898, *The Daily Chronicle* had another instalment of this story, describing more outrageous fines and stating that "it is clear that shopkeepers regard themselves free to break the Truck Act with impunity – a view which is encouraged by the Home Secretary's statement of his intention not to enforce the Act in shops." The newspaper also addressed a common defence of disciplinary fines, both in retail shops and in factories and workshops, which was that fining a worker was a more merciful form of discipline than dismissal. The author observed that in practice the ability of an employer to fine in no way diminished his ability to fire, stating that "the Houses which fine most unscrupulously are the readiest to threaten dismissal, and fines or no fines, the least successful assistants are dismissed light-heartedly when the end of the season comes."[304] On 17 May 1898, Herbert Asquith told the annual conference of the Women's National Liberal Association that

> the conditions of service of shop assistants, more particularly, female shop assistants, constituted in his opinion a crying social and industrial scandal, and the time had come for a searching investigation into those conditions and for that intelligent agitation which . . . was the necessary precursor of reform.[305]

In addition to being fined in the shop, many male and female shop assistants lived under the rule of their employers even after the working day had ended. Some shop assistants who came from rural areas sometimes stayed in rooms over the shop or in dormitories located nearby that were provided by employers as part of the employee's remuneration. This was known as "living in." These workers had deductions taken from their wages for room and board and sometimes for the library, doctor, breakages in the house and many other services. They were also subject to the rules of the dormitories. Shop assistants could be fined 6d for making unnecessary noise or 3d for leaving clothing or boots lying about the bedrooms.[306] Shop assistants working for a store in South Wales laboured under a code of 83 fineable rules while at work and then came home to live under an additional 40 fineable offenses governing their domestic lives.[307] In one extraordinary case, a shop assistant in the employ of Messrs. Arding and Hobbs of Clapham was fined 5s for leaving meat on his plate. The fine represented more than a quarter of his weekly wage. He contended that the meat was overdone and he ate all that he could but the manager of the house said that "he could not get exactly what he wanted, so he hacked his meat about and positively refused to eat it." The manager informed the firm and recommended his dismissal, but the employers "took a lenient view of the matter and proposed that he should be fined 5s, as it might do him good." The shop assistant quit rather than pay the fine, and the firm retaliated by dismissing his brother.[308] The case was taken up by the executive of the United Shop Assistants' Union, which resolved to have its general secretary, William Arnold, write to the Home Office and request an inquiry. The Home Office officials agreed that the fine did not seem reasonable but felt that the United Shop Assistants' Union should prosecute the case.[309] It appears that the matter went no further.

At the end of the nineteenth century and during the first decade of the twentieth, shop assistants agitated for better protections from Parliament. On 30 July 1899, a mass meeting at Hyde Park was organized by the NAUSAWC, where those assembled listened to speeches delivered from two platforms. The meeting resolved that it

> emphatically protests against 'living in,' a survival of the truck system (with its deductions from wages for library, doctor, breakages, etc.), and is of opinion that it is maintained as a profit-making department at the cost of the moral, social, and political degradation of those affected. It also strongly condemns the arbitrary fines so frequently inflicted.[310]

The first decade of its enforcement exposed many flaws in the 1896 Truck Act, including the lack of an inspectorate with jurisdiction to enforce Section one for shop assistants, who had to take their own initiative to use the law. Some shop workers who were compelled to "live in" as a condition of employment lamented the fact that the 1831 and 1887 Truck Acts did not apply to their work and therefore they could not easily challenge their employers paying part of their wages in room and board some thought was inadequate.

The "bonus system"

Some employers circumvented the requirements of the Truck Act for fines and deductions by making part of the employee's remuneration a "bonus" that was paid for being punctual or doing perfect work. Employers argued that "the amount of the bonus forms no part of the wage contract, but is simply a gratuity to be paid or withheld in individual cases as the firm chose."[311] In her 1904 report, Inspector Mary Paterson found that in practice the bonus was less a gratuity and more understood as part of the worker's ordinary wage. She wrote, "There seemed, however, on investigation, no doubt that it was part of an unwritten agreement, and that in withholding the bonus the firm virtually made a deduction under the Truck Act."[312] This "bonus" was not an "in addition to wages" prize but was an amount of money that brought the wages up to the subsistence level that the employees expected to receive. For this reason, losing the "bonus" was not losing an "extra" but having wages that one anticipated taken away. Deane reported that with the bonus system "the point is that . . . these sums, which when withheld operate – and are intended to operate – as fines, are exempt from all regulation under the Act."[313] Whitelegge thought the bonus system was illegal because if an employer is at liberty to escape from the provisions of the Truck Act with regard to fines by simply calling a portion of the wages he pays a bonus instead of calling it wages, then the effect of Section 1 of the Act of 1896 is very largely nullified.[314]

Inspector Harriet Martindale conducted an investigation into the operation of the "bonus system," which was especially prevalent in the spinning and weaving mills of the Northern Ireland.[315] There she found ten flax-spinning mills and eight weaving factories that used a bonus as high as 2s to go with a weekly wage of 8s, but for spinners it was most often an arrangement of 9s a week of wages and 1s a week bonus. Workers told Martindale they thought of the bonus as simply part of their wages, and, in fact, few could tell her the size of the bonus or its proportion of their take-home pay. In one large factory, each week about 90% of the female employees were able to earn their bonus, and they told her that they budgeted on the assumption that they would receive it.[316] Of managers interviewed, some thought that the bonus was part of the workers' wages because "we are virtually obliged to give it" while some others who were more aware of the 1896 Truck Act insisted that it was not part of the standard wages. Martindale also reported that during a recent strike in Belfast, many owners when publicizing the wages they paid to their workers included the bonus as simply part of the weekly wages, and when the workers won a raise part of it was a larger bonus.[317] Some factories used the bonus to help insure punctuality. For example, at one factory, weavers could earn a bonus of 2s 6d every fortnight for arriving to work on time. If a weaver was late once, he or she would forfeit 1s 6d of the bonus. For a second offence, the entire bonus would be lost.

Martindale investigated another factory where the bonus of 2s 6d per fortnight was used to insure the quality of the weaving. If a foreperson found fault or damage to a piece of cloth, 1s 6d of the bonus would be lost. For a second error the entire bonus was taken.[318] It was clear that the bonus system operated as fines or deductions for bad work, but it had the advantage of not being subject to the requirements of the 1896 Truck Act. Therefore, employers using the bonus system did not need to post the specific offences for which parts of the bonus could be withheld, nor did they need to keep a register or provide employees with written particulars of why they did not receive the entire bonus. Weavers at one factory informed her that they

> do not receive any pay docket with their wages, even with such a complicated system of deductions, and they complained to me that they were hardly ever able to earn the bonus. I am obliged, however, to tell these workers that these deductions are not regulated by the law.[319]

Inspector Deane was determined to test the legality of the bonus system in Ireland, so on 25 April 1906 she brought charges to Newry Petty Sessions against Abraham Wilson and Co. Spinning Factory for deducting 2s from the wages of Theresa Dixon without providing her with written particulars. Dixon had worked for the firm since she was a child and in a normal week she earned 10s for 55½ hours of labour. One day in February of 1906, she arrived to work at 9:45 a.m. instead of the normal start time of 6:30 a.m. At the next pay period her wages were 2s 4d less than normal: 4d because of the quarter day during which she was absent and unable to earn wages and 2s for having forfeited the bonus given for working full hours. The prosecution argued that the 2s bonus was wages within the meaning of the Truck Acts, which the firm had violated by making the deduction without providing Dixon with written particulars. The defence argued that Dixon's actual wages were 1s 4d per day, which over 6 days of work would total 8s, and she received an additional 2s bonus for working the full 55½ hours during the week. The firm had a posted rule stating that "[a]ny person absent without reason, and not assigning satisfactory reason, shall lose bonus." Her failure to perform 55½ hours of work meant that she had not earned the 2s bonus. The magistrates agreed with the defence, ruling "the 2s per week was given as a bonus or prize in special consideration for full time of 55 ½ hours kept by the worker each week" but this sum was not to be "computed as 'wages' as it was not given for excellence of, nor for extra, work, but was a premium for full time." For this reason "no fine had been inflicted" but Dixon had failed to earn the 2s. Deane requested a case for the higher courts.[320]

Nine days later, Cunynghame testified to a Parliamentary Committee about the magistrates' ruling, saying,

> I submit it is erroneous. If the 2s is not wages I should like to know what it is. I think on that point they will be overridden. I hope they will because it is perfectly plain it is a clear evasion of the act. If you are allowed to do that, instead of saying your wages are 7s 6d a week and for being late we will fine you 2d, you will be allowed to say, your wages shall be 7s 4d with a bonus of 2d if you are in time. I cannot believe that the courts ever will allow a juggle with words to take place.[321]

As was often the case when predicting how the judiciary would interpret the 1896 Act, Home Office officials could not have been more wrong.

The case was heard in the Irish King's Bench Division on 15 May 1906 before Lord Chief Justice O'Brien, Justice Andrews and Justice Kenny. The solicitor general represented the state and argued that the two shillings was a penalty taken from the sum contracted to be paid, contrary to the 1896 Truck Act, and calling it a bonus was just a device used to evade this legislation. Defence counsel argued that the 2s did not represent a fine but was part of a clear contract stating if the employee worked 55½ hours during the workweek she was to receive 10s and if she failed to do so would be paid 8s. The 2s could not be wages that were owed to Dixon because she had not earned them.

On 27 June 1906 Justice Andrews delivered his ruling and agreed with the defence. He concluded, "I am unable to hold that the non-payment of 2s, which was not earned, and never became due, was a deduction from the sum contracted to be paid to the worker. There was no contract to pay it unless it was earned." He continued, "the non-payment took nothing from her to which in any view she had become entitled. . . . [I]t was simply withholding payment of what she had not earned."[322] Justice Kenny agreed, dismissing the argument that the bonus system was a transparent evasion of the Truck Act, noting, "It was suggested in the course of the argument that this arrangement for a bonus to those workpeople who worked their full week . . . was really a device or contrivance for evading the provisions of the Act of Parliament. I cannot for a moment think so." He described the inter-connectedness of labour in a factory and how the absence of one worker prevented other workers from earning a living. Because punctuality was important, "I believe the offer of a bonus in the present case for punctual and regular attendance to be a perfectly *bona fide* effort on the part of the company to ensure the latter – that it in no respect savours of a device or contrivance to evade the provisions of the Truck Acts." The ruling of the magistrates was upheld.[323]

In 1908, the Departmental Committee on the Truck Acts heard testimony about the bonus system, particularly in Northern Ireland, and reached a conclusion that was contrary to that of the Irish King's Bench. The report stated

> in its actual operation the system was merely a system of fining in disguise, which had been adopted to evade the restrictions of the Truck Act of 1896; the bonus not being a real addition to the wage, but a part of the wage, and so regarded by the worker.[324]

Inspector Paterson complained after the ruling, in practice

> [W]e, therefore, find this curious condition, that while the contracts relating to fines and deductions imposed on workers in one factory are open to investigation and subject to regulation and control, there is the adjoining workplace where the contract is on the bonus system and is outside any jurisdiction.[325]

Deane argued in favour of Parliament outlawing the bonus system, which she insisted was "simply a fine turned round the other way."[326]

Williams and Others v. Norths Navigation Collieries (1904–1906)

Many trade union officials remained insistent that the 1896 Truck Act had been a step backwards for workers because it "legalized fines" by giving them statutory recognition. These people contended that under section three of the 1831 Truck Act, which required that the entirety of wages owed be paid in the current coin of the realm (except for those deductions explicitly permitted with a written contract by section 23 of the same Act), fines and deductions for damaged work had been illegal until the 1896 Truck Act became law. This seemed doubtful given the rulings of *Chawner v. Cummings (1846)* and *Redgrave v. Kelly (1889)*, the latter of which treated fines as the non-payment of wages rather than a payment in truck. Defenders of the 1896 Act contended that the legislation prohibited fines except under strictly regulated conditions. However, in

1906 the House of Lords delivered a verdict in a case that could be interpreted as vindicating the trade union position on this question.

In December 1903, at Wyndham Colliery, owned by Messrs. North Navigation Collieries Ltd., a haulier, Taliesin Williams, had 8s 5d deducted from his pay packet on the grounds that he had been overpaid by that amount in a previous pay period. There was confusion because there were at least three men with the last name Williams employed at the colliery. Williams protested vigorously and was given vague promises by management that the matter would be investigated. On 22 December, at 6:30 a.m., Williams went to the manager and said that if his 8s 5d were not paid, the hauliers would not work that day. After some haggling, the manager hastily wrote out an order for a payment of the sum, but by this point the hauliers had gone home for the day and the pit was left idle. The mining agent estimated that this stoppage cost the firm £49 9s 2d.[327]

In mid-January, North's Navigation Collieries Ltd. brought suit against Williams and 29 other hauliers under the 1875 Employer and Workmen's Act for breach of contract. The magistrate found fault with the management of the colliery for allowing a conflict over such a trifling amount to escalate but reprimanded the miners for not pursuing their grievances in court. He delivered a judgement against the defendants, ordering them to pay the company 30s each, to be divided into in three 10s fortnightly instalments.[328]

At the next payday the firm deducted 10s from the wages of each of the defendants. Williams and six other miners then brought an action against the firm to recover the amounts deducted, claiming that these deductions were illegal under the 1831 Truck Act. On an application to Justice Bunknill at chambers, an injunction was granted to stop the firm from making any further deductions until the case was heard. The defendants appealed, and by agreement, the appeal was treated as the trial of the action. This case was heard in April 1904.

The defendants in the case argued that the purpose of the 1831 Truck Act was to prevent the payment of wages in goods and "not at the non-payment of wages." They told the three judges that "[t]t is treating it in a manner altogether foreign to the general scope of the Act to read it as prohibiting the employer on payment of wages from deducting an amount legally due from the workman to him." This was clearly not the intention of the legislature when passing the 1831 Act, and

> [i]f the plaintiff's contention is correct, it was quite unnecessary to pass the Truck Act, 1896 (59 & 60 Vict., c.44), which prohibits deductions for fines, except in certain specified cases, for such deductions would have been unlawful under the Truck Act, 1831.

The plaintiffs countered that the purpose of the 1831 Truck Act was to ensure that the total amount of wages owed be paid in money, "subject only to the deductions authorized by s. 23, leaving it open to the employer to recover any legal cross-claim which he may have against the workman by proceedings in the appropriate court." The fact that the 1831 Act legalized specific deductions in section 23 "tends to show that other deductions from wages without the assent of the workman are forbidden."[329] The three judges ruled that it was not an offense against the 1831 Truck Act to deduct from wages a sum due by law from the employee to the employer. The case was dismissed and costs were granted to the firm. Williams appealed to the House of Lords.[330]

On 20 March 1906, the case was heard in the House of Lords. The counsel for Williams and others quoted Justice Bowen in *Hewlett v. Allen (1892)* to argue for a literal interpretation of the 1831 Truck Act. Bowen had said "[t]he statute insists . . . on actual payment in coin. Payment in account will not do. Payment in goods will not do. Nothing is to discharge the wages debt except actual payment in coin." They stressed that in the cases of *Chawner v. Cummings (1846)* and *Archer v. James (1862)* the deductions had been part of the contract of employment which had been carried out by the employer. In this case there was no written agreement to carry out the deductions. The counsel for North's Navigation Collieries countered that "[t]he Act simply declares that the amount payable must be paid in coin. The employer owes only what he can be made to pay by process of law: he does not owe the wages without deducting the set-off."

Lord Chancellor Loreburn agreed with the counsel for Williams. Loreburn read section three of the 1831 Act and stated, "I cannot think this means that it shall be paid as to part in coin and as to the remainder in account." Against the suggestion that the employer only needed to pay the wages in coin after deducting cross claims, Loreburn answered that section 23, with its precise listing of the deductions that an employer could take with a contract, "would be wholly unnecessary if an employer were already authorized by s. 3 to deduct anything that the workman owed him and to pay in coin merely his balance." He recognized that by ruling for Williams he would be creating a legal anomaly because if the employer had refused to pay Williams any wages at all and was sued by his employee, he could set off the sums that were owed to him against the claim, gaining an advantage that would be denied to him under the 1831 Truck Act. Loreburn said, "No doubt this would be an anomaly, as are the Truck Acts themselves . . . which interfere in a limited degree with freedom to contract." However, "the fact that the provision is anomalous does not permit us to disregard the plain meaning of the words used." Lord MacNaghten, Lord Davey, Lord Robertson and Lord Atkinson all agreed. Atkinson stated that "there is no ambiguity in the words of the section used. They are precise and clear, and require that the entire amount of the wages earned shall be 'actually paid in the current coin of this realm.'" Atkinson added, "The whole principle on which this legislation is based is that the workman requires protection, that if not protected he may be over-reached." Therefore, the employer should have to claim debts owed to him through a separate legal tribunal to "prohibit the master from, as it were, substituting himself for the legal tribunal, investigating his own claim against his workman in his own office and deciding in his own favour." Nothing in the case law permitted an employer to unilaterally make this 10s deduction from the wages of his workers. The House of Lords ordered the repayment of 10s to each of the plaintiffs as well as the full costs for the entire legal proceedings.[331]

Most observers interpreted this ruling narrowly, believing that its implications did not extend beyond an employer deducting non-contracted debt owed to him from his employees. However, it appeared that this ruling could be interpreted to mean that trade unions were correct all along in believing that deductions from their wages for fines were illegal because they were not authorized by section 23 of the 1831 Truck Act. Indeed, among the clippings collected by WTUL president Gertrude Tuckwell is a newspaper article about this case and attached to it is a typed note reading, "[T]he judgement confirms the view of Lancs. against ourselves in supporting the H.O. in '96," suggesting that the Lancashire Cotton Weavers' unions had been right all along in opposing the 1896 Truck Act.[332] Legal scholar John Romanes argued in 1906 that the cases of *Redgrave v. Kelly (1889)* and *Archer v. James* (1862) "must now, however, be held to be definitely overruled by the recent case of *Williams v. the North Navigation Collieries*." Romanes quoted the Lord Chancellor, who, in his ruling, stated,

> It appears to me that an obligation rests upon the employer, under the Truck Act, 1831, sect. 3, to pay in coin . . . all the money payable as wages, and that in ascertaining how much is payable as wages, he can subtract nothing except the deductions expressly sanctioned by section 23.

This meant that in the absence of the 1896 Truck Act, fines would be illegal under the 1831 Truck Act. Romanes, however, also pointed out that Section eight of the 1896 Truck Act states that nothing in it shall make lawful a contract or payment that would be illegal under the 1831 or 1887 Truck Acts. This caused Romanes to conclude that "[f]ines, therefore, . . . must now be pronounced illegal; and as to a fair and reasonable extent, they are obviously called for in the legitimate interests of the masters, any impending legislation should make provision for their rehabilitation."[333] Other legal scholars, ignoring section eight of the 1896 Act, recognized that this ruling changed that law from one that mostly prohibited deductions to one that legalized them.

Most employers and government officials continued to believe that the deductions from wages for fines were legal because they were the means of arriving at the wages that were owed to the worker which then had to be paid in coin. Given the desperation with which organized labour sought legislation that would explicitly prohibit fines and deductions from wages, most of their leadership understood that these remained legal under the current law, whatever they said in public. Yet given the battering that the 1896 Truck Act had taken before the high courts and this uncertain ruling from the House of Lords, by 1906 there was a growing desire for reform. This will be explored in the next chapter.

Notes

1 *Departmental Committee on the Truck Acts: Minutes of Evidence Taken Before the Truck Committee, Vol. II: Minutes of Evidence (Days 1–37)* (London: HM Stationary Office, 1908), p. 17, Question 193.
2 *Daily News*, 1 January 1911; *The Challenge*, 8 May 1914. Gertrude Tuckwell Papers, London Metropolitan University Archives. *Departmental Committee on the Truck Acts: Report of the Truck Committee, Vol. I: Report and Appendices* (London: HM Stationary Office, 1908), p. 35.
3 *Factories and Workshops: Annual Report of the Chief Inspector of Factories and Workshops for the Year 1899, Part II: Reports* (London: H.M. Stationary Office, 1900), p. 181. Parliamentary Papers [cd.223]. Also see 1905 remarks of Inspector Parkes of Nottingham. *Factories and Workshops: Annual Report of the Chief Inspector of Factories and Workshops for the Year 1905, Reports* (London: H.M. Stationary Office, 1906), p. 105. Parliamentary Papers [cd. 3036].
4 *Departmental Committee on the Truck Acts: Minutes of Evidence, Vol. II* (1908), p. 65, Questions 1323–1328.
5 *Departmental Committee on the Truck Acts: Minutes of Evidence, Vol. II* (1908), p. 67, Question 1388.
6 *Departmental Committee on the Truck Acts: Minutes of Evidence, Vol. II* (1908), p. 22, Question 271.
7 Anderson, *Women in the Factory*, p. 22; *Departmental Committee on the Truck Acts: Minutes of Evidence Vol. II* (1908), p. 37, Questions 605–609.
8 Anderson, *Women in the Factory*, pp. 59–60; *Departmental Committee on the Truck Acts: Minutes of Evidence, Vol. II* (1908), pp. 63, 69, Question 1436.
9 *Departmental Committee on the Truck Acts: Minutes of Evidence Vol. II* (1908), p. 63, Question 1291–1293.
10 *Hansard Parliamentary Debates Online, House of Commons*, 8 July 1901.
11 *Departmental Committee On the Truck Acts: Minutes of Evidence Vol. II* (1908), pp. 19, 67 Questions 226–227, 1397–1405.
12 *Departmental Committee On the Truck Acts: Minutes of Evidence Vol. II* (1908), p. 67, Question 1397.
13 *Departmental Committee On the Truck Acts: Minutes of Evidence Vol. II* (1908), p. 65, Question 1329.
14 Squire, *Thirty Years in the Public Service*, p. 100.
15 *Factories and Workshops: Annual Report of the Chief Inspector of Factories and Workshops for the Year 1898, Part II: Reports* (London: H.M. Stationary Office, 1900), p. 183. Parliamentary Papers [cd.27]
16 *Departmental Committee on the Truck Acts: Minutes of Evidence, Vol. II* (1908), p. 20, Question 242.
17 *Factories and Workshops: Annual Report of the Chief Inspector of Factories and Workshops for the Year 1898, Part II: Reports* (London: H.M. Stationary Office, 1900), p. 74. Parliamentary Papers [cd.27]; *Factories and Workshops: Annual Report of the Chief Inspector of Factories and Workshops for the Year 1899, Part II: Reports* (London: H.M. Stationary Office, 1900), p. 18. Parliamentary Papers [cd.223]
18 *Annual Report of the Chief Inspector of Factories . . . for the Year 1898, Part II: Reports*, p. 74; *Annual Report of the Chief Inspector of Factories . . . for the Year 1899, Part II: Reports* (1900), p. 180; *Factories and Workshops: Annual Report of the Chief Inspector of Factories and Workshops for the Year 1905, Reports* (London: H.M. Stationary Office, 1906), p. 179. Parliamentary Papers [cd.3036]
19 *Annual Report of the Chief Inspector of Factories . . . for the Year 1900* (1901), p. 190.
20 For examples, see Major Roe, Factory Inspector for Manchester in 1901: *Factories and Workshops: Annual Report of the Chief Inspector of Factories and Workshops for the Year 1901, Part II: Reports* (London: H.M. Stationary Office, 1902), p. 122. Parliamentary Papers [cd.1112]; In 1905 Inspector Owner of Bristol also reported the successful use of warnings and cautions: *Annual Report of the Chief Inspector of Factories . . . for the Year 1905, Reports* (1906), p. 57; Also see: *Factories and Workshops: Annual Report of the Chief Inspector of*

Factories and Workshops for the Year 1904, Part I: Reports (London: H.M. Stationary Office, 1905), pp. 42, 174. Parliamentary Papers [cd.2569]; *Annual Report of the Chief Inspector of Factories . . . for the Year 1906, Reports and Statistics* (1907), p. 138.

21 *Departmental Committee on the Truck Acts: Minutes of Evidence, Vol. II* (1908), p. 36, Question 595.

22 Anderson, *Women in the Factory,* pp. 71–72.

23 *Departmental Committee On the Truck Acts: Minutes of Evidence, Vol. II* (1908), pp. 84–85, Questions 1810–1818.

24 *Annual Report of the Chief Inspector of Factories . . . for the Year 1901, Part II: Reports* (1902), p. 148.

25 *Departmental Committee on the Truck Acts: Minutes of Evidence, Vol. II* (1908), p. 37, Question 609.

26 *Annual Report of the Chief Inspector of Factories . . . for the Year 1905, Reports* (1906), p. 323.

27 *Annual Report of the Chief Inspector of Factories . . . for the Year 1900* (1901), p. 404.

28 *Annual Report of the Chief Inspector of Factories . . . for the Year 1905, Reports* (1906), pp. 255–256; *Departmental Committee on the Truck Acts: Minutes of Evidence, Vol. II* (1908), p. 20, Questions 243. For other examples, see: *Annual Report of the Chief Inspector of Factories . . . for the Year 1900* (1901), p. 242; *Annual Report of the Chief Inspector of Factories . . . for the Year 1901, Part II: Reports* (1902), pp. 82–83.

29 *Annual Report of the Chief Inspector of Factories . . . for the Year 1898, Part II: Reports* (1900), p. 75.

30 *Annual Report of the Chief Inspector of Factories . . . for the Year 1898, Part II: Reports* (1900), p. 184.

31 Anderson, *Women in the Factory,* p. 69.

32 *Annual Report of the Chief Inspector of Factories . . . for the Year 1901, Part II: Reports* (1902), p. 190.

33 *Annual Report of the Chief Inspector of Factories . . . for the Year 1899, Part II: Reports* (1900), p. 281.

34 *Annual Report of the Chief Inspector of Factories . . . for the Year 1904, Part I: Reports* (1905), p. 42; *Departmental Committee on the Truck Acts: Minutes of Evidence, Vol. II* (1908), p. 85, Questions 1836–1840, p. 114, 118, Questions 2564, 2571, 2721, p. 132, Questions 3256–3260, p. 176, Question 4599. Also see: *The Total Abolition of Fines in Factories and Workshops: A Deputation from the United Textile Factory Workers Association. Thursday June 10, 1909. Official Report* (Ashton-Under-Lyne: Cotton Factories Times, 1909). HD 4931. London Metropolitan University Archives.

35 *Departmental Committee on the Truck Acts: Minutes of Evidence Vol. II* (1908), p. 200, Questions 5169.

36 *Annual Report of the Chief Inspector of Factories . . . for the Year 1898, Part II: Reports* (1900), p. 184.

37 *Departmental Committee on the Truck Acts: Minutes of Evidence, Vol. II* (1908), p. 106, Question 2362.

38 *Departmental Committee on the Truck Acts: Minutes of Evidence, Vol. II* (1908), p. 236, Questions 6116.

39 *Annual Report of the Chief Inspector of Factories . . . for the Year 1898, Part II: Reports* (1900), p. 184.

40 *Annual Report of the Chief Inspector of Factories . . . for the Year 1900* (1901), p. 242; for similar testimony, see: *Departmental Committee on the Truck Acts: Minutes of Evidence Vol. II* (1908), p. 233, Questions 6030–6035.

41 *Morning Post,* 4 January 1909. Also see: *Saturday Review,* 29 February 1896 and *The Challenge,* 8 May 1914. Gertrude Tuckwell Papers, London Metropolitan University Archives.

42 *Annual Report of the Chief Inspector of Factories . . . for the Year 1905, Reports* (1906), p. 140.

43 *Annual Report of the Chief Inspector of Factories . . . for the Year 1906, Reports and Statistics* (1907), p. 104.

44 *Annual Report of the Chief Inspector of Factories . . . for the Year 1899, Part II: Report* (1900), p. 405.

45 *Annual Report of the Chief Inspector of Factories . . . for the Year 1898, Part II: Reports* (1900), p. 75.

46 *Annual Report of the Chief Inspector of Factories . . . for the Year 1901, Part II: Reports* (1902), p. 190. Also see: *Annual Report of the Chief Inspector of Factories . . . for the Year 1898, Part II: Reports* (1900), p. 75.

47 *Annual Report of the Chief Inspector of Factories . . . for the Year 1900* (1901), p. 275.

48 *Annual Report of the Chief Inspector of Factories . . . for the Year 1898, Part II: Reports* (1900), p. 75.

49 The deterrent effect of public opinion upon employers was further suggested in 1906 when A.F.Yarrow expressed to Factory Inspector Redgrave that one way of decreasing the number of retail firms that disciplined shop workers with fines would be for Parliament to require notices of fines not only to be posted in the workplace, but also in the window of the shop so "that the public who make purchases in the shop could form an opinion as to the labour conditions at that establishment." After all, "If an employer objected to that play, would it not be some evidence that he had reason to be ashamed of his methods?" *Departmental Committee on the Truck Acts: Minutes of Evidence, Vol. II* (1908), p. 45, Questions 792–793.

50 59 & 60 Victoria, c. 44, s.3 (1896).

51 *Annual Report of the Chief Inspector of Factories . . . for the Year 1903: Part I: Reports* (1904), p. 234.

52 *Annual Report of the Chief Inspector of Factories . . . for the Year 1906, Reports and Statistics* (1907), p. 138.

53 *Departmental Committee on the Truck Acts: Minutes of Evidence, Vol. II* (1908), p. 48, Question 844, p. 77, Questions 1607–1610.

54 *Annual Report of the Chief Inspector of Factories . . . for the Year 1898, Part II: Reports* (1900), p. 74

55 *Annual Report of the Chief Inspector of Factories . . . for the Year 1898, Part II: Reports* (1900), p. 183.

56 *Annual Report of the Chief Inspector of Factories . . . for the Year 1906, Reports and Statistics* (1907), p. 45.

57 *Annual Report of the Chief Inspector of Factories . . . for the Year 1906, Reports and Statistics* (1907), p. 138.

58 *Annual Report of the Chief Inspector of Factories . . . for the Year 1903: Part I: Reports* (1904), p. 80.

59 Anderson, *Women in the Factory,* p. 74. Also see report from Rose Squire: *Annual Report of the Chief Inspector of Factories . . . for the Year 1901, Part II: Reports* (1902), p. 190.

60 *Annual Report of the Chief Inspector of Factories . . . for the Year 1898, Part II: Reports* (1900), p. 74.

61 *Annual Report of the Chief Inspector of Factories . . . for the Year 1905, Reports* (1906), p. 55.

62 *Annual Report of the Chief Inspector of Factories . . . for the Year 1905, Reports* (1906), p. 326.

63 Squire, *Thirty Years in Public Service,* pp. 111–112; For a similar case, see *Annual Report of the Chief Inspector of Factories . . . for the Year 1905, Reports* (1906), p. 56.

64 *Annual Report of the Chief Inspector of Factories . . . for the Year 1900* (1901), p. 242. A year later he was able to inform his superiors that in the majority of factories and workshops in Walsall deductions from wages for materials and gas were no longer made. *Annual Report of the Chief Inspector of Factories . . . for the Year 1901, Part II: Reports* (1902), p. 84.

65 *Annual Report of the Chief Inspector of Factories . . . for the Year 1901, Part II: Reports (1902),* p. 36.

66 *Annual Report of the Chief Inspector of Factories . . . for the Year 1901, Part II: Reports (1902),* p. 190.

67 *Annual Report of the Chief Inspector of Factories . . . for the Year 1905, Reports* (1906), pp. 106, 179 (Quote).

68 *Annual Report of the Chief Inspector of Factories . . . for the Year 1903: Part I: Reports* (1904), p. 234.
69 Home Office Note, 17 January 1898; Rose Squire to Adelaide Anderson, 27 November 1897, TNA HO 45 9930 B25943.
70 Rose Squire to Adelaide Anderson, 27 November 1897, TNA HO 45 9930 B25943.
71 Rose Squire to Adelaide Anderson, 8 January 1898, TNA HO 45 9930 B25943.
72 Extract from Weekly Report of Rose Squire, 28 December 1897, TNA HO 45 9930 B25943.
73 Rose Squire to Adelaide Anderson, 6 March 1898, TNA HO 45 9930 B25943.
74 Quote from Home Office Note, 2 March 1898; Treasury Solicitor to Under Secretary of State for the Home Department, 22 February 1898, TNA HO 45 9930 B25943.
75 *Annual Report of the Chief Inspector of Factories . . . for the Year 1898, Part II: Reports* (1900), pp. 74, 183. Also See Inspector Jackson of Walsall for another example of an employer prepared to go to great lengths to evade the spirit of the 1896 Truck Act.
76 *Departmental Committee on the Truck Acts: Minutes of Evidence, Vol. II* (1908), p. 65, Questions, 1325–1327.
77 For an example of a confusing and complex prosecution under the Truck Acts, see Factory Inspector Gerald Snape's prosecution of the Belfast Flax Spinning and Weaving Company November of 1897 under the 1896 Truck Act. See: TNA HO 45 9929 B25591.
78 *Departmental Committee on the Truck Acts: Minutes of Evidence, Vol. II* (1908), p. 28, Questions 390–396, Quote from 392.
79 McFeely, "The Lady Inspectors: Women at Work 1893–1921," p. 51.
80 Squire, *Thirty Years in the Public Service*, p. 101.
81 *Nottingham Gazetter,* 18 June 1913. Gertrude Tuckwell Papers, London Metropolitan University Archives.
82 *Annual Report of the Chief Inspector of Factories . . . for the Year 1904, Part I: Reports* (1905), p. 42. Also see: *Daily Telegraph,* 25 October 1911; *Birmingham Post,* 28 March 1914. Gertrude Tuckwell Papers, London Metropolitan University Archives.
83 *Belfast Newsletter,* 2 March 1910; *Yorkshire Weekly Post,* 30 April 1910; *Western Daily Press,* 20 January 1911. Gertrude Tuckwell Papers, London Metropolitan University Archives. For a contrary example, see: *Annual Report of the Chief Inspector of Factories . . . for the Year 1901, Part II: Reports* (1902), p. 36.
84 *Annual Report of the Chief Inspector of Factories . . . for the Year 1899, Part II: Reports* (1900), p. 277.
85 *Departmental Committee on the Truck Acts: Minutes of Evidence, Vol. II* (1908), p. 19, Question 230.
86 *Departmental Committee on the Truck Acts: Minutes of Evidence, Vol. II* (1908), p. 27, Questions 384–385.
87 *Departmental Committee on the Truck Acts: Minutes of Evidence, Vol. II* (1908), p. 67, Questions 1393.
88 Anderson, *Women in the Factory,* pp. 2–3.
89 TNA HO 45 9989 X79124; *Departmental Committee on the Truck Acts: Minutes of Evidence, Vol. II* (1908), p. 119, Questions 2774–2780.
90 TNA HO 45 9989 X79124.
91 *Freeman's Journal,* 8 April 1904. Gertrude Tuckwell Papers, London Metropolitan University Archives.
92 *Annual Report of the Chief Inspector of Factories . . . for the Year 1898, Part II: Reports* (1900), p. 182.
93 *Departmental Committee on the Truck Acts: Minutes of Evidence, Vol. II* (1908), p. 79, Question 1677; Squire, *Thirty Years in the Public Service,* p. 79; *Times,* 4 March 1897, p. 10.
94 Desmond Greer has described these prosecutions in two outstanding articles: Desmond Greer, "'Middling Hard on Coin': Truck in Donegal in the 1890s," Presidential Address to the Annual General Meeting of the Irish Legal History Society, Dublin, 2000; Desmond Greer and James Nicolson, "The Fair Payment of Wages," in *The Factory Acts in Ireland, 1802–1914* (Dublin: Four Courts Press, 2003).

95 Squire, *Thirty Years in the Public Service,* p. 89; Greer, "Middling Hard on Coin," p.294.

96 Greer, "Middling Hard on Coin," pp. 284–285.

97 *Annual Report of the Chief Inspector of Factories . . . for the Year 1899, Part II: Reports,* 1900), p. 18.

98 *Annual Report of the Chief Inspector of Factories . . . for the Year 1899, Part II: Reports,* 1900), p. 275.

99 Desmond Greer, "Middling Hard on Coin," pp. 281–287; Squire, *Thirty Years in Public Service,* pp. 78–79; *Departmental Committee on the Truck Acts: Minutes of Evidence, Vol. II* (1908), pp. 80–81, Question 1712–1715; *Annual Report of the Chief Inspector of Factories . . . for the Year 1899, Part II: Reports* (1900), p. 276; *Departmental Committee on the Truck Acts: Minutes of Evidence, Vol. III* (1908), pp. 219–222.

100 Squire, *Thirty Years in the Public Service,* p. 79; Greer, "'Middling Hard on Coin," pp. 287–288. Quote from Squire.

101 *Departmental Committee on the Truck Acts: Minutes of Evidence, Vol. II* (1908), p. 103, Question 2263 (quote), and 2266.

102 *Annual Report of the Chief Inspector of Factories . . . for the Year 1899, Part II: Reports* (1900), p. 276.

103 Squire, *Thirty Years in the Public Service,* p. 84.

104 Greer, "'Middling Hard on Coin," pp. 288–289.

105 *Annual Report of the Chief Inspector of Factories . . . for the Year 1899, Part II: Reports* (1900), p. 276.

106 Greer, "'Middling Hard on Coin," p. 289; Squire, *Thirty Years in the Public Service,* pp. 82–83.

107 Squire, *Thirty Years in the Public Service,* p. 83.

108 Squire, *Thirty Years in the Public Service,* pp. 85–87; *Departmental Committee on the Truck Acts: Minutes of Evidence, Vol. II* (1908), p. 80, Question 1699–1703; Kevin James, "Outwork, Truck and the Lady Inspector: Lucy Deane in Londonderry and Donegal, 1897," pp. 115–116.

109 Squire successfully prosecuted two other firms under the Truck Act in November of 1899, and a third in December 1899. Greer, "'Middling Hard on Coin,'" pp. 292–293; *Departmental Committee on the Truck Acts: Report of the Truck Committee, Vol. I: Report and Appendices* (London: HM Stationary Office, 1908), p. 11.

110 Greer, "'Middling Hard on Coin," pp. 289–290; *Departmental Committee on the Truck Acts: Minutes of Evidence, Vol. III* (1908), p. 19, Questions 10438–10439.

111 *Departmental Committee on the Truck Acts: Minutes of Evidence, Vol. II* (1908), p. 79, Question 1678 (quotation), 1686–1690.

112 *Hansard Parliamentary Debates Online, House of Commons,* 9 July 1900.

113 Squire, *Thirty Years in the Public Service,* pp. 93–94.

114 Greer, "'Middling Hard on Coin,'" pp. 291–292.

115 Squire, *Thirty Years in the Public Service,* p. 94; Frank, "Let But One of Them Come Before Me, and I'll Commit Him," pp. 64–91; Douglas Hay, "Dread of the Crown Office: The Magistracy and the King's Bench, 1740–1800," in N. Landau (ed.), *Law, Crime and English Society, 1660–1830* (Cambridge: Cambridge University Press, 2002).

116 *Departmental Committee on the Truck Acts: Minutes of Evidence, Vol. III* (1908), p. 19, Question 10465. The firm had two members, John Sweeney and his brother, Morris Sweeney.

117 *Departmental Committee on the Truck Acts: Minutes of Evidence, Vol. III* (1908), p. 19, Question 10465.

118 Greer, "Middling Hard on Coin," pp. 292–293.

119 Greer, "Middling Hard on Coin," p. 294; *Annual Report of the Chief Inspector of Factories . . . for the Year 1900* (1901), p. 29.

120 Greer, "Middling Hard on Coin," pp. 295–297; Squire, *Thirty Years in the Public Service,* pp. 94–96.

121 Squire, *Thirty Years in the Public Service,* pp. 95–96; Greer, "Middling Hard on Coin."

122 *Hansard Parliamentary Debates Online, The House of Commons,* 9 July 1900.

123 38 & 39 Victoria, c.90, s.10.

124 *Report of the Departmental Committee on the Truck Acts* (1908), p. 111; Greer, "Middling Hard on Coin," p. 299; Squire, *Thirty Years in the Public Service*, pp. 96–97; *Annual Report of the Chief Inspector of Factories . . . for the Year 1900* (1901), p. 30.

125 Greer, "Middling Hard on Coin," pp. 301–302; *Hansard Parliamentary Debates Online, House of Commons*, 23 July 1900.

126 *Annual Report of the Chief Inspector of Factories . . . for the Year 1900* (1901), pp. 358–359.

127 *Hansard Parliamentary Debates Online, The House of Commons*, 9 July 1900. Also see: *Hansard Parliamentary Debates Online, The House of Commons*, 31 July 1900.

128 *Annual Report of the Chief Inspector of Factories . . . for the Year 1900* (1901), p. 359.

129 Greer, "Middling Hard on Coin," pp. 302–303; Squire, *Thirty Years in the Public Service*, p. 97.

130 *Annual Report of the Chief Inspector of Factories . . . for the Year 1900* (1901), pp. 403–404.

131 *Departmental Committee on the Truck Acts: Minutes of Evidence, Vol. II* (1908), p. 103, Question 2276–2283 (quote 2276).

132 *The Annual Report of the Chief Inspector of Factories for the Year 1903 – Part I: Reports* (1904), p. 233.

133 *Freeman's Journal*, 18 February 1908; *Freeman's Journal*, 4 January 1909. Gertrude Tuckwell Papers, London Metropolitan University Archives. Also see: *Departmental Committee on the Truck Acts: Report of the Truck Committee, Vol. I: Report and Appendices* (London: HM Stationary Office, 1908), pp. 11–12; *Departmental Committee on the Truck Acts: Minutes of Evidence, Vol. III* (1908), pp. 247–252.

134 *New Statesman*, 11 July 1914. Gertrude Tuckwell Papers, London Metropolitan University Archives.

135 "Truck in Ireland" *Woman Worker* 1 (5 June 1908), p. 30. Nineteenth Century Collections Online. Web. 15 January 2015.

136 *Departmental Committee on the Truck Acts: Minutes of Evidence, Vol. II* (1908), p. 99, Question 2150–51; Also see *Hansard Parliamentary Debates Online, House of Commons*, 2 May 1901. Liberal M.P. H.J. Tennant worried that because the decision in *Squire v. Sweeney (no.2) (1900)* was based in part on an English precedent *(Ingram v. Barnes)*, the Irish ruling might have implications for the Administration of the Truck Acts in England and Wales. *Hansard Parliamentary Debate Online, House of Commons*, 17 May 1901.

137 *Annual Report of the Chief Inspector of Factories . . . for the Year 1900* (1901), p. 404. Also see Inspector Edwards' similar prosecution in Southampton, *Annual Report of the Chief Inspector of Factories . . . for the Year 1905, Reports* (1906), p. 56.

138 *Departmental Committee on the Truck Acts: Minutes of Evidence, Vol. II* (1908), pp. 82–83, Question 1678 (quotation), 1743–1756; *Departmental Committee on the Truck Acts: Report of the Truck Committee, Vol. I: Report and Appendices* (London: HM Stationary Office, 1908), p. 12; *The Guardian*, 10 March 1909, Gertrude Tuckwell Papers, London Metropolitan University Archives.

139 *Annual Report of the Chief Inspector of Factories . . . for the Year 1900* (1901), p. 359.

140 Lynn Abrams, "Knitting, Autonomy and Identity: The Role of Hand-Knitting in the Construction of Women's Sense of Self in an Island Community, Shetland, c.1850–2000," *Textile History* 37:2 (2006):156.

141 *Departmental Committee on the Truck Acts: Minutes of Evidence, Vol. II* (1908), pp. 134–135, Questions 3323–3380; Abrams, "Knitting, Autonomy and Identity," p. 157.

142 *Annual Report of the Chief Inspector of Factories . . . for the Year 1900* (1901), p. 344.

143 *Departmental Committee on the Truck Acts: Minutes of Evidence, Vol. II* (1908), p. 135, Question 3381; *Annual Report of the Chief Inspector of Factories . . . for the Year 1901, Part II: Reports* (1902), p. 148.

144 *Departmental Committee on the Truck Acts: Minutes of Evidence, Vol. II* (1908), p. 136, Questions 3382–3393; *Annual Report of the Chief Inspector of Factories . . . for the Year 1902, Part I: Reports* (1903), p. 139.

145 *Annual Report of the Chief Inspector of Factories . . . for the Year 1905, Reports* (1906), pp. 326–327.

146 Scottish National Archives, AD.59.30.

147 "Industrial Prosecutions: Small Penalties: Contraventions of the Truck Act" *The Woman Worker* 3 (19 June 1908), p. 91. Nineteenth Century Collections Online. Web. 15 January 2015.

148 *The Scotsman,* 20 January 1909. Gertrude Tuckwell Papers, London Metropolitan University Archives.

149 *Departmental Committee on the Truck Acts: Minutes of Evidence, Vol. II* (1908), p. 139, Questions 3506; Also see: *Departmental Committee on the Truck Acts: Report of the Truck Committee, Vol. I: Report and Appendices* (London: HM Stationary Office, 1908), p. 12.

150 *Annual Report of the Chief Inspector of Factories . . . for the Year 1906, Reports and Statistics* (1907), p. 173.

151 *Departmental Committee on the Truck Acts: Minutes of Evidence, Vol. II* (1908), Testimony of the Duchess of Sutherland, pp. 165–170.

152 *Departmental Committee on the Truck Acts: Minutes of Evidence, Vol. II* (1908), p. 140, quote from. Question 3518, also see Questions 3537; Also see: *Departmental Committee on the Truck Acts: Report of the Truck Committee, Vol. I: Report and Appendices* (London: HM Stationary Office, 1908), pp. 12–13.

153 59 & 60 Victoria, c.44 (1896), s.2.

154 Squire, *Thirty Years in the Public Service,* p. 105.

155 Squire, *Thirty Years in the Public Service,* pp. 106–107.

156 Anderson, *Women in the Factory,* pp. 72–73; Squire, *Thirty Years in the Public Service,* p. 106.

157 *Annual Report of the Chief Inspector of Factories . . . for the Year 1899, Part II: Reports* (1900), p. 281.

158 *Departmental Committee on the Truck Acts: Minutes of Evidence, Vol. II* (1908), p. 86, Question 1846; Also see: *Annual Report of the Chief Inspector of Factories . . . for the Year 1902: Part I: Reports* (1903), pp. 189–191.

159 Smith v. Walton (1877) 3 C.P. 190–113; *Departmental Committee on the Truck Acts: Minutes of Evidence, Vol. II* (1908), pp. 23, 291; p. 27, Questions 360–364; p. 71, Question, 1471; p. 99, Question 2145.

160 Smith v. Walton (1877) 3 CP 109–113.

161 HO 45 9937 B27536; *Annual Report of the Chief Inspector of Factories . . . for the Year 1898, Part II: Reports* (1900), p. 152; *Departmental Committee on the Truck Acts: Minutes of Evidence, Vol. II* (1908), p. 87, Questions 1880–1881. *The Annual Report of the Chief Inspector of Factories . . . for the Year 1903 – Part I: Reports* (1904), p. 235.

162 *Annual Report of the Chief Inspector of Factories . . . for the Year 1905: Reports and Statistics* (1906), p. 324.

163 See the reports of London Inspector Good, Manchester Inspector W.J. Law and Inspector Rogers of Blackburn. *Annual Report of the Chief Inspector of Factories and Workshops for the Year 1906, Reports and Statistics* (1907), pp. 45, 138; Also see: *Millgate Monthly,* May 1910. Gertrude Tuckwell Papers, London Metropolitan University Archives.

164 *Nottingham Gazetter,* 18 June 1913. Gertrude Tuckwell Papers, London Metropolitan University Archives.

165 *Departmental Committee on the Truck Acts: Minutes of Evidence, Vol. II* (1908), p. 197, Questions, 5092–5093.

166 Anderson, *Women in the Factory,* p. 72.

167 *The Times,* 23 December 1910 in London Metropolitan University Archives, HD 4928. CA.45. Truck Box. Trades Council Material.

168 *Annual Report of the Chief Inspector of Factories . . . for the Year 1906: Reports and Statistics* (1907), p. 239.

169 *Departmental Committee on the Truck Acts: Minutes of Evidence, Vol. II* (1908), p. 22, Questions 285–286.

170 *Departmental Committee on the Truck Acts: Minutes of Evidence, Vol. II* (1908), p. 87, Question 1867.

171   *Departmental Committee on the Truck Acts: Minutes of Evidence, Vol. II* (1908), p. 68, quote from Question 1418, also see Questions 1416–1418; Also see the testimony of J.A. Redgrave, p. 42, Questions 713–721.

172   *Departmental Committee on the Truck Acts: Minutes of Evidence, Vol. II* (1908), p. 88, Question 1884–1888; p. 99, Question 2158–2164.

173   *Belfast News Letter,* 4 April 1903, from London Metropolitan University Archives, HD 4928.CA.45 Truck Box. Trades Council Material; *Departmental Committee on the Truck Acts: Minutes of Evidence, Vol. II* (1908), p. 93, Questions 2012–2020.

174   *Annual Report of the Chief Inspector of Factories . . . for the Year 1904, Reports* (1905), p. 282.

175   *Departmental Committee on the Truck Acts: Minutes of Evidence, Vol. II* (1908), p. 204, Questions 5277–5283; p. 222, Questions 5797–5800.

176   *Departmental Committee on the Truck Acts: Minutes of Evidence, Vol. II* (1908), p. 205, Questions 5291.

177   *Departmental Committee on the Truck Acts: Minutes of Evidence, Vol. II* (1908), pp. 51–52, Questions 936–942, Quote from 939; also p. 88, Question 1888.

178   *Departmental Committee on the Truck Acts: Minutes of Evidence, Vol. II* (1908), pp. 105–106, Questions 2331–2345.

179   *Annual Report of the Chief Inspector of Factories . . . for the Year 1901, Part II: Reports* (1902), p. 190.

180   *Annual Report of the Chief Inspector of Factories . . . for the Year 1898, Part II: Reports,* 1900), p. 185; Squire, *Thirty Years in the Public Service,* p. 69.

181   For some additional examples see: *Times,* 16 August 1899; *Annual Report of the Chief Inspector of Factories . . . for the Year 1901, Part II: Reports* (1902), p. 190; *Annual Report of the Chief Inspector of Factories . . . for the Year 1904, Reports* (1905), p. 201; *Annual Report of the Chief Inspector of Factories . . . for the Year 1906: Reports and Statistics* (1907), p. 106.

182   *Annual Report of the Chief Inspector of Factories . . . for the Year 1902: Part I: Reports* (1903), pp. 189–191; Squire, *Thirty Years in the Public Service,* p. 106.

183   *Departmental Committee on the Truck Acts: Minutes of Evidence, Vol. II* (1908), p. 20, Question 242.

184   *Departmental Committee on the Truck Acts: Minutes of Evidence, Vol. II* (1908), p. 67, Question 1394.

185   *Departmental Committee on the Truck Acts: Minutes of Evidence, Vol. II* (1908), p. 84, Questions 1804–1807.

186   *Departmental Committee on the Truck Acts: Minutes of Evidence, Vol. II* (1908), p. 68, Questions, 1425.

187   *Times,* 25 January 1899.

188   *Yorkshire Weekly Post,* 30 April 1910. Gertrude Tuckwell Papers, London Metropolitan University Archives.

189   *Annual Report of the Chief Inspector of Factories . . . for the Year 1901, Part II: Reports* (1902), pp. 147–148.

190   *Annual Report of the Chief Inspector of Factories . . . for the Year 1899, Part II: Reports* (1900), p. 281. For a similar observation by Gertrude Tuckwell, see *Departmental Committee on the Truck Acts: Minutes of Evidence, Vol. II* (1908), p. 222, Questions 5783–5790.

191   *Annual Report of the Chief Inspector of Factories . . . for the Year 1898, Part II: Reports* (1900), p. 184.

192   *Departmental Committee on the Truck Acts: Report of the Truck Committee, Vol. I: Report and Appendices* (London: HM Stationary Office, 1908), p. 37.

193   Squire, *Thirty Years in the Public Service,* pp. 106–107 (Quote from 107).

194   Adelaide Anderson to Arthur Whitelegge, 16 March 1898; Arthur Whitelegge to Kenelm E. Digby, 19 March 1898; HO 45 9932 B26427.

195   Arthur Whitelegge to Kenelm E. Digby, 19 March 1898; HO 45 9932 B26427.

196   Home Office Notes, TNA HO 45 9932 b26427.

197   *Squire v. Midland Lace Company (1905),* 2 K.B. 448; *Annual Report of the Chief Inspector of Factories . . . for the Year 1904, Reports* (1905), p. 281; *Annual Report of the Chief Inspector of*

Factories . . . for the Year 1905: Reports and Statistics (1906), p. 323; *Departmental Committee on the Truck Acts: Minutes of Evidence, Vol. II* (1908), p. 92, Questions 1980–1986.

198 *Squire v. Midland Lace Company (1905)*, 2 K.B. 488.

199 *Annual Report of the Chief Inspector of Factories . . . for the Year 1904, Reports* (1905), p. 281.

200 *Squire v. Midland Lace Company (1905)*, 2 K.B. 488.

201 *Departmental Committee on the Truck Acts: Minutes of Evidence, Vol. II* (1908), p. 177, Questions 4623.

202 *Departmental Committee on the Truck Acts: Minutes of Evidence, Vol. II* (1908), p. 25, Question 337.

203 *Annual Report of the Chief Inspector of Factories . . . for the Year 1905: Reports and Statistics* (1906), pp. 323–324.

204 *Departmental Committee on the Truck Acts: Minutes of Evidence, Vol. II* (1908), p. 92, Question 1994.

205 *Departmental Committee on the Truck Acts: Minutes of Evidence, Vol. II* (1908), p. 66, Question 1382.

206 *Departmental Committee on the Truck Acts: Minutes of Evidence, Vol. II* (1908), p. 6, Question 48, p. 88, Questions 1888–1889. Anderson echoed this sentiment. p. 66, Question 1357.

207 *Departmental Committee on the Truck Acts: Minutes of Evidence, Vol. II* (1908), p. 114, Question 2559.

208 *Departmental Committee on the Truck Acts: Minutes of Evidence, Vol. II* (1908), p. 106, Question 2530.

209 *Departmental Committee on the Truck Acts: Minutes of Evidence, Vol. II* (1908), p. 106, Question 2368.

210 *Departmental Committee on the Truck Acts: Minutes of Evidence, Vol. II* (1908), p. 105, Question 2333.

211 *Departmental Committee on the Truck Acts: Minutes of Evidence, Vol. II* (1908), p. 23, Question 296.

212 See the remarks of Clementina Black, of the Women's Industrial Council and Factory Inspector Rose Squire. *Departmental Committee on the Truck Acts: Minutes of Evidence, Vol. II* (1908), p. 97, Question 5102; *Annual Report of the Chief Inspector of Factories . . . for the Year 1898, Part II: Reports* (1900), p. 184.

213 *Yorkshire Post*, 14 January 1909. Gertrude Tuckwell Papers, London Metropolitan University Archives.

214 *Annual Report of the Chief Inspector of Factories . . . for the Year 1901, Part II: Reports* (1902), p. 83.

215 *The Annual Report of the Chief Inspector of Factories for the Year 1903 – Part I: Reports* (1904), p. 87.

216 *Departmental Committee on the Truck Acts: Minutes of Evidence, Vol. II* (1908), p. 38, Question 631.

217 *Annual Report of the Chief Inspector of Factories . . . for the Year 1906, Reports and Statistics* (1907), p. 239.

218 *Annual Report of the Chief Inspector of Factories . . . for the Year 1904, Reports* (1905), p. 174.

219 *Bristol Times*, 5 January 1911; *Western Daily Press*, 6 January 1911; *Western Daily Press*, 20 January 1911. Gertrude Tuckwell Papers, London Metropolitan University Archives.

220 For some additional examples, see: *Birmingham Post*, 13 February 1912, *The Leicester Post*, 10 January 1913, *John Bull*, 30 August 1913. Gertrude Tuckwell Papers, London Metropolitan University Archives; *Times*, 19 December 1910. London Metropolitan Archives, Truck Box, Trades Council Material. HD 4928.CA.45; *Times*, 22 March 1900, p. 12; *The Annual Report of the Chief Inspector of Factories for the Year 1903 – Part I: Reports* (1904), p. 36.

221 *Annual Report of the Chief Inspector of Factories . . . for the Year 1904, Reports* (1905), p. 43.

222 *Departmental Committee on the Truck Acts, Report of The Truck Committee . . .* (1908), p. 39.

223 *Departmental Committee on the Truck Acts, Report of The Truck Committee . . .* (1908), p. 39.

224 National Archives, LAB 14/47.

225 *Departmental Committee on the Truck Acts: Minutes of Evidence, Vol. II* (1908), p. 38, Question 629; p. 48, Question 846. Also see Squire, *Thirty Years in Public Service*, p. 111.
226 TNA, LAB 14/49.
227 TNA, LAB 14/47.
228 *Annual Report of the Chief Inspector of Factories . . . for the Year 1904, Reports* (1905), pp. 282–283.
229 Anderson, *Women in the Factory*, p. 73.
230 Squire, *Thirty Years in Public Service*, p. 110.
231 *Annual Report of the Chief Inspector of Factories . . . for the Year 1898, Part II: Reports* (1900), pp. 182–183.
232 For another example see: *Yorkshire Post*, 14 January 1909. Gertrude Tuckwell Papers, London Metropolitan University Archives.
233 *Annual Report of the Chief Inspector of Factories . . . for the Year 1905: Reports and Statistics* (1906), pp. 56, 105, 140, 209.
234 *Annual Report of the Chief Inspector of Factories . . . for the Year 1905: Reports and Statistics* (1906), pp. 139, 179.
235 *Annual Report of the Chief Inspector of Factories . . . for the Year 1905: Reports and Statistics* (1906), p. 179.
236 *Annual Report of the Chief Inspector of Factories . . . for the Year 1905: Reports and Statistics* (1906), p. 325.
237 "Owner v. Hooper," *Times Law Reports* 19:30 (1903), 601–602; *Departmental Committee on the Truck Acts, Report of The Truck Committee . . .* (1908), p. 125, Questions 2967–2982.
238 *Annual Report of the Chief Inspector of Factories . . . for the Year 1901, Part II: Reports* (1902), p. 190.
239 59 & 60 Victoria, c.44, Section 1.
240 *Departmental Committee on the Truck Acts, Report of The Truck Committee . . .* (1908), pp. 20–21.
241 Squire, *Thirty Years in the Public Service*, p. 100; *Manchester Dispatch*, 5 November 1910. Gertrude Tuckwell Papers, London Metropolitan University Archives.
242 *Annual Report of the Chief Inspector of Factories . . . for the Year 1899, Part II: Reports* (1900), pp. 277–280; *Departmental Committee on the Truck Acts: Minutes of Evidence, Vol. II* (1908), p. 209, Question 5416.
243 *Annual Report of the Chief Inspector of Factories . . . for the Year 1899, Part II: Reports* (1900), p. 280.
244 *Departmental Committee on the Truck Acts: Minutes of Evidence, Vol. II* (1908), p. 126, Questions, 3009–3021.
245 *Departmental Committee on the Truck Acts: Minutes of Evidence, Vol. II* (1908), p. 175, Questions 4582–4586. In another similar case he was less successful, see: p. 176, Question 4587.
246 Anderson, *Women in the Factory*, pp. 68–69; *Daily Chronicle*, 13 November 1911. Gertrude Tuckwell Papers, London Metropolitan University Archives.
247 *Departmental Committee on the Truck Acts: Minutes of Evidence, Vol. II* (1908), pp. 177–178, Questions 4634, 4635, 4685; *Departmental Committee on the Truck Acts: Report of the Truck Committee, Vol. I: Report and Appendices* (London: HM Stationary Office, 1908), p. 20.
248 *Departmental Committee on the Truck Acts: Minutes of Evidence, Vol. II* (1908), p. 203, Questions, 5255–5257; p. 209, Questions 5268–5269, 5417–5419.
249 *Departmental Committee on the Truck Acts: Minutes of Evidence, Vol. II* (1908), p. 211, Question 4558.
250 *Annual Report of the Chief Inspector of Factories . . . for the Year 1905: Reports and Statistics* (1906), p. 326.
251 Squire, *Thirty Years in the Public Service*, p. 102.
252 *Annual Report of the Chief Inspector of Factories . . . for the Year 1899, Part II: Reports* (1900), p. 281.
253 *Annual Report of the Chief Inspector of Factories . . . for the Year 1905: Reports and Statistics* (1906), p. 326.

254 *Departmental Committee on the Truck Acts: Minutes of Evidence, Vol. II* (1908), p. 211, Question 280.

255 *Annual Report of the Chief Inspector of Factories . . . for the Year 1901, Part II: Reports* (1902), p. 162; Squire v. Bayer & Co. (1901), 2 K.B. 299–303.

256 *Departmental Committee on the Truck Acts: Minutes of Evidence, Vol. II* (1908), p. 6, Question 46.

257 *Departmental Committee on the Truck Acts: Minutes of Evidence, Vol. II* (1908), p. 21, Question 260.

258 *Departmental Committee on the Truck Acts: Minutes of Evidence, Vol. II* (1908), p. 66, Questions 1358–1359.

259 *Departmental Committee on the Truck Acts: Minutes of Evidence, Vol. II* (1908), p. 65, Questions 1351.

260 *Squire v. Bayer (1901),* 2 K.B. 300.

261 *Squire v. Bayer & Co. (1901),* 2 K.B. 302; *Annual Report of the Chief Inspector of Factories . . . for the Year 1901, Part II: Reports* (1902), p. 162.

262 *Squire v. Bayer & Co. (1901),* 2 K.B. 302; *Annual Report of the Chief Inspector of Factories . . . for the Year 1901, Part II: Reports* (1902), p. 162.

263 *Annual Report of the Chief Inspector of Factories . . . for the Year 1901, Part II: Report* (1902), pp. 103–104; Squire, *Thirty Years in the Public Service,* p. 104. Quote from Squire.

264 Squire, *Thirty Years in the Public Service,* p. 104.

265 *Annual Report of the Chief Inspector of Factories . . . for the Year 1901, Part II: Report* (1902), p. 189.

266 *Star,* 21 July 1914; *Darlington Echo,* 22 July 1914; *Mary Bull,* 4 July 1914. Gertrude Tuckwell Papers, London Metropolitan University Archives. Quote from *Mary Bull.*

267 *Departmental Committee on the Truck Acts: Minutes of Evidence, Vol. II* (1908), p. 65, Questions 1345–1355, Quote from 1345.

268 *Departmental Committee on the Truck Acts: Minutes of Evidence, Vol. II* (1908), p. 85, Question 1836.

269 *Annual Report of the Chief Inspector of Factories . . . for the Year 1904, Part I: Report* (1905), p. 283; *Departmental Committee on the Truck Acts: Minutes of Evidence, Vol. II* (1908), p. 41, Questions 698–700, p. 45, Question 773, p. 47, Questions 823–824. Also see, p. 211, Questions 5448–5453.

270 *Departmental Committee on the Truck Acts: Minutes of Evidence, Vol. II* (1908), p. 190, Questions 5060–5061.

271 *Labour Leader,* 23 July 1914. Gertrude Tuckwell Papers, London Metropolitan University Archives.

272 *Departmental Committee on the Truck Acts: Minutes of Evidence, Vol. II* (1908), p. 85, Questions 1831–1835; *Departmental Committee on the Truck Acts, Report of The Truck Committee. . .* (1908), pp. 19–20.

273 *Departmental Committee on the Truck Acts, Report of The Truck Committee . . .* (1908), pp. 19–20.

274 *Truck Act of 1986: Contract in respect of deductions and other conditions subject to which all workers are employed in this weaving factory.* London Metropolitan University Archives, Truck Box, Trades Council Materials, HD 4928.CA.45.

275 *Annual Report of the Chief Inspector of Factories . . . for the Year 1905: Reports and Statistics* (1906), p. 56 (Quote); *Departmental Committee on the Truck Acts: Minutes of Evidence, Vol. II* (1908), p. 174, Questions 4528–4530; p. 176, Question 4590.

276 *Annual Report of the Chief Inspector of Factories . . . for the Year 1906, Reports and Statistics* (1907), p. 45.

277 *Departmental Committee on the Truck Acts: Minutes of Evidence, Vol. II* (1908), p. 196, Question 5062.

278 *Birmingham Post,* 4 January 1909. Gertrude Tuckwell Papers, London Metropolitan University Archives.

279 *Departmental Committee on the Truck Acts, Report of The Truck Committee. . .* (1908), p. 19.

280 *Departmental Committee on the Truck Acts: Minutes of Evidence, Vol. II* (1908), p. 209, Question 5393.

281 *Departmental Committee on the Truck Acts: Minutes of Evidence, Vol. II* (1908), p. 196, Question 5062.

282 *Departmental Committee on the Truck Acts: Minutes of Evidence, Vol. II* (1908), p. 208, Question 5378.

283 *Staffordshire Sentinel,* 16 June 1910, 23 June 1910; *Birmingham Post,* 17 June 1910. Gertrude Tuckwell Papers, London Metropolitan University Archives.

284 *The Common Cause,* 25 April 1913. Gertrude Tuckwell Papers, London Metropolitan University Archives.

285 *Departmental Committee on the Truck Acts: Minutes of Evidence, Vol. II* (1908), pp. 72, 74, Question 1488–1490, 1538–1542.

286 *Departmental Committee on the Truck Acts: Minutes of Evidence, Vol. II* (1908), p. 85, Question 1837.

287 *Departmental Committee on the Truck Acts: Minutes of Evidence, Vol. II* (1908), pp. 86, 89, Question 1838–1840, 1925–1929.

288 *Departmental Committee on the Truck Acts: Minutes of Evidence, Vol. II* (1908), pp. 91–92, Question 1977.

289 *Departmental Committee on the Truck Acts: Minutes of Evidence, Vol. II* (1908), p. 125, Questions 2964–2966, 4721.

290 Stephen Fox and J.R. MacDonald, "Shop Assistants and the Truck Acts," *Women's Industrial News,* New Series, No.3 (March 1898):17. Nineteenth Century Collections On Line. Web. 15 January 2015.

291 Fox and MacDonald, "Shop Assistants and the Truck Acts," pp. 17–20.

292 *Departmental Committee on the Truck Acts: Minutes of Evidence, Vol. III* (1908), p. 137, Questions 13464.

293 *Departmental Committee on the Truck Acts: Minutes of Evidence, Vol. III* (1908), p. 113, Questions 13093–13097; p. 136, Questions 13464–13468.

294 *The Daily Chronicle,* 24 March 1898, 31 March 1898 in TNA HO 45 9986 X68918; Margaret Bondfield, P.C. Hoffman, Frank Tilley, *Truck Enquiry Committee, Evidence Given on Behalf of the National Amalgamated Union of Shop Assistants, Warehousemen and Clerks* (London: The Twentieth Century Press, 1907), p. 2.

295 *The Daily Chronicle,* 31 March 1898 in TNA HO 45 9986 X68918; Also see Fox and MacDonald, "Shop Assistants and the Truck Acts," pp. 19–20; *Departmental Committee on the Truck Acts: Minutes of Evidence, Vol. II* (1908), p. 47, Questions 830–834.

296 *The Daily Chronicle,* 24 March 1898 in TNA HO 45 9986 X68918.

297 *The Daily Chronicle,* 24 March 1898 in TNA HO 45 9986 X68918.

298 *Departmental Committee on the Truck Acts: Minutes of Evidence, Vol. II* (1908), p. 47, Questions 834.

299 *The Daily Chronicle,* 24 March 1898 in TNA HO 45 9986 X68918.

300 *The Daily Chronicle,* 31 March 1898 in TNA HO 45 9986 X68918.

301 Fox and MacDonald, "Shop Assistants and the Truck Acts," p. 19.

302 Folio 3, TNA HO 45 9986 X68918.

303 Folio 3, Home Office note, TNA HO 45 9986 X68918; *Hansard Parliamentary Debates Online: House of Commons,* 25 March 1898.

304 *The Daily Chronicle,* 31 March 1898 in TNA HO 45 9986 X68918.

305 *Times,* 18 May 1898, p. 13.

306 *The Daily Chronicle,* 24 March 1898 in TNA HO 45 9986 X68918; Bondfield, Hoffman, and Tilley, *Truck Enquiry Committee,* pp. 3–5.

307 *Departmental Committee on the Truck Acts: Minutes of Evidence, Vol. II* (1908), p. 47, Questions 833.

308 *The Daily Chronicle,* 18 March 1898, in TNA HO 45 9986 X68918.

309 William Arnold to Home Office, 18 March 1898; Home Office note, 21 March 1898; TNA HO 45 9986 X68918.

310 *The Times,* 31 July 1899.

311 *Annual Report of the Chief Inspector of Factories . . . for the Year 1904, Part II: Report* (1905), p. 282.

312 *Annual Report of the Chief Inspector of Factories . . . for the Year 1904, Part II: Report* (1905), p. 282.

313 *Annual Report of the Chief Inspector of Factories . . . for the Year 1906, Part I: Report* (1907), p. 240.

314 *Departmental Committee on the Truck Acts: Minutes of Evidence, Vol. II* (1908), p. 25, Question 332.

315 *Annual Report of the Chief Inspector of Factories . . . for the Year 1904, Part I: Report* (1905), p. 283; *Annual Report of the Chief Inspector of Factories . . . for the Year 1906, Part I: Report* (1907), pp. 241–243.

316 *Annual Report of the Chief Inspector of Factories . . . for the Year 1906, Part I: Report* (1907), p. 241.

317 *Annual Report of the Chief Inspector of Factories . . . for the Year 1906, Part I: Report* (1907), pp. 241–243.

318 *Annual Report of the Chief Inspector of Factories . . . for the Year 1906, Part I: Report* (1907), p. 242.

319 *Annual Report of the Chief Inspector of Factories . . . for the Year 1906, Part I: Report* (1907), pp. 241–243.

320 *Deane v. Wilson (1906),* Irish Reports, K.B.D. (1906), Vol. II, pp. 405–413.

321 *Departmental Committee on the Truck Acts: Minutes of Evidence, Vol. II* (1908), p. 8, Question 67.

322 Deane v. Wilson, Irish Reports, K.B.D. (1906), Vol. II, pp. 405–413.

323 Deane v. Wilson, Irish Reports, K.B.D. (1906), Vol. II, pp. 405–413.

324 *Departmental Committee on the Truck Acts, Report of The Truck Committee. . .* (1908), pp. 19–27.

325 *Annual Report of the Chief Inspector of Factories . . . for the Year 1906, Part I: Report* (1907), p. 240.

326 *Departmental Committee on the Truck Acts: Minutes of Evidence, Vol. II* (1908), p. 107, Questions, 2374–2378, quote from 2375.

327 *Cardiff Times and South Wales Weekly News,* 23 January 1904.

328 *Cardiff Times and South Wales Weekly News,* 23 January 1904.

329 *Williams and Others v. North's Navigation Collieries (1889), Ltd. (1904),* 2 K.B. pp. 44–48.

330 Ibid., pp. 48–57.

331 *Williams and Others v. North's Navigation Collieries (1889), Ltd. (1906),* A.C. House of Lords and Privy Council, pp. 136–147.

332 HD 4928.CA.45 Truck Box, Trades Council Material. London Metropolitan University Archives.

333 John H. Romanes, "The Truck Acts," *Juridical Review* 18 (1906–1907), pp. 247–258.

6 The factory inspectorate, organized labour, and the debate over fines and deductions from wages, 1906–1914

The departmental committee on the Truck Acts

By 1906, government officials and trade union leaders had come to the conclusion that the 1896 Truck Act was not sufficient for protecting workers from exploitative deductions from their wages. In fact, after a decade of mixed results, a number of trade union leaders felt vindicated for opposing its passage and insisted it had "legalized fines."[1] *Williams and Others v. North's Navigation Collieries, Ltd. (1906)* appeared to transform the 1896 Truck Act from legislation that limited fines to an act that enabled them. These perceptions were shaped by the prosecutions under the 1896 Act that were lost on appeal before the high courts that removed outworkers from the protections of the Act, allowed employers to evade its regulations of fines by adopting the "bonus system" and accepted such an expansive definition of the term "fair and reasonable" that it seemed nearly any fine was legal. While inspectors won 75% of the cases that they prosecuted during the first decade of the Act's existence, their annual reports revealed that they struggled to convince magistrates that excessive deductions from wages were not fair and reasonable or that when considering "all the circumstances of the case" they should take into account factors beyond the loss to the employer. Even when victorious in court the inspectors could not always secure large enough penalties to deter similar violations. In 1904, the female factory inspectors lost more than 40% of the cases that they brought before magistrates under the 1896 Truck Act, and they became reluctant to prosecute cases. For shop assistants, who were outside the jurisdiction of factory inspectors, the law had always been a dead letter. There were legitimate reasons why politicians, factory inspectors and labour leaders felt that reform was overdue.

Yet, the 1896 Truck Act was more successful than the case law suggests. Assistant Under-Secretary of State at the Home Office Henry Cunynghame argued in 1906 that

> in spite of some adverse circumstances and some difficulties I think a very good record can be shown by the inspectors of their exertions. The number of cases on that point by no means represents of course the evil put down. For one person who has fought the Home Office, hundreds have given

way, so that there has been undoubtedly in factories and workshops very considerable truck reductions.[2]

In 1908 when the Departmental Committee on the Truck Acts reported to Parliament, the majority insisted, "We entertain no doubt, as a result of the evidence we have taken ... that the provisions of the Act of 1896 have been productive of a large amount of good, notwithstanding the existence of certain defects."[3] Inspectors convinced large numbers of employers to conform to the requirements of the 1896 Act by reducing, and more transparently defining, fines and deductions. Many employers chose to abandon them altogether, gradually changing customs in some industries and regions.[4] Statute law and state regulation can play a significant role in the creation, encouragement or confirmation of new norms and expectations and can stigmatize behaviours that were once widely practiced.

Even unsuccessful prosecutions confronted the public with the dubious pretences employers used to claw back the wages of the lowest paid workers. Just because the high courts ruled that it was legal for employers to fine workers for dancing on their dinner break, to pay poor outworkers in truck or to charge employees the cost of insurance required for complying with the Workmen's Compensation Act did not mean that the public felt that these were honourable practices.[5] The annual reports of factory inspectors and the press coverage of the cases they prosecuted raised awareness about the ways in which poor workers were cheated out of their wages.

The voices of female factory inspectors were amplified through their correspondence and cooperation with female trade union leaders such as Gertrude Tuckwell, Clementina Black and Mary MacArthur. These women passed information back and forth about abusive practices in the workplace and the shortcomings of the 1896 Act. Tuckwell, Black and MacArthur, who each conducted investigations into the condition of sweated female workers, spread this knowledge through publications, lectures and testimony before Parliament. In 1904, 27% of the complaints received by the WTUL from female workers were about violations of the Truck Acts.[6] These women communicated examples of hardship caused by exploitative practices that the 1896 Act had been ineffective at preventing with allies in Parliament, particularly Sir Charles Dilke and H.J. Tennant. This information was disseminated against the backdrop of active public campaigns for improving the conditions of women in sweated labour and agitation for a minimum wage.[7]

On 27 February 1906, Dilke proposed a resolution in Parliament: "That it is the opinion of this House that it is necessary to put an end to fines and deductions from wages." Because "timid legislation" had repeatedly failed, "the time had come for heroic legislation." He asserted that the 1831 and 1887 Truck Acts had been "killed by judge-made law," and the 1896 Act "unfortunately has been a complete failure." He described outrageous cases of deductions for damaged work and fines for trivial offences that had been supplied by Tuckwell, Black and female factory inspectors. Dilke cited the factory inspectors, who "declared conclusively that fines were not necessary to discipline, and that in the best factories and workshops there were no fines." He argued that rather than deducting from workers' wages for fines or damaged work, the remedy for serious misconduct or damage should be the 1875 Employer and Workmen Act. This would prevent employers from acting as prosecutor and judge in their own cause. He argued that a report from The Board of Trade that found that the fining of workers was a significant cause of labour disputes, declaring it was time to end this "fruitful source of tyranny."[8]

In the February 1906 election, 29 members of the Labour Party were elected to Parliament, and many spoke in support of Dilke's resolution. David Shackleton, who was also the general secretary of the Textile Factory Workers' Association, agreed that the "time had arrived when the legislature should prohibit fines of every description."[9] Labour MP and president of the National Amalgamated Union of Shop Assistants and Clerks, James Seddon, added that any new legislation should include greater protections for shop assistants, who experienced fines with "special severity." Labour Party leader Keir Hardie insisted that "[n]o fines or deductions should be allowed which benefit the employer."[10]

Under-Secretary of State for the Home Department Herbert Samuel reassured the House that this "question belonged to a class of subjects that the new Parliament would take a special interest," and truck "legislation would certainly be introduced." He praised the work of the factory inspectors whose efforts had been undermined by weak statutes and reported additional examples of workers who faced excessive deductions from wages. He informed the House that the bill would not be introduced during the present session, because the government intended to prioritize the Trade Union Bill and the Workmen's Compensation Bill. He suggested that the time could be used to have a Departmental Committee investigate the issue, especially the conditions of shop assistants and the living-in system. Because the government did not yet know the conclusions of this inquiry, it could not accept Dilke's resolution.[11] Home Secretary Herbert Gladstone reiterated Samuel's sentiments, acknowledging the consensus that a more stringent Truck Act was required, as well as a desire to reduce fines and deductions. At the same time Gladstone insisted that "drastic legislation cannot be proposed without careful preliminary consideration." He proposed amending Dilke's resolution by adding the words "other than such as may be specifically legalized by Parliament." Dilke agreed to the qualification, and his resolution passed the House.[12]

On 5 April 1906, Gladstone appointed a Departmental Committee to inquire into the Truck Acts and consider what amendments or changes in their enforcement were necessary. He instructed the committee to consider whether employers taking fines and deductions from the wages of workers should be prohibited and whether the practice of shop assistants being lodged and boarded by employers was being abused. The chair of the Committee was Liberal MP and Lord Advocate of Scotland, Thomas Shaw. Other members of the Committee included Liberal MP and Lancashire cotton merchant Frederick Cawley, shipbuilder Sir Alfred F. Yarrow, chemical manufacturer and Unionist MP Edward

Brotherton, and Labour MP and future prime minister Ramsay MacDonald. MacDonald resigned from the Committee and was replaced in October 1906 by Labour MP Stephen Walsh, a long-time opponent of fines and deductions. The only woman named to the Committee was May Tennant, who had served as the first female factory inspector until resigning after the birth of her first child. Home Office official Malcolm Delevingne was chosen to serve on the committee because of his expertise in factory law and occupational welfare and safety and was joined by Thomas Bettany, who acted as secretary.[13] Although violations of the Truck Acts were thought to be particularly rampant in Ireland, there were no Irish MPs on the Committee. It was initially thought that the Committee might complete its work in less than a year, but the range of issues it investigated meant that they did not present their report to Parliament until 14 December 1908.[14]

The first meeting of the Departmental Committee on the Truck Acts took place on 2 May 1906, and, over the next two years and eight months, it met 82 times and interviewed 118 witnesses.[15] The Committee compiled the relevant case law, compared the laws against truck that existed in the colonies and foreign countries and also personally visited living-in establishments.[16] Thirteen of the first 15 witnesses interviewed were officials from the Home Office or inspectors of the mines and factories. These witnesses provided the commissioners with first-hand accounts of the injustices uncovered while enforcing the Truck Acts. A number of common themes emerged in their testimony. There was a consensus that the 1896 Truck Act had reduced the number of fines and deductions, but the vagueness of the terms "fair and reasonable," the unwillingness of magistrates to consider the wages of workers when evaluating the legality of fines and deductions and setbacks before the high courts had prevented further progress.[17] Nearly all of the first 15 witnesses recommended that the Truck Acts be expanded to cover outworkers, arguing that rulings in *Squire v. Sweeney (no. 2) (1900)* and *Squire v. Midland Lace (1905)* were contrary to the intentions of the legislature and caused great suffering among poor women.[18] Many disagreed with the judgement in *Owner v. Hooper (1903)*, insisting that employers should not force workers to pay for statutory obligations imposed on owners by Parliament.[19]

While none of the factory inspectors thought that fines and deductions were fair to workers, and all agreed that in the best-run workplaces they were not used, they were divided over whether they should be more strictly regulated or prohibited. Chief Inspector Whitelegge and Principal Lady Inspector Anderson thought that there should be a limit on the percentage of a worker's weekly wage that an employer could take for all deductions, suggesting 5% as the maximum. Some inspectors worried that if fining were abolished it might force employers to more frequently resort to suspensions or dismissals. Some were also concerned about instances where employees' actions endangered the safety others or wilfully damaged employers' property.[20]

Inspectors Squire, Deane, Paterson and Owner all took the position that fines and deductions for damaged work should be abolished, even if it meant that employers would more regularly suspend or dismiss workers.[21] They doubted that a spike in sackings would be the result of abolishing fines, because well-managed firms could handle minor transgressions with reprimands. Furthermore, inspectors emphasized that these sanctions were not necessarily alternatives to one another, as the factories that imposed heavy fines also discharged workers more frequently than non-fining firms.[22] Three female inspectors argued that in addition to being a hardship for low paid workers, deductions for fines and damaged work failed to improve discipline and only increased tensions between employers and workers.[23] Inspectors Squire, Paterson, Deane, Redgrave, Owner and Edwards also thought that most deductions for materials should be made illegal as well. Many thought that workers should receive their wages free of deductions and should then be able to make separate bargains for materials, tools or services provided by the employer. These witnesses expressed deep scepticism about the need to charge workers for power, heat, light or standing room.[24]

Inspectors Anderson, Deane, Paterson and Martindale, who had the most experience investigating the bonus system, argued for its abolition as well.[25] Deane informed the Committee that when investigating how the bonus system operated in practice, it became obvious that it was a *de facto* fine.[26] Inspector Martindale testified that this was not merely her interpretation, as "two employers have told me they adopted the bonus system in order to evade the Truck Acts."[27]

In contrast to the factory inspectors, the inspectors of the mines opposed further regulation or prohibition of fines and deductions from wages. During the previous decade the inspectors of the mines had devoted much less energy to the enforcement of the 1896 Truck Act than the inspectors of the factories. Inspector of the Mines for Lancashire and North Wales District Henry Hall and his colleague for the Midland District, A.H. Stokes, explained in their testimony that fines in the mines were important for workplace safety, and many offences for which miners could be fined were also violations of the Special Rules of Coal Mines Regulation Act of 1887, so it was less harsh for an employer to impose a fine than to prosecute the offending miner before a magistrate. In most mines the proceeds of fines went to a sick club or charity.[28] Inspectors also asserted that miners were represented by powerful trade unions that could protect their interests.[29]

However, the testimony of the inspectors revealed that mine owners under their jurisdiction only dubiously conformed to the requirements of the 1896 Act. These owners fined their workers without describing in a written contract or a posted notice the specific offences for which they could be fined and the amounts that could be taken, as required by the 1896 Act.[30] When a miner was fined, he would be presented with a slip that he was required to sign (on pain of dismissal) stating that he agreed to pay the fine and authorized the employer to deduct the amount from his wages. Thomas Ellis, the solicitor and law clerk for the Mining Association of Great Britain, an organization for employers in the industry, testified that it would be "impossible" for mine owners to catalogue a list of offences and amounts of fines because of the large number of possible transgressions each with a potentially wide degree of seriousness.[31]

Ellis supported the testimony of the inspectors, stating that in the absence of fines, each instance where miners violated the Special Rules under the Coal Mines Regulation Act would have to be brought before magistrates, costing time and expense to both management and employees. Fines involved no lost time and usually were smaller sums than the penalties inflicted by magistrates.[32] The testimony of Ellis was followed by directors of mines who agreed that the abolition of fines would undermine safety and discipline and result in the adoption of more severe forms of discipline. They also insisted that deductions for tools, supplies and house rent were beneficial to the miners.[33]

Thomas Greenall and Henry Twist of the Lancashire and Cheshire Miners' Federation challenged the suggestion that coal miners were satisfied with fines and deductions. In fact, Greenall described instances where the Miners' Federation supported men financially who were dismissed for refusing to sign the authorization for deducting a fine.[34] Twist stated that in addition to complaining to employers on behalf of individual miners who had been fined, the union approached the Coal Owners' Association about abolishing fines but was unsuccessful.[35] Greenall testified his union

> are of the opinion that the fines ought not to be imposed, that they do not achieve the object which we expect the mine officials have in view, . . . and also it rather lends itself to undue advantage being taken of the man by under-officials.[36]

Greenall, encouraged by the questions of Walsh, himself a former Lancashire miner, disputed the observation that fines promoted better discipline or safety.[37] He insisted that if a miner violated the special rules of the Coal Mines Regulation Act, he thought "the proper course would be to take the offender before the magistrate."[38] Greenall opposed deductions from miners' wages for tools and materials, proposing that miners should receive their wages in full and then purchase items as they needed.[39] Greenall stated that while the miners trusted the inspectors to enforce the Coal Mines Regulation Act, they were reluctant to approach them about violations of the Truck Act because "the inspectors do seem to lean to the employers' side with regard to the amount, and some are very favourable to deductions being made from the wages."[40] Other miners expressed fear that if they reported Truck Act violations to the inspectors they might be dismissed.[41] The inspectors of the mines received few complaints under the Truck Act not because pitmen accepted the right of their employers to take fines and deductions but rather because they did not trust these officials to enforce the Act. Greenall and Twist were supported by Robert Smillie, a representative of both the Scottish Miners' Federation and the Parliamentary Committee of the TUC. Based upon his 20 years' experience as a Lanarkshire miner, he found that

> the miners, so far as I can gather their opinions, are absolutely opposed to any deductions whatever being taken from their wages with the exception of those contributions which might be taken off wages at the miners' request, and handed over to their committees for their own purposes.[42]

Greenall, Twist and Smillie were not the only trade union officials interviewed by the Departmental Committee. Representatives of organized labour
were, for the most part, in agreement the 1896 Act had been a failure. Only
Herbert Withey of the Amalgamated Union of Clothing Operatives and Ben
Turner of the General Union of Weavers and Textile Workers thought that the
1896 Act had reduced workplace fines and deductions.[43] Richard Bell, secretary
of the Amalgamated Railway Servants Association, and Moses Sclaire, of the
Amalgamated Jewish Tailors, Machinists and Pressers Trade Union, described
the 1896 Act as a "dead letter" in their trades.[44] William Drew, the secretary of
the Bradford Trades Council, remained persistent in his belief that the 1896
Act had "legalized fines." Because of the power of trade unions in some trades
"in the old days, although there was no schedule published, an employer was
chary of inflicting fines, because of the ease in which bother could be made
about it, but now the employer hides himself behind the schedule" posted in
the workplace.[45] David Shackleton, representing the Northern County Weavers
Association, described why his union had worked with the employers to get
cotton weavers in the north exempted from the 1896 Truck Act, explaining
"we feared we should lose the right which we had always claimed of examining whether the fault was that of the weaver or not. . . . [I]f it was found the
weaver was not to blame we should refuse to admit liability." Under the 1896
Truck Act, the posting of a notice of fines and deductions for damaged work
"might be regarded as an implied contract under which we might lose our right
to insist that every fine might be made a question of examination and proof."[46]
Both men thought that prior to the 1896 Act their unions could contest fines
and deductions with greater success than after its passage. However, the 1896
Truck Act was intended to protect those workers who were unorganized and
less able to challenge unfair treatment.[47] In its final report to Parliament, the
majority of the Committee stated, "we conclude from this evidence, and that
of other representatives of the organized trades, that the unions in these trades
are able as a rule to protect their members against unreasonable fines," but "it is
in the unorganized trades that the abuses chiefly occur."[48]

Nearly every representative of organized labour who testified thought that
the only way forward was the complete abolition of fines and deductions for
damaged work.[49] They provided examples of the unfairness of these exactions
to working people and testified that they poisoned industrial relations without
improving discipline or the quality of work.[50] While most union representatives
doubted that the abolition of fines or deductions for bad work would lead to
more suspensions and dismissals, they were prepared to accept that outcome
over the current system.[51] Many union representatives called for the abolition
of all deductions from wages for materials and services provided by employers.[52]

Female trade unionists also gave evidence before the committee. Clementina Black had spent nearly three decades advocating on behalf of low-paid
female workers and represented the position of the Women's Industrial Council
(WIC).[53] The WIC had conducted a study of deductions from wages for disciplinary fines, damaged work, materials, goods supplied by employers and sick

and benefit clubs. They also inquired into the experiences of shop assistants as they related to the Truck Acts.[54] Black had written and lectured extensively on the Truck Acts and was able to provide the committee with specific cases of the misery caused by deductions taken from low-paid workers.[55] Black's personal views differed from the organization that she was representing before the Committee. The Council advocated making it illegal to deduct wages for power or room, for the purchase spoiled work and for work damaged by juvenile workers, but it voted that in some narrow circumstances deductions from the wages of adults should be permitted, if limited to a maximum proportion of the weekly pay packet. This would be preferable to the alternatives of dismissal or suspension.[56] Encouraged by the questions of May Tennant, Black revealed that "I myself think that it is a mistake on the part of my Council. . . . I should go further than they do; for my own part I should like to see disciplinary fines abolished by law."[57] She also disputed that in their absence employees would be more frequently dismissed, observing of women workers subjected to fines, "I do not think it is possible that they could be discharged more readily than they are now."[58]

The most informed testimony of any witness before the Committee was provided by Gertrude Tuckwell of the WTUL, who had long been involved in the struggle over fines and deductions. During her preparation for testifying she wrote that her goal was to show

> that no legislation short of the abolition of all fines and deductions, all suspensions, and all payments by workers to their employers, direct or indirect, will be effective. The failure of the present law will be shown and some objections v. abolition dealt with.[59]

Tuckwell provided the committee with a list of nearly 80 cases of unjust fines and deductions that the WTUL had sent to Principal Lady Inspector Anderson between April 1904 and May 1906, which was included as an Appendix to the final report. These fines either were for trivial offences or represented an outrageous proportion of the workers' wages.[60] Tuckwell was the most forceful and convincing witness in favour of the total prohibition of fines, deductions from wages and the bonus system. She argued that these exactions were ineffective and unnecessary.[61] When the chairman attempted to get her to concede that capping deductions as a percentage of the weekly wage would be an improvement, she replied,

> I am afraid I cannot bring my mind to contemplate any of these palliatives; they do seem to me to leave such loopholes for abuses. One has seen the breakdown of the 1896 Act. . . . It seems to me that nothing short of abolition will do . . . the fines ought to go.[62]

She also reminded the committee that the prohibition of workplace fines and deductions was not only what she wanted, but it was what working women wanted as well.[63] When Committee members challenged her by suggesting that the abolition of fines would lead to more suspensions and discharges, Tuckwell disagreed, arguing that if employees were certain that their position depended upon adherence to the rules, they would transgress them less frequently.[64]

Mary Galway of the Textile Operatives Society of Ireland, an organization which had a membership of over 3,000 workers, also gave strong evidence in favour of the prohibition of fines. During her ten-and-a-half years as organizing secretary, her union had represented workers in 66 cases of unfair fines or deductions for damaged work. Sometimes they remonstrated with the employer and succeeded in getting the exaction returned to the worker and in others they went to court under the Truck Act.[65] Galway provided stories of deductions for spoiled work that supported her assertion that "fines should be absolutely abolished."[66] In June of 1908, Galway convinced the Irish Trades Union Congress to pass a resolution demanding "that all deductions from wages in the form of fines, inflicted as punishment for alleged offences or as indemnities for spoiled work, should be rendered illegal."[67]

Not all advocates for female labour favoured a stronger Truck Act. Edith Lawson testified on behalf of the Freedom of Labour Defence, an organization "formed to protect adult women from undue restrictive legislation which we think will hamper their interests in obtaining work."[68] Lawson's organization was opposed to further reform, citing cases where firms had abandoned fines for lateness but instead locked tardy workers out of the workplace until the next break time, which cost piece workers more money than the fines.[69] Tennant questioned Lawson aggressively, especially over Lawson's assertion that "no authentic cases of unreasonable fines have been met with." Tennant directed Lawson's attention to the reports of the factory inspectors, causing her to concede, "Yes, I wrote that in a great hurry. I did not mean it to apply to the factory inspectors' work." Tennant also grilled Lawson about the thoroughness and methodology of her investigations, which the former factory inspector thought were superficial.[70]

Strengthening the arguments of trade unionists was the testimony of employers who had abandoned the system of fining workers and taking deductions for damaged work and achieved positive results. Thomas Ferrens, MP for East Hull, had spent 40 years as managing director of Messrs. Reckitt and Sons, starch and blue manufacturers.[71] Decades earlier, because the leaders for the firm found that "fines and deductions from the wages were very obnoxious to the workpeople . . . we concluded . . . to try the entire abolition of fines." Instead of fining, the firm hired skilled foremen and forewomen and provided greater oversight.[72] Ferrens stated that dismissals had not increased since his firm had changed the system. Warning and cautions were used, with discharge as the ultimate sanction for repeat offences, which had been under the fining system as well.[73] Edward Cadbury, one of the managing directors of Cadbury Brothers, Ltd., testified that in 1898 the firm eliminated all fines for its 4,000 employees because they discovered that they did not deter lateness or bad behaviour.[74] Like Ferrens, Cadbury reported that punctuality and discipline improved after the prohibition, and dismissals did not increase.[75] Other employers suggested that in recent years many firms had been moving away from fining because it embittered workers.[76]

Not all employers, however, thought that fines and deductions were unnecessary, and the Committee heard their testimony as well. These employers emphasized that fines were essential to the maintenance of discipline and safety.[77] They stressed that it was imperative that employers have an intermediate sanction available when employees were unpunctual or engaged in behaviour that hindered the firm. If such penalties were abolished, they would resort to dismissal.[78] Some textile manufacturers anticipated significant losses if they could not make deductions for spoiled work.[79] Even when confronted with the examples of employers in their own industries who had eliminated fines, they refused to concede that they could run their businesses under a different disciplinary system.[80]

Employers of low-paid workers defended the fining system by suggesting that it was the only way to keep a "low class" of employee punctual and focused. Laundry owner Charles Marshall stated that "[my]y own feeling is that I would much sooner see no fines at all, . . . but into the laundry trade drifts every unsuccessful person from every possible class of business."[81] With tough questioning, Walsh made Marshall acknowledge that the majority of launderers, drawing from the same pool of workers, did not use fines. Marshall insisted that those firms had poor discipline and "the hands practically do what they like."[82] Another laundry proprietor, Hugh Trenchard, used fines because his employees "are largely undisciplined young girls . . . that we take soon after they leave school. . . . [T]he difficulty is to get them in to time."[83] When a committee member asked Trenchard whether he had considered locking the women out until the next break period when they were late, Trenchard replied, "My dear sir, do not suggest that! We have hard enough work as it is to get the work out without indulging in the luxury of stopping anybody."[84] This statement reveals the real reason why some employers kept insisting that a system of fines was preferable to one of cautions, suspensions and dismissals. Employers did not object to suspensions and dismissals because they would be harder on employees but rather because they would be harder upon them. In cases of suspensions and dismissals, the employer lost the labour of the worker, so unless that labour was no longer worth the trouble, it was preferable to fine and have the work continue at a reduced cost. Alexander Siemens, of the Engineering Employers' Federation, told the Committee that it was undesirable to abolish fines because "you cannot use dismissal in the same way, because you hurt yourself more than you hurt the men."[85]

There were some apparent contradictions in the testimony of the employers. John Aspinall, the general manager of the Lancashire and Yorkshire Railway, testified that fines were essential for the maintenance of safety and discipline, but he also swore that they were not oppressive because so few were imposed by the company. In 1906, his company collected £121 of fines from 33,000 employees, an amount that averaged one-one hundredth of a penny per week per employee. Walsh asked Aspinall, "Does not this suggest that you could nearly do away with the fines, when the total gets so low?" Aspinall insisted that it was the moral effect of the fine that made workers adhere to the rules.[86] Alexander Butterworth, manager of the North Eastern Railway, argued that fines were not unjust because most were for small amounts. This prompted Walsh to ask whether these "matters might very well have been met by an admonition on behalf of officials?" Butterworth replied, "I do not really think mere cautions would act as the check that the man wants. It is like water running off a duck's back."[87] There were many of these exchanges during the testimony of employers, who believed strongly in the moral power of fining workers.[88] Female factory inspectors had repeatedly shown that, in fact, fines were not a moral deterrent and that it left workers with the impression that they could "purchase" a certain amount of bad behaviour.

Another important mandate of the Departmental Committee on the Truck Acts was to investigate the conditions of shop assistants, particularly the living-in system. Shop workers were outside of the protections of the 1831 and 1887 Truck Acts but were covered by Section 1 the 1896 Truck Act. Four full days of testimony came from representatives of the NAUSAWC, including Margaret Bondfield, Frank Tilley, P.C. Hoffman and J.A. Seddon. Their evidence was published and distributed in pamphlet form, and in the evenings after their testimony they held public meetings to discuss the issues that they raised before the Committee.[89] An additional day was given to M. J. O'Lehane, of the Irish Drapers Assistants' Benefit and Protective Association, and Aubrey Rees, of the National Association of Grocery Assistants.

Bondfield and Hoffman testified that their constituents wished to see fines abolished.[90] Shop assistants laboured under large codes of fines that often only dubiously conformed to the "fair and reasonable" standards of the 1896 Truck Act, because there was no inspectorate to enforce the legislation.[91] In addition to heavy fines for unpunctuality and minor transgressions, many of the rules in shops were vague and highly subjective.[92] Under such rules the question of whether an employee had committed an offence sometimes "just depends on whether the shop walker is in a temper or not."[93] Hoffman added, "It very largely depends upon the shopwalker, whether he is of an amiable disposition or not . . . it depends on whether he has any animosity against you or not."[94] Bondfield insisted that the trend was moving away from fines and that many of the most respected establishments did not use them.[95]

Many witnesses also advocated prohibiting the living-in system for shop assistants.[96] In some establishments accommodation provided by the employer was treated as a condition of employment, and it represented a portion of the employee's remuneration.[97] Many shop assistants would have preferred a larger wage and the freedom to choose their own food and housing. As with truck in other contexts, they argued that the arrangement undermined their freedom and independence and left them continually under the control of their employers. Hoffman stated that "there cannot be the least doubt but that the living-in system is a survival of truck."[98] Although the living-in system was not used in Scotland, it was estimated that as many as 400,000, or half of the total shop workers in the United Kingdom, lived in.[99] The scale of this system was an argument against reform, as its abolition would lead to short-term disruption. The witnesses from NAUSAWC gave detailed accounts of conditions in different establishments, describing crowded and poorly ventilated sleeping facilities, lack of privacy and bad food.[100] Many shop assistants believed that employers profited from boarding their workers because they were able to reduce wages by more than what they actually spent on accommodation.[101] Exacerbating this were additional deductions taken from shop assistants who resided in employer's housing, such as charges for breakages, access to a doctor, maintenance of a library or boot cleaning.[102]

Committee members pointed out that prohibiting the living-in system did not necessarily mean that employers would raise the wages of shop assistants by the amount that they claimed to spend providing board and lodging.[103] Even if they were able to raise their wages by that amount, some doubted whether it would be enough to find lodging in expensive cities such as London. In some cases, employers had economies of scale that allowed them to house and board workers more cheaply than they could their own. The witnesses in support of abolishing the living-in system noted that workers in other trades with similar wages were able to find lodging.[104]

For shop assistants, the monetary losses that came from living in were secondary to the issue of independence.[105] When living in was a condition of employment, one could never have a separate life from work, or, as Aubrey Rees testified, there was "no escape from the atmosphere of the shop." This left the employee with "[a]n overpowering sense of being fettered."[106] Bondfield thought that living in "robs the assistant, whether man or woman, of that sense of . . . ordering and controlling one's own life."[107] Many employers used the living-in system to pressure shop assistants to work unpaid overtime, because "the fact that they are living on premises makes it possible for the employers to keep their assistants in up to ten or eleven o'clock, or even till midnight, dressing windows and getting ready for the next day's sales."[108]

While living in, the shop assistant was compelled to continue living under the rules of the employer even after work day had ended. In addition to the list of fines that were enforced at work, there were also fines for violating the rules of their lodgings.[109] For example, employees could be fined 2s 6d for not eating their supper in the correct room.[110] O'Lehane argued that living in

> is an infringement of their social rights and of their ordinary rights as citizens, and as men who are responsible for their actions. Men are timed going out and coming in, spied upon, fined, dismissed, and generally worried. In fact, it is more difficult to conform to the various rules and avoid the pains and penalties attendant upon the 'living in' system than it is to go through a day's work.[111]

In this atmosphere of continual supervision it was difficult to develop an independent life.[112] Because so many shop assistants were young men and women, opponents of the system argued that it undermined their development into full adults. Tilley told the committee, "An assistant who lives in never handles part of his wages, everything is done for him, he is treated like a child, and it discourages the growth of all manly and womanly characteristics in shop workers."[113] Witnesses thought this interfered with the ability of shop assistants to get married and become full citizens.[114] Living in cost many male shop assistants the ability to vote, and Seddon lamented to the Committee that it "deprives men from taking any part in the life of the community; not having votes, they are cut off from political life."[115] Rees thought that this made "men more effeminate who live in" and had observed among them "a nervousness and shaking of the limbs; they seem as if afraid of things are going to happen."[116]

Ernest Debenham, of Debenhams Ltd., reported to the Committee that his firm, by voluntary agreement with the employees, had been steadily reducing the number of employees who lived in and currently housed only a few under special circumstances.[117] This was partially from the desire of employees and partially from the will of the firm to rid itself of the challenges of housing employees.[118] He informed the Committee that his shop assistants had no troubles in finding accommodations, experienced no detrimental moral effects.[119]

Other representatives of drapers, grocers and retail shops, however, defended the living-in system, and they were supported by the testimony of six shop workers who were pleased with the conditions and food provided.[120] Most employers were willing to submit their premises to a regime of inspection, though they were decidedly less enthusiastic about bringing their industry within the provisions of the 1831 and 1887 Truck Acts.[121] They described the pleasant amenities provided to employees, such as libraries, reading rooms, smoking rooms, sitting rooms, billiards rooms, pianos, athletic clubs, sports teams and opportunities for recreation.[122] Arthur Cole, a Sheffield draper, told the Committee that the "living in encourages the social side of a business house" and without the "pleasant and helpful recreation" it provided the "necessary *esprit de corps* would be absent."[123] Many employees, particularly young and female employees, came from the countryside with no experience of urban life and benefitted from the moral supervision and protection.[124] In the absence of living in, many parents would be reluctant to permit their children to work as shop assistants.[125] They defended the value of the lodging and food provided for the shop assistants.[126] Benjamin Evans, the chair of the Drapers' Chamber of Trade, said that the workers themselves were quite pleased with the arrangements and in terms of the agitation against the living-in system: "The whole thing in my opinion is a political agitation to gain members of the union."[127]

One of the reasons why the Departmental Committee on the Truck Acts was unable to report back to Parliament within the expected time frame was because their inquiry touched upon a range of different interests whose views needed to be considered. Five representatives from various regional accident and relief societies for miners testified to the Committee about their opposition to any changes to the Truck Act. Much of their funding came from deductions taken from the wages of workers, and they feared, just as they had in 1887, that if this were made illegal it would have a very detrimental effect upon their membership.[128] The Committee also heard two days of testimony on the issue of "Cider Truck" in agricultural districts, which had been a controversial question for truck reformers since at least the 1860s.[129]

The divided report of the Departmental Committee, 1908

In December of 1908 a divided Departmental Committee finally reported back to Parliament, presenting both a Majority and a Minority Report. The Majority Report, which was supported by six members of the committee, contained 32 recommendations.[130] It recommended that the Truck Acts be extended to outworkers and that the authority of factory inspectors be expanded to include docks and warehouses. The Majority Report stated that in 1896 "when legislating on the subject of truck, Parliament intended that outworkers as a class should have the benefit of the protection of the Acts" and observed that the rulings in *Squire v. Sweeney (no. 2) (1900)* and *Squire v. Midland Lace (1905)* "produced widespread dissatisfaction and the social effects of such a state of the law are such that we think it our duty as a Committee to call attention to them" because they left the workers who needed the Truck Acts outside of its protections.[131]

The Majority Report acknowledged the extensive testimony, revealing fines were often imposed upon workers for "the most trivial offenses" that "it is difficult to see with regard to many of these offenses, in what way loss or hindrance is caused to the employer's business."[132] Against this evidence the majority weighed the possibility that a prohibition might lead to increases in suspensions, wages reductions and dismissals.[133] For this reason the majority recommended tighter regulation of fines rather than their abolition.[134] Because it was unfair to fine a young and inexperienced worker who was just learning the trade, the majority proposed prohibiting fines on those 16 years old and younger.[135] For adults, the majority recommended making the maximum amount of accumulated fines imposed during any week not exceed 5% of the wages owed to the worker. Deductions for the payment of fines should only be made in the pay period in which the fine was imposed, so employers could no longer impose outrageously large fines and then deduct them in instalments over many pay periods. The majority were also opposed to compelling a coal miner to sign an agreement to deduct a fine from his wages after the fact, stating "whether this system is technically in compliance with the provisions of Section 1 of the Act of 1896 or not, the intention of the Act was clearly to require an antecedent contract."[136] In cases involving the "bonus system," which "from the evidence placed before us, we believe is abused," they proposed that magistrates should be given the discretion to decide whether the system in the particular workplace was a *bona fide* bonus or an evasion the Truck Act.[137] The majority observed that the fining system among shop assistants was disappearing on its own, but because some shop assistants laboured under very considerable codes of fines and had no inspectorate to act on their behalf, the majority proposed that the inspectors who enforced the Shop Hours Act also be given the additional powers to enforce the Truck Acts.[138]

After reviewing examples of crippling deductions from the wages of poor employees for damaged work, it was obvious that, "serious abuses still exist, chiefly in the unorganized trades, and ... the present statutory powers are insufficient to deal with them." The majority was reluctant to leave the employer without any remedy for damaged work, because carelessness could destroy costly materials; but they also wanted to eliminate deductions that were out of proportion to the wages paid. Therefore, they recommended that the provisions for deductions for bad work or damaged materials in section two of the 1896 Truck Act be repealed and deductions for negligent work be treated as fines with the same proposed limits upon the maximum percentage of the weekly wages for cumulative deductions. It would not be permitted for an employer to fine a worker under 16 for damaged work because "if an employer for his own purposes sets an inexperienced hand to work, . . . the risk should be the employer's."[139] More serious damage to materials could be pursued in civil court and decided by an independent party.

The Majority Report recommended that employers not be permitted to charge workers for materials that went into the product sold, though they suggested that the Home Secretary be permitted to grant exemptions to particular trades.[140] Likewise, no deductions should be permitted for machinery, standing room, light, heat "or anything else which might be considered to be part of the general equipment of the works."[141] Deductions for tools that become the property of the worker should be permitted subject to the requirements of Section three of the 1896 Truck Act. There should be no deductions for benefit societies except for those certified under the Shop Clubs Act (1902). No deductions should be permitted for the provisions of mess rooms or house rent but rather these should be a part of a separate agreement between employers and workers. Deductions for medical care should be subject to section 23 of the 1831 Truck Act, but workers should be able to choose their own medical attendant. Deductions for fuel and food and drink (not intoxicating), consumed on premises, should be permitted.[142]

The Departmental Committee heard a great deal of contradictory evidence about living in, and the majority sided with those in favour of its continuance. Committee members personally visited many of the establishments complained about by the shop assistants' unions, and the majority found that while there was a range in the quality, abuses did not appear widespread.[143] The majority expressed doubt that the sum an employer would allow to employees in lieu of living in would be enough to secure lodgings of a comparable quality in London. They also thought that the system provided security for young women.[144] Rather than abolish the living-in system, they instead proposed a mild regime of local inspection.[145]

Had the Departmental Committee been able to make the Majority Report unanimous, it would have represented an ideal compromise solution for the Liberal government. The recommendations retained the basic principles of 1896 Truck Act, while repairing its most obvious flaws. Limiting the cumulative total fines and deductions for damaged work charged to a worker at 5% of the weekly wages and prohibiting fines being carried over from the pay period in which they were charged would mean that the overall size of an employee's wage would automatically be one of the "circumstances of the case" that had to be considered. When combined with abolishing all fines and deductions for damaged work on employees under the age of 16, it would prevent the most egregious examples of unfairness. At the same time, these proposals would involve minimal interference with the authority of employers.

The majority did not seem to appreciate how strongly opponents objected to the very principle of employers having the authority to make fines and deductions from wages. Furthermore, for workers in non-organized and low wage trades, every penny mattered to the struggle for survival. If past practice were any guide, the 5% cumulative weekly total would not be a maximum but rather the new norm for fines and deductions for damaged work.

The majority's recommendations for the living-in system also offered the least disruptive solution that still had the potential to check the worst accommodations for shop assistants. The majority was convinced that this system provided good value to the worker and some moral protections for young people. The arguments that living in robbed employees of their independence were ignored by the majority. The recommendations of the majority had enough compromises to make legislation politically possible. However, the dissent of two Committee members significantly changed the political prospects for Parliament acting on this Report.

The Minority Report was written by May Tennant and Stephen Walsh. Tennant and Walsh disagreed with many points in the Majority Report, but their primary differences were in three critical areas: fines, deductions from wages for damaged or negligent work and the living-in system. They saw absolutely no useful purpose for fines, which embittered workers, and did nothing to improve discipline or punctuality. Tennant and Walsh relied upon the testimony of not only the female factory inspectors and trade unionists but also prominent employers, who stated that better supervision and training eliminated the need for fining workers.[146] The Minority Report stressed the obvious fact that in the United Kingdom "the majority of firms have no recourse to fines."[147] In answer to the contention of the majority of the Departmental Committee that in the absence of fines employers would fire workers for errors, Walsh and Tennant again looked to the testimony of employers, who asserted that this had not been their experience. The Minority Report asserted that "[d]ismissal is too generally considered to be an alternative to fining: it is its accompaniment. Supervision, with cautioning as one of its incidents, is the true alternative."[148] Walsh and Tennant also believed that this argument was a bluff by employers because suspension and dismissal "is of great inconvenience to manufacturers.

While their machinery is running inside, few employers will indulge in the luxury of keeping their workers standing outside."[149] The Minority Report conceded that under the Majority Report

> many of the abuses of the present legalized system would disappear. But many would remain. The sense of injustice, the irritation that is the essence of the system, the friction, the substantial grievance of the loss where the maximum penalty becomes the standard penalty, or where the wages are already low, all this would remain.[150]

Walsh and Tennant objected to treating deductions for bad work as disciplinary fines. Under this new regime, employees would remain helpless to argue that the fault was caused by a defect in materials, machinery or other workers. It would not eliminate the injustices inherent in the current system. They insisted that deductions for spoiled or damaged work be prohibited and employers be compelled to use their civil remedies.[151]

Walsh and Tennant were also unable to accept the position of the majority regarding the living-in system. They argued that "[a] system where workers are compelled to lodge and board in a particular place must, in itself, stand condemned." Workers had no powers to shop around to find the best possible lodgings, which reduced incentives for employers to improve these establishments. Supported by the evidence given by employers such as Derry and Debenham, they also challenged the argument that workers would be unable to find adequate lodging.[152]

The Departmental Committee's division in its recommendations significantly changed the political calculus of proposing reforms for the Liberal government. The division of the Committee and the production of two official reports undermined the credibility and authority of both. Trade unions and the Labour Party would support the Minority Report and in fact most resolved to oppose anything else. This meant that if the Liberal government prepared legislation based upon the Majority Report, it would get no credit from organized labour for having improved conditions for workers and, indeed, might engender greater hostility. Legislation based upon the Majority Report would probably be grudgingly acceptable to some employers and Liberals, but some would object to new regulations as a matter of principle. To provoke the irritation of employers and the opposition of much of organized labour would be a high price to pay for reform. Embracing the Minority Report would be difficult for the government because it meant rejecting a bi-partisan Majority Report in favour of one written by a radical former coal miner and a retired female factory inspector, both of whom had a long history of activism. The recommendations of the Minority Report would force some workplaces to dramatically transform disciplinary regimes, which would be opposed by most employers and Conservative MPs and many Liberals as well. Another factor which blunted the force of the 1908 Report of the Departmental Committee on the Truck Acts was the timing of its presentation to Parliament: in December of 1908.

Had the Committee been able to complete its work even six or eight months earlier there might have been an opening for the introduction of legislation. In April of 1909, David Lloyd George introduced his controversial "People's Budget," which occupied much of Parliament's agenda, eventually leading to the even more divisive and time-consuming issue of Parliamentary reform. In 1909 and 1910, there was little space on the political agenda for truck reform.

Public reactions to the 1908 report of the Departmental Committee

After The Report of the Departmental Committee on the Truck Act was presented to Parliament on 21 December 1908, its conclusions were widely reported upon in the press, which often expressed shock at the revelations that truck, workplace fines and dubious deductions from the wages of workers continued to exist.[153] The *Irish Times* told its readers that

> the whole report with regard to Ireland raises questions of grave importance to the people of this country . . . and the national discourse will undoubtedly receive a shock from these disclosures. It may be hoped that prompt and adequate measures will be taken.[154]

The *Bolton Evening News* argued, "[W]hatever differences of opinion there be generally on the reports, there can be only one opinion as to the proved need of some reforms, and the material cause is now to design the best scheme."[155] All agreed that outworkers should be protected by the law and, at the very least, fines and deductions should be limited by Parliament.

Much of the press embraced the relative moderation of the Majority Report, which as the *Birmingham Gazette* editorialized "will commend itself at once bearing the stamp of impartial research and clear thinking on common sense lines." On the other hand, it considered that the Minority Report "will scarcely command serious attention except from those who believe in state interference for its own sake."[156] The *Times* asserted that "in spite of its dissenting postscripts, the report of the majority will necessarily carry much weight."[157] Many provincial papers reached very similar conclusions.[158] The *Factory and Workshops Times* reluctantly endorsed many of the recommendations of the Majority Report while severely condemning the Minority Report. It wrote of May Tennant that her "experience is undeniably great, if her zeal, perhaps, is even greater." It complained of "the appetite for state intervention of Mr. Walsh and his lady colleague" and stated that abolishing fines "is completely in accordance with the general socialist hostility to the development of efficiency and competition."[159]

Walsh and Tennant had supporters, such as Clementina Black, who warned MPs not to make the same errors that undermined the effectiveness of the 1896 Truck Act. Black warned that "compromise too often means confusion; to attempt to stand with one foot on each side of a dividing line is in effect to leave the shaping of the law in the hands of magistrates and judges." Black asserted that with fines, deductions from wages and the living-in system, there was "a clear line of principle," which was "to give workers a larger proportion of that independence which ought to be theirs." She insisted that "the point is that the mere fact of paying B to do certain work does not entitle A to regulate B's private life and expenditure."[160] Mary MacArthur wrote an editorial that denounced fines, deductions for damaged work and charges for materials, and like Black she warned the government against a "window dressing type of legislation which gives the sanction of law to the very abuses it claims to remedy."[161] *The Woman Worker* said of the Minority Report,

> [I]t is clearly more important than the report of the majority, for it has the greater weight of expert opinion to back its unhesitating arguments against fines and the living-in system. Resolutions everywhere should be sent to the Home Office and to Members of Parliament.

The article foregrounded the testimony of the female factory inspectors and reiterated all of the arguments against fines, deductions from wages for damage and the living-in system.[162] *The Manchester Guardian* also endorsed the proposals of the Minority Report. The editorial criticized the majority for focusing solely on the material conditions of living in, suggesting that they "have disregarded the one all-important fact that shop assistants, as far as their desires can be ascertained, do not like the system, and are quite powerless to escape it." *The Nation* agreed and, after reviewing the revelations of the Departmental Committee on the Truck Acts with respect to living in, stated that "the recommendation of the Majority Report is timid and disappointing; it seems to also run contrary to the texture of the Report itself."[163] In addition to some newspapers, most of the labour movement supported the findings of the Minority Report.[164] At the annual meeting of the TUC, resolutions were passed insisting that no legislation which failed to abolish the living-in system would be satisfactory to shop workers and that the Parliamentary Committee should push the government to introduce truck legislation based upon the Minority Report.[165]

There were also reactions that rejected both the Majority and the Minority Reports, finding any reform an unwarranted interference with the freedom to contract. *The Journal of Commerce* concluded that "many of the recommendations . . . are of a drastic character and most of them may be said to infringe on the once sacred principle of freedom to contract." The article complained that if the regulations of the Majority Report were implemented it would contribute to a trend where

> [t]he employer is no longer master. His predecessors may have been tyrants, but he has paid for their alleged sins and is now not only no longer master of his own house, but carries on his own business absolutely on sufferance. He is to be the loser from unpunctuality, disobedience, damage to materials or machinery. Already he has to run the risk of accidents, and the burden of the Workmen's Compensation Acts. Already he has to pay his share of

the state pensions which have been given to aged workers. Already he is regulated as to the hours, place, and conditions in which he may carry on his business.[166]

The *Newcastle Journal* wondered "whether the Departmental Committee on the Truck Act . . . has considered what the full effect of its recommendations will be" for employers. The author thought that if the regulations suggested by even the Majority Report became law, unemployment would increase because negligent workers would be dismissed.[167]

Efforts for reform, 1908–1914

In their *History of British Trade Unionism*, H.A. Clegg, Alan Fox and A.F. Thompson claim that the reports of the 1908 Departmental Committee on the Truck Acts were "completely ignored."[168] This is not correct and, in fact, prior to the outbreak of the Great War, there was strong momentum for legislation. Organized labour made repeated efforts to keep the abolition of fines and deductions, as well as the living-in system, on the Parliamentary agenda. On 19 February 1909, a deputation from the TUC waited upon Home Secretary Gladstone and requested the abolition of fines. The next day in the House of Commons, J.A. Seddon asked the Home Secretary whether the opportunity would be granted to debate the Reports of the Departmental Committee on the Truck Acts. Gladstone informed him that he hoped there would be time.[169]

On 10 June 1909, another deputation, of 120 representatives, from the United Textile Factory Workers Association, which was led by MP David Shackleton, met Gladstone in the reception room at the Home Office. Shackleton was concerned that contradictory evidence given to the Departmental Committee on the Truck Acts might obscure the fact that there was overwhelming support among workers in the northern textile industry for the abolition of fines and deductions from wages for spoiled work.[170]

Shackleton introduced J.W. Odgen, who represented the cotton weavers. Ogden brought attention to resolutions passed in 1905 and 1908 by unions representing over 100,000 textile workers that called for the abolition of fines. He explained that weavers had always objected to these fines and deductions.[171] Ogden then explained the weaver's work to Gladstone, emphasizing the ways in which errors could be made through no fault of the weaver. He described the sheer quantity of material each weaver worked with, some of which was of an inferior quality, as well as the problems that could arise with the machinery. Despite the employee's best efforts there was "no such thing as a perfect cloth." When supervisors determined that a cloth was spoiled, "we have no say in this matter. We have to accept the employer's verdict. If he keeps any part of our wages under any pretext whatever, we can only go to the county court." Ogden insisted that if an employer thought a worker was at fault, he should pursue his remedies in civil court and not be judge in his own cause. Ogden stated, "[W]e are told that if these fines were removed we should have more discharges. Well, we have no guarantee of employment even with fines, and our answer to the contention is we are prepared to face that danger."[172] He also argued that the 5% cap on cumulative weekly fines "would leave us worse than we are today" because "in the hands of an unscrupulous employer, such a proviso would in practice mean a 5% reduction of wages." Ogden told Gladstone that the textile workers in Lancashire would be grateful to him if he would use his influence to secure legislation enacting the recommendations of the Minority Report. He also warned Gladstone, however, that

> if we cannot get this reformed by legal means we shall have to seek it by way of the strike. But that is a weapon we have no desire to use – our wish is to keep the machines running, and secure a settlement by peaceful methods.[173]

Thomas Ashton reiterated that "fines must be abolished," describing how for among spinners 30 years earlier fines and deductions were serious problems but because of the strength of their organization they had been able to have these ended. He lamented, however, that the cotton weavers had weaker organization and included a significant proportion of juvenile and female workers in its ranks. Employers have "taken advantage of in their weakness. The employers are persistent in nibbling at their wages for the most trivial causes." He pleaded that because organized labour could not end these practices by itself, "surely you, with your wide sympathy and influence in the House of Commons, will induce that assembly to pass a measure to put an end to it once and for all."[174]

Gladstone replied to the deputation by conceding that the system of fines and deductions was "irritating and galling." He could not promise prompt action, however, because

> the budget, with all its pervading influences and scope – is inevitably blocking many avenues usually open in the way of legislation, and although I hope to deal with this question this session, it must be sorrowfully admitted that the whole time of Parliament up to Christmas, if not until next Easter, will be occupied in discussing the budget.

The budget he was referring to was David Lloyd George's controversial "People's Budget," which used a variety of progressive taxes to fund old-age pensions. Gladstone also stated that the inability of the Committee to arrive at unanimous recommendations complicated legislating: "the matter has been made rather more complex by the fact that there has been a division on the Committee. . . . [T]hese are differences which have to be got over."[175] Despite renewed agitation by the weavers and ongoing revelations of abuse from the reports of factory inspectors, there was no legislative activity on the issue in 1909 or 1910.[176]

While Parliament did not pass legislation based upon the conflicting recommendations of the Departmental Committee on the Truck Acts, it did pass a new law that provided some assistance to a small number of poor workers who had been susceptible to having their wages reduced by fines and deductions. In 1909 Parliament passed the Trade Boards Act, which applied to workers in ready-made and bespoke tailoring, domestic chain making, card-box making and machine-made lace making and finishing. These fields represented around 250,000 low-paid workers. The legislation, influenced by laws passed in Australia and New Zealand, allowed for the creation of Trade Boards in the named industries, where wages were deemed unacceptably low. These boards consisted of representatives of labour, representatives of employers and independent members appointed by the government. These boards were empowered to establish minimum time rates of wages, or minimum piece rates. The law contained a number of loopholes and limitations, but it did lead to significant improvements in pay for workers in these jobs.[177] Of particular relevance was section six of the Trade Boards Act, which stated that the minimum wage rate decided by a Trade Board must be paid to the employee "clear of all deductions." Factory Inspector Constance Smith later emphasized the significance of this section:

> These four words relieve the poorest class of workers from a burden that has long weighed heavily upon them. The provision does not, it should be observed, sweep away the whole system of fines and deductions in all workplaces where the minimum rate is in operation, for it does not – and indeed cannot – deal with any earnings beyond the minimum wage which is contemplated by the Trade Boards Act. But it does at least secure the worker in absolute and undiminished possession of this minimum wage.[178]

Inspector Anderson agreed with this assessment in her 1922 memoirs, stressing the important role that female factory inspectors played in producing evidence that led to the passage of this legislation. She observed the Trade Boards Act had a "striking effect in steadily sweeping away many of the deductions from low wages with which we were specially concerned."[179] Inspector Squire thought that the Trade Boards Act reduced the most abusive fines and deductions.[180] In 1913, additional Trade Boards were established in the sugar confectionery, food preserving, shirt-making, tin-box making and linen and cotton embroidery industries. In 1918, a new Trade Boards Act was passed and by 1921 nearly three million labourers were covered by these Acts.[181]

There was overlap between efforts to eliminate unfair fines and deductions from workers' wages and the anti-sweating movement which worked to raise low wages and improve working conditions. Sir Charles Dilke, Clementina Black, George and Edward Cadbury, Rose Squire and Mary MacArthur had been active in both struggles. In June of 1907, a Select Committee on Homework was created and when it reported in July of 1908 it recommended the creation of wage boards. Another recommendation of that Committee was that "the full protection of the Truck Acts should be secured to homeworkers," nearly identical to a conclusion reached in both the Majority and Minority

Reports of the Departmental Committee on the Truck Acts.[182] The Trade Boards Bill was introduced into Parliament on 24 March 1909 by Winston Churchill, and he was assisted in shepherding it through the House of Commons by H.J. Tennant, the husband of May Tennant.[183] Even though advocates of Truck Acts reform were unable to secure new legislation based upon the work of the Departmental Committee, they did win a qualified victory in the form of the Trade Boards Act, which, as Jessica Bean and George Boyer demonstrated, reduced household poverty rates among women in these trades.[184]

In 1911 the issue of truck received renewed attention in Parliament, as labour leaders, particularly those representing workers in cotton factories and female trade unions, pushed hard to keep this issue in the public eye. On 30 May 1911, Albert Smith introduced a bill to make all deductions from the wages of workers in cotton factories – including for fines and charges for damaged work – illegal. The bill did not advance in the House of Commons.[185] The TUC and organized labour worked to support this bill with resolutions, lobbying and petitions.[186] In March of 1912, Smith asked the new Home Secretary, Reginald McKenna, whether he intended to introduce legislation to abolish fines in factories and workshops. McKenna informed Smith that the government would not legislate on the subject during the present session and that the Majority Report of the Departmental Committee on the Truck Acts opposed the abolition of fines.[187] Unsatisfied with this answer, for the second time, Smith introduced a bill to abolish fines and deductions in cotton factories.[188] The bill's co-sponsor, Labour MP A.H. Gill of Bolton, tried to win the support of the entire industry by organizing a conference between the Lancashire Cotton Spinners and Manufacturers' Association and the Textile Workers' Association in November of 1912. The conference was unable to bridge the difference of opinion on the need for fines. Employers claimed that they needed to retain fines for ensuring quality work.[189] There was, however, some good news for some Lancashire weavers in 1912. Employers in Bacup agreed to extend their year-long experiment in abolishing all fines, having found the results satisfactory.[190]

In the House of Commons, Unionist MP Lord Henry Cavendish-Bentinck of Nottingham kept the pressure on the Home Secretary by asking him in question time whether he was aware of the resolution of the International Association for Labour Legislation that was meeting in Zurich, which declared that legislation should be introduced to abolish fines and deductions from wages. McKenna stated that he was aware of this resolution and hoped to introduce a truck bill in the next session of Parliament but at this point was unable to provide details.[191]

By the end of February 1913, a TUC deputation waited upon McKenna and raised the question of fines and deductions from wages. Andrew Conley presented McKenna with the TUC resolution demanding an amendment to the Truck Act to make fines and deductions illegal. He explained to the Home Secretary that while some employers, including those in the Leeds Wholesale Clothiers Association, had agreed to stop fining workers (after a strike led by female workers), among unorganized employees "the system of fines and deductions in this trade have been growing more unreasonable year after year." He described deductions were taken from women's wages for materials, power and water and even to pay the wages of other women who cleaned the factory. McKenna thought that some of these deductions were probably illegal under the current law and was not optimistic that there would be time for a Truck Amendment Bill in the current session.[192]

This deputation included no female trade unionists, and this outraged suffragist Isabella Ford, who wrote an article connecting women's exclusion from these deliberations to their exclusion from the franchise. Ford described fines and deductions that were taken primarily from female workers, insisting that their unique vulnerability to these exactions were because "men have votes." She observed: "We see everywhere that the people who need the most help or protection of the law are the most neglected" by both the state and male trade unionists. Ford's answer was for more working-class women to join the suffrage movement.

> Their menkind are not helping them as they should – men alas, are men – it is we women who must help them. Mr. McKenna must be made to see how monstrously unjust he is to them when he does not take the trouble to ascertain their wishes about this truck bill, and when he casually says there may be 'no time' for its introduction this session. He probably knows nothing about women's lives – why should he? Who studied the conditions of working men's lives before 1867? The condition of working women's lives can only be remedied when, by means of the vote, they have the power themselves to insist that their wishes shall be attended to.[193]

Margaret Llewellyn Davies of the Manchester, Salford and District Women's Trade Union Council agreed, arguing that the elimination of fines and deductions from wages depended upon winning female suffrage because "MPs were apt to run where there was the chance of a vote."[194] In the spring of 1913, a deputation of female labour leaders met with Prime Minister Asquith to discuss these issues. Asquith stated that while he was sympathetic to their arguments, he "had no intention to make promises that he had no power to perform."[195]

This did not stop members of the opposition parties from introducing private members' bills on the subject. In April 1913, Smith, supported by Gill and Walsh, for the third session in a row introduced a bill to abolish fines and deductions in cotton factories. He informed the House of Commons that an estimated £20,000 per year was deducted from the wages of weavers in the form of fines and deductions for damaged work. He pointed to individual manufacturers and, indeed, entire towns such as Bacup, which abolished fines and discovered no deterioration in the quality of work.[196] Sir Edmund Denniss, a Conservative MP from Oldham, also promised his support of the measure because "fines were very hard on the operatives and he had come to the conclusion that they were not necessary."[197] Later that year, a deputation of weavers convinced cotton merchant and Liberal MP Gordon Harvey to announce his support for the total abolition of fines and deductions.[198] However, many cotton textile employers in Lancashire continued to oppose abolition, which meant that despite cross-party support, the private member's bill again failed to move forward.

In the summer of 1913, the WTUL published a report with fresh examples of low-waged female workers suffering from the infliction of fines for trivial offences or damaged work that was not their fault. Combined with the reports of factory inspectors, press accounts and pamphlet literature, there was evidence that the problem remained serious.[199] Prosecutions under the 1896 Truck Act undertaken by female factory inspectors and private individuals also helped to keep the issue in the public eye, though by 1911 there were many cases that inspectors investigated but took no action due to the uncertain state of the law.[200]

In the House of Commons, Cavendish-Bentinck asked the Home Secretary if had read the report of the female factory inspectors and seen "the numerous instances of unfair and capricious fines and deductions from wages inflicted on women workers; and whether he intends to introduce a Bill to strengthen the powers . . . to remedy this hardship?" McKenna replied that the issue was one "which I hope to be able to deal in the near future." Cavendish-Bentinck was not satisfied with this answer and on 30 July 1913 introduced a "Bill to Amend and Extend the Truck Acts, 1831 to 1896." This bill would abolish all fines and deductions from wages and extend the Truck Acts to include outworkers.[201] The member from Nottingham South explained that his bill was inspired by the Minority Report of the Departmental Committee on the Truck Acts of 1908, and he believed the conclusions in that report had been strengthened by subsequent revelations from female factory inspectors, female trade union leaders and the press. He conceded that his

> Bill has no chance of passing into law this session, but it is intended as a gentle reminder to the Government that they have been very lax in the matter. I hope that when the Government do bring in a Bill they will decide to sweep away fines and deductions, first, as a relic of barbarism, and second, as a sign of a badly organized and inefficiently conducted business.[202]

The *Manchester Guardian* thought that Cavendish-Bentinck's argument was "unimpeachable." The *Freeman's Journal* observed that Cavendish-Bentinck, "despite his rank and party, has already proved himself an advanced social reformer."[203] In September 1913, the TUC once again unanimously passed a resolution to abolish all deductions from wages.[204]

While no legislation on truck advanced in the House of Commons during 1913, at the end of the year the *Shields Gazette* reported that from Prime Minister Asquith "we have a pretty definite promise, however, that . . . the question of Truck will be brought forward soon after parliament meets again next month."

The legislation created by the Home Secretary would embody the recommendations of the Majority Report of the 1908 Committee.[205] *The Daily Citizen* reported that the prime minister had written to WTUL president Gertrude Tuckwell promising legislation that would address the question of fines and deductions from wages, but it was unclear "whether the proposals regarding truck promised by the Prime Minister are deemed satisfactory by the societies interesting themselves or not."[206]

With the prospect of the government introducing new truck legislation, 1914 saw a flurry of efforts to influence its contents. Writing in the *Manchester Guardian* (an article which was later reprinted in the *Women's Liberal Federation Monthly News* and the *Birmingham Post*), Tuckwell responded to the prime minister's letter by urging him not to make the same error of regulating fines and deductions rather than abolishing them, which he made as Home Secretary in 1894–1895, when he began the process that resulted in the 1896 Truck Act.[207] Even if ending fines would lead to more dismissals, she proclaimed "wholeheartedly that this risk we are prepared to face, for its plausibility is destroyed by the evidence of good employers" who imposed no fines. She stated, "[O]ur industrial laws are not aimed at the good employer, who is always ahead of the demands of protective legislation; they are intended to standardize protection and to bring the laggard up to the mark."[208]

In March of 1914 Home Secretary McKenna met with deputations of both trade unions and employers from Lancashire, who were anxious influence truck law reform. Although McKenna favoured modelling the government bill on the Majority Report of the Departmental Committee, the arguments of the textile workers made a much better impression on him than those of the owners. He again met with the United Textile Factory Workers Association, and their representatives pressed their strong desire for legislation that would abolish fines and deductions. McKenna promised that in the current session he would introduce a new truck bill that would deal with fines and assured the deputation that "I frankly admit you have made a great impression on" the subject of fines. His instincts were overall that "the bill as introduced by me ought, I think, in the first instance . . . to be based on the Majority Report of the Committee" that reported in 1908. While he did not plan on totally abolishing fines, he would not make the question of how the law applied to individual trades a government matter, so an amendment to eliminate fines for textile workers was possible.[209]

McKenna also met with representatives of the Cotton Spinners and Manufacturers Association and the Federation of Master Spinners. They drew his attention to the fact that between a quarter and a third of the value of all British exports were cotton products. They stated that among 425 firms employing 90,000 workers, the average fine per worker per week was less than a halfpenny. However, without them employers would have no choice but fire workers for errors. McKenna asked the deputation if they were aware that over 200 Lancashire mills had abolished fines. A factory owner informed McKenna that "the workers themselves did not demand the abolition of fines." An incredulous

Home Secretary, who had repeatedly met with deputations of textile workers demanding precisely that, responded, "That is a very serious statement. Do you really say workers don't demand it?" At the end of the meeting McKenna informed the deputation, "Employers admitted that fining was not effective, and the case for it did not seem strong."[210]

The Factory Times stated that the workers' deputation left the meeting with the Home Secretary with "mingled feelings as to its success," but they thought McKenna's "tone was hopeful, though we are a little uneasy on that question." The editorial stated, "We trust the Home Secretary understands that nothing short of legal prohibition will suit the Lancashire textile operatives. Fines and deductions must be legally forbidden." The argument that the abolition of fines would lead to more dismissals was the same as saying "the weaver must be hanged or drown when she is deserving of neither." It demanded that the system of fines be abolished "root and branch."[211] MacArthur wrote of the prospect of new truck legislation:

> [M]uch as we desire redress, long as we have worried and waited for it, we shall not be satisfied with any more patchwork. We demand . . . the entire abolition of all fines and deductions. Any measure that falls short of this will not satisfy, since we know from bitter experience that it would be twisted and distorted by employers and the law courts.[212]

These sentiments demonstrate the complex politics that McKenna and his department faced in crafting new legislation. Any measure that did not abolish fines and deductions would be opposed by trade unions, the Labour Party and some Liberals. Throughout the spring of 1914 many newspapers published articles endorsing the complete abolition of fines and deductions. Tuckwell was especially active, writing in the *Westminster Gazette* that

> there is no protection for the class we represent except that complete abolition. We urge on the Home Secretary to give us in his promised Truck Bill the abolition of all fines, deductions, charges on wages, and the abolition of the living in system.[213]

In *The Challenge*, she argued that in the six years since the Departmental Committee reported "much has occurred to strengthen the position of the abolitionists, whose principles are set forth in the Report of the Minority," including the number of small and large employers who had abandoned fines and the growing worker opposition. She also argued that "in all, the sharp rise in the cost of living has rendered any nibbling at wages more acutely painful to wage earners."[214] Another writer called fines "childish, tyrannical, and cowardly – childish because fines fail in their ostensible purpose of preventing bad work; tyrannical because they are imposed by virtue of an arbitrary power; cowardly because they are inflicted upon women and children."[215] *The New Statesman* editorialized that "the remedy for all these abuses is clear. The worker is entitled to receive the reward of his labour in the current coin of the realm, clear of all deductions whatsoever – just as the Trade Boards minimum wage must be." For this reason, "we therefore endorse heartily the demands of the Minority Report of the Truck Committee."[216] Other papers wrote in favour of the abolition of fines and deductions.[217] In May 1914, May Tennant, one of the two authors of the 1908 Minority Report, defended her position on truck and workplace deductions from wages before the Women's Liberal Conference.[218]

Some employers were equally insistent that any further regulatory burdens on them would be unacceptable. *The Drapers' Record* reported on the workers' deputation to the Home Secretary by complaining that "it is time a protest is made regarding the improper interference of Parliament with the legitimate liberty of subjects." The journal argued that "the evils of the system are often grossly exaggerated by labour organizers" and "if fairly administered, there is nothing to be said against it."[219] Such contrasting views on the merits of a new truck bill left the Home Secretary with a very limited legislative field with which to work.

By the end of March 1914, Cavendish-Bentinck, Smith, Walsh and Gill were asking the Home Secretary on a weekly basis when new truck legislation could be expected. The Home Secretary always informed them that they were working to have it ready soon.[220] Not content to wait, on 12 March 1914 Smith again introduced a bill to abolish fines and deductions from wages for workers in cotton factories. There was an effort to win support for this bill from employers in Lancashire, but the bill's supporters were unsuccessful.[221] On 18 May 1914, Lord Cavendish-Bentinck introduced his own bill to prohibit fines, deductions and the bonus system for the second session in a row.[222]

Supporters of abolishing fines supplemented their publishing and petitioning strategy with a series of large public meetings held during the spring and summer of 1914. At the end of May a large meeting at Queen's Hall in London was held to "express a determination to refuse to accept as satisfactory any measure which did not make illegal all fines and deductions from wages and abolish the living in system." The meeting was addressed by the Bishop of Oxford, Lord Henry Cavendish-Bentinck, May Tennant, Stephen Walsh, Albert Smith and Joseph Devlin, who assured the crowd that the Irish Parliamentary Party fully supported the proposal, chanting "hands off the workers' wages!"[223] In July, MacArthur led a mass meeting of the National Federation of Women Workers in Southeast London. The meeting began at Deptford Park, where women, supported by male trade unionists, marched with banners and music in procession to Southwark Park, where they listened to a full program of speakers who criticized the Home Secretary for not yet fulfilling his promise of a new truck bill. MacArthur told the audience many stories of oppressive fines and deductions and the meeting closed with a resolution that "this mass meeting of Deptford workers calls on the government to fulfill its promise and introduce a truck bill, and further demands the abolition of fines, deductions, and the living-in system."[224] That same month, the Hyde, Hadfield, and District Weavers, Winders and Warpers' Association concluded that "the only safe remedy for operatives is the total abolition of fines and deductions from weavers' wages" and that "the abolition of fines and deductions . . . is a question that we must fight to the bitter end."[225]

By the middle of July, supporters of a new truck bill were pressing the Home Secretary as to whether the private members' bills of either Smith or Cavendish-Bentinck would receive facilities from the government so they could advance. McKenna replied, "I hope very shortly to introduce a bill for this purpose."[226] McKenna and the Home Office had been working very slowly to craft legislation based upon the Majority Report of the 1908 Committee, despite the concerns that this would fall short of the expectations of many who had been pushing for reform. In less than two weeks after McKenna made his promise, however, Austria-Hungary declared war upon Serbia, and soon the United Kingdom itself was drawn into the Great War. Almost immediately, all discussion of truck, fines and deductions from wages disappeared from the parliamentary and newspaper record, and many advocates of further legislation found themselves deeply immersed in the war effort. For many workers, particularly women, the war eventually brought opportunities for higher paying work and, when combined with greater state intervention, this temporarily made fines and deductions from wages a less pressing grievance. The significant growth in trade union membership that occurred during the Great War, particularly among women, was also helpful on this front.

The failure to successfully pass legislation based upon the findings of the 1906–1908 Departmental Committee on the Truck Acts had many causes. One was simply bad timing, as the momentum for reform was halted first by the busy and consequential legislative sessions of 1909–1911 and then by the outbreak of the Great War. Another cause of the failure might have been the unwillingness of the labour movement to accept further incremental change, as they rather sought nothing short of a complete abolition of fines and deductions. The experience of the 1896 Truck Act had taught workers, trade unionists and factory inspectors that in the face of hostile courts, as long as fines and deductions were legal, they could be abused, no matter what limitations or regulations were placed upon them. Still, it is likely that the insistence on nothing less than the full abolition of fines and deductions made the government reluctant to legislate on the topic at all. Finally, even though the trend among many industrialists and shop owners appeared to be moving away from the use of disciplinary systems that relied upon deductions from wages, their instincts were strongly against the imposition of new regulations and rules. Workers had to settle for a more indirect method for reducing the burden of fines through the introduction of the Trade Boards Act of 1909 and the temporary transformation of the economic and regulatory landscape brought about by the Great War.

Concluding remarks

It is common knowledge among British labour historians that during the nineteenth and twentieth centuries, many working men and women struggled very hard for meagre rewards offered by employers. This book has demonstrated that the most vulnerable of those workers were not even able to secure the whole value of these rewards. For the entirety of the nineteenth century there were employers who paid workers at long intervals, forcing them to endure the costs of borrowing against future paydays either from employers or from retail shopkeepers. Many employers used company stores and the workers' need for advances to reduce their contractual obligations to employees by substituting overvalued goods and services for cash wages. For an even longer period, employers encroached upon their workers' wages by requiring them to pay for materials, tools, heat, light, power, lunches, tea, sick club contributions, government mandates and the use of basic amenities in the workplace. It was labour rather than capital that bore the risks of errors in production, reimbursing their employers in amounts vastly greater than their rates of pay for mistakes at work. The most marginal workers were reminded of their powerlessness in the workplace by the constant threat of excessive fines for tardiness or trivial offences taken at the discretion of the foreperson or employer.

However, contemporaries were increasingly aware of these injustices thanks to the protests of workers, trade unions and their allies. To understand how workers felt about these practices we merely have to read their words, expressed in speeches, petitions, pamphlets, public rallies and marches, industrial actions, newspaper investigations, court proceedings, the reports of government inspectors and testimony before select committees. Workers who thought that truck was "mutually beneficial" were hard to find. Beyond the loss of pennies and shillings that were desperately necessary for survival, labourers paid in truck objected to the loss of independence, autonomy and freedom. They often invoked comparisons to serfdom or slavery to describe the extent to which these practices allowed their masters' authority to penetrate the entirety of their lives. Employers had long since shed any paternalistic obligations toward their workers yet were not above using its language to justify interfering in their consumption and controlling their choices away from work.

Workers who experienced unfair deductions from wages for materials, fines or errors in production often referred to them as a form of tyranny, and, even after the 1896 Truck Act, the seeming one-sidedness and arbitrariness of these exactions lends itself to that description. Fines were defined vaguely enough that employers and forepersons had considerable discretion in deciding what acts or omissions justified deductions from employees' wages. They alone determined when work was bad, having only rarely to prove the defect or justify the amount of money deducted before an independent third party. They decided what to charge for tools and equipment needed for work or materials that went into the product, all of which could only be purchased from them. They set the price of the workers' lunch, the cost for using the cloakroom and the fees for heat, light or the power that ran machinery. They determined that employees would join the sick club that they ran rather than one chosen by the workers. In theory, workers could decide not to take employment on such terms but in practice many non-unionized or unskilled men and women had to take work on undesirable terms to survive. Without the help of strong trade unions or the Factory Inspectorate, the individual employee took a great risk when challenging these deductions.

Yet many did, and they had strongly committed allies who pursued a range of strategies to help workers keep the wages they earned. The most effective strategy, of course, was industrial action and union organizing. As repeated throughout this book, where unions were powerful, truck was less likely and deductions from wages were comparatively few and carefully negotiated. Other strategies included campaigning and lobbying for legislation outlawing truck and regulating deductions from wages, legal efforts to try and bring these laws into force and communicating injustices and hardships caused by these practices to the public to raise awareness and convince employers to voluntarily forego them.

The state and its agents were central to all of these strategies, yet how important was state action in reducing truck and wage theft? The author of the only other monograph on the British truck system, economist George Hilton, nearly 60 years ago came to the conclusion that they were not important at all. Hilton, in *The Truck System*, which was published shortly after the passage of the 1960 Payment of Wages Act, expressed frustration at the debate over this legislation. In particular, he observed that "members of both parties in 1960 typically argued that the Truck Act of 1831 had been for many years a valuable safeguard to the British labourer. This is an indefensible interpretation. . . . [T]he Truck Act of 1831 was a virtually total failure."[227] Hilton also considers the 1887 Act to have come too late to have had a meaningful impact. He does not explore the 1896 Truck Act at all.[228] Hilton argued that the most important factors in the decline of the truck system were the intensity of workers' dislike of it and the decline of industries where it was most widely practiced. Truck was defeated by economic forces, not state action.

In this book, I have rehabilitated the seemingly indefensible interpretation that state action was important in the struggle for fair wages over the long term. In the fight against truck, fines and deduction, Seymour Tremenheere, William Duignan, Alexander MacDonald, Charles Bradlaugh, May Tennant, Adelaide Anderson, Rose Squire, Lucy Deane, Mary Paterson, Gertrude Tuckwell, Clementina Black, Sir Charles Dilke and many others put faith in the power of the state and law to prevent injustice and protect the poor. Despite the setbacks and humiliations that they endured, I contend that in the long run they were not wrong. A parliament where employer interests were strongly represented was always going to be unlikely to impose stringent regulations on themselves, yet in the process of lobbying and agitating for new laws, advocates publicized and exposed injustices in how workers were paid. Facts and knowledge generated by government inspectors, Home Office officials and stakeholders contributed to a shift in attitudes, which can be seen in the growing tendency of opponents of truck legislation to qualify their position by stating their personal abhorrence to truck and arbitrary fines before expounding upon the importance of freedom to contract. The gradual effect of the dissemination of knowledge about the plight of marginal workers on accepted norms of respectable business is manifest in the effectiveness of factory inspectors promoting the idea that modern managements did not discipline through fines and convincing employers to voluntarily abandon many deductions from wages. The courts were hostile terrain for labour when litigating the Truck Acts. Although private individuals and government inspectors won a high percentage of the cases brought under the Truck Acts, magistrates were generally loathe to impose heavy penalties on members of their own class, and the high courts, concerned about limiting legislation that interfered with freedom to contract, provided many setbacks for those using these laws to stop employers from cheating workers out of their pay. However, courts are places where stories are told, and, even in cases where employers won, these stories were often very embarrassing for them. An employer convincing the high courts of his right to fine young women for dancing during their dinner hour in the long term probably shamed more employers into abandoning fines than it convinced to adopt them.

While the rise of organized labour was more decisive in the decline of truck and deductions from wages, the state and the law had an influence that was greater than the number of prosecutions under the Truck Acts. They provided the means for workers and their allies to expose and publicize the numerous ways that employers clawed back the wages of the lowest paid workers. The government and the statute law increased the legitimacy of those who demanded that workers receive the full value of the wages they earned and gradually helped to establish new norms so that these dubious practices were seen as disreputable. It is essential to tell their stories so that truck, fines and unfair deductions from wages will remain unacceptable for future generations of workers.

Notes

1 *Times,* 11 August 1897, p. 11; 8 September 1897, p. 8; 6 October 1899, p. 11; 6 July 1899, p. 12; 3 March 1900, p. 14.
2 *Departmental Committee on the Truck Acts, Report of The Truck Committee. . .* (1908), pp. 9–10.
3 *Departmental Committee on the Truck Acts, Report of The Truck Committee. . .* (1908), p. 17.
4 *Departmental Committee on the Truck Acts: Minutes of Evidence, Vol. II* (1908), p. 69, question 1442; p. 73, questions 1507–1511; pp. 76–77, questions 1593–1596; pp. 84–85, Questions 1810–1817; p. 96, question 2087; p. 111, Questions 2477–2478; p. 112, Question 2502.
5 *Departmental Committee on the Truck Acts: Minutes of Evidence, Vol. II* (1908), p. 84, questions 1805–1807.
6 *Women's Trade Union League Annual Reports* (1904), p. 11. Nineteenth Century Collections online. Web 15 January 2015.
7 Clementina Black, *Sweated Industry and the Minimum Wage* (London: Duckworth and Co, 1907); B.L. Hutchins, *Home Work and Sweating* (1907); *Slum Travelers: Ladies and London Poverty, 1860–1920,* ed: Ellen Ross (Berkeley: University of California Press, 2007).
8 *Hansard Parliamentary Debates Online, House of Commons,* 27 February 1906; *Times,* 28 February 1906, p. 7; *Western Daily Press, Bristol,* 28 February 1906.
9 *Hansard Parliamentary Debates Online, House of Commons,* 27 February 1906; *Times,* 28 February 1906, p. 7; *Western Daily Press, Bristol,* 28 February 1906.
10 *Hansard Parliamentary Debates Online, House of Commons,* 27 February 1906; *Times,* 28 February 1906, p. 7; *Western Daily Press, Bristol,* 28 February 1906.

11 *Hansard Parliamentary Debates Online, House of Commons,* 27 February 1906; *Times,* 28 February 1906, p. 7; *Western Daily Press, Bristol,* 28 February 1906.

12 *Hansard Parliamentary Debates Online, House of Commons,* 27 February 1906; *Times,* 28 February 1906, p. 7; *Western Daily Press, Bristol,* 28 February 1906.

13 MacMillan, Shaw, Thomas, first Baron Craigmyle (1850–1937)," rev. H.C.G. Matthew, *Oxford Dictionary of National Biography* (Oxford University Press, 2004); Online edn, Sept. 2014; "Tennant, Margery Mary Edith Josephine Pia (1869–1946)," *ODNB,* Oxford University Press, 2004; Online edn, 2009; P.W.J. Bartrip, "Delevingne, Sir Malcolm (1868–1950)," *ODNB,* Oxford University Press, 2004; Lionel Alexander Ritchie, "Yarrow, Sir Alfred Fernandez, first baronet (1842–1932)," *ODNB,* Oxford University Press, 2004; James Donnelly, "Brotherton, Edward Allen, Baron Brotherton (1856–1930)," *ODNB,* Oxford University Press, 2004, online edn., 2006.

14 *Hansard Parliamentary Debates Online, House of Commons,* 10 July 1906.

15 *Wigan Observer,* 31 July 1909, Gertrude Tuckwell Papers, London Metropolitan University Archives.

16 *Departmental Committee on the Truck Acts, Report of The Truck Committee. . .* (1908), p. 4.

17 *Departmental Committee on the Truck Acts: Minutes of Evidence, Vol. II* (1908), p. 6, question 51; p. 19, question 228; p. 20, Question 245; p. 21, questions 256–264; p. 36, Questions 585–591; p. 69, Question 1442; p. 73, Question 1507–1511; pp. 76–77, Question 1593–1597; p. 111, questions 2477–2478; p. 112, Question 2502; 174, questions 4521–4523.

18 *Departmental Committee on the Truck Acts: Minutes of Evidence, Vol. II* (1908), pp. 7–8, questions 54–66, p. 25, question 336; p. 26, question 340; p. 28, questions 398, 406; p. 33, questions 499–503; p. 63, Question 1286; p. 83, questions 1776–1780; p. 91, Question 1948, 1955–1963; pp. 92–93, Questions 1996–2003; pp. 107–108, Questions 2391–2397; p. 137, question 3443; p. 177, Questions 4623–4626.

19 *Departmental Committee on the Truck Acts: Minutes of Evidence, Vol. II* (1908), p. 125, questions 2967–2987.

20 *Departmental Committee on the Truck Acts: Minutes of Evidence, Vol. II* (1908), p. 22, questions 273–274; p. 23, questions 295–297; p. 29, questions 424–428; p. 30, Questions 439–447, 506; pp. 34–35, questions 530–533, 548–550; p. 32, Questions 487–489; p. 41, Questions 694, 708; p. 43, question 743; p. 66, questions 1368–1369; p. 73, Question 1501–1502; p. 74, Questions 1524–1526, 1539–1546, 1565; p. 71, questions 1467; p. 72, Questions 1489–1492; p. 175, Questions 4567–4571; p. 176, Questions 4593–4597, 4609–4613; p. 178, Questions 4655–4661, 4671–4672; p. 179, Question 4700. Anderson thought that the proceeds that employers collected from fines should be given to charities that benefited workers: p. 70, Question 1452; p. 71, Question 1467, 1474; pp. 74–75, Questions 1544–1547.

21 *Departmental Committee on the Truck Acts: Minutes of Evidence, Vol. II* (1908), pp. 85–86, questions 1837–1840; p. 87, Questions 1874–1876; p. 88, questions 1888–1892; p. 93, questions 2008–2009; p. 94, questions 2031–2032; p. 96, questions 2082–2085; p. 97, Question 2118; p. 98, Question 2128; p. 100, Questions, 2171, 2191; pp. 105–107, Questions 2333, 2348, 2356, 2387; pp. 112–113, Questions 2518–2520; p. 114, questions 257–2571; p. 115, Questions 2629–2630, 2638; p. 117, questions 2718–2720; pp. 124–125, questions 2953–2963; p. 130, Questions 3149–3171; p. 131, questions 3188–3189.

22 *Departmental Committee on the Truck Acts: Minutes of Evidence, Vol. II* (1908), p. 95, Question 2061; pp. 96–97, Question 2086–2102; p. 98, Questions 2126–2127; p. 101, Question 2205–2206; p.106, Question 2357; pp. 108–109, Questions 2414–2416, 2434–2436; p. 128, Questions 3071, 3075; p. 129, Questions 3133–3136; p. 131, Questions 3217–3222.

23 *Departmental Committee on the Truck Acts: Minutes of Evidence, Vol. II* (1908), pp. 96–97, Question 2103–2105; p. 101, Question 2218; pp. 105–106, Questions 2330, 2331–2348; pp. 113–114, questions 2550–2551, 2558–2564, 2571; p. 118, questions 2721; p. 120, questions 2860–2861; p. 125, Questions 2964–2966; p. 130, Questions 3177–3179; p. 131, questions 3185–3187.

24 *Departmental Committee on the Truck Acts: Minutes of Evidence, Vol. II* (1908), p. 41, Questions 694–697; p. 43, Questions 737–738, 742–743; p. 49, Questions 875–879, 883; p. 50, Questions 900, 909; p. 88, Question 1895–1906; p. 110, Quests 2467–2468; p. 116, questions 2680–2682; p. 127, Questions 3066–3068; p. 175, Questions 4550–4553, 4580–4581; p. 177, Questions 4640.

25 *Departmental Committee on the Truck Acts: Minutes of Evidence, Vol. II* (1908), p. 107, Questions 2374, 2387; p. 108, Questions 2412–2413; p. 110, Question 2454; p. 114, Question 2589.

26 *Departmental Committee on the Truck Acts: Minutes of Evidence, Vol. II* (1908), p. 69, Question 1444, p. 107, Question 2375.

27 *Departmental Committee on the Truck Acts: Minutes of Evidence, Vol. III* (1908), p. 255, Questions 16655.

28 *Departmental Committee on the Truck Acts: Minutes of Evidence, Vol. II* (1908), pp. 144–146, Questions 3645–3647, 3660, 3667, 3679, 3681–3682, 3689; p. 153, Question 3861; p. 157, Questions 3999–4001; pp. 162–163, Questions 4177–4178.

29 *Departmental Committee on the Truck Acts: Minutes of Evidence, Vol. II* (1908), p. 147, Question 3730–3734; p. 152, Questions 3833–3836; p. 154, Questions 3900–3905; p. 156, Questions 3986–3988; pp. 162–163, Questions 4171–4176, 4195.

30 They did have a prior contract that specified deductions for tools and materials, but not fines.

31 *Departmental Committee on the Truck Acts: Minutes of Evidence, Vol. II* (1908), p. 145, Questions 3649–3666; p. 343, Questions 9187–9195.

32 *Departmental Committee on the Truck Acts: Minutes of Evidence, Vol. II* (1908), p. 344, Questions 9197–9217, p. 352, Questions 9349–9367, p. 355, Question 9437.

33 *Departmental Committee on the Truck Acts: Minutes of Evidence, Vol. III* (1908), pp. 39–49.

34 *Departmental Committee on the Truck Acts: Minutes of Evidence, Vol. II* (1908), pp. 283–284, Questions 7443–7459; p. 288, Questions 7556–7566.

35 *Departmental Committee on the Truck Acts: Minutes of Evidence, Vol. II* (1908), p. 303, Questions 7985–7991, 7995–7996; p. 305, Questions 8073–8080.

36 *Departmental Committee on the Truck Acts: Minutes of Evidence, Vol. II* (1908), p. 284, Question 7462.

37 *Departmental Committee on the Truck Acts: Minutes of Evidence, Vol. II* (1908), p. 284, Questions 7460–7473; p. 286, Question 7516–7519; p. 288, Questions 7556–7572.

38 *Departmental Committee on the Truck Acts: Minutes of Evidence, Vol. II* (1908), p. 288, Question 7574, p. 305, Question 8060. Also see Questions 8053–8060 and *Departmental Committee on the Truck Acts: Minutes of Evidence, Vol. III* (1908), p. 262, Questions 16831–16838.

39 *Departmental Committee on the Truck Acts: Minutes of Evidence, Vol. II* (1908), p. 285, Questions 7484–7491; p. 287, Questions, 7529–7542; p. 289, Questions 7592–7600.

40 *Departmental Committee on the Truck Acts: Minutes of Evidence, Vol. II* (1908), p. 288, Quote from Question 7552, also see Questions 7550–7552; p. 289, Question 7609–7610.

41 *Departmental Committee on the Truck Acts: Minutes of Evidence, Vol. II* (1908), p. 299, Question 7873; p. 300, Questions 7894–7895; p. 307, Question 8129.

42 *Departmental Committee on the Truck Acts: Minutes of Evidence, Vol. III* (1908), pp. 259–260, Question 16778.

43 *Departmental Committee on the Truck Acts: Minutes of Evidence, Vol. II* (1908), p. 215, Question 5589; p. 216, Question 5632–5635; p. 258, Questions 6776–6778.

44 *Departmental Committee on the Truck Acts: Minutes of Evidence, Vol. II* (1908), p. 184, Questions 4809–4810; p. 192, Question 4961–4962, 4965; p. 229, Question 5943.

45 *Departmental Committee on the Truck Acts: Minutes of Evidence, Vol. II* (1908), p. 232, Question 6010, 6016, p. 240, Questions 6248–6250.

46 *Departmental Committee on the Truck Acts: Minutes of Evidence, Vol. II* (1908), p. 241, Question 6275.

47 *Departmental Committee on the Truck Acts: Minutes of Evidence, Vol. II* (1908), p. 248, Questions 6421–6429.

48 *Departmental Committee on the Truck Acts, Report of The Truck Committee* (1908), p. 21.
49 *Departmental Committee on the Truck Acts: Minutes of Evidence, Vol. II* (1908), p. 180, Questions 4716–4719; p. 185, Question 4821; p. 192, Question 4972; p. 212, Question 5484; p. 213, Question 5506–5507; p. 228, Questions 5926–5931; p. 235, Questions 6089, 6094–6098; p. 237, Question 6140; p. 242, Question, 6285, 6291–6295; p. 243, Question 6302; p. 258, Question 6786; p. 259, Questions 6801–6805; pp. 261–262, Questions 6849–6852, 6858–6859; p. 265, Questions 6951–6952; p. 277, Questions 7269–7270.
50 *Departmental Committee on the Truck Acts: Minutes of Evidence, Vol. II* (1908), pp. 181–182, Questions 4734–4746; p. 185, Questions 4823–4826; p. 187, Questions 4853–4855; p. 190, Question 4909; p. 191, 4927; p. 199, Question 5153; p. 211, Questions 5448–5457; p. 230, Question 5956–5958; p. 233, Question 6030; p. 234, Question 6055; p. 243, Question 6297; p. 244, Questions 6316–6318; p. 247, Question 6395–6396; p. 258, Questions 6779–6780, 6788; p. 259, Question 6795; p. 260, Questions 6806–6810, 6816–6819; pp. 280, Questions 7340–7343; pp. 281–282, Questions 7383–7388; p. 283, Questions 7424–7425. *Departmental Committee on the Truck Acts: Minutes of Evidence, Vol. III* (1908), p. 267, Question 16972; p. 269, Question 17037.
51 *Departmental Committee on the Truck Acts: Minutes of Evidence, Vol. II* (1908), p. 211, Questions 5461; p. 215, Questions 5579–5587; p. 236, Questions 6111–6118; p. 242, Questions 6293–6294; p. 244, Questions 6335–6336; pp. 245–246, Questions 6357–6360; p. 259, Questions 6790–6794; p. 260, Questions 6814–6816; p. 262, Questions 6860–6862; p. 264, Questions 6924–6927; p. 265, Questions 6974–6976; p. 267, Questions 7000–7010, 7023–7024; p. 277, Questions 7267–7268; p. 278, Questions 7303.
52 *Departmental Committee on the Truck Acts: Minutes of Evidence, Vol. II* (1908), p. 212, Questions 5469–5471; 5475–5476; p. 339, Questions 9091–9092, 9100, 9104, 9124.
53 *Slum Travelers: Ladies and London Poverty, 1860–1920,* Eds: Ellen Ross (Los Angeles: University of California Press, 2007), pp. 52–54; "Black, Clementina," in Jennifer S. Uglow, Frances Hinton, and Maggy Hendry (eds.), *Palgrave Macmillan Dictionary of Women's Biography* (London: Macmillan Publishers, Ltd., 2005).
54 *Departmental Committee on the Truck Acts: Minutes of Evidence, Vol. II* (1908), p. 195, Question 5042–5049; *The Labour Record,* May 1906, p. 71. Nineteenth Century Collections Online. Web 15 January 2015.
55 *Departmental Committee on the Truck Acts: Minutes of Evidence, Vol. II* (1908), pp. 196–201.
56 *Departmental Committee on the Truck Acts: Minutes of Evidence, Vol. II* (1908), p. 197, Questions 5086, 5091–5092, 5102; pp. 200–201, Questions 5181–5188; p. 202, Questions 5220–5224.
57 *Departmental Committee on the Truck Acts: Minutes of Evidence, Vol. II* (1908), p. 199, Question 5149–5150 (Quote); p. 202, Question 5215.
58 *Departmental Committee on the Truck Acts: Minutes of Evidence, Vol. II* (1908), p. 202, Questions 5216–5217.
59 TRADES COUNCIL MATERIAL, HD4928, CA.45 "TRUCK" BOX, London Metropolitan University Library.
60 *Truck Committee, Appendix to Evidence: Deductions in Respect of Disciplinary Fines: List of Complaints ('Truck) Sent to Miss Anderson, HM Principal Lady Inspector of Factories, April 1904 up to date May 1906.* TRADES COUNCIL MATERIAL, HD4928, CA 45 "TRUCK" BOX. London Metropolitan University Library.
61 *Departmental Committee on the Truck Acts: Minutes of Evidence, Vol. II* (1908), p. 204, Questions 5272–5277; p. 206, Questions 5309–5314, 5317–5324, 5328–5335; p. 208, Questions 5362–5365, 5374–5377; p. 209, Questions 5394–5400; pp. 224–225, Questions 5845–5848.
62 *Departmental Committee on the Truck Acts: Minutes of Evidence, Vol. II* (1908), p. 207, Question 5345. Also see Questions 5349–5351.
63 *Departmental Committee on the Truck Acts: Minutes of Evidence, Vol. II* (1908), p. 208, Questions 5365, 5368; p. 226, Question 5882.

64 *Departmental Committee on the Truck Acts: Minutes of Evidence, Vol. II* (1908), pp. 207–208, Questions 5341–5344, 5358–5366; p. 224, Questions 5823–5835.
65 *Departmental Committee on the Truck Acts: Minutes of Evidence, Vol. III* (1908), p. 256, Questions 16665–16683.
66 Ibid., Quote from p. 256, Question 16684. Also see pp. 256–257, Questions 16685–16701.
67 *Woman Worker,* 3 (1908), p. 91. Nineteenth Century Collections Online. Web 15 January 2015.
68 *Departmental Committee on the Truck Acts: Minutes of Evidence, Vol. III* (1908), p. 243, Question 16413.
69 *Departmental Committee on the Truck Acts: Minutes of Evidence, Vol. III* (1908), pp. 243–244, Question 16418, 16441.
70 *Departmental Committee on the Truck Acts: Minutes of Evidence, Vol. III* (1908), p. 245, Questions 16474–16490; *Departmental Committee on the Truck Acts: Minutes of Evidence, Vol. II* (1908), p. 247, Questions 16529–16537.
71 *Departmental Committee on the Truck Acts: Minutes of Evidence, Vol. II* (1908), p. 290, Question 7629–7630.
72 *Departmental Committee on the Truck Acts: Minutes of Evidence, Vol. II* (1908), p. 291, Questions 7662, 7666–7668, p. 292, Questions 7675, 7691–7696; p. 293, 7708–7709.
73 *Departmental Committee on the Truck Acts: Minutes of Evidence, Vol. II* (1908), p. 293, Questions 7715–7718.
74 *Departmental Committee on the Truck Acts: Minutes of Evidence, Vol. II* (1908), p. 309, Questions 8177–8200; p. 313, Questions 8350–8352.
75 *Departmental Committee on the Truck Acts: Minutes of Evidence, Vol. II* (1908), pp. 309–310, Questions 8204, 8208–8209, 8218–8219; p. 311, Questions 8243–8249.
76 *Departmental Committee on the Truck Acts: Minutes of Evidence, Vol. II* (1908), pp. 268–269, Questions 7041–7042, 7049–7063; p. 271, Questions 7116–7118; pp. 272–273, Questions 7129, 7151–7166, 7169–7173, 7190–7194; p. 275, Question 7236–7238.
77 *Departmental Committee on the Truck Acts: Minutes of Evidence, Vol. II* (1908), p. 367, Question 9743. *Departmental Committee on the Truck Acts: Minutes of Evidence, Vol. III* (1908), p. 33 Question 10964; p. 36, Question 11063; p. 51, Question 11519–11520; p. 55, Question 11607; p. 58, Questions 11685–11686, 11697; p. 67, Question 11913; p. 285, Question 17471; p. 291, Question 17656.
78 *Departmental Committee on the Truck Acts: Minutes of Evidence, Vol. II* (1908), p. 367, Questions 9752–9755; p. 369, Question 9792; p. 370, Questions 9806–9808, 9811–9812, 9814. *Departmental Committee on the Truck Acts: Minutes of Evidence, Vol. III* (1908), p. 33, Questions 10961–10875; p. 34, Questions 10982–10984; p. 36, Questions 11054–11060, p. 38, 11111–11117; pp. 51–52, Question 11522–11523; p. 55, Questions 11599–11603; p. 67, Question 11915; p. 233, Question 16025; p. 277, Question 17276; p. 290, Questions 17639–17641; p. 291, Question 17657.
79 *Departmental Committee on the Truck Acts: Minutes of Evidence, Vol. II* (1908), pp. 32–33, Question 10947, 109054; pp. 64–71.
80 *Departmental Committee on the Truck Acts: Minutes of Evidence, Vol. II* (1908), p. 32, Questions 10977–10979; p. 231, Question 15979; p. 280, Questions 17314–17320.
81 *Departmental Committee on the Truck Acts: Minutes of Evidence, Vol. II* (1908), p. 231, Question 15973.
82 *Departmental Committee on the Truck Acts: Minutes of Evidence, Vol. II* (1908), p. 231, Question 15979.
83 *Departmental Committee on the Truck Acts: Minutes of Evidence, Vol. II* (1908), p. 232, Question 16019; p. 278, Question 17242.
84 *Departmental Committee on the Truck Acts: Minutes of Evidence, Vol. II* (1908), p. 233, Question 16030.
85 *Departmental Committee on the Truck Acts: Minutes of Evidence, Vol. II* (1908), p. 289, Question 17601. Also see 17597, 17602.

86 *Departmental Committee on the Truck Acts: Minutes of Evidence, Vol. II* (1908), p. 369, Questions 9788–9792; p. 370, Question 9813.

87 *Departmental Committee on the Truck Acts: Minutes of Evidence, Vol. III* (1908), p. 55, Question 11588.

88 *Departmental Committee on the Truck Acts: Minutes of Evidence, Vol. II* (1908), p. 60, Question 11701; p. 291, Question 17653. Quote from p. 278, Question 17242. *Departmental Committee on the Truck Acts: Minutes of Evidence, Vol. III* (1908), p. 34, Question, 10985.

89 *Departmental Committee on the Truck Acts: Minutes of Evidence, Vol. III* (1908), pp. 113–153; p. 133, Question 13405; Bondfield, Hoffman, and Tilley, *Truck Enquiry Committee*. HD 4928, London Metropolitan University Archives.

90 *Departmental Committee on the Truck Acts: Minutes of Evidence, Vol. III* (1908), p. 115, Question 13134; p. 117, Question 13163; p. 151, Questions 13780–13781.

91 *Departmental Committee on the Truck Acts: Minutes of Evidence, Vol. III* (1908), p. 136, Questions 13464–13469.

92 *Departmental Committee on the Truck Acts: Minutes of Evidence, Vol. III* (1908), p. 114, Questions 13112–13120; p. 115, Questions 13131; p. 116, Questions 13141–13146, 13151–13158 (Quote from 13157); p. 117, Questions 13164–13181.

93 *Departmental Committee on the Truck Acts: Minutes of Evidence, Vol. III* (1908), p. 116, Question 13157.

94 *Departmental Committee on the Truck Acts: Minutes of Evidence, Vol. III* (1908), p. 151, Question 13782.

95 *Departmental Committee on the Truck Acts: Minutes of Evidence, Vol. III* (1908), p. 115, Questions 13122–13126, 13128, 13132–13133; p. 133, Questions 13401–13402; p. 181, Questions 14589–14591.

96 *Departmental Committee on the Truck Acts: Minutes of Evidence, Vol. III* (1908), p. 128, Question 13308; p. 130, Questions 13336–13337; p. 132, Questions 13385–13386; p. 140, Question 13555; pp. 146–149, Questions 13711–13717.

97 *Departmental Committee on the Truck Acts: Minutes of Evidence, Vol. III* (1908), p. 139, Question 13553.

98 *Departmental Committee on the Truck Acts: Minutes of Evidence, Vol. III* (1908), p. 146, Question 13711.

99 *Departmental Committee on the Truck Acts: Minutes of Evidence, Vol. III* (1908), p. 136, Questions 13484, 13487; p. 133, Question 13391; p. 154, Questions 13863–13864.

100 *Departmental Committee on the Truck Acts: Minutes of Evidence, Vol. III* (1908), p. 123, Questions 13268–13271; p. 125, Question 13274; pp. 125–126, Questions 13270–13276; p. 129, Questions 13315–13329; p. 135, Questions 13447–13449; p. 139, Question 13553; pp. 146–148, Question 13711; p. 149, Questions 13733, 13737–13740; p. 154, Questions 13870–13871; pp. 161–162, Question 14037; p. 166, Questions 14143–14150; p. 168, Questions 14197–14198, 14203.

101 *Departmental Committee on the Truck Acts: Minutes of Evidence, Vol. III* (1908), p. 119, Question 13209 (Quote); p. 152, Question 13817; p. 156, Question 13899; p. 163, Question 14047.

102 *Departmental Committee on the Truck Acts: Minutes of Evidence, Vol. III* (1908), pp. 118–119, Questions 13193–13204.

103 *Departmental Committee on the Truck Acts: Minutes of Evidence, Vol. III* (1908), p. 138, Questions 13535–13536; p. 163, Questions 14054–14082; p. 156, Question 13901, p. 128, Questions 13308; p. 133, Question 13389.

104 *Departmental Committee on the Truck Acts: Minutes of Evidence, Vol. III* (1908), p. 134, Question 13429; p. 139, Question 13538; p. 141, Questions 13562–13564.

105 *Departmental Committee on the Truck Acts: Minutes of Evidence, Vol. III* (1908), p. 156, Question 13900.

106 *Departmental Committee on the Truck Acts: Minutes of Evidence, Vol. III* (1908), p. 168, Questions 14203–14204, 14207.

107 *Departmental Committee on the Truck Acts: Minutes of Evidence, Vol. III* (1908), p. 120, Question 13224; p. 132, Question 13388.

108 *Departmental Committee on the Truck Acts: Minutes of Evidence, Vol. III* (1908), p. 137, Question 13492.

109 *Departmental Committee on the Truck Acts: Minutes of Evidence, Vol. III* (1908), p. 166, Question 14166. See also 14158–14161.

110 *Departmental Committee on the Truck Acts: Minutes of Evidence, Vol. III* (1908), p. 117, Question 13182.

111 *Departmental Committee on the Truck Acts: Minutes of Evidence, Vol. III* (1908), p. 162, Question 14037.

112 *Departmental Committee on the Truck Acts: Minutes of Evidence, Vol. III* (1908), p. 128–129, Questions 13309–13314.

113 *Departmental Committee on the Truck Acts: Minutes of Evidence, Vol. III* (1908), p. 142, Question 13584; p. 143, Questions 13615–13616; p. 148, Question 13718.

114 *Departmental Committee on the Truck Acts: Minutes of Evidence, Vol. III* (1908), p. 140, Question 13555; p. 162, Question 14037.

115 *Departmental Committee on the Truck Acts: Minutes of Evidence, Vol. III* (1908), p. 155, Question 13883; p. 162, Question 14037.

116 *Departmental Committee on the Truck Acts: Minutes of Evidence, Vol. III* (1908), p. 168, Questions 14218–14219.

117 *Departmental Committee on the Truck Acts: Minutes of Evidence, Vol. III* (1908), p. 192, Questions 14921; p. 193, Questions 14951–14958.

118 *Departmental Committee on the Truck Acts: Minutes of Evidence, Vol. III* (1908), p. 192, Question 14922, 14938, 14940; p. 204, Question 15307.

119 *Departmental Committee on the Truck Acts: Minutes of Evidence, Vol. III* (1908), p. 193, Questions 14958–14959, 14971; p. 194, Questions 14976; p. 194, Question 15021; For other stores that had abandoned living in, see: pp. 296–297, Questions 17768–17778, 17817–17833; p. 298, Question 17837.

120 *Departmental Committee on the Truck Acts: Minutes of Evidence, Vol. III* (1908), pp. 312–322; pp. 269–270, Questions 14257–14282; p. 184, Questions 14648–14651; p. 197, Question 15063; p. 308, Question 18174. General Manager John Forbes told the committee that he would favour an inspection regime provided that the inspectors were men. He found that "the ladies were frequently faddy and irritating. I have often heard complaints made about the lady inspectors." p. 313, Question 18305.

121 *Departmental Committee on the Truck Acts: Minutes of Evidence, Vol. III* (1908), p. 185, Question 14659–14661; pp. 234–235, Question 16116; p. 308, Question 18174.

122 *Departmental Committee on the Truck Acts: Minutes of Evidence, Vol. III* (1908), pp. 170–171, Questions 13283–14286, 14290, 14295; p. 198, Questions 15097, 15102, 15107, 15120, 15133; p. 205, Questions 15329–15334; p. 303, Questions 18002–18009; p. 308, Question 18174; p. 313, Question 18305.

123 *Departmental Committee on the Truck Acts: Minutes of Evidence, Vol. III* (1908), p. 308, Question 18174.

124 *Departmental Committee on the Truck Acts: Minutes of Evidence, Vol. III* (1908), p. 171, Questions 14311–14314; p. 173, Questions 14358–14363; p. 185, Questions 14669–14671; p. 189, Questions 14799–14800; p. 199, Question 15140–15148; p. 200, Question 15171; p. 201, Questions 15194–15197; p. 202, Question 15214–15216; p. 207, Questions 15399–15400; p. 208, Questions 15417–15418, 15439; pp. 302–303, Questions 17987, 17994; p. 311, Question 18264; p. 315, Question 18376; p. 321, Question 18554.

125 *Departmental Committee on the Truck Acts: Minutes of Evidence, Vol. III* (1908), p. 188, Question 14757.

126 *Departmental Committee on the Truck Acts: Minutes of Evidence, Vol. III* (1908), p. 185, Question 14668; p. 186, Question 14684–16490; p. 188, Questions 14785–14787; p. 198, Questions 15110–15116; p. 235, Question 16128; p. 313, Question 18315.

127 *Departmental Committee on the Truck Acts: Minutes of Evidence, Vol. III* (1908), p. 177, Question 14459, pp. 176–177, Questions 14450, 14460, 14465–14468, 14473–14474. p. 187, Question 14736–14739; Also see p. 189.
128 *Departmental Committee on the Truck Acts: Minutes of Evidence, Vol. II* (1908), pp. 248–258, 294–298. Also see similar arguments from various medical associations, pp. 1–11.
129 *Departmental Committee on the Truck Acts: Minutes of Evidence, Vol. II* (1908), pp. 317–338.
130 Two of the six committee members who signed the majority report did so with slight qualifications. Malcolm Delevingne disagreed with the idea that deductions for bad or negligent work should be treated as fines. Instead he thought there should be a tribunal of workers and employers to judge damaged work. He thought that there should be a maximum deduction from the weekly wage, perhaps 10% of the wage for damaged work. Delevingne also disagreed with the decision of the majority to prohibit deductions for rent, mess rooms and for benefit societies not covered by the Shop Clubs Act. Mr. Yarrow thought that it should be required that all employers who maintained fines post a notice outside of the workplace so potential employees and consumers could know the conditions and policies of the firm. He disagreed with a ban deduction for mess halls or rent. *Departmental Committee on the Truck Acts: Report of the Truck Committee (1908)*, pp. 78–83.
131 *Departmental Committee on the Truck Acts: Report of the Truck Committee (1908)*, p. 10–12.
132 *Departmental Committee on the Truck Acts: Report of the Truck Committee (1908)*, p. 19.
133 *Departmental Committee on the Truck Acts: Report of the Truck Committee (1908)*, pp. 22–25.
134 *Departmental Committee on the Truck Acts: Report of the Truck Committee (1908)*, p. 28.
135 *Departmental Committee on the Truck Acts: Report of the Truck Committee (1908)*, 30.
136 *Departmental Committee on the Truck Acts: Report of the Truck Committee (1908)*, p. 30.
137 *Departmental Committee on the Truck Acts: Report of the Truck Committee (1908)*, p. 28.
138 *Departmental Committee on the Truck Acts: Report of the Truck Committee (1908)*, pp. 31–32.
139 *Departmental Committee on the Truck Acts: Report of the Truck Committee (1908)*, pp. 35–38.
140 *Departmental Committee on the Truck Acts: Report of the Truck Committee (1908)*, p. 41.
141 *Departmental Committee on the Truck Acts: Report of the Truck Committee (1908)*, p. 48.
142 *Departmental Committee on the Truck Acts: Report of the Truck Committee (1908)*, pp. 78–81.
143 *Departmental Committee on the Truck Acts: Report of the Truck Committee (1908)*, p. 75.
144 *Departmental Committee on the Truck Acts: Report of the Truck Committee (1908)*, pp. 75–77.
145 *Departmental Committee on the Truck Acts: Report of the Truck Committee (1908)*, pp. 78–80.
146 *Departmental Committee on the Truck Acts: Report of the Truck Committee (1908)*, pp. 84–85.
147 *Departmental Committee on the Truck Acts: Report of the Truck Committee (1908)*, p. 85.
148 *Departmental Committee on the Truck Acts: Report of the Truck Committee (1908)*, p. 85.
149 *Departmental Committee on the Truck Acts: Report of the Truck Committee (1908)*, p. 85.
150 *Departmental Committee on the Truck Acts: Report of the Truck Committee (1908)*, p. 85.
151 *Departmental Committee on the Truck Acts: Report of the Truck Committee (1908)*, p. 86.
152 *Departmental Committee on the Truck Acts: Report of the Truck Committee (1908)*, p. 87.
153 *Hansard Parliamentary Debates Online, House of Commons*, 3 November 1908; 18 November 1908. *Freeman's Journal*, 4 January 1909; *Birmingham Post*, 4 January 1909; *Morning Post*, 4 January 1909; *Welsh Gazette*, 4 January 1909; *Dublin Express*, 4 January 1909; *Factories and Workshops Times*, 5 January 1909; *Dublin Express*, 4 January 1909; *The Saturday Review*, 16 January 1909; *Morning Post*, 11 February 1909; *The Guardian*, 10 March 1909; *The People's Friend*, 3 May 1909; Gertrude Tuckwell Papers. London Metropolitan University Archives. *The Woman Worker*, 6 January 1909; *The Woman Worker*, 20 January 1909; *Women's Industrial News*, January 1909; *Gloucestershire Echo*, 2 January 1909, 14 January 1909; *Lancashire Evening Post*, 2 January 1909; *Lincolnshire Echo*, 2 January 1909; *Western Chronicle*, 8 January 1909; *Derby Daily Telegraph*, 2 January 1909, *Nottingham Evening Post*, 4 January 1909; *Taunton Courier and Western Advertiser*, 6 January 1909; *Western Gazette*, 8 January 1909; *Preston Herald*, 6 January 1909; *Shipley Times and Express*, 8 January 1909; *Belfast Telegraph*, 18 January 1909; *Larne Times*, 9 January 1909; *Shields Daily News*, 2 January 1909; *Sheffield Evening Telegraph*, 2 January 1909; *The Scotsman*, 4 January 1909; *Yorkshire Post*, 4 January 1909.

154 *Irish Times,* 28 May 1909.
155 *Bolton Evening News,* 4 January 1909.
156 *Birmingham Gazette,* 4 January 1909. Gertrude Tuckwell Papers. London Metropolitan University Archives.
157 *Times,* 5 January 1909.
158 *Birmingham Post,* 4 January 1909. *Leicester Post,* 4 January 1909. Gertrude Tuckwell Papers. London Metropolitan University Archives.
159 *Factory and Workshops Times,* 5 January 1909. Gertrude Tuckwell Papers. London Metropolitan University Archives.
160 Clementina Black, "Report of the Departmental Committee on the Truck Acts," *The Economic Journal* 19:74 (June 1909):315–319.
161 *The Woman Worker,* 3:4 (27 January 1909), p. 93.
162 *The Woman Worker,* 3:3 (20 January 1909), p. 54.
163 *The Nation,* 9 January 1909. Gertrude Tuckwell Papers. London Metropolitan University Archives.
164 *Shoreditch Observer,* 23 January 1909.
165 *Report of the Proceedings of the 42nd Annual Trades Union Congress held at Public Hall in Ipswich* (London: London Co-operative Printing Society, 1909), p. 139.
166 *Journal of Commerce,* 9 January 1909. Gertrude Tuckwell Papers. London Metropolitan University Archives.
167 *Newcastle Journal,* 9 January 1909. Gertrude Tuckwell Papers. London Metropolitan University Archives.
168 Clegg, Fox, and Thompson, *A History of British Trade Unionism Since 1889, Vol. I, 1815–1914,* p. 403.
169 *Times,* 20 February 1909.
170 *The Total Abolition of Fines in Factories and Workshops: A Deputation from the United Textile Factory Workers' Association, Thursday, June 10, 1909. Official Report.* (Ashton-Under Lyne: Cotton Factory Times, 1909); *Morning Advertiser,* 11 June 1909. Gertrude Tuckwell Papers. London Metropolitan University Archives.
171 *The Total Abolition of Fines; Morning Advertiser,* 11 June 1909. Gertrude Tuckwell Papers. London Metropolitan University Archives.
172 *The Total Abolition of Fines; Morning Advertiser,* 11 June 1909.
173 *The Total Abolition of Fines; Morning Advertiser,* 11 June 1909.
174 *The Total Abolition of Fines; Morning Advertiser,* 11 June 1909.
175 *The Total Abolition of Fines; Morning Advertiser,* 11 June 1909.
176 *Hansard Parliamentary Debates Online, House of Commons* 25 August 1909, 1 December 1909. *Blackburn Telegraph,* 18 June 1909. Gertrude Tuckwell Papers. London Metropolitan University Archives.
177 Blackburn, "Curse or Cure?" pp. 214–239; Blackburn, "Must Low Pay Always Be with Us?" pp. 61–101; Deakin and Green, "One Hundred Years of British Minimum Wage Legislation," pp. 205–213; Blackburn, "'Between the Devil of Cheap Labour Competition and the Sea of Family Poverty?" pp. 91–101; Bean and Boyer, "The Trade Boards Act of 1909 and the Alleviation of Household Poverty," pp. 240–264.
178 Constance Smith, "The Working of the Trade Boards Act in Great Britain and Ireland," *Journal of Political Economy* 22:7 (22 July 1914), p. 615.
179 Anderson, *Women in the Factory,* pp. 60–61.
180 Squire, *Thirty Years in the Public Service,* pp. 112–113.
181 Bean and Boyer, "The Trade Boards Act of 1909 and the Alleviation of Household Poverty," p. 241; Deakin and Green, "One Hundred Years of British Minimum Wage Legislation," p. 206; Squire, *Thirty Years in the Public Service,* p. 113.
182 *Report from the Select Committee on Home Work: Together with the Proceedings of the Committee, Minutes of Evidence, and Appendix* (London: H.M. Stationary Office, 1908), p. xxxvi; Anderson, *Women in the Factory,* 60–61; Blackburn, "The Origins of Britain's Minimum Wage," pp. 68–75.

183 Blackburn, "The Origins of Britain's Minimum Wage," pp. 68–75.

184 Bean and Boyer, "The Trade Boards Act of 1909 and the Alleviation of Household Poverty." Also see: Smith, "The Working of the Trade Boards Act in Great Britain and Ireland," p. 617.

185 *Cotton Factories (Fines) (Abolition). A Bill to make it illegal for any employer in a cotton factory to impose a fine on a workman for alleged spoiled work or for any other cause.* Bill 241. House of Commons Parliamentary Papers Online.

186 Gertrude Tuckwell Papers. London Metropolitan University Archives.

187 *Hansard Parliamentary Debates Online, House of Commons,* 19 March 1912.

188 *Cotton Factories (Fines) (Abolition). A Bill to make it illegal for any employer in a cotton factory to impose a fine on a workman for alleged spoiled work or for any other cause.* Bill 110. House of Commons Parliamentary Papers Online.

189 *Manchester Evening Chronicle,* 19 November 1912; *Daily Dispatch,* 19 November 1912. Gertrude Tuckwell Papers, London Metropolitan University Archives.

190 *Manchester Evening Chronicle,* 28 November 1912. *Daily Dispatch,* 10 October 1913. Gertrude Tuckwell Papers, London Metropolitan University Archives. This experiment ultimately became permanent. *Manchester Guardian* 24 October 1914. Gertrude Tuckwell Papers. London Metropolitan University Archives.

191 *Hansard Parliamentary Debates Online, House of Commons,* 6 November 1912.

192 *Trades Union Congress Parliamentary Committee: Reports of Deputations to Ministers* (London: Cooperative Printing Society, Ltd, 1913), pp. 90–91. HD 6661 1913 London Metropolitan University Archives.

193 *The Common Cause,* 25 April 1913. Gertrude Tuckwell Papers. London Metropolitan University Archives.

194 *The Manchester Courier,* 5 February 1913. Gertrude Tuckwell Papers. London Metropolitan University Archives.

195 *The Draper and Drapery Times,* 5 May 1913. Gertrude Tuckwell Papers. London Metropolitan University Archives.

196 *Cotton Factories (Fines Abolition). A Bill to Abolish the System of Fining in Cotton Factories.* Parliamentary Papers, 1913. Bill 121; *Hansard Parliamentary Debates Online, House of Commons* 23 April 1913; *Manchester Courier,* 24 April 1913, 30 April 1913; *Liverpool Courier,* 24 April 1913; *Manchester Guardian,* 1 May 1913. Gertrude Tuckwell Papers. London Metropolitan University Archives.

197 *Manchester Courier,* 26 April 1913. Gertrude Tuckwell Papers. London Metropolitan University Archives.

198 *Daily Dispatch,* 14 November 1913. Gertrude Tuckwell Papers. London Metropolitan University Archives.

199 *Daily News and Leader,* 23 July 1913; *The Star,* 23 July 1913; *Mary Bull,* 12 August 1913; *The Weekly Dispatch,* 16 November 1913. *Liverpool Weekly Post,* 21 March 1914. Gertrude Tuckwell Papers. London Metropolitan University Archives; B.L. Hutchins, "Truck, Fines and Deductions," *Women's Industrial News,* 16:60 (1913):89–100.

200 *Manchester Courier,* 13 September 1913; *Morning Post,* 13 September 1913; *Daily Citizen,* 13 September 1913; *The Morning Advertiser,* 13 September 1913; *Liverpool Daily Post and Mercury,* 13 September 1913; *Manchester Guardian,* 13 September 1913; *Western Morning News,* 2 April 1914; *Draper and Drapery Times,* 4 April 1914; *Hardware Trade Journal,* 17 April 1914; *Dundee Courier,* 1 May 1914; *South Wales Daily News,* 11 June 1914; *Northern Whig,* 3 June 1914. Gertrude Tuckwell Papers. London Metropolitan University Archives; *Women's Industrial News* 16:60 (1913):99.

201 *Truck. A Bill to Amend and Extend the Truck Acts 1831 to 1896.* 1913. Parliamentary Papers. Bill 289.

202 *Hansard Parliamentary Debates Online, House of Commons.* 7 July 1913; 30 July 1913; *Daily News and Leader,* 31 July 1913; *Manchester Evening Chronicle,* 15 January 1914; Gertrude Tuckwell Papers. London Metropolitan University Archives.

203 *The Manchester Guardian*, 31 July 1913; *Freeman's Journal*, 31 July 1913; *The Draper*, 9 August 1913. Gertrude Tuckwell Papers. London Metropolitan University Archives.

204 *Daily Dispatch*, 6 September 1913. Gertrude Tuckwell Papers. London Metropolitan University Archives.

205 *Shields Gazette*, 30 December 1913. Gertrude Tuckwell Papers. London Metropolitan University Archives.

206 *Daily Citizen*, 1 January 1914. Gertrude Tuckwell Papers. London Metropolitan University Archives.

207 *Manchester Guardian*, 5 January 1914; *Catholic Times*, 9 January 1914; *Women's Liberal Federation Monthly News* 5:3 (1 March 1913), p. 5. Gertrude Tuckwell Papers. London Metropolitan University Archives.

208 *Manchester Guardian*, 5 January 1914; *Catholic Times*, 9 January 1914; *Women's Liberal Federation Monthly News* 5:3 (1 March 1913), p. 5; *Birmingham Post*, 28 March 1914. Gertrude Tuckwell Papers. London Metropolitan University Archives.

209 *Factory Times*, 6 March 1914; *The Textile Mercury*, 7 March 1914; *Mary Bull*, 28 March 1914. Gertrude Tuckwell Papers. London Metropolitan University Archives.

210 *Times*, 3 March 1914; *Morning Advertiser*, 3 March 1914; *Factory Times*, 6 March 1914; *The Textile Mercury*, 7 March 1914 Gertrude Tuckwell Papers. London Metropolitan University Archives.

211 *Factory Times*, 5 March 1914. Gertrude Tuckwell Papers. London Metropolitan University Archives.

212 *Daily News and Leader*, 26 March 1914. Gertrude Tuckwell Papers. London Metropolitan University Archives.

213 *Westminster Gazette*, 18 May 1914. Gertrude Tuckwell Papers. London Metropolitan University Archives.

214 *The Challenge*, 8 May 1844. Gertrude Tuckwell Papers. London Metropolitan University Archives.

215 *Sunday Chronicle*, 8 March 1914. Gertrude Tuckwell Papers. London Metropolitan University Archives.

216 *The New Statesman*, 16 May 1914. Gertrude Tuckwell Papers. London Metropolitan University Archives.

217 *Cardiff Times*, 23 May 1914; *Ideas*, 24 April 1914; *Mackirdy's Weekly*, 4 April 1914; *Daily Herald*, 30 June 1914; *The New Statesman*, 11 July 1914; *Mary Bull*, 4 July 1914; *Darlington Echo*, 22 July 1914; *The Star*, 21 July 1914. Gertrude Tuckwell Papers. London Metropolitan University Archives.

218 *Daily Chronicle*, 21 May 1914. Gertrude Tuckwell Papers. London Metropolitan University Archives.

219 *The Drapers' Record*, 7 March 1914. Gertrude Tuckwell Papers. London Metropolitan University Archives. Furthermore, a number of benefit societies began to agitate against new truck legislation which might undermine their access to contributions deducted from the wages of workers. *Daily Telegraph*, 20 June 1914; *Manchester Courier*, 23 May 1914; *Timber Trades Journal*, 27 June 1914; *Colliery Guardian*, 3 July 1914. Gertrude Tuckwell Papers. London Metropolitan University Archives.

220 *Hansard Parliamentary Debates Online, House of Commons*, 26 March 1914; 1 April 1914; 20 May 1914; *Morning Post*, 18 June 1914. Gertrude Tuckwell Papers. London Metropolitan University Archives.

221 *Cotton Factories (Fines Abolition). A Bill to Abolish the System of Fining in Cotton Factories*. 1914. Parliamentary Papers. Bill 117; *Liverpool Courier*, 13 March 1914; *Northern Daily Telegraph*, 28 May 1914. Gertrude Tuckwell Papers. London Metropolitan University Archives.

222 *Truck. A Bill to Amend and Extend the Truck Acts 1831 to 1896*. 1914. Parliamentary Papers. Bill 260.

223 *Reynold's Newspaper*, 24 May 1914. Gertrude Tuckwell Papers. London Metropolitan University Archives.

224 *The Star,* 20 July 1914; *Citizen,* 17 July 1914; *Daily Herald,* 17 July 1914; *Yorkshire Observer,* 20 July 1914; *Darlington Echo,* 20 July 1914; *Daily News Leader,* 20 July 1914; *Manchester Guardian,* 20 July 1914; *Standard,* 20 July 1914; *Daily News,* 17 July 1914, 21 July 1914; *Leicester Daily Post,* 20 July 1914; *Morning Advertiser,* 20 July 1914; *The Schoolmistress,* 27 August 1914. Gertrude Tuckwell Papers. London Metropolitan University Archives; *Times,* 19 July 1914, pp. 8, 15; *Sussex and Essex Free Press,* 22 July 1914; *Walsall Advertiser,* 25 July 1914.

225 *Daily Dispatch,* 14 July 1914. Gertrude Tuckwell Papers. London Metropolitan University Archives.

226 *Hansard Parliamentary Debates Online, House of Commons,* 16 July 1914; *Men's Wear,* 25 July 1914. Gertrude Tuckwell Papers. London Metropolitan University Archives; *Belfast News Letter,* 25 July 1914; *Larne Times,* 17 July 1914.

227 Hilton, *The Truck System,* p. 154.

228 He devotes 2 paragraphs to the 1896 Act. Hilton, *The Truck System,* pp. 147–148.

Bibliography

Primary sources arranged by archive

British Newspaper Library, Colindale

The British Workman and Friend of the Sons of Toil
The Cambrian or General Weekly Advertiser for the Principality of Wales
Cardiff and Merthyr Guardian, Glamorgan, Monmouth, and Brecon Gazette
The Charter
The Commonwealth, Lately Entitled the Workman's Advocate
Glasgow Examiner
Glasgow Saturday Post
Glasgow Sentinel and Journal of the Industrial Interests
The Glamorgan, Monmouth and Brecon Gazette Cardiff Advertiser, and Merthyr Guardian
Liverpool Daily Post
Manchester Guardian
The Merthyr and Cardiff Chronicle, and South Wales Advertiser
The Merthyr Express and Advertiser for the Iron and Coal Districts of Wales
The Merthyr Telegraph, and General Advertiser for the Iron Districts of South Wales
The Miner
The Miners' Advocate
The Miner and Workman's Advocate
The Monmouthshire Merlin and South Wales Advertiser
North British Daily Mail
The Northern Star
Pontypool Free Press
The Sheffield Free Press
The Sheffield and Rotherham Intelligencer
The Silurian or South Wales General Advertiser
South Wales Reporter and General Advertiser
Staffordshire Advertiser
The Swansea Journal and Llanelly, Neath, Aberavon, Bridgend and South Wales Advertiser
The Welshman, General Advertiser for the Principality of Wales
Wolverhampton Chronicle
Wolverhampton Journal
The Workman's Advocate With Which is Incorporated the Miner
Yorkshire Gazette

Gwent Country Record Office

Blaenavon Company Minute Book, 1837–1864. D751/356

London Metropolitan University Archives

Byrne, Dominic. *Low Pay Report: Reforming the Truck Acts*. London: TUC Low Pay Unit, 14 November, 1983., TUC Collections, HD 5017.

Central Policy Review Staff. *Cashless pay: Alternatives to Cash in Payment of Wages*. London: HM Stationary Office, 1981. Trades Union Congress Papers, Cashless Pay, HD 4926.

Department of Employment. *The Law on the Payment of Wages and Deductions, A Guide to Part 1 of the Wages Act 1986*. London: HM Stationary Office, 1986. Trades Union Congress Papers, Cashless Pay, HD 4926 Gertrude Tuckwell Papers, Box 16.

Suter, Erich and Phil Long. *Cashless Pay and Deductions: Implications of the Wages Act, 1986* London: Chartered Institute of Personnel Management and Development, 1987.

Trades Council Material, "Truck Box" HD 4928, CA.45

Trades Union Congress. *The TUC Guide to The Wages Act 1986*. London: TUC, 1986. Trades Union Congress Papers, Cashless Pay, HD 4926

Trades Union Congress Collection, TUC Pamphlets, 1872–1919, HD 6661

Tuckwell, Gertrude, Constance Smith, Mary MacArthur, May Tennant, Nettie Adler, Adelaide Anderson, Clementina Black. *Woman in Industry: From Seven Points of View*. London: Duckworth and Co, 1908.

Modern Records Centre, University of Warwick

Ironworkers Journal, 1869–1892, MSS.36.AMI.1–5

Trades Union Congress, First Deposit, 1920–1960, MSS 292/20/188–193

Amalgamated Society of Railway Servants Proceedings and Reports, 1877–1878, 1887, MSS/127/AS/1/1/3–4, 13

Leaving work without notice, wages withheld, 1940–1956, MSS.200/B/3/2/c630 pt.2

Trades Union Congress Reports, MSS/292/4/10/4–6, 13

Trades Union Congress, Parliamentary Committee, 1875–1878, MSS/292/20a/1

Pratt v. Cook and Sons, Ltd., 1939, Truck Act Litigation, MSS/292/42/05/11

Protection of wages, MSS/292/115/1/3

Payment of wages act 1960, MSS/292b/190/3

Payment of wages by cheque. 1965-aug 1970, mss/292b/190/4

The National Archives, Kew

Home Office Papers Series 44, 45, 52

Inland Revenue Papers, Series 40

Ministry of Health, Series 12

Ministry of Labour Papers, Series 10, 11, 14, 46

Ministry of Transportation, Series 9

RAIL, Series 487, 783, 1014, 1016, 1057

Treasury, Series 520

Treasury Solicitor, Series 18, 25

National Archives of Scotland

Ayrshire Miners' Union (1886). FS/7/18

Bill to abolish arrestment on the dependence in all actions before the small debts courts of Scotland and to regulate arrestment of wages etc.: Petitions memorials, etc. AD/58/368

Copies and drafts of various bills. AD/56/234/1

The Dunfermline Press newspaper containing article Wemyss-the mining population. GD/172/905

Easdale Slate Quarries, Miscellaneous Papers. GD/112/18/12/4.

Letters to Sir George Clerk regarding the recovery of small debts bill and the arrestment of wages for payment of debts (1844). GD.18.3615.

Lord Advocates' Department Correspondence and Papers. Miscellaneous Matters: Shetland Truck Act . . . 1906. AD/59/30

Papers relating to the payment of wages. GD/44/51/403/2

Truck Act 1887, Amendment Bill. HH/1/850

National Library of Scotland

Anderson, George. *Arrestment of Wages: An Exposure of Its Impolicy and Injustice. Revised from Letters Originally Published in the Reformers' Gazette and the North British Daily Mail.* Glasgow: Thomas Murray and Son, 1853.

Bailey, David. *The Truck System: A Book For Masters and Workmen.* London: Fred Pitman, 1859.

Johnson, Robert L. *A Shetland Country Merchant: A Biography of James Williamson of Mid Yell: 1800–1872.* Shetland: Shetland Publishing co. Ltd, 1979.

Vindex. *Remarks on the Proposed Abolition of the Law of Arrestment of Wages in Scotland.* Edinburgh: Alex Elder, 1853.

Staffordshire Record Office

Cuttings on the Truck System, 1850s. D 260/M/F/5/18

"Addition to Truck Shop at Cannock and Rugeley Colliery Co." D 3766/1/8/17/18 (1892)

Letters of Edward Littleton, 1821–1841. D 593/ P/22/1/3/10

Letters of Frederick Harrison, D 615.P(P) 44.4

Memorandum Upon the Truck Acts. London: HM Stationary Office, 1924. D 5476/B.8/21

"Notice to the Tradesmen and Shopkeepers of Hanley, Stoke, Lane-End and Potteries in General . . . will be waited on in the course of a few days by a committee from the Tradesmen of Burslem to consider the most effectual means of putting a stop to the manufacturers paying their servants in truck." (1821) D 593/V/10/59

Unrest in Mines in the Potteries, 1824–1842. D 4216/F/18

Walsall Free Press, 1856–1858, 1862–1863, 1914

Walsall Library

William Duignan Travel Correspondence, 48/1/32, 46–47

William Duignan Travel Diaries, 48/1/1–48.

William Salt Library, Staffordshire

Speech of E.J. Littleton Esq., M.P. for Staffordshire in the Commons on Weds. 17 March on Moving Leave to Bring in a Bill to Render More Effectual Laws Requiring the Payment of Wages in Money (London: Hatchard and Son, 1830). SUBPBOX A/3/1.

Working Class Movement Library Salford

Amalgamated Society of Engineers, Annual Reports, 1851–1866.

The Barefoot Aristocrats: A History of the Amalgamated Association of Operative Cotton Spinners, Alan Fowler and Terry Wyke, (eds.). Littleborough: George Kelsall, 1987.

Brassey, Thomas. *On Work and Wages.* London: George Bell and Sons, 1874.

Davis, James Edward. *The Master and Servant Act, 1867: With an Introduction, Notes and Forms and Tables of Offences.* London: Butterworths, 1868.

Durham Chronicle. 1844.

Felkin, W. An Account of the Machine-Wrought Hosiery Trade: Its Extent, and the Condition of the Framework Knitters; Being A Paper Read in the Statistical Section at the Second York Meeting of the British Association, held 18 Sept. 1844 together with Evidence Given Under the Hosiery Commission Inquiry. London: W. Strange, 1845.

Hopwood, Edwin. *A History of the Lancashire Cotton Industry and the Amalgamated Weavers' Association.* Manchester: Cooperative Press, Inc., 1969.

Levi, Leone. *The Wages and Earnings of the Working Classes.* London: John Murray, 1867, 1885.

MacDonald, Alexander. *Handybook of the Law Relative to Masters, Workmen, Servants and Apprentices, in all trades and occupations. With notes of decided cases in England, Scotland and Ireland.* (1868)

Miners' Journal. October–November 1843.

Report of the Colliery Cause Williamson v. Taylor and Others Tried at the Northumberland Assizes August 4, 1843 Before Mr. Justice Wightman. Newcastle: John and James Selkirk, 1843.

Trades Union Congress. Annual Reports, 1877–1896.

Trades Union Congress Papers, 1873–1883.

Walker, Francis A. *The Wages Question: A Treatise on Wages and the Wages Class.* London: MacMillan and Co., 1886.

Parliamentary papers

House of Commons Parliamentary Papers Online

Arrests for debt, Scotland. Returns to several addresses to His Majesty, dated 3d April 1828; – for returns of the number of warrants granted by the Judge Admiral, sheriffs, magistrates of burghs, and justices of the peace, in Scotland, respectively, against individuals, as being in meditation to avoid payment of debts: – of the number of letters of horning and caption issued from the Signet Office, Edinburgh: – of the number of acts of warding issued by the magistrates of royal burghs, Scotland: – of the number of persons incarcerated on warrants, as being in meditation to avoid payment of debt; and, of those imprisoned where the sums exceeded. 8. sterling, in the different gaols of Scotland; – for the last five years: – also, returns of the number of decrees in small debt cases that have been made in each sheriff court in Scotland since the passing of the act 6 Geo. IV. c. 24: – of the number of the said decrees that have been put in execution against the moveable property of the defenders: – and, of the number of the said decrees that have been enforced by imprisonment. London: HM Stationary Office, 1830. Cd.115–116.

A Bill to Alter and Amend the Act Which Prohibits the Payment of Wages in Goods, Commonly Called the Truck Act. House of Commons, 21 July 1853. Cd. 798.

A Bill to Alter and Amend the Act Which Prohibits the Payment of Wages in Goods, Commonly Called the Truck Act. House of Commons, 21 February 1854. Cd. 21.

A Bill to Amend the law relating to the payment of wages. House of Commons, January 1958. Cd. 59.

A Bill to Restrain Stoppages from the Payment of Wages in Hosiery Manufacture. House of Commons, 2 March 1854. Cd.33

A Bill to Secure the Payment of Wages Without Stoppages. House of Commons, 3 March 1853. Cd. 188.

Children's Employment Commission. First report of the commissioners. Mines. London: HM Stationary Office, 1842. Cd.380–382.

Children's Employment Commission. Second report of the commissioners. Trades and manufactures. HM Stationary Office, 1843. Cd.430–432.

Commission to inquire into Truck System. Volume I. Report, Schedules, Supplement; Volume II. Minutes of Evidence. London: HM Stationary Office, 1871. Cd.326–327.

Cotton factories (fines) (abolition). A bill to make it illegal for any employer in a cotton factory to impose a fine on a workman for alleged spoiled work or for any other cause. House of Commons, 1911. Cd.241.

Cotton factories (fines) (abolition). A bill to make it illegal for any employer in a cotton factory to impose a fine on a workman for alleged spoiled work or for any other cause. House of Commons, 1912–1913. Cd. 110.

Cotton factories (fines abolition). A bill to abolish the system of fining in cotton factories. House of Commons, 1913. Cd.121.

Cotton factories (fines abolition). A bill to abolish the system of fining in cotton factories. House of Commons, 1914. Cd.117.

Departmental Committee on the Truck Acts. Report of the Truck Committee. Vol. I. – Report and appendices. London: HM Stationary Office, 1908. Cd.4442.

Departmental Committee on the Truck Acts. Minutes of evidence taken before the Truck Committee. Vol. II. – Minutes of evidence (days 1–37). London: HM Stationary Office, 1908. Cd.4443.

Departmental Committee on the Truck Acts. Minutes of evidence taken before the Truck Committee. Vol. III. – Minutes of evidence (days 38–66) and index. London: HM Stationary Office, 1908. Cd.4444.

Factories and workshops. Annual report of the Chief Inspector of Factories and Workshops for the year 1898. Part II. – Reports. London: HM Stationary Office, 1900. Cd.27.

Factories and workshops. Annual report of the Chief Inspector of Factories and Workshops for the year 1899. London: HM Stationary Office, 1900. Cd.223.

Factories and workshops. Annual report of the Chief Inspector of Factories and Workshops for the year 1900. London: HM Stationary Office, 1901. Cd. 668.

Factories and workshops annual report of the Chief Inspector of Factories and Workshops for the year 1901. Part I. – Reports. London: HM Stationary Office, 1902. Cd.1112.

Factories and workshops. Annual report of the Chief Inspector of Factories and Workshops for the year 1902. Part I. – Reports. London: HM Stationary Office, 1903. Cd.1610.

Factories and workshops. Annual report of the Chief Inspector of Factories and Workshops for the year 1903. Part I. Reports. London: HM Stationary Office, 1904. Cd.2139.

Factories and workshops. Annual report of the Chief Inspector of Factories and Workshops for the year 1904. Part I. – Reports. London: HM Stationary Office, 1905. Cd. 2569.

Factories and workshops. Annual report of the Chief Inspector of Factories and Workshops for the year 1905. Reports and statistics. London: HM Stationary Office, 1906. Cd.3036.

Factories and workshops. Annual report of the Chief Inspector of Factories and Workshops for the year 1906. Reports and statistics. London: HM Stationary Office, 1907. Cd. 3586.

Home Office. Shop Clubs. Report to Her Majesty's Principal Secretary of State for the Home Department, with reference to complaints made by certain Friendly Societies that men are compelled by employers, as a condition of employment, to join shop clubs and to discontinue their membership of other benefit societies. London: HM Stationary Office, 1899. Cd.9203.

Hosiery manufacture (wages) (no. 2). A bill to make provision respecting deductions from wages in the hosiery manufacture. House of Commons, 1871. Cd. 275.

Justices of peace, Scotland. Returns of the number of quarter sessions of the peace and Courts of Justices of the Peace, held for the recovery of small debts, under 39 & 40 Geo. 3. c. 46. in

Scotland; during the years 1821, 1822, and 1823. London: HM Stationary Office, 1825. Cd.183.

Labour statistics. Returns of wages published between 1830 and 1886. London: HM Stationary Office, 1887. Cd. 5172.

Lords Amendments to the Payment of Wages Bill. House of Commons, 1959–1960. Cd. 120.

Lords amendments to the Truck Bill. House of Lords, 1887. Cd. 377.

Master and servant (wages). A bill to amend the law with respect to the payment of wages to workmen in certain trades. House of Commons, 1872. Cd. 65.

Master and servant (wages). A bill [as amended by the select committee] to amend the law with respect to the payment of wages to workmen in certain trades. House of Commons, 1872. Cd.149.

Memorandum on the Laws Relating to Truck, With Appendix of Statutes and Decided Cases; and Checkweighing Clauses in Coal Mines Regulation Act, With an Appendix of Decided Cases. London: HM Stationary Office, 1896. Cd. 8048.

Memorandum Relating to the Truck Acts for Use of HM Inspectors of Mines and Factories. London: HM Stationary Office, 1897. Cd. 8330

Miners' wages payment. A bill to amend the law relating to the payment of wages of miners. House of Commons, 1887. Cd. 140.

Payment of wages in public-houses prohibition. [H.L.]. A bill intituled an act to prohibit the payment of wages to workmen in public-houses and certain other places. House of Commons, 1882. Cd. 185.

Payment of Wages. A bill to remove certain restrictions imposed by the Truck Acts, 1831 to 1940, and other enactments, with respect to the payment of wages; and for purposes connected therewith. House of Commons, 1959–1960. Cd. 49.

Payment of Wages. A bill [as amended by standing committee] to remove certain restrictions imposed by the Truck Acts, 1831 to 1940, and other enactments, with respect to the payment of wages; and for purposes connected therewith. House of Commons, 1959–1960. cd. 74.

Payment of wages in public-houses prohibition. [H.L.] A bill intituled an act to prohibit the payment of wages to workmen in public-houses and certain other places. House of Commons, 1883. Cd. 126.

Preferential payment of wages. A bill to provide for the preferential payment of wages in bankruptcy and other cases. House of Commons, 1888. Cd. 234.

Preferential payment of wages (no. 2). A bill to amend the law with respect to preferential payments in bankruptcy, and in the winding-up of companies. House of Commons, 1888. Cd. 381.

Report on the Administration of the Law in the Justice of the Peace Court Held in the City of Glasgow, 1841. London: HM Stationary Office, 1842. Cd. 9.

Report of Alexander Redgrave, HM Chief Inspector of Factories, Upon the Truck System in Scotland. London: HM Stationary Office, London, 1887. Cd. 4982.

Report on Arrestment of Wages, Effect of abolishing Imprisonment for Small Debts, and Practice of Truck in Scotland. London: HM Stationary Office, 1854. Cd. 03

Report on the Commissioners Appointed to Inquire into the Truck System, Volume I: Report, Schedules, Supplement. Volume II: Minutes of Evidence. London: HM Stationary Office, 1871. Cd. 326–327.

Report of the Commissioner Appointed Under the Provisions of the Act 5 & 6 Victoria c. 99 to Enquire into the Operation of that Act and into the State of the Population in the Mining Districts, 1845. London: HM Stationary Office, 1846. Cd. 670.

Report of the Commissioner Appointed Under the Provisions of the Act 5 & 6 Victoria c. 99 to Enquire into the Operation of that Act and into the State of the Population in the Mining Districts, 1850. London: HM Stationary Office, 1851. Cd. 1248.

Report of the Commissioner Appointed Under the Provisions of the Act 5 & 6 Victoria c. 99 to Enquire into the Operation of that Act and into the State of the Population in the Mining Districts, 1851. London: HM Stationary Office, 1852. Cd. 1406.

Report of the Commissioner Appointed Under the Provisions of the Act 5 & 6 Victoria c. 99 to Enquire into the Operation of that Act and into the State of the Population in the Mining Districts, 1852. London: HM Stationary Office, 1853. Cd. 1525.

Report of the Commissioner Appointed Under the Provisions of the Act 5 & 6 Victoria c. 99 to Enquire into the Operation of that Act and into the State of the Population in the Mining Districts, 1853. London: HM Stationary Office, 1854. Cd.1679.

Report of the Commissioner Appointed Under the Provisions of the Act 5 & 6 Victoria c. 99 to Enquire into the Operation of that Act and into the State of the Population in the Mining Districts, 1854. London: HM Stationary Office, 1855. Cd. 1838.

Reports of Inspectors of Coal Mines, 1865. London: HM Stationary Office, 1867. Cd. 3768.

Report of the Select Committee on Home Work: together with the Proceedings of the Committee, Minutes of Evidence and Appendix. London: HM Stationary Office, 1908. Cd. 246.

Report of the Committee on the Truck Acts. London: HM Stationary Office, 1961.

Reports of Inspectors of Factories to Secretary of State for Home Department. London: HM Stationary Office, November 1868–1869. Cd. 4093-II.

Return of Convictions in Counties of York and Lancaster of Persons guilty of illegally paying Wages of Workpeople in Goods instead of current Coin of Realm. London: HM Stationary Office, 1842. Cd. 330.

Royal Commission on Children's Employment in the Mines and Manufactories, First Report, 1842. London: HM Stationary Office, 1843. Cd. 430–432.

Royal Commission on Children's Employment in the Mines and Manufactories, Second Report, 1843. London: HM Stationary Office, 1844. Cd. 430–432.

Royal Commission on Employment of Children in Trades and Manufactures not Regulated by Law. First Report, Appendix, 1863. London: HM Stationary Office, 1863. Cd. 3170.

Royal Commission on Employment of Children, Young Persons and Women in Agriculture, Second Report, Appendix (Evidence from Assistant Commissioners). London: HM Stationary Office, 1868–1869. Cd. 4202.

Royal Commission to inquire into Condition of Framework Knitters: Report, Appendices. London: HM Stationary Office, 1845. Cd. 609.

Royal Commission to inquire into Condition of Framework Knitters Appendix to Report, Part I., Leicestershire. London: HM Stationary Office, 1845. Cd. 618.

Royal Commission to inquire into Condition of Framework Knitters Appendix to Report, Part II., Nottinghamshire and Derbyshire. London: HM Stationary Office, 1845. Cd. 641.

Royal Commission to Inquire into Licensing System and Sale of Excisable Liquors in Scotland, Report, Minutes of Evidence, Index. London: HM Stationary Office, 1860. Cd. 2684, 2684-I.

Royal Commission to Inquire into Organization and Rules of Trade Unions and Other Associations, Seventh Report, Minutes and Evidence, 1867–1868. London: HM Stationary Office, 1869. Cd. 3980-III.

Royal Commission to Inquire into Organization and Rules of Trade Unions and Other Associations, Eighth Report, Minutes and Evidence, 1867–1868. London: HM Stationary Office, 1869. Cd. 3980-IV.

Royal Commission to Inquire into Organization and Rules of Trade Unions and Other Associations, Eleventh and Final Report, Minutes and Evidence, 1868–1869. London: HM Stationary Office, 1869. Cd. 4123, 4123-I.

Select Committee on Payment of Wages Bill, and Payment of Wages (Hosiery) Bill: Report, Proceedings, Minutes of Evidence, Index. London: HM Stationary Office, 1854. Cd.382.

Select Committee on Payment of Wages in Goods: Report, Minutes of Evidence, Appendix, Index. London: HM Stationary Office, 1842. Cd. 471.

Select Committee on Railway Labourers. Report, Minutes of Evidence, Index. London: HM Stationary Office, 1846. Cd. 530.

Select Committee to consider Stoppage of Wages in Hosiery Manufacture: Report, Proceedings, Minutes of Evidence, Appendix, Index. London: HM Stationary Office, 1854–55. Cd.421.

Select Committee to Inquire into the Expediency of Establishing Equitable Tribunals for Amicable Adjustment of Differences between Masters and Operatives: Report, Proceedings, Minutes of Evidence, Appendix, Index. London: HM Stationary Office, 1856. Cd. 343.

Select Committee to Inquire into the Regulation and Inspection of Mines, and Complaints in Petitions from Miners in Great Britain. Report, Proceedings, Minutes of Evidence, Appendix, Index, 1866. London: HM Stationary Office, 1867. Cd. 431, 431-I.

Select Committee to Inquire into the Regulation and Inspection of Mines, and Complaints in Petitions from Miners in Great Britain. Report, Proceedings, Minutes of Evidence, Appendix, Index, 1867. London: HM Stationary Office, 1868. Cd. 496, 496-I.

Select Committee to inquire into the State of the Law as Regards Contracts of Service Between Master and Servant. Report, Proceedings, Minutes of Evidence, Appendix, Index. London: HM Stationary Office, 1866. Cd. 449.

Sheriff clerks, Scotland. Copy of the report of the committee of the judges of the Court of Session, on the fees of the sheriff clerks in Scotland. London: HM Stationary Office, 1837. Cd. 119.

Small debt courts, Scotland. Returns from justice of peace clerks, Scotland, showing the names of counties and places where small debt courts have been held, &c. London: HM Stationary Office, 1839. Cd. 276.

Special report from the Select Committee on Mines, &c. Assessment Bill; together with the proceedings of the committee, and minutes of evidence. London: HM Stationary Office, 1867. Cd. 321.

Standing Committee A. Minutes of Proceedings on the Payment of Wages Bill. House of Commons, 1959–1960. Cd. 135.

Truck Amendment Act (1887) amendment (no. 2). A bill to amend the Truck Amendment Act, 1887. House of Commons, 1889. Cd. 99.

Truck Acts amendment. A bill to amend the Truck Acts. House of Commons, 1895. Cd.154.

Truck Acts amendment. A bill to amend the Truck Acts. House of Commons, 1897. Cd. 115.

Truck Acts amendment. A bill to amend the Truck Acts. House of Commons, 1898. Cd. 235.

Truck Acts amendment. A bill to amend the Truck Acts. House of Commons, 1900. Cd. 116.

Truck Acts amendment (no. 2). A bill to amend the Truck Acts. House of Commons, 1899. Cd.156.

Truck Acts amendment (no. 3). A bill to amend the Truck Acts. House of Commons, 1899. Cd. 167.

Truck Acts amendment (No. 2). A bill to amend the Truck Acts, and to make it illegal for employers to compel their workmen, as a condition of employment, to become or remain members of, or to leave, any benefit or friendly society or club. House of Commons, 1898. Cd. 274.

Truck Acts amendment. A bill to amend the Truck Acts, and to make it illegal for employers to compel their workmen, as a condition of employment, to become or remain members of, or to leave, any benefit or Friendly Society or club. House of Commons, 1899. Cd. 75.

Truck. A bill to amend the law relating to truck. House of Commons, 1887. Cd. 21.

Truck. A bill to amend and extend the law relating to truck. House of Commons, 1887. Cd. 109.

Truck. A bill to amend the Truck Acts. House of Commons, 1896. Cd. 184.

Truck. A bill [as amended in committee] to amend and extend the law relating to truck. House of Commons, 1887. Cd. 299.

Truck. A bill [as amended by the Standing committee of Trade] to amend the Truck Acts. House of Commons, 1896. Cd. 259.

Truck. A bill to amend and extend the Truck Acts, 1831 to 1896. House of Commons, 1913. Cd. 289.

Truck. A bill to amend and extend the Truck Acts, 1831 to 1896. House of Commons, 1914. Cd. 260.

Truck. A bill [as amended by the Standing committee of Trade] to amend the Truck Acts. House of Commons, 1896. Cd. 259.

Truck Bill. Lords reasons for insisting on certain amendments and their consequential amendment to the bill. House of Lords, 1887. Cd. 389.

Truck Commission. A bill for appointing a commission to inquire into the alleged prevalence of the truck system, and the disregard of the acts of Parliament prohibiting such system, and for giving such commission the powers necessary for conducting such inquiry. House of Commons, 1870. Cd. 252.

Truck Law amendment. A bill to amend the law relating to truck. House of Commons, 1887. Cd. 21.

Wages. A Bill to Amend the Law Relating to the Payment of Wages. House of Commons, 1958–1959. Cd. 25.

Wages. A Bill to Make Fresh Provision with Respect to the Protection of Workers in Relation to the Payment of Wages; To Make Further Provision with Respect to Wages Councils; To Restrict Redundancy Rebates to employers with Less than Ten Employees and to Abolish Certain Similar Payments; and For Connected Purposes. House of Commons, 1985–1986. Cd. 70.

Wages. A Bill [as amended by Standing Committee K] to Make Fresh Provision with Respect to the Protection of Workers in Relation to the Payment of Wages; To Make Further Provision with Respect to Wages Councils; To Restrict Redundancy Rebates to employers with Less than Ten Employees and to Abolish Certain Similar Payments; and For Connected Purposes. House of Commons, 1985–1986. Cd. 148.

Waitresses. A bill to amend the law relating to the employment of waitresses in restaurants. House of Commons, 1898. Cd.244.

Weekly wages. A bill to provide for weekly payment of wages in Great Britain and Ireland. House of Commons, 1888. Cd. 208.

Weekly wages. A bill to provide for the payment of wages weekly. House of Commons, 1889. Cd. 66.

Weekly wages. A bill to provide for the payment of wages weekly. House of Commons, 1890. Cd. 45.

Printed/online primary sources

Bondfield, Margaret, P.C. Hoffman, and Frank Tilley. *Truck Enquiry Committee, Evidence Given on Behalf of the National Amalgamated Union of Shop Assistants, Warehousemen and Clerks.* London: The Twentieth Century Press, 1907.

Bradlaugh, Charles. *Speeches by Charles Bradlaugh.* London: Freethought Publishing Co., 1890.

Labour and the Poor in England and Wales, 1849–1851: The Letters to the Morning Chronicle from the Correspondents in the Manufacturing and Mining Districts, the Towns of.

Liverpool and Birmingham, and the Rural Districts: Vol II, Northumberland and Durham, Staffordshire, the Midlands. J. Ginswick (ed). London: Frank Cass, 1983.

Labour and the Poor in England and Wales, 1849–1851: Letters to the Morning Chronicle from the Correspondents in the Manufacturing and Mining Districts, the towns of Liverpool and Birmingham and the rural districts: Vol. III. The mining and manufacturing districts in South Wales and North Wales. J. Ginswick (ed.). London: Frank Cass, 1983.

Transactions of the National Association for the Promotion of Social Science York Meeting 1864. George W. Hastings (ed.). London: Longman, Green, Roberts, Longman and Green, 1865.

British Newspaper Archive, Online

Aberdeen Evening Express
Aberdeen Journal
Ballymena Observer
Birmingham Daily Post
Birmingham Journal
Birmingham Evening Post
Buckinghamshire Advertiser and Free Press
Bury Free Press
Cardiff Times
Commonwealth
Daily Gazette for Middlesbrough
Derby Daily Telegraph
Dundee Advertiser
Dundee Courier
Dundee Evening Telegraph
Dundee Observer
Dunfermline Saturday Press
Edinburgh Evening News

Evening Telegraph
Exeter and Plymouth Gazette
Essex Newsman
Express and Echo
Falkirk Herald
Fife Herald
Glasgow Evening Herald
Glasgow Herald
Glasgow Observer
Hackney Express and Shoreditch Observer
Hartlepool Northern Daily Mail and South Durham Herald
Hull Daily Mail
Irish Times
Isle of Wight Observer
Lancashire Evening Post
Leamington Spa Courier and Warwickshire Standard
Leicester Chronicle
Leeds Times
Liverpool Mercury
London Daily News
London Evening Standard
Manchester Courier
Manchester and Salford Advertiser
Merthyr Express
Motherwell Times
North Devon Gazette
Northampton Mercury
Northeastern Daily Gazette
Northern Daily Mail
Nottingham Evening Post
Pall Mall Gazette
Potters' Examiner and Workman's Advocate
Preston Chronicle and Lancashire General Advertiser
Reynolds Newspaper
St. James Gazette
Sevenoaks Chronicle
Sheffield Daily Telegraph
Shetland Times
Shields Daily Gazette
Shoreditch Observer
South Wales Echo
The Star
Sunderland Echo
Western Daily Press, Bristol
Western Mail
Western Times
Whitstable Times
Worcester Chronicle
Yorkshire Post

Goldsmith-Kress Library of Economic Literature

Briggs, Jeremiah. *Advocate of the Poor for the Security of Wages: The Universal Anti-Truck.* Derby, 1846. Goldsmith Kress Library of Economic Literature, Reel 3368.

Cases of Distress and Oppression in the Staffordshire Potteries; By Labourers Wages Being Paid in Truck. Market Place, Burslem: Brougham Printer, 1830. Goldsmith Kress Library of Economic Literature, Reel. 26355.

A Dispassionate and Succinct View of the Truck System as it Affects the Labourer, the Capitalist, the Landlord and the State; With an Attempt to Answer the Query, "Is it a subject for Legislative Interference?" Being a Reply to the Objectors to the System. Birmingham: Printed by Thomas Knott Jr., 1830. Goldsmith Kress Library of Economic Literature, Reel 26456.

Reflections on the Injustice and Impolicy of the Truck System by a Staffordshire Morelander. London: Holdsworth and Ball, 1830. Goldsmith Kress Library of Economic Literature, Reel 26435.

A Report of the Proceedings of the Anti-Truck Meeting for the Staffordshire Potteries Held on the Pottery Race Ground on Monday 18 October 1830. William Ridgway, Esq. Chief Bailiff of Hanley and Shelton, in the Chair. Hanley: Printed at the Mercury Office by T. Allbut, 1830. Goldsmith Kress Library of Economic Literature, Reel 26439.

Some Remarks on the Injurious Effect of the Truck System with an Appendix Consisting of Affidavits. Dudley: Stanley, Printer, Albion Office, 1830. Goldsmith Kress Library of Economic Literature, reel 26437.

Rogers, Jasper W. *The Potato Truck System of Ireland, the Main Cause of Her Periodical Famines and of the Non-Payment of Her Rents.* London: J. Ridgway, 1847. Goldsmith- Kress Library of Economic Literature, Reel 35384.

The Tommy, or Truck System, Exposed in Three Letters to the Editors of Birmingham Journal. Dudley: The Office of Hinton's Executors, 1829. Goldsmith-Kress Library of Economic Literature, Reel 25792.

The Truck System: The Speech of E.J. Littleton, Esq. MP (For Staffordshire) In the House of Commons, on Wednesday, March 17, On Moving for Leave to Bring in A Bill "To Render More Effectual the Laws Requiring Payment of Wages in Money. Taken from the Mirror of Parliament and Published by the Dudley Anti-Truck Committee. London: Published by Hatchard and Son, Piccadilly. Stanley, Printer, Wolverhampton, Dudley, 1830. Goldsmith Kress Library of Economic Literature, Reel 26408.

George White, *A Few Remarks on the State of the Laws, At Present Existence, for Regulating Masters and Workpeople, Intended as a Guide for the Consideration of the House, in their Discussion on Repealing the Several Acts Relating to the Combinations of Workmen* (London, 1823) – Goldsmith Kress, Library of Economic Literature, Reel, #23943

Hansard Parliamentary Debates Online: House of Commons and House of Lords

Oxford Dictionary of National Biography Online

NINETEENTH CENTURY COLLECTIONS ONLINE

"Alderman Copeland, a Few Days Ago, in Speaking of the Truck System in the House of Commons, Stated That It Is Carried." *Watchman* 15 June 1842: 192. Nineteenth Century Collections Online. Web. 15 Jan. 2015.

"The Alleged Breaches of the Truck Act in Scotland, to Which Attention Has Been Called Both in and out of Parliament by Mr. Bradlaugh, M. P." *Labour Tribune* 18 Sept. 1886: 4.

Nineteenth Century Collections Online. Web. 15 Jan. 2015. "Anti-Truck." *Leader* 30 Aug. 1851: 816+. Nineteenth Century Collections Online. Web. 15 Jan. 2015.

"It appears from the reports of inspectors of factories that there are still some dark corners of the country in which the infamous truck system is in full vogue." *Workman's Times* 15 May 1891: [1]. Nineteenth Century Collections Online. Web. 15 Jan. 2015.

"The Ballast Heavers and the Truck System." *Pioneer; and Weekly Record of Movements* 17 May 1851: 69+. Nineteenth Century Collections Online. Web. 15 Jan. 2015.

"Complaints." *Women's Trade Union League Annual Reports* (1899): 10. Nineteenth Century Collections Online. Web. 15 Jan. 2015.

"Complaints." *Women's Trade Union League Annual Reports* (1904): 11+. Nineteenth Century Collections Online. Web. 15 Jan. 2015.

"The Explanation of These Preposterous Fines and Deductions Just Now Is to Be Found in the Reactionary Truck Act of the Tory Government, Which Came into Operation on January 1st." *Londoner* 8 Jan. 1897: 6. Nineteenth Century Collections Online. Web. 15 Jan. 2015.

Fox, Stephen N., and J.R. MacDonald. "Shop Assistants and the Truck Acts." *Women's Industrial News* 3 (1898): [17]+. Nineteenth Century Collections Online. Web. 15 Jan. 2015.

"Great Anti-Truck Meeting at Dudley." *Leader* 27 July 1850: 418. Nineteenth Century Collections Online. Web. 15 Jan. 2015.

Hutchins, B.L. "Truck, Fines, and Deductions." *Women's Industrial News* 16:60 (1913): 89–100.

"House of Commons. – Wednesday, July 4." *Watchman* 11 July 1855: 223. Nineteenth Century Collections Online. Web. 15 Jan. 2015.

"I Write Feelingly, Because It Has Been My Lot to Look on at the Latest Attempt Which Legislators Are Making to Render the Truck Act Intelligible and Effective." *The Commonwealth* I.6 (1896): 228. Nineteenth Century Collections Online. Web. 15 Jan. 2015.

"Important Trial. – Truck Act." *Cabinet Newspaper* 30 July 1859: 6. Nineteenth Century Collections Online. Web. 15 Jan. 2015.

"Industrial Prosecutions." *The Woman Worker* 3 (1908): 91. Nineteenth Century Collections Online. Web. 15 Jan. 2015.

"Labour." *Londoner* 19 Feb. 1897: 6. Nineteenth Century Collections Online. Web. 15 Jan. 2015.

"Legislative Work." *Women's Trade Union League Annual Reports* (1897): 5. Nineteenth Century Collections Online. Web. 15 Jan. 2015.

MacArthur, Mary R. "Life and Labour." *The Woman Worker* III.4 (1909): 93. Nineteenth Century Collections Online. Web. 15 Jan. 2015.

"Miss Tuckwell on Factory Life." *The Woman Worker* 20 (1908): 493. Nineteenth Century Collections Online. Web. 15 Jan. 2015.

"The Truck Act." *The Woman Worker* 28 (1908) 702. Nineteenth Century Collections Online. Web. 15 January 2015.

"The Truck Acts." *Anti-Sweater* Feb. 1887: 2. Nineteenth Century Collections Online. Web. 15 Jan. 2015.

"The Truck Acts." *Labour Record* May 1906: 71. Nineteenth Century Collections Online. Web. 15 Jan. 2015.

"The Truck Acts." *The Woman Worker* 3:1 (1909): 21. Nineteenth Century Collections Online. Web. 15 Jan. 2015.

"The Truck Acts Report." *The Woman Worker* 3:3 (1909):54. Nineteenth Century Collections Online. Web. 15 Jan. 2015.

"Truck Amendment Act, 1887." *Labour Record* 1 Mar. 1894: 2+. Nineteenth Century Collections Online. Web. 15 Jan. 2015.

"The Truck Commission in the Shetland Isles." *Watchman* 10 July 1872: 221. Nineteenth Century Collections Online. Web. 15 Jan. 2015.

"Truck and Fair Wages." *Women's Industrial News* 46 (1909): 12. Nineteenth Century Collections Online. Web. 24 June 2015.

"Truck in Ireland." *Woman Worker* 1 (5 June 1908): 30. Nineteenth Century Collections Online. Web. 15 January 2015.

"The Truck System." *Douglas Jerrold's Weekly Newspaper* 25 Sept. 1847: 1201. Nineteenth Century Collections Online. Web. 15 Jan. 2015.

"The Truck System." *Leader* 3 Aug. 1850: 445. Nineteenth Century Collections Online. Web. 15 January 2015.

"The Truck System." *The Trade Unionist* (18 July 1891). Nineteenth Century Collections Online. Web. 15 January 2015.

"The Truck System." *The Women's Journal* (24 April 1875): 135. Nineteenth Century Collections Online. Web. 15 January 2015.

"The Truck System in Leicester." *Women's Union Journal* 8:90 (1883): 59. Nineteenth Century Collections Online. Web. 15 January 2015.

"The Truck System in Scotland." *Women's Union Journal* 12:134 (1887): 22. Nineteenth Century Collections Online. Web. 15 January 2015.

"Unequal Sentences." *The Woman Worker* 1 (1908): 30. Nineteenth Century Collections Online.

Web. 15 January 2015.

"Wages without Stoppages." *Weekly Telegraph* 25 Feb. 1860: 4. Nineteenth Century Collections Online. Web. 15 January 2015.

"Women and the Truck System in Shetland." *Women's Suffrage Journal* 19:224 (1888): 83. Nineteenth Century Collections Online. Web 15 January 2015.

The Times of London Online

Secondary sources

Abrahams, Gerald. *Trade Unions and the Law*. London: Cassell and Co., 1968.

Abrams, Lynn. "Knitting Autonomy and Identity: The Role of Hand-Knitting in the Construction of Women's Sense of Self in An Island Community, Shetland, c. 1850-2000." *Textile History* 37:2 (2006):156.

Abrams, Lynn. "There Is Many a Thing That Can Be Done with Money: Women, Barter, and Autonomy in a Scottish Fishing Community in the Nineteenth and Twentieth Centuries." *Signs* 37:3 (Spring 2012):602–609.

Aikin, Olga. "Payment of Wages Act 1960." *Modern Law Review* 24:1 (January 1961):155–157.

Allen, G.C. *The Industrial Development of Birmingham and the Black Country, 1860–1927*. London: George Allen and Unwin, Ltd., 1929.

Allen, V.C. *Trade Unions and the Government*. London: Longmans, 1960.

Anderson, Adelaide Mary. "Truck Legislation in England and on the Continent." *Journal of the Society of Comparative Legislation* 1:3 (1899):395–406.

Anderson, Adelaide Mary. *Women in the Factory: An Administrative Adventure, 1893 to 1921*. London: John Murray, 1922.

Arlington, David. "A Squire's Examples: The Persistent Persuasion of Edward J. Littleton." *Western Speech* 38 (1974):162–169.

Arnstein, Walter. *The Bradlaugh Case: A Study in Late Victorian Opinion and Politics*. Oxford: Oxford University Press, 1965.

Balnave, Nikola and Greg Patmore. "The Politics of Consumption in Labour History." *Labour History* 100 (2011):145–166.

Barnsby, George B. *The Social Conditions in the Black Country, 1800–1900*. London: Integrated Publishing Services, 1987.

Barnsby, George B. *The Working Class Movement in the Black Country from 1760 to 1867*. Wolverhampton: Integrated Publishing Services, 1977.

Barrett, Brenda. "The Truck Acts in a Modern Context." *Modern Law Review* 39:1 (January 1976):101–105.

Bean, Jessica and George R. Boyer. "The Trade Boards Act of 1909 and the Alleviation of Household Poverty." *British Journal of Industrial Relations* 47:2 (June 2009):240–264.

Benson, John. "The Thrift of English Coal-Miners, 1860–1895." *Economic History Review* 31:3 (1978):410–418.

Benson, John. "Working Class Consumption, Saving, and Investment in England and Wales, 1851–1911." *Journal of Design History* 9:2 (1996):87–99.

Black, Clementina. "Report of the Departmental committee on the Truck Acts." *The Economic Journal* 17:94 (June 2009):315–319.

Black, Clementina. *Sweated Industry and the Minimum Wage*. London: Duckworth and Co., 1907.

Blackburn, Sheila. "'Between the Devil of Cheap Labour Competition and the Sea of Family Poverty?' Sweated Labour in Time and Place, 1840–1914." *Labour History Review* 71:2 (August 2006):91–101.

Blackburn, Sheila. "Curse or Cure? Why Was the Enactment of the Trade Boards at So Controversial?" *British Journal of Industrial Relations* 47:2 (June 2009):214–239.

Blackburn, Sheila. "Must Low Pay Always Be with Us? The Origins of Britain's Minimum Wage Legislation." *Historical Studies in Industrial Relations* 23/24 (June 2009):61–101.

Bonner, Hypatia Bradlaugh. *Charles Bradlaugh: A Record of His Life and Work by His Daughter Hupatia Bradlaugh Bonner*. Vol. II. London: T. Fisher Unwin, 1894.

Bourke, Joanna. "Housewifery in Working Class England, 1860–1914." *Past and Present* 143 (May 1994):167–197.

Boyd, Robert Nelson. *Coal Mines Inspection: Its History and Results*. London: W.H. Allen and Co., 1879.

Bradlaugh, Charles. *Labour and the Law: With a Memoir and Two Portraits*. London: R. Forder, 1891.

Campbell, Alan B. *The Lanarkshire Miners: A Social History of their Trade Union, 1775–1974*. Edinburgh: John Donald Publishers, Ltd., 1979.

Carson, W.G. "Early Factory Inspectors and the Viable Class Society: A Rejoinder." *International Journal of the Sociology of the Law* 8 (1974):187–191.

Carson, W.G. "Some Instrumental and Symbolic Dimensions of the 1833 Factory Act." In *Crime, Criminology and Public Policy: Essays in Honor of Sir Leon Radzinowicz*. R. Hood (ed.). New York: Free Press, 1974.

Challinor, Raymond. *Radical Lawyer in Victorian England: W.P. Roberts and the Struggle for Workers' Rights*. London: I.B. Taurus, 1990.

Challinor, Raymond. *The Miners' Association: A Trade Union in the Age of Chartists*. London: Lawrence and Wisehart, 1968.

Chase, Malcolm. *Early Trade Unionism: Fraternity, Skill and the Politics of Labour*. Aldershot: Ashgate, 2000.

Church, R. *History of the British Coal Industry, Vol 3, 1830–1913*. Oxford: Clarendon Press, 1986.

Clark, Anna. *The Struggle for the Breeches: Gender and the Making of the English Working Class*. Berkley: University of California Press, 1995.

Clegg, H.A., Alan Fox and A.F. Thompson. *A History of British Trade Unions since 1889*. Vol. I. Oxford: Clarendon Press, 1964.

"Constitutionality of Statutes Requiring Corporations to Pay Employees' Wages in Money." *University of Pennsylvania Law Review* 56:3 (1908):194–197.

Crowley, John E. "Empire versus Truck: The Official Interpretation of Debt and Labour in the Eighteenth Century Newfoundland Fishery." *Canadian Historical Review* 70:3 (1989):311–336.

Curthoys, Mark. *Governments, Labour and the Law in Mid-Victorian Britain: Trade Union Legislation of the 1870s*. Oxford: Clarendon Press, 2003.

Daunton, M.J. "The Dowlais Iron Company in the Iron Industry, 1800–1850." *Welsh History Review* 6 (1972):16–48.

Davies, Alvin Eurig. "The Condition of Labour in Mid-Cardiganshire in the Early Nineteenth Century." *Ceridigion* 4:4 (1963):321–335.

Davies, Alvin Eurig. "Wages, Prices and Social Improvement in Cardiganshire, 1750–1850." *Ceredigion* 10:1 (1984):31–55.

Davies, John. *A History of Wales*. London: Penguin, 1990.

Davies, Russell. *Hope and Heartbreak: A Social History of Wales and the Welsh, 1776–1871*. Cardiff: University of Wales Press, 2005.

Deakin, Simon and Francis Green. "One Hundred Years of British Minimum Wage Legislation." *British Journal of Industrial Relations* 47:2 (June 2009):205–213.

Dolding, Lesley. "The Wages Act of 1986: An Exercise in Employment Abuse." *The Modern Law Review* 51:1 (1988):89.

Dyble, David. *The Turbulent Squire of Apedale: Richard Edensor Heathcote (1780–1850)*. Audley: Audley and District Family History Publications, 2010.

Edwards, N. *The History of the South Wales Miners*. London: C. Tirling and Co., 1926.

Egan, David. *Coal Society: A History of the South Wales Mining Valleys, 1840–1980*. Llandysul: Gomer Press, 1987.

Engels, Friedrich. *The Condition of the Working Class in England*. Translated and Edited by W.O. Henderson and R.H. Challinor. Stanford: Stanford University Press, 1958, original: 1845.

Englander, David. "Wages Arrestment in Victorian Scotland." *Scottish Historical Review* 60 (1981):68–75.

Evans, E.W. *The Miners of South Wales*. Cardiff: University of Wales Press, 1961.

Feurer, Rosemary. "The Meaning of Sisterhood: The British Women's Movement and Protective Labour Legislation." *Victorian Studies* 31:2 (1988):235.

Finn, Margot. *The Character of Credit: Personal Debt in English Culture 1740–1914*. Cambridge: Cambridge University Press, 2003.

Fishback, Price. "Did Coal Miners 'Owe Their Souls to the Company Store'? Theory and Evidence from the Early 1900s." *The Journal of Economic History* 46:4 (1986):1011–1029.

Flinn, M. *History of the British Coal Industry, Vol. 2, 1700–1830*. Oxford: Clarendon Press, 1984.

Frank, Christopher. "'Let But One of Them Come Before Me and I'll Commit Him.': Trade Unions, Magistrates, and the Law in Mid-Nineteenth Century Staffordshire." *Journal of British Studies* 44:1 (2005):64–91.

Frank, Christopher. *Master and Servant Law: Chartists, Trade Unions, Radical Lawyers and the Magistracy in England, 1840–1865*. Farnham: Ashgate Press, 2010.

Frank, Christopher. "The Sheriff's Court or Company Store: Truck, The Arrestment of Wages and Working Class Consumption in Scotland, 1830–1870." *Labour History Review* 79:2 (Summer 2014):139–164.

Frank, Christopher. "Truck or Trade? Anti-Truck Prosecution Associations and the Campaign Against the Payment of Wages in Goods in Mid-Nineteenth Century Britain." *Historical Studies in Industrial Relations* 27/28 (Spring/Autumn 2009):1–40.

Fraser, W. Hamish. *The Coming of the Mass Market 1850–1914.* London: Palgrave, 1982.

Fyson, Richard. "The Crisis of 1842: Chartism, the Colliers' Strike, and the Outbreak in the Potteries." In *The Chartist Experience: Studies in Working Class Radicalism and Culture, 1830–1860.* Dorothy Thompson and James Epstein (eds.). London: MacMillan, 1982.

Goriely, Tamara. "Arbitrary Deductions from Pay and the Proposed Repeal of the Truck Acts." *Industrial Law Journal* 12:1 (June 1983):236–250.

Gray, Robert and Donna Loftus. "Industrial Regulation, Urban Space and the Boundaries of the Workplace: Mid-Victorian Nottingham." *Urban History* 26:2 (1999):211–229.

Greer, Desmond. "Middling Hard on Coin: Truck in Donegal in the 1890s." Presidential Address to the Annual General Meeting of the Irish Legal History Society in Dublin, 2000.

Greer, Desmond and James Nicholson. *The Factory Acts in Ireland, 1802–1914.* Dublin: Four Courts Press, 2003.

Griffin, Colin P. "The Standard of Living in the Black Country in the Nineteenth Century: A Comment." *Economic History Review*, New Series 26:3 (1973):510–513.

Gurney, Peter. *Cooperative Culture and the Politics of Consumption in England.* Manchester: Manchester University Press, 1996.

Gurney, Peter. "Exclusive Dealing in the Chartist Movement." *Labour History Review* 74:1 (April 2009):90–110.

Gurney, Peter. *Wanting and Having: Popular Politics and Liberal Consumerism In England, 1830–1870.* Manchester: Manchester University Press, 2015.

Hammond, J.L. and Barbara Hammond. *The Skilled Labourer, 1760–1832.* London: Longmans, Green and Co., 1919.

Hammond, J.L. and Barbara Hammond. *The Town Labourer, 1760–1832.* London: Longmans, Green and Co., 1917.

Handley, James Edmund. *The Navvy in Scotland.* Cork: Cork University Press, 1970.

Hay, Douglas. "Dread of the Crown Office: The Magistracy and the King's Bench, 1740–1800." In *Law, Crime and English Society, 1660–1830.* Norma Landau (ed.). Cambridge: Cambridge University Press, 2002.

Hay, Douglas. "England, 1562–1875: The Law and Its Uses." In *Masters, Servants, and Magistrates in Britain and the Empire, 1562–1955.* Douglas Hay and Paul Craven (eds.). Chapel Hill: University of North Carolina Press, 2004.

Highfield, William. "The Great Tim Plate Workers' Strike." *The Blackcountryman*, 5 (April 1972):49–56.

Hilton, George. "The Truck Act of 1831." *The Economic History Review* 10:3 (1958):470–479.

Hilton, George. "The Truck System in the Nineteenth Century." *The Journal of Political Economy* 65:3 (January 1957):237–256.

Hilton, George. *The Truck System Including a History of the British Truck Acts, 1465–1960.* Cambridge: Heffer and Sons, 1960.

Historical Meanings of Work. Edited by Patrick Joyce. Cambridge: Cambridge University Press, 1987.

Howarth, David. "Truck Acts." *Industrial Law Journal* 15:3 (1986):190–194.

Howarth, David. "The Truck Act 1896 – Last Rites." *Cambridge Law Journal* 45:1 (1986):30–32.

Hughes, Mervyn. "A Truck Shop at Dinas, Near Betwys-y-Coed, on Telford's London to Holyhead Road." *Caem. Historical Society Transactions* 27 (1966):139–148.

Hunt, Cathy. "Gertrude Tuckwell and the British Labour Movement, 1891–1921: A Study in Motives and Influences." *Women's History Review* 22:3 (2013):478–496.

Hunt, E.H. *British Labour History, 1815–1914.* Atlantic Highlands, NJ: Humanities Press, 1981.

Hutchins, B.L. *Home Work and Sweating: The Cause and Remedies.* London: Fabian Society, 1907.

James, Kevin J. "Outwork, Truck and the Lady Inspector: Lucy Deane in Londonderry and Donegal, 1897." In *Essays in Irish Labour History: A Festschrift for Elizabeth and John W. Boyle.* Frances Devine, Fintan Lane and Niamh Purséil (eds.). Dublin: Irish Academic Press, 2008. pp. 103–117.

Johnson, Howard. "A Modified Form of Slavery: The Credit and Truck Systems in the Bahamas in the Nineteenth and Early Twentieth Centuries." *Comparative Studies in Society and History* 28:4 (1986):729–753.

Johnson, Paul. "Creditors, Debtors, and the law in Victorian and Edwardian England." In *Private Law and Social Inequality in the Industrial Age: Comparing the Legal Cultures of Britain, France, Germany and the United States.* Willibald Steinmetz (ed.). Oxford: Oxford University Press, 2000.

Johnson, Paul. *Saving and Spending: The Working Class Economy in Britain, 1870–1939.* Oxford: Oxford University Press, 1985.

Johnson, Robert. *A Shetland Country Merchant: Being An Account of the Life and Times of James Williamson of Mid Yell, 1800–1872.* Shetland: Shetland Publishing, 1972.

Jones, D.J.V. "Distress and Discontent in Cardiganshire, 1814–1819." *Ceredigion* 5:3 (1966):280–289.

Jones, Helen. "Women Health Workers: The Case of the First Women Factory Inspectors in Britain." *Social History of Medicine* 1 (1988):167–171.

Jones, Ieuan Gwynedd. "Merthyr Tydfil: The Politics of Survival." *Llafur* 2:1 (1976):18–31.

Jones, Thomas. *Rhymney Memories.* Newtown: The Welsh Outlook Press, 1938.

Kahn-Freund, Otto. "The Tangle of the Truck Acts." *Industrial Law Review* 2 (July 1949):1–9.

Keast, Horace. "A Commentary on the Truck Acts." *Industrial Law Review* 3 (1949):223.

Knowles, L.C.A. *Industrial and Commercial Revolutions in Great Britain During the Nineteenth Century.* London: George Routledge and Sons, Ltd., 1933.

Laybourne, Keith. *A History of British Trade Unionism.* London: Sutton Publishers, 1997.

Lester, M. *Victorian Insolvency: Bankruptcy, Imprisonment for Debt, and Company Winding Up in Nineteenth Century England.* Oxford: Clarendon Press, 1995.

Lewis, D. "A Great Blessing to the People Employed: Conflicting Views of the Truck System in Llynfi Valley, 1840–1870." *Morgannwg* 48 (2004):35–46.

Livesey, Ruth. "The Politics of Work: Feminism, Professionalism and Women Inspectors of Factories and Workshops." *Women's History Review* 13:2 (2004):233–245.

Machin, Frank. *The Yorkshire Miners: A History.* Barnsley: National Union of Mineworkers, 1958.

MacRaild, Donald and David E. Martin. *Labour in British Society, 1830–1914.* London: MacMillan, 2000.

Martin, Ross. *TUC: The Growth of a Pressure Group.* Oxford: Clarendon Press, 1980.

Martindale, Hilda. *Women Servants of the State, 1870–1938: A History of Women in the Civil Service.* London: George Allen and Unwin, 1938.

Masters, Servants and Magistrates in Britain and Empire, 1562–1955. Edited by Douglas Hay and Paul Craven. Chapel Hill: University of North Carolina Press, 2004.

Mather, F.C. "The General Strike of 1842: A Study in Leadership, Organization and the Threat of Revolution During the Plug Plot Disturbances." In *Popular Protest and Public Order: Six Studies in British History 1790–1920.* John Stevenson and Roland Quinault (eds.). New York: St. Martin's Press, 1974.

McCready, H.W. "British Labour Lobby, 1867–1875." *Canadian Journal of Economics and Political Science* 22:2 (1956):160.

McFeely, Mary Drake. *Lady Inspectors: The Campaign for a Better Workplace, 1893–1921.* Oxford: Basil Blackwell, 1991.

McFeely, Mary Drake. "The Lady Inspectors: Women at Work, 1893–1921." *History Today* 36 (1986).

McMullen, John. "Recent Legislation: The Wage Act of 1986." *Industrial Law Review* 15:1 (1986):267.

Mellor, John. *The Company Store.* Toronto: Doubleday Canada Ltd., 1987.

Mitchell, B.R. *Economic Development of the British Coal Industry, 1800–1914.* New York: Cambridge University Press, 1984.

Morgan, Carol. *Women Workers and Gender Identities, 1835–1913: The Cotton and Metal Industries in England.* London: Routledge, 2001.

Morris, J.H. and L.J. Williams. *The South Wales Coal Industry, 1841–1875.* Cardiff: University of Wales Press, 1958.

Mostyn, F.E. *The Truck Acts and Industry.* London: Thames Bank Publishing Co. Ltd., 1950.

Murray, Norman. *The Scottish Handloom Weavers, 1750–1850: A Social History.* Edinburgh: John Donald Publishers, Ltd., 1978.

Murray, S.H. "Pratt v. Cook, Son & Co. (St. Paul's) Limited (56 TLR 363)." *Modern Law Review* 4:1 (July 1940):56–60.

Napier, Brian. "The Contract of Service: The Concept and its Application." D. Phil Thesis, Cambridge University, 1975.

Olcott, Teresa. "Dead Centre: The Women's Trade Union Movement in London, 1874–1914." *London Journal* 2:1 (1976):33–50.

Ommer, Rosemary E. *Merchant Credit and Labour Strategies in Historical Perspective.* Fredericton: Acadiensis Press, 1990.

Ommer, Rosemary E. "The Truck System in Gaspé, 1822–1877." *Acadiensis* 19:1 (1989):91–114.

Orth, John. *Combination and Conspiracy: A Legal History of Trade Unionism, 1721–1906.* Oxford: Clarendon Press, 1991.

Orth, John. "The Contract and the Common Law." In *The State and Freedom to Contract.* N. Scheiber (ed.). Stanford: Stanford University Press, 1998.

Palgrave MacMillan Dictionary of Women's Biography. Jennifer S. Uglow, Frances Hinton and Maggy Hendry. London: Macmillan Publishers, Ltd., 2005.

Philips, David. "The Black Country Magistracy, 1835–1860: A Changing Elite and the Exercise of its Power." *Midland History* 3:2 (1976):161–190.

Price, Richard. *Labour In British Society: An Interpretive History.* London: Croom Helm, 1986.

Private Law and Social Inequality in the Industrial Age: Comparing the Legal Cultures of Britain, France, Germany and the United States. Edited by Willibald Steinmetz. Oxford: Oxford University Press, 2000.

Richards, W.M. "Some Aspects of the Industrial Revolution in South East Caernarvonshire." *Transactions of the Caernavornshire Historical Society* 5 (1944):71–87.

Rights and Wrongs of Women. Edited by J. Mitchell and A. Oakley. London: Penguin, 1976.

Roberts, B.C. *The Trades Union Congress, 1868–1921.* London: George Allen and Unwin, 1958.

Roberts, R.O. "Financial Developments in Early Modern Wales and the Emergence of the First Banks." *Welsh History Review* 16 (1992–1993):291–307.

Romanes, John H. "The Truck Acts." *Juridical Review* 18 (1906–1907):247–258.

Rubin, G.R. "Law, Poverty and Imprisonment for Debts, 1869–1914." In *Law, Economy and Society, 1750–1914.* G.R. Rubin and D. Sugarman (eds.). Ann Arbor: Abingdon Books, 1984.

Rule, John. *The Experience of Labour in Eighteenth Century English Industry.* New York: St. Martin's Press, 1981.

Rule, John. *The Labouring Classes in Early Industrial England, 1750–1850.* London: Longman, 1986.

Shoemaker, Robert. *Gender in English Society 1650–1850: The Emergence of Separate Spheres?* London: Longmans, 1998.

Slum Travelers: Ladies and London Poverty, 1860–1920. Edited by Ellen Ross. Berkeley: University of California Press, 2007.

Smith, Constance. "The Working of the Trade Boards Act of 1909 and the Alleviation of Household Poverty." *Journal of Political Economy* 22:7 (22 July 1914):615.

Squire, Rose. *Thirty Years in the Public Service: An Industrial Retrospect.* London: Nisbet and Co., 1927.

Steinberg, Marc. "Capitalist Development, the Labour Process, and the Law." *American Journal of Sociology* 109:2 (September 2003):445–495.

Steinberg, Marc. *England's Great Transformation: Law, Labour, and the Industrial Revolution.* Chicago: University of Chicago Press, 2016.

Steinfeld, Robert. *Coercion, Contract and Free Labor in the Nineteenth Century.* Cambridge: Cambridge University Press, 2001.

Stevens, Simon. "A Social Tyranny: The Truck System in Colonial Western Australia, 1829-99." *Labour History* 80 (2001):83–98.

Strange, Keith. "The Conditions of the Working Classes in Merthyr Tydfil, Circa 1840–1850." University of Wales Swansea, Ph.D. Thesis, 1982.

Swift, Roger. "The English Urban Magistracy and the Administration of Justice During the Early Nineteenth Century: Wolverhampton, 1815–1850." *Midland History* 17 (1992):75–92.

Tan, Elaine. "Ideology, Interest Groups, and Institutional Change: The Case of the British Prohibition of Wages In Kind." *Journal of Institutional Economics* 1:2 (2005):175–191.

Tan, Elaine. "Regulating Wages in Kind: Theory and Evidence from Britain." *Journal of Law, Economics, and Organization* 22:2 (2006):442–458.

Tan, Elaine. "Script as Private Monopoly, Monetary Monopoly, and the Rent-Seeking State In Britain." *The Economic History Review* 64:1 (2011):237–255.

Tebbutt, M. *Making Ends Meet: Pawnbroking and Working Class Credit.* New York: St. Martin's Press, 1983.

Thompson, Edward. *The Making of the English Making Class.* London: Penguin, 1963.

Tuckwell, Gertrude. *Constance Smith: A Short Memoir.* London: Duckworth, 1931.

Warburton, William H. *The History of Trade Union Organization in the North Staffordshire Potteries.* London: George Allen and Unwin, 1931.

Webb, Sidney and Beatrice Webb. *The History of Trade Unionism.* London: Augustus M. Kelley, 1894.

Wedgewood, Josiah. *The Staffordshire Pottery and its History.* London: Sampson, Low, Marston & Co., 1913.

Williams, David. *John Frost: A Study in Chartism.* London: Augustus M. Kelley, 1969.

Williams, Gwyn. "The Making of Radical Merthyr, 1800–1836." *The Welsh History Review* 1:2 (1961):161–192.

Williams, J.E. *The Derbyshire Miners: A Study in Industrial and Social History*. London: George Allen and Unwin Ltd., 1962.

Wilson, Gordon M. *Alexander McDonald: Leader of the Miners*. Aberdeen: Aberdeen University Press, 1982.

Women and Work Culture, Britain 1850–1950. Edited by Krista Cowman and Louise Jackson. Aldershot: Ashgate, 2005.

Woods, D.C. "The Borough Magistracy and the Authority Structure in the Black Country, 1858-1875." *West Midland Studies* 12 (1979).

Young, Craig. "Geography, Law and the Centralizing State: Wages Arrestment in Nineteenth and Twentieth Century Scotland." *Area* 36:3 (2004):287–297.

Zangerl, Carl. "The Social Composition of the County Magistracy in England and Wales, 1831-1887." *Journal of British Studies* 11 (1971):113–125.

Index

8

Printed in the United States
by Baker & Taylor Publisher Services